SONGWRITER'S MARKET

40TH EDITION

Cris Freese, *Editor*

Andrea Williams, Contributing Editor

WD
WRITER'S DIGEST
BOOKS
WritersDigest.com
Cincinnati, Ohio

Publisher: Phil Sexton

Writer's Market website: www.writersmarket.com
Writer's Digest website: www.writersdigest.com

Distributed in Canada by Fraser Direct
100 Armstrong Avenue
Georgetown, Ontario, Canada L7G 5S4
Tel: (905) 877-4411

Distributed in the U.K. and Europe by F&W Media International
Brunel House, Newton Abbot, Devon, TQ12 4PU, England
Tel: (+44) 1626-323200, Fax: (+44) 1626-323319
E-mail: postmaster@davidandcharles.co.uk

ISSN: 0161-5971
ISBN-13: 978-1-4403-4779-5
ISBN-10: 1-4403-4779-4

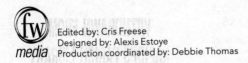

Edited by: Cris Freese
Designed by: Alexis Estoye
Production coordinated by: Debbie Thomas

CONTENTS

INDEXES

FROM
THE EDITOR

In the previous edition of *Songwriter's Market*, I focused on returning the book to the craft of songwriting, because at the heart of any song that stands the test of time is good writing. This year, though, I found it best to turn the approach back to the songwriter.

I think this approach makes this edition of *Songwriter's Market*, now in its 40th year, as unique as ever. And it starts with the number of songwriters featured in this book. You'll find more than ten interviews with a variety of songwriters, such as hall-of-fame songwriter Chip Taylor and up-and-coming star Erik Blu2th Griggs. These are the people every songwriter should want to hear from. Read closely: Their advice and stories are as important as any you'll find in the industry. Because they've made it. And they've been where you are now.

With expert advice from songwriters of varying success and experience levels, I think anyone is going to find something useful in these pages. And beyond that, you'll find helpful articles on crowdfunding, useful tips on networking via Twitter, advice on how to co-write, and the importance of breaking into Nashville.

And if you're looking for more, be sure to check out a unique video from the masterful Pat Pattison (Berklee College of Music) at www.writersmarket.com/sm17-webinar. In this video, he walks through a student's song, showing precisely how to tighten her song and perfect her form.

Take Pat's advice—and the advice in this book—and tighten your own work. Make yourself a complete songwriter. You may just find yourself closer to a breakthrough.

Cris Freese
Associate Editor, Writer's Digest Books

HOW TO USE *SONGWRITER'S MARKET*

Before diving into the *Songwriter's Market* listings, it's a good idea to take time to research—you want to be in the best possible position for success before submitting. As you read through the articles and advice in this book's opening sections, ask yourself if you currently have what it takes to succeed: strong songs, a well-recorded demo, a professional presence both online and in person, the ability and desire to network, the patience to learn new technologies and skills, and, perhaps most important, the commitment to your craft and to researching the business aspects of the music industry. By educating yourself and constantly assessing your needs and skills, you'll be better prepared when you actually do submit your songs.

Now, let's take a look at what is inside *Songwriter's Market*, why these articles were put into the book in the first place, and how they can help your career.

THE LISTINGS

Beyond the articles, which we highly encourage you to read first, there are eight market sections in this book, including Music Publishers, Record Companies, Contests & Awards, and Managers & Booking Agents. Each section begins with an introduction detailing how the different markets function—what part of the music industry they work in, how they make money, and what you need to think about when approaching them with your music.

These listings are the heart of *Songwriter's Market*. They are the names, addresses, and contact information of music markets looking for songs and artists, as well as descriptions of the types of music they are looking for.

How do I use *Songwriter's Market*?

The quick answer is that you should use the indices to find markets that are interested in your type of music; then read the listings for details about how they want the music submitted. For support and help, join a songwriting or other music industry association (see the Organizations section at the back of this book). Also, read everything you can about songwriting (see the Publications of Interest section), and talk to other songwriters. Always conduct your own research (using this book is a great starting point), especially since businesses can change contact information and location between a book's publication and when you pick it up. The industry moves fast!

How does *Songwriter's Market* work?

The listings in *Songwriter's Market* are packed with information. It can be intimidating at first, but they are structured for ease of use. Take a few minutes to get used to how the listings are organized, and you'll save time in the long run. For more detailed information about how the listings are put together, read the section "Where Should I Send My Songs?"

The following are general guidelines about how to use the listings:

READ THE ENTIRE LISTING to decide whether to submit your music. Please *do not* use this book as a mass mailing list. If you blindly send out demos by the hundreds, or e-mail links to your website or social media profile at random, you'll waste a lot of time and annoy a lot of people.

PAY CLOSE ATTENTION TO THE "MUSIC" SECTION IN EACH LISTING. This will tell you what kind of music the company is looking for. If it wants rockabilly only, and you write heavy metal, don't submit to that company. That's just common sense.

FOLLOW THE SUBMISSION INSTRUCTIONS shown under How to Contact. Many listings are particular about how they want submissions packaged. If you don't follow their instructions, your submission will probably be discarded. If you are confused about a listing's instructions, contact the company for clarification. Some companies will also list their submission instructions on their website.

IF IN DOUBT, CONTACT THE COMPANY FOR PERMISSION TO SUBMIT. Some companies don't mind if you send an unsolicited submission, but others may require you to get special permission prior to submitting. Others still may be currently closed to unsolicited submissions, in which case they are legally forbidden from even listening to your music. Pay attention to these guidelines and act accordingly. Contacting a company first is also a good way to determine its latest music needs, while also briefly making contact on a personal level—you'll be more likely to get a response to your submission if you've already been in contact with someone at the company.

BE COURTEOUS, BE EFFICIENT, AND ALWAYS HAVE A PURPOSE to be in touch with your personal contact. Don't waste a contact's time. If you call, always have a legitimate reason: seeking permission to submit, checking on guidelines, following up on a demo, etc. Once you have someone's attention, don't wear out your welcome, and always be polite.

CHECK FOR A PREFERRED CONTACT. Some listings designate a contact person after the bolded Contact heading. This is the person you should contact with questions or address your submission to. Again, you may want to use the listing as a starting point and then look up the company online to verify that the contact person is still there. Double-checking never hurts!

READ THE TIPS SECTION. This part of the listing provides extra information about how to submit or what it might be like to work with the company.

FREQUENTLY ASKED QUESTIONS

How do companies get listed in *Songwriter's Market*?

No company pays to be included—all listings are free. The listings come from a combination of research the editor does on the music industry and questionnaires filled out by companies who want to be listed (many of them contact us to be included). All questionnaires are screened for known sharks and to make sure they meet our requirements.

Why aren't other companies I know about listed in this book?

There are many possible reasons. Perhaps they did not reply to the questionnaire we sent, were removed due to reader complaints, went out of business, specifically asked not to be listed, could not be contacted for an update, or were left out because of space restrictions.

What's the deal with companies that don't take unsolicited submissions?

In the interest of completeness, the editor will sometimes include listings of crucial music companies and major labels you should be aware of. We want you to at least have some idea of their policies. And, you never know: Their submission policies may change.

A listed company claimed that it accepts unsolicited submissions, but my demo came back unopened. What happened?

Needs can change rapidly. This may be the case for the company you submitted to. That's why it's a good idea to contact a company before submitting.

So that's it. You now have the power and resources at your fingertips to begin your journey. Let us know how you're doing. Drop us a line at marketbookupdates@fwmedia.com and tell us about any successes you have had thanks to the materials in this book.

WHERE SHOULD I SEND MY SONGS?

This question depends a lot on whether you write mainly for yourself as a performer or if you want someone else to pick up your song to record (often the case in country music, for example). These two types of songwriters may have different career trajectories, so it's important to assess whom you'd like to write for and what you'd like to write. This is important for figuring out what kind of companies to contact, as well as how you contact them.

What if I'm strictly a songwriter/lyricist?

Many well-known songwriters are not performers. Some are not skilled instrumentalists or singers, but they understand melody, lyrics, and harmony, and how those elements go together. They can write great songs, but they need someone else to bring their words to life through skilled musicianship. This type of songwriter will usually approach music publishers first for access to artists looking for songs. Music publishers are to songwriters what literary agents are to authors. They take great songs and find homes for them while managing the rights and money flow for you. Some producers and record companies may also seek out songwriters directly, but music publishers might be your best bet. Additionally, you can reach out to artists directly—especially indie artists—and offer your songs for their upcoming projects. (For more details on the different types of companies and the roles they play for songwriters and performing artists, see the section introductions for Music Publishers, Record Companies, Record Producers, and Managers & Booking Agents.)

What if I am a performing artist/songwriter?

Famous songwriters can also be famous performers. They are skilled interpreters of their own material and know how to write to their own particular talents as musicians. In this case, songwriters' intentions are usually to sell themselves as performers in the hope of recording and releasing an album. They could also have an album already recorded and simply be trying to find gigs and people who can help guide their careers. After working independently to maximize opportunities in their local markets, these songwriters will likely benefit from the assistance of booking agents and managers.

However, a music publisher can still be helpful for this kind of artist, especially in managing a catalog of music and securing licensing opportunities in TV, film, and advertisements. Some music publishers in recent years have also taken on the role of developing artists as both songwriters and performers, or are connected to a major record label, so performing songwriters might go to them for these reasons, too.

ADDITIONAL RESOURCES

Songwriter's Market lists music publishers, record companies, producers, and managers (as well as advertising firms, play producers, and classical performing-arts organizations) along with specifications about how to submit your material to each. Trade publications such as *Billboard* and *Variety*, available at most local libraries and bookstores, are great sources for up-to-date information. These periodicals list new companies and the artists, labels, producers, and publishers for each song on the charts.

Band websites, social media pages, and album liner notes can also be valuable sources of information, providing the name of the record company, publisher, producer, and usually the manager of an artist or group. Use your imagination in your research, and be creative with your results—any contacts you make in the industry may help your career as a songwriter in some way. See the "Publications of Interest" section for more details.

How do I use *Songwriter's Market* to narrow my search?

Once you've identified whether you are primarily interested in getting others to perform your songs or want to perform your own songs and get a record deal, there are several steps you can take:

IDENTIFY WHAT KIND OF MUSIC COMPANY YOU SHOULD APPROACH. As mentioned earlier, deciding whether you're a performing artist or strictly a songwriter will affect whom you want to contact. Songwriters may wish to contact a music publisher for a publishing deal first. Performing artists may prefer to first contact record companies, managers, and record producers to find a record deal or record an album, and reaching out to music publishers might be a secondary, though still important, option.

CHECK FOR COMPANIES BASED ON LOCATION. Maybe you need a manager located near you. Maybe you need to find as many Nashville-based companies as you can because you write country music and that's where most country publishers are. You can also recognize Canadian and foreign companies by the icons in the listing (see A Sample Listing Decoded, located in this section).

LOOK FOR COMPANIES BASED ON THE TYPE OF MUSIC THEY WANT. Some publishers want country. Some record labels want only punk. Read the listings carefully to make sure you're maximizing your time and submitting your work to the appropriate markets.

LOOK FOR COMPANIES BASED ON HOW OPEN THEY ARE TO BEGINNERS. Some companies are more open than others to beginning artists and songwriters. If you are a beginner, it may help to approach these companies first. Some music publishers are hoping to find that wild card hit song and don't care if it comes from an unknown writer. A good song is a good song no matter who writes it. Maybe you are just starting out looking for gigs. In this case, try finding a manager willing to help build your band's career from the ground up.

BEWARE OF FALSE ADVERTISEMENTS. It is important to note that some companies out there are actually service companies for songwriters and not actual "markets." For example, many demo-recording companies that charge songwriters to professionally record their demos are legitimate, but there are others that may present themselves misleadingly as potential "markets" and overpromise exposure. Make sure you perform appropriate research before committing to any company for any reason.

TYPES OF MUSIC COMPANIES

MUSIC PUBLISHERS evaluate songs for commercial potential, find artists to record them, find other uses for the songs (such as in film or television), collect income from songs, and protect copyrights from infringement.

RECORD COMPANIES sign artists to their labels, finance recordings, promotion, and touring, and release songs/albums to radio and television.

RECORD PRODUCERS work in the studio and record songs (independently or for a record company), may be affiliated with a particular artist, sometimes develop artists for record labels, and locate or co-write songs for artists who do not write their own.

MANAGERS & BOOKING AGENTS work with artists to manage their careers, find gigs, and locate songs to record for artists who do not write their own.

A SAMPLE LISTING DECODED

What do the symbols at the beginning of the listings mean?

These icons give you quick information about a listing with one glance. Here's what they mean:

Openness to Submissions

○ The company is open to beginners' submissions, regardless of past success.

◑ The company is mostly interested in previously published songwriters or well-established acts, but will consider beginners.

● The company does not want submissions from beginners, only from previously published songwriters/well-established acts.

⊘ The company only accepts material referred by a reputable industry source.

Other Icons

✪ The market is Canadian.

↺ The market is located outside of the United States and Canada.

⊕ The market is new to this edition.

✪ The market places music in film/television.

EASY-TO-USE REFERENCE ICONS —

E-MAIL AND WEBSITE INFORMATION —

TERMS OF AGREEMENT —

DETAILED SUBMISSION GUIDELINES —

WHAT THEY'RE LOOKING FOR —

INSIDER ADVICE —

○ RUSTIC RECORDS

6337 Murray Lane, Brentwood, TN 37027. (615)371-8397. Fax: (615)370-0353. E-mail: rusticrecordsam@aol.com. Website: www.rusticrecordsinc.com. President: Jack Schneider. Executive VP & Operations Manager: Nell Schneider. VP Publishing and Catalog Manager: Amanda Mark. VP Marketing and Promotions: Ross Schneider. Videography, Photography, and Graphic Design: Wayne Hall. Image consultant: Jo Ann Rossi. Independent traditional country music label and music publisher (Iron Skillet Music/ASCAP, Covered Bridge/BMI, Old Town Square/SESAC). Estab. 1979. Staff size: 6. Releases 2-3/year. Pays negotiable royalty to artists on contracts, statutory royalty to publisher per song on record.

DISTRIBUTED BY CD Baby.com and available on iTunes, MSN Music, Rhapsody, and more.
HOW TO CONTACT Submit professional demo package by mail. Unsolicited submissions are OK. CD only, no MP3s or e-mails. Include no more than 4 songs with corresponding lyric sheets and cover letter. Include appropriately sized SASE. Responds in 4 weeks.
MUSIC Good combination of traditional and modern country. 2008-09 releases: *Ready to Ride*—debut album from Nikki Britt, featuring "C-O-W-B-O-Y," "Do I Look Like Him," "Long Gone Mama," and "I'm So Lonesome I Could Cry."
TIPS "Professional demo preferred."

DEMO RECORDINGS

What is a "demo"?

The demo, shorthand for demonstration recording, is the most important part of your submission package. Demos are meant to give music-industry professionals a way to hear all the elements of your song as clearly as possible so they can decide if it has commercial potential.

What should I send?

Some music-industry people will still want CDs or DVDs, but most now request digital files or MP3 files via e-mail, a Dropbox account, or other electronic means. Others accept submissions through a contact form on their website, rather than giving out an e-mail address. You should also consider having your songs available on a streaming site, such as YouTube, which allows you to easily share your music via a link, without sending any materials. Some companies would prefer to receive a link to a YouTube video, rather than physical (or digital) files. If a listing isn't specific, contact the company or check its website for details. For more information, see the next chapter, "How Do I Submit My Demo?"

How many songs should I send, and in what order?

Up to three is enough, but the number varies. Most music professionals are short on time, and if you can't catch their attention in three songs, your songs probably don't have hit potential. Put complete songs on your demo, not just snippets. Make sure your best, most commercial song is first. An up-tempo number is usually best.

Should I sing my own songs on my demo?

If you can't sing well, you may want to hire someone who can. There are many resources for locating singers and musicians, including songwriter organizations, music stores, and songwriting magazines. The Organizations section of this book is a good resource. Some aspiring professional singers will perform on demos in exchange for a copy they can use as a demo to showcase their talent.

Should I use a professional demo service?

Many songwriters find professional demo services convenient if they don't have the time or resources to hire musicians on their own. For a fee, a demo service will produce your songs in its studio using in-house singers and musicians. (This is fairly common in Nashville.) Many of these services advertise in music magazines and songwriting newsletters, and on bulletin boards at music stores. Perform thorough research before selecting a service. Make sure to listen to samples of prior work, and look for reviews of the service online. Some are mail-order businesses—you send a rough recording of your song or the sheet music, and they produce and record a demo within a couple of months. Be sure to find a service that will allow some control over how the demo is produced, and explain exactly how you want your song to sound. As with studios, look for a service that fits your needs and budget. Some will charge as low as $300 for three songs, while others may go as high as $3,000 and boast a higher-quality sound. Shop around and use your best judgment!

Should I buy equipment and record demos myself?

If you have the drive and focus to learn good recording techniques, yes. Digital multi-track recorders are readily available and affordable, and many artists can set up a passable home studio using just some software, a laptop, and basic recording equipment. If this is not something you feel comfortable doing yourself, it might be easier to have someone else do it; thus, a demo-recording service becomes handy. For performing songwriters in search of record deals, the actual sound of their recordings can be an important part of their artistic concept. Having the "means of production" within their grasp can be crucial to artists pursuing the independent route. But if you don't know how to use the equipment, it may be better to utilize a professional studio.

How elaborate and full should the demo production be if I'm not a performing artist?

Many companies listed in *Songwriter's Market* tell you what types of demos they're looking for. If in doubt, contact them and ask. In general, country songs and pop ballads can be recorded with just a vocal plus a guitar or piano, although many songwriters in those genres still prefer a more complete recording with drums, guitars, and other backing instruments. Up-tempo pop, rock, and dance demos usually require a full production. If you write for a chorus, you will need a number of vocalists to help you create your demo.

What kind of production do I need if I'm a performing artist?

If you are a band or artist looking for a record deal, you will need a demo that is as fully produced as possible. Many singer/songwriters record their demos as if they are going to be released as an album. That way, if they don't get a deal, they can still release it on their own. Also, professionally pressed CDs are now easily within reach of performing songwriters, and many companies offer graphic-design services for a professional-looking product.

What should I send if I'm seeking management?

Some companies want a video of an act performing their songs. Check with the companies for specific requirements. If they don't list this on their website, send them an e-mail through their contact form.

HOW DO I SUBMIT MY DEMO?

You have three basic options for submitting your songs: by mail, in person, and via the Internet.

SUBMITTING MATERIAL BY MAIL

Should I call, write, or e-mail first to ask for submission requirements?

This is always a good idea, and many companies require being contacted first. Be sure to check the company's website so you can respect its wishes regarding phone calls. If you call, be polite, brief, and specific. If you send a letter, make sure it is typed and to the point. Include a typed SASE (self-addressed stamped envelope) for reply. If you send an e-mail, again, be professional and concise. Proofread your message before you send it, and then be patient. Give the company some time to reply. Do not send out mass e-mails or repeated requests.

What do I send with my demo?

Most companies have specific requirements, but here are some general pointers:

- Read the listing carefully and submit *exactly* what it asks for. It's also a good idea to check online in case the submission policies have changed.
- Listen to each demo to make sure it sounds right and is in the right order. (See the previous section, Demo Recordings.)
- Enclose a *brief*, typed cover letter to introduce yourself. Indicate what songs you are sending and why you are sending them. If you are pitching your songs to a particular artist, say so in the letter. If you are an artist/songwriter looking for a record deal, you should say so. Be specific.

SUBMISSION MAILING POINTERS

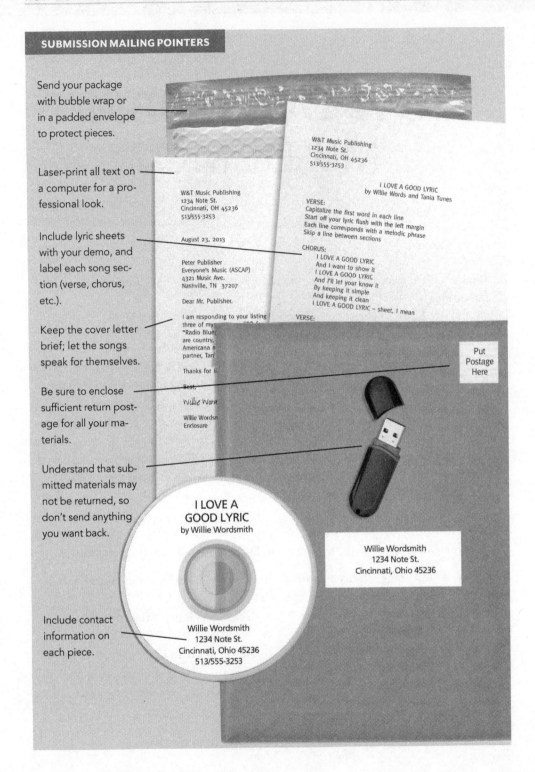

Send your package with bubble wrap or in a padded envelope to protect pieces.

Laser-print all text on a computer for a professional look.

Include lyric sheets with your demo, and label each song section (verse, chorus, etc.).

Keep the cover letter brief; let the songs speak for themselves.

Be sure to enclose sufficient return postage for all your materials.

Understand that submitted materials may not be returned, so don't send anything you want back.

Include contact information on each piece.

W&T Music Publishing
1234 Note St.
Cincinnati, OH 45236
513/555-3253

August 23, 2013

Peter Publisher
Everyone's Music (ASCAP)
4321 Music Ave.
Nashville, TN 37207

Dear Mr. Publisher,

I am responding to your listing
three of my
"Radio Blue
are country,
Americana
partner, Tan

Thanks for li

Best,

Willie Words

Willie Wordsn
Enclosure

W&T Music Publishing
1234 Note St.
Cincinnati, OH 45236
513/555-3253

I LOVE A GOOD LYRIC
by Willie Words and Tania Tunes

VERSE:
Capitalize the first word in each line
Start off your lyric flush with the left margin
Each line corresponds with a melodic phrase
Skip a line between sections

CHORUS:
I LOVE A GOOD LYRIC
And I want to show it
I LOVE A GOOD LYRIC
And I'll let your know it
By keeping it simple
And keeping it clean
I LOVE A GOOD LYRIC – sheet, I mean

VERSE:

Put
Postage
Here

I LOVE A
GOOD LYRIC
by Willie Wordsmith

Willie Wordsmith
1234 Note St.
Cincinnati, Ohio 45236
513/555-3253

Willie Wordsmith
1234 Note St.
Cincinnati, Ohio 45236

- Include *typed* lyric sheets or lead sheets, if requested. Make sure your name, address, and phone number are on each sheet.
- Neatly label each CD with your name, address, e-mail, and phone number, along with the song names in the order they appear on the recording.
- Include a SASE with sufficient postage, and make sure it's large enough to return all your materials. **WARNING:** Many companies do not return materials, so read each listing carefully. Be sure to double-check information on their website.
- If you submit to companies in other countries, include a self-addressed envelope (SAE) and International Reply Coupon (IRC), available at most post offices. Make sure the envelope is large enough to return all your materials.
- Pack everything neatly. Clearly type or print the company's address and your return address. Your package is the first impression a company has of you and your songs, so neatness counts!
- Stamp or write "First Class Mail" on the package and the SASE you enclose.
- Do not use registered or certified mail unless requested. Most companies will not accept or open demos sent by registered or certified mail for fear of lawsuits.
- Keep records of the dates, songs, and companies you submit to.

Is it okay to send demos to more than one person or company at a time?

It is usually acceptable to make simultaneous submissions. One exception is when a publisher, artist, or other industry professional asks you to put your song "on hold."

What does it mean when a song is "on hold"?

This means someone intends to record the song and doesn't want you to give it to anyone else. This is not a guarantee, though. Your song may eventually be returned to you, even if it's been on hold for months.

How can I protect my song from being put "on hold" indefinitely?

One approach is to establish a deadline for the person who asks for the hold in writing: "You can put my song on hold for three months." Or you can modify the hold to specify that you will still pitch the song to others but won't sign another deal without allowing the person with the song on hold to make you an offer. Once you sign a contract with a publisher, it has exclusive rights to your song, and you cannot pitch it to others.

SUBMITTING MATERIAL IN PERSON

Do I need to visit New York, Nashville, or Los Angeles to submit in person?

A trip to one of the major music hubs can be valuable if you are organized and prepared to make the most of it. You should have specific goals and set up appointments before you go. Some industry professionals are difficult to see and may not consider meeting out-of-town writers a high priority. Others are more open and even encourage face-to-face meetings. By taking the time to travel, organize, and schedule meetings, you may appear more professional than songwriters who submit blindly through the mail.

What should I take?

Take several copies of your demo and typed lyric sheets of each of your songs. More than one company you visit may ask you to leave a copy for them to review. A person may cancel an appointment but want you to leave a copy of your songs. (Never give someone the only copy of your demo, though.)

Where should I network?

Coordinate your trip with a music conference or make plans to visit ASCAP, BMI, or SESAC offices while you are there. For example, the South by Southwest Music Conference in Austin and the NSAI Spring Symposium in Nashville often feature demo listening sessions, where industry professionals hear demos submitted by songwriters attending the seminar. ASCAP, BMI, and SESAC also sometimes sponsor seminars or allow aspiring songwriters to make appointments with counselors who can give them solid advice.

How do I deal with rejection?

Many good songs are rejected simply because they are not what the publisher or record company is looking for at that particular point. Do not take it personally. If few people like your songs, it does not mean they are not good. On the other hand, if you have a clear vision for what your particular songs are trying to convey, specific comments can teach you a lot about whether your concept is coming across as you intend. If you hear the same criticisms of your songs over and over—for instance, that the feel of the melody isn't right or the lyrics need work—give the advice serious thought. Listen carefully, and use what reviewers say constructively to improve your songs.

SUBMITTING MATERIAL VIA THE INTERNET

Is it okay to submit via the Internet?

This is becoming standard practice, but many companies still require regular mail submissions, so make sure you verify which process the company prefers. Web-based companies like Songspace.com and TAXI, among many others, are making an effort to connect songwriters and industry professionals via the Internet. The Internet is important for networking. Garageband.com has extensive bulletin boards and allows members to post audio files of songs for critique. Some companies' websites also feature a contact form through which songwriters can submit their material. This eliminates the possiblity of spam and viruses coming from e-mail attachments.

If I want to try submitting via the Internet, what should I do?

First, send an e-mail to confirm whether a music company is equipped to stream or download audio files properly (whether MP3 or streaming at Bandcamp, Soundcloud, etc.). If it does accept demos online, it is possible to use sites such as Dropbox to set up an online folder for sharing. Many e-mail services also have larger maximum file sizes for attachments than they used to, making it easier to e-mail songs. Another strategy is to build a website with audio files that can be streamed or downloaded, or make YouTube videos using just a band photo or album cover image. Better yet, upload a memorable video. (For those companies that only have contact forms, just the link to your YouTube videos may be sufficient.) Then, when you have permission, send an e-mail with links to that website or to particular songs. All they have to do is click on the link, and it launches their Web browser to the appropriate page. Do not try to send MP3s or other files as attachments if the company doesn't accept them or doesn't request them—this is an almost sure-fire way to receive an immediate rejection.

THE ANATOMY OF A HIT

....

Robin Frederick

Robin Frederick has written and produced more than 500 songs for television, records, theater, and audio products.

No matter how much you write songs solely because it's your passion, every songwriter dreams of earning a living from his notebook, full of lyrics and melodies. I know because I've spent my career writing and producing hundreds of songs and teaching others how to do it. I also know that the best way to realize your dream of being a successful (and well-paid) songwriter is with a hit record.

In today's industry, writing a hit song has become more elusive than ever, but the good news is that all chart toppers share similar characteristics. Simply put, a hit song is one that moves a lot of people. It connects with listeners and makes them feel something, whether it gives them an intense emotional experience or an unshakeable urge to get to the dance floor. If your song can do that, then it has the potential to become a hit.

That sounds simple enough, but the difficulty is in understanding how to use the craft of writing a song to create that emotional connection every time you sit down.

THE THREE ELEMENTS OF A HIT

Start with these three basics—and execute them well—and your song will have the same components of your favorite chart toppers.

The Right Mix

Hit songs tend to have a strong, memorable chorus section that lyrically and musically expresses the energy and emotional heart of the song. Listeners love a great chorus, so it might be repeated four or five times during the song, giving them a powerful anchor to come back to that will stick with them long after the song is over. You can hear choruses like this in mega-hits such as Katy Perry's "Roar," John Legend's "All Of Me," and Luke Bryan's "Play It Again." But just repeating a chorus, no matter how good it is, can become predictable. Listeners might tune out pretty quickly if they were hearing the same thing over and over, so we put verses between the choruses and a bridge in the latter portion of the song to break up the repetition with some variety.

....

[Your song structure] needs to be sturdy and able to connect with listeners who may not pay attention until the first or second chorus.

....

This idea of mixing repetition with variety is a crucial part of a hit song's success. Each section—verse, chorus, and bridge—has its own identity and function. We put them together in a way that creates enough repetition to make the song easy to remember and enough variation to keep it interesting. A good song structure, with a mix of repetition and variation, is a great example of how song craft keeps listeners involved. It's not just an arbitrary set of rules designed to make life miserable for songwriters. It really works.

The song structure that today's listeners love best is, in its simplest form: Verse - Chorus - Verse - Chorus - Bridge - Chorus.

Often, we add an extra section called a "pre-chorus," which builds anticipation between each verse and chorus. Listeners really like that. You can hear pre-choruses in all the hits I just mentioned. Or maybe you'll want to start your song with a chorus instead of a verse, like Meghan Trainor's "All About That Bass." You don't need to feel that a song structure limits your creativity. Be creative within it.

When we talk about the "anatomy" of a hit, think of song structure as the basic skeleton the song is built on. It needs to be sturdy and able to connect with listeners who may not pay attention until the first or second chorus. Listen to your favorite hit songs to hear how successful songwriters build strong, resilient song structures.

The Perfect Title

A good title is one thing that can really give birth to a great song, set it in motion, and keep it focused. Make your title something you feel passionate about and something that listeners will want to know about. It can evoke an image or a question, or just be an intriguing statement. Remember, radio listeners don't know you, so you've got to make a powerful impression right away and give them a reason to listen. Titles like Beyoncé's "Halo," Jason Aldean's "Tattoos on This Town," or Justin Bieber's "What Do You Mean?" all suggest interesting situations or questions that might make a listener stick around to check out the song.

A good title is also crucial in creating a catchy "hook"—that all-important line that grabs the listener's attention and sticks with her when the song is over. In each of the hit songs I just mentioned, the title is part of the hook—a lyric and melody line that's prominently featured (and repeated) in the chorus of the song.

Once you have an idea for a title, you can build your lyric on it. Think of a few questions your title suggests, or questions you can answer in your song: What does the title mean? What caused this to happen? Who is involved? What's likely to happen next? And most important: How does the singer feel about it? If you do that, I guarantee you won't run out of things to write about before you get to your second verse.

A Memorable Melody

A hit song needs an irresistibly memorable melody, the kind that listeners can't get out of their heads. Fortunately, there's a crafting tool for doing just that. Hit song melodies—like song structure—are a mix of repetition with variation. It's not uncommon to hear a melody line repeated two or three times in a row as the lyrics change. You can hear this in recent pop hits like Adele's "Hello" and Tim McGraw's "Highway Don't Care." Listen through the verse and chorus of these songs and notice which melody lines are repeated and how the lyrics change over them.

We also use melody to create a dynamic build-up, increasing emotional tension and then releasing it. Without that, a song can feel static, like it's stuck in a rut. For example, a verse might have a melody in a low, conversational note range, while a chorus is likely to be in a higher note range, giving it more emotional impact and setting it apart from the verse. Kelly Clarkson's "Stronger (What Doesn't Kill You)" is a great example. Or check out a timeless hit like The Police's "Every Breath You Take," with its restrained verse melody and big upward swing into the two different, very emotional bridge sections.

FIVE WAYS TO TURN LISTENERS OFF

Now that you know the main elements you need to add to a hit song, you need to know what to leave out. It can be pretty easy to lose listeners if you're not careful—all they have to do is push a button to change the radio station, or cruise on over to another YouTube video. Avoid these things and you have a good chance to keep them tuned in.

Too Many Personal Details

If you're writing a song based on a personal story—something we all do, and should do— think about which details listeners need to know to feel what you're feeling. Include the emotional details, the ones that everyone can relate to: "You asked me to be your friend, but I want to be your lover." "I felt the cold winter of your embrace." Just skip over the fact that you were at a restaurant when it happened and you ordered the penne pasta. Listen to a hit song like Adele's "Set Fire to the Rain" to hear a great example of emotional details, imagery, and actions—with no distractions.

... try to mix those difficult lines with others that are more straightforward and conversational, ones that clearly tell the listener what's going on.

A Wandering Melody

Another thing that will have listeners changing the station is a melody that feels aim- less or has little structure. One big characteristic of hit song melodies is contrast between verse and chorus. Whether it's a difference in note range (a low verse and a high chorus) or note pace (a choppy verse and a smooth chorus), the melody makes it clear that the song has moved from one section to another. Check out a country hit like Lee Brice's "I Drive Your Truck" to hear contrast in note range and pace between the verse and chorus melodies. You always know right where you are in a hit song like this.

Title Not in the Lyric

A title that isn't used in the song lyric, like "Iris" by the Goo Goo Dolls, is only a good idea if you've already sold about a million records. Then your fans will find your song no matter what you call it. But if you're just starting out and you want an audience to be able to locate and buy your song, be sure to feature your title prominently.

Lyrics That Are Too Obscure

It's okay to be ultrapoetic sometimes. We all occasionally need to write those gorgeous, image-laden lyric lines that are difficult to decipher. But keep in mind that these lyrics don't work well in hit songs. At the very least, try to mix those difficult lines with others that are more straightforward and conversational, ones that clearly tell the listener what's going on. A great example from a few years ago is Rob Thomas's "Ever the Same," a huge hit single and a beautiful love song. The first verse is extremely poetic—a long, extended image of a moonlit battlefield. Then the last line of the verse basically says in case you didn't understand, I'm going to tell you what I mean right now. And then he does.

Your best teachers are right in front of you. They're the hit songs on the music charts, the songs that listeners are excited about right now.

FIVE MORE WAYS TO INCREASE YOUR "HIT POTENTIAL"

If you've followed the previous steps, there's a good chance that you have a good song on your hands. But hit songs aren't just good—they're great. Use these final tips to ramp up your song's hit potential a few more notches and score a better chance of appealing to listeners, music publishers, and record labels.

Give Your Title a Boost

Make your title step out from the crowd by including an image, action verb, or question. A music publisher might be more likely to listen to a song called "I Can Kiss You Better," "Thunder in the Rain," or "What's in It for You?" than a song called "You're Special." This doesn't mean one song is better than the other, just that your song might move closer to the top of the pile if it sounds intriguing. Also, it's a good idea to limit the length of your title to make it easy to remember. The usual range is one to five words.

Add Momentum to Your Melody

Today's hit song melodies build momentum from verse to chorus. The verse melody is often relaxed and conversational, with plenty of pauses between lines. But as the melody moves through the pre-chorus and into the chorus, the pauses grow shorter, and there are fewer of them. The effect is one of increased energy and emotion in the chorus, and of thoughts tumbling out. You can hear this type of melody in big hits like Taylor Swift's "Style," Sam Hunt's "House Party," Shawn Mendes's "Stitches," and Kelly Clarkson's "Stronger (What Doesn't Kill You)."

Give Your Chorus a Memorable Payoff Line

The payoff line is the last line of your chorus, and it's the line that makes the deepest impression on listeners. Use that line to express the single most important thing that the singer needs to say. Listen to some of your favorite hit songs and notice how the final line of the chorus conveys a sense of importance, of finality.

Use a Bridge Section

I sometimes call the bridge "Area 51 for songwriters," because no one knows what goes on there. But it's really pretty straightforward. The bridge can be the place where the singer drops all pretense. It's a moment of truth. Think of it as "the reveal." If there's something you haven't said in the rest of the lyrics, here's the place to put it. You can hear a great example of a bridge in the rock genre in Foo Fighters' "The Pretender." John Legend has a simple two line reveal in "All of Me" that really works, and Tim McGraw's hit "Live Like You Were Dying" is a good country example.

Use Song Sections Properly

This is a simple one, but it's very important: Do your explaining in the verses, and keep your chorus focused on how the singer feels.

THE BEST OVERALL ADVICE FOR WRITING HIT SONGS

Study success to be successful. That's the best advice I can give you. Your best teachers are right in front of you. They're the hit songs on the music charts, the songs that listeners are excited about right now.

If you don't like to listen to radio, then check out the top hits on the music charts. Preview them on Amazon or iTunes, and buy the ones you want to study. Of course, no one likes everything on the charts. You may only find one or two songs you like, but that's enough.

Listen to the songs that move you and ask yourself these questions: Why do I like this? What are the lyrics and music doing that draws my attention or makes me feel something? Are there techniques here that I could use in songs of my own?

Finally, stay open. Keep learning and growing; the best songwriters always do. And above all, listen. Then listen more. Write. Then write more. And may your songs flow!

ROBIN FREDERICK has written and produced more than 500 songs for television, records, theater, and audio products. She is a former director of A&R for Rhino Records, the executive producer of more than 60 albums, and the author of top-selling songwriting books, including *Shortcuts to Hit Songwriting*, *Shortcuts to Songwriting for Film & TV*, *Study the Hits*, and *The 30-Minute Songwriter*. Her books are used in top universities and music schools in the United States to teach all levels of songwriting, from beginning to advanced.

HOW DO I PITCH MY SONGS?

....

Andrea Williams

///

Once you've learned how to write hit songs and how you'll get paid from them, the next step is to get them in the hands of people who can record them and generate income for you. While every pitch is different based on the recipient and his specific needs (see the listings in the back of this book for more info), there are some pitching tips that are universal. Follow these suggestions to increase your chances for success.

DON'T BE AFRAID TO START SMALL

When songwriter/producer, sound engineer, and instrumentalist Kevin Kadish started co-writing with a young, unheard-of Meghan Trainor, he had no way of knowing that their collaborations would become the uber-successful "All About That Bass" and "Lips Are Movin." As it turns out, some of the most successful songs are born this way, so if you want the chance to write with pop music's next big star, your best chance of doing so is actually *before* she becomes a star. "In your neighborhood or in your state is probably the next Carrie Underwood or Christina Aguilera," says Sheree Spoltore, founder and president of the Global Songwriters Connection. "You find the up-and-coming talent and you grow together and learn together. And that's how these circles form around the artists where other people are trying to get in, but it's too tight at that point. They've already been working with those writers and producers, and they know one another and have that relationship."

Not sure how to find the Christina Aguilera in your neck of the woods? Try checking out ReverbNation.com, Spoltore suggests. ReverbNation is an online platform developed to help artists and bands connect with fans and promote live shows. It's also a way for songwriters to find acts to write for. "A lot of people are putting their music up on ReverbNation, but they never think of it as a pitch sheet," she says. "The cool thing about the site is that it ranks all these great performers, so you can look and hear the voices of the people you want to pitch to, and you can search it by your state. There's some incredible up-and-coming talent on ReverbNation, and if someone is doing twenty-five or thirty dates a year, you need to be pitching to them, because not only could you get a cut, but you could also get paid every time they perform your song."

The key for success in these markets ... is sounding similar without being copycat or derivative. And the only way to achieve that is by studying what's already out there.

DELIVER THE BEST QUALITY

Grabbing your acoustic and pressing record on your iPhone might work for a rough demo of a song, but when it comes to pitching, quality is everything. You'll have to use professional software like Pro Tools or Logic Pro, and you may need to pay a producer and/or engineer who can record your demo for you. If you feel you can't be completely objective about whether your songs meet commercial standards, enlist the help of a focus group to get the truth. Just don't take the chance of sending out anything that's less than great, because you may never get a chance to redeem yourself.

"In most cases, songs need to be fully produced and delivered at a level that is commensurate with the songs you hear on the radio," says Aurora Pfeiffer, co-founder of the Los Angeles-based artist and songwriter management firm Rolen Music Group. "Managers, publishers, and A&Rs listen to thousands of songs a year, and every song you send is in competition with the song next to it. The same artist you are submitting to is most likely one of the same artists that the top 5 percent of songwriters in the world are submitting to as well."

Quality also refers to your ability to meet the exact needs of the market you're pitching. Obviously, a song you write for a teenage Disney pop star will be vastly different from a song you want to pitch for a beer ad. "Watch TV shows, movies, trailers, and ads, and play video games," says Jennifer Yeko of True Talent Management in Beverly Hills. "Pay careful attention to the type of music that is being used in these mediums. Of course, you should write what inspires you, but I often tell songwriters to make an album that just speaks to you, and then write another EP or album with songs and lyrics specifically geared towards licensing."

The key for success in these markets, says Yeko, is sounding similar without being copycat or derivative. And the only way to achieve that is by studying what's already out there. "Songwriters will think that's selling out, but it's really just being savvy about the type of music that gets used in these formats," she says. "It needs magic and creativity without losing the edge. There is definitely a certain style of songwriting and song that gets licensed, and either you're able to create that or you aren't."

BRING SOMETHING TO THE TABLE BESIDES YOUR MUSIC

We've talked a lot about how competitive the music industry is for songwriters right now, even for those with great songs. And while that reality should certainly cause you to take your craft more seriously and keep working to reach your full potential, it shouldn't leave you fearful or worried. There are still plenty of songwriters getting album cuts and signing publishing deals. The key differentiator between those who are getting opportunities and those who aren't is that successful writers bring value to the table. It is the music *business*, after all, so if you can communicate how a potential buyer will benefit from working with you, your odds of landing a deal or a cut will increase exponentially.

Case in point: From early 2006 to early 2014, Nashville-based Big Loud Shirt Music Publishing didn't sign any new writers who hadn't previously signed at least one other publishing deal. That's *eight years* of only signing veteran songwriters. Unfortunately, many executives just can't afford to take risk, says Seth England, Big Loud Shirt's creative manager.

As England explains, one of the major costs of doing business for publishers is recording demos and it's one of the quickest ways writers can get upside down in their deals—that's when the publisher is continuing to front the money for the demos, yet the writer hasn't earned any money. But when England met with a talented songwriter who was also able to produce his own demos, the decision to sign him came easy. "It's just smarter business," says England. "And the demos end up coming out better sometimes, too, because he can produce the feel of the song he had in his head, and he's talented enough to play multiple instruments and understand rhythms and melodies."

If you want an advantage over your competition when pitching, determine what sets you apart and push that with fervor.

BUILD YOUR BRAND

Many songwriters who are not also artists fail to take the time to establish their personal brand. But with the Internet at your fingertips and numerous free platforms at your disposal, there's no reason for you *not* to do so—and, in fact, it can make all the difference in your career.

"It's always best to have a strong social media presence across all platforms," says Pfeiffer. "You don't need to have a website, but it does add value to your brand if you do. There's so much competition in this business that it's best to utilize as many platforms as you can to make yourself visible. SoundCloud is a great platform to share music on and can easily be linked to a website if you choose to create one."

Yeko agrees about the importance of establishing a brand and encourages songwriters to define their niche. "Songwriters should absolutely brand themselves, because, like it or not, people get known for writing a certain type of song very well, whether it's pop or rock or country," she says. "Focus on becoming amazing in one genre first, before branching out into others."

Another tip from Pfeiffer when you're setting up shop on the Internet: "Be careful to not publicly put out any songs that you plan on placing with other artists in the future, as most artists want songs that were never previously released or shared with others."

GET HELP

The act of writing songs can be a lonely venture, but getting them out to potential buyers shouldn't be. Actually, bringing a professional on board to help you pitch your songs can generate more success for your efforts. "Having a manager helps connect the dots, and it keeps a songwriter organized and on track," explains Pfeiffer. "A manager helps filter talent and put her client in the right rooms. The right manager works with the songwriter, not *for* the songwriter. They help bring opportunities to the table, and negotiate and close deals. They build a strategy and execute ideas together."

By now, you've no doubt experienced the uncertainty and heartbreak of reaching out to a contact via e-mail and never hearing anything back. Well, the secret to getting on a manager's radar and best positioning yourself for possible representation—and a return e-mail—is to have someone refer you and vouch for your work, says Pfeiffer. When that isn't possible, you should still reach out, but you must remember that first impressions are everything. "When approaching via a cold e-mail, the best way is to reach out with a product that's undeniable," says Pfeiffer. "It's all in the way your e-mail is worded. You need to learn how to sell yourself and make an undeniable pitch that makes the recipient intrigued to know more."

Even if you can't convince a manager to work with you, Pfeiffer says having a third party reach out on your behalf is still possible—just recruit a friend or family member in a manager's stead. "I know a few writers who pursue this route, and both parties seem to learn as they go if they don't have a music business background," she says. "If you don't have the luxury of having a close friend or relative representing you, then a clever way around that is to create an e-mail [address] just for pitches ... I've seen that route also [taken] before, and it can open up doors if it's done right."

ANDREA WILLIAMS is an author, celebrity ghostwriter, and journalist living in Nashville, Tennessee. She has written hundreds of articles for numerous publications, including CNNMoney.com, *Pregnancy and Newborn* magazine, USNews.com, *Vegetarian Times*, and MediaBistro.com, and she has several books in various stages of publication with traditional and independent publishers. Along the way, Andrea has interviewed everyone from stay-at-home moms and multimillionaire entrepreneurs, to megachurch pastors and award-winning athletes—and she's always on the lookout for the next great story. Though currently residing in the South with her husband and four children, Andrea's heart will always remain in her hometown of Kansas City, Missouri—constantly feasting on Kansas City Royals baseball and Gates & Sons Bar-B-Q.

AVOIDING THE RIP-OFFS

Andrea Williams

Since you're reading this book, there's a high likelihood that you're one of the thousands, if not millions, of songwriters looking to ramp up their career. And as you may not have realized thus far, there are tons of shady outfits at the ready to prey on your ambition. Luckily, getting ripped off as a naïve, unsuspecting songwriter is not a forgone conclusion. There are, in fact, specific steps that you can follow to help you preserve your dignity— and your earning potential—on your way to stardom.

GET SOME LEVERAGE

Most songwriters are dreaming of the days when they can live fabulously off fat advances and ever-streaming royalty checks, and relish in the luxury of working (that is, writing songs) only because they want to—not because they *have* to. The reality, however, is that it takes years for songwriters to reach that elite status, if they ever do. In the meantime, bills still need to be paid, and there is nary a collector who will accept "proof of potential fame and riches" as sufficient payment. In short: Don't quit your day job.

You may have already been advised to maintain a steady income while you're building your music career so that you can sleep on an actual mattress and have a full belly at night. That's most important, but there's another issue at stake: When you're worried about keeping the lights on in your dingy apartment, you aren't in the best state of mind for negotiations. All of a sudden, $250 seems perfectly reasonable for five cuts on an indie album, or you're willing to sign over all your authorship for a publishing deal that may only net a $10,000 advance.

That's not to say you won't have to work for little or nothing in the early stages of your career, because you probably will. But there's a difference between strategically pursuing opportunities that provide little present value but have a major upside in the long run versus signing the first deal that comes along because you feel you have to—or, worse, you're *desperate*. It comes down to being in a position of power in business deals. In that sense, power doesn't mean that you have more money, or clout, or influence than the other party. It means, simply, that you understand your value and worth as a songwriter (even if you're just starting out) and don't need to accept any offer that's dangled before you. Entertainment attorney Barry Chase, of Miami, Florida-based ChaseLawyers, says it like this:

> If the other party—a producer, publishing company, artist, or business seeking a jingle; let's call them the "buyer"—has approached the songwriter, rather than vice versa, that suggests that something about the songwriter's previous work or personality has specially appealed to the buyer. Or, if some higher-up on the buyer's side has already recommended the songwriter, that also equalizes the bargaining leverage somewhat. The worst situation, from the point of view of the songwriter's bargaining leverage, is one where the songwriter approaches the buyer, hat-in-hand, desperate for a gig. It is almost impossible to maintain one's rights and respect when you need to pay the rent tomorrow.

So how can you avoid begging for opportunity and instead entice music industry bigwigs to come knocking on your door? The answer, says Chase, is to launch your own career, DIY-style. As our State of the Industry report in the next section mentions, in the history of recorded music, there has never been a time greater than today to be a songwriter. Yes, there's more competition than ever, and incomes across the board have decreased. But no longer are songwriters beholden to the merciless gatekeepers who've historically cherry-picked those they deemed worthy enough to have a career. Now, more than ever, you can get started, do some co-writes, put your songs out, and build your own brand. Ultimately, if you've also taken time to hone your skills and refine your craft, bigger doors may start to open. And if they do, you'll have evidence of your talent and drive, which you will be able to effectively communicate, and could be offered a deal that honors that.

INVEST IN YOURSELF, BUT DO IT WISELY

If you're going to get serious about launching your career independently (at least to start), you need to be aware that you'll have to spend some cash along the way. That's not a bad thing; after all, where there's no risk, there's no reward. And if you aren't willing to bank on your own songwriting ability, it's unlikely that anyone else will be, either. Unfortunately, coming to terms with that reality isn't as difficult as determining where you can actually invest your hard-earned money to reap the greatest return in your career.

From third-party A&R companies that screen songs and claim to forward those that pass muster on to record labels, producers, ad agencies, and other buyers looking for music, to song pluggers who promise to use their connections to secure album cuts and licensing opportunities for writers, a quick Internet search will yield numerous opportunities to spend cash in hopes of furthering your career.

Some experts believe that, while newbie songwriters should generally expect to pay some dues when starting, those dues shouldn't necessarily be in the form of hundreds of dollars spent upfront for a service. "I would avoid it altogether or, at the very least, tread extremely carefully in any situation where someone is requesting large sums of upfront money to review or pitch your work," says Atlanta-based entertainment attorney John Seay. "You should pay attention to the exclusivity of the service. Is it open to pretty much anyone, or is the client list curated? If someone has reached out to you, have they demonstrated legitimate interest in your work, or was it a form e-mail? If the service is not very exclusive and no one has expressed legitimate excitement about your music, then do you really think they're going to spend much time pitching your songs? In my experience, if someone thinks you can make them money, they are much more willing to work for a piece of the back end versus charging a fee upfront."

That said, not all industry veterans condemn upfront fees. "There are many legitimate song pluggers in Nashville and in other major music centers," says Steve Weaver, an entertainment attorney in Music City with more than thirty years of experience representing songwriters. "A few pluggers work on a percentage only, but the top pluggers charge a retainer and sometimes bonuses and/or a percentage, depending on certain measurable levels of success of a song placement."

At *Songwriter's Market*, we believe every songwriter's situation is unique and should be treated as such. If you're siphoning from your trust fund and have cash to burn, signing up for one of these services may not be a terrible option. It certainly won't hurt your career, and you may land a decent opportunity in the process. Before you start, though, ask around and get an objective take on the individual or business, and if something doesn't feel right, go with your gut. "The contract for these services should have clear ways to measure and determine the efforts of the plugger or other service, and an easy way to terminate the contract if the service or plugger is not performing as agreed," adds Weaver.

For those songwriters who are tight on cash and can't afford to invest in an A&R service or professional song plugger without guarantee of success, we advise caution. It is those who are caught between a rock and a student loan (or phone, or gas, or credit card bill) who will most likely feel cheated or ripped off should things not pan out. And there are safer investments for your money anyway. Songwriting organizations like Nashville Songwriters Association International and Global Songwriters Connection charge fees, but there are so many guaranteed benefits built into the membership plans, including networking events, opportunities to pitch to publishers and other decision makers *directly*, and educational resources that teach the ins and outs of the music business, that the costs are more than worth it.

DO YOUR HOMEWORK; KNOW WHEN TO HIRE HELP

You've heard about unscrupulous car mechanics who take advantage of little old ladies who don't know the difference between a carburetor and a carport. Well, the same ruthless behavior happens all the time in the music industry. In the end, the best protection against rip-offs is education.

Become well versed in the usage of split sheets when working with co-writers. "Remember," says Seay, "in the absence of a written agreement to the contrary, under United States copyright law, each writer of the song automatically owns an undivided interest in the entire song. That could get messy if a writer only contributed to a small part of the song, but nevertheless claims an equal share to the royalties generated from the song." And get a good grasp on independent contractor and work-for-hire agreements, whether you're executing one with a session musician or producer you're hiring or if you, yourself, are brought in as a work-for-hire songwriter, which means, basically, that you forfeit all ownership rights to the song.

Once you've started putting songs out for the public, research and register with one of the performing rights organizations to ensure that no one can use your work without your permission. And, perhaps more important, be savvy enough to understand when you need to recruit the services of an attorney.

"Although you may not need to hire a lawyer early on in your career, it might be a good idea to consult with one initially," says Seay. "Regardless of whether you take advantage of an early consultation, though, you should absolutely consider consulting with an attorney as soon as a contract is introduced into the equation. Remember that many contracts last forever, or for so long that it might as well be forever. An attorney can help you draft, review, and negotiate those agreements. I speak from experience saying that it's much better and cheaper for you to address any potential issues on the front end than it is to hire an attorney to try to extricate you from, or enforce, a bad deal."

The key, adds Weaver, is to hire your own attorney who is experienced in the entertainment industry and intellectual property matters. "It should go without saying, but a writer should never rely on the producer's or publisher's lawyer to tell them that the contract is okay," he says. "I have seen writers do this, and the end result was never good. And the attorney should be an entertainment attorney—not a generalist or attorney with some other specialty. Sure, the writer's father's business attorney can read a publishing contract and tell the writer what it says, but it is not likely that the nonentertainment lawyer will know if its terms are acceptable. And, more important, the nonentertainment lawyer probably will not know what is *not* in the contract that should be there."

Finally, it also helps to research the typical career trajectory of a songwriter in your chosen genre. How long does it typically take for someone to "make it"? We'd like to believe that you are the exception and not the rule, and you may very well be. But just in case, having conservative expectations for your career will save you the heartache of being bamboozled by some sleazy suit who promises you the world two weeks after you've penned your first full song.

"Be realistic about the fact that you are trying to make a living in a way that almost everyone on earth would like to if they could," says Chase. "You shouldn't expect to get Paul Simon's deal until you have demonstrated that you are a bankable talent. At the end of the day, I'm afraid, it's a business, and the sooner a new talent reconciles herself to that ugly fact, the better."

HOW DO I SUBMIT A COMPLAINT TO *SONGWRITER'S MARKET*?

Write the *Songwriter's Market* editor at: 10151 Carver Road, Suite 200, Blue Ash, OH 45242. Include:

- a complete description of the situation, as best you can describe it
- copies of any materials the company sent you that we can keep on file

---

STATE OF
THE INDUSTRY

....

Andrea Williams

When the American economy crashed in 2008 following the housing crisis, there were millions of families who quite literally lost everything. Wall Street's charade of packaging bogus loans and passing around funny money blew up, and the general public was left holding the bag. But while much of Middle America spent years trying to recover and to clean up the mess, there were others who saw nothing but opportunity. As foreclosures mounted in neighborhoods across the country, these savvy investors swooped in, bolstering their portfolios and their profits with properties that they scored for pennies on the dollar.

So what does this have to do with the 2017 music industry? Well, everything, actually. If our 2016 report was the warning that streaming and other twenty-first century factors had turned the music industry on its head and were forcing songwriters to rethink their career strategies, this year's report is evidence that it's possible to not just survive the record business flux but to thrive on it.

Case in point: The cover of the November 25, 2014, issue of *Bloomberg Businessweek* featured a heavily mascaraed, red-lipsticked Taylor behind the dubious headline "Taylor Swift Is The Music Industry." And while the accompanying article did a good job of detailing her ascent to the top of the (country and pop) charts, the bigger story was that of her label head, Scott Borchetta.

It was the visionary Borchetta who launched Big Machine Records in 2006, with Swift as his flagship artist, reaping commercial and financial success as every album she released raced to No. 1, each one faster than the one before. "We never had a year when we lost money," he told the magazine. And when it seemed streaming sites were encroaching on songwriter and artist profits, he encouraged her to pull her entire catalog from Spotify just prior to the release of her most recent project, "1989."

But Borchetta's savvy extends far beyond the blonde superstar who, like Madonna and Beyoncé, is now on first-name status, worldwide. After noticing the rabid young female fans hanging on Taylor's every guitar chord, he gave the boys something to groove to by signing the massive country crossover duo Florida Georgia Line. Then, as the ABC television network readied its primetime country music soap *Nashville*, he negotiated for the right to market and distribute the show's original music. And when Jimmy Iovine, chairman of Interscope Geffen A&M, vacated his position as mentor on Fox's *American Idol*, Borchetta swooped in, eager to discover his next great act.

Even in country music, where radio still matters and fans still buy entire albums, Borchetta's success is unmatched. He operates an independent label in a sea of Capitols, Sonys, and Universals, yet when he sees an opportunity, he strikes without restraint. Because Borchetta and company are passionate enough about their product—and so willing to zig while everyone else zags—success is nothing but a foregone conclusion. In short, if the music industry is in a state of ruin, Borchetta simply didn't get the memo.

With experts spewing industry doom and gloom and all but insisting would-be music makers to choose another career path, songwriters could do worse than to follow Borchetta's lead.

Not much that we reported last year has changed. Executive Director of the nonprofit Nashville Songwriters Association International, Bart Herbison, explained that:

> ... songwriters get paid under two sets of government rules. The first is the mechanical royalty, which pays artists and songwriters anytime there is a purchase of physical CDs or legal downloads. "Those rules are from 1909," he says, "and they were created for player piano rolls. They've never worked effectively, and they certainly don't work in the digital era." The second set of rules is related to performance royalties, which are paid whenever a song is played on terrestrial radio (local stations), in a bar or restaurant, in any live venue, or on the aforementioned streaming services. Those rules, while not as dated, still go back to 1941.
>
> In both cases, the royalty rates are set by the federal government—mechanical royalties reset once every five years by a Copyright Royalty Board (CRB) in what is similar to a trial, while performance royalties are set by a rate court. The problem, explains Herbison, is that once rates are set, songwriters are under a compulsory license, which means they have to license songs for the rates the government sets, whether they agree or disagree with the terms. And most don't.
>
> "So here's the result of all that, as it relates to the streaming sites," says Herbison. "If you get a song played on a regular radio station, it averages 5 to 6 cents every time it spins, for the songwriter and the music publisher. When it plays on a streaming service, it's 8/10,000ths of a penny."
>
> That wouldn't signal as big of a crisis if the digital streams had only supplemented an already robust industry. But as Forbes Executive Editor Zack O'Malley Greenburg noted in an article appearing in the May 2015 issue of the magazine, the industry has never really recovered from the days of piracy. Total U.S. albums sold hit a peak of 785 million in 2000, the year after Napster's launch. But, Greenburg writes, "By 2008 annual album sales had plummeted

45%. Between then and now, even as the labels reined in illegal downloading, sales dropped another 40% to 257 million. That means, at $15 per album, the industry is currently taking in $7.9 billion less in annual retail sales than it was a decade and a half ago."

Herbison and others are working earnestly to shift the tide. John Poppo, Chairman of the Board of the National Academy of Recording Arts and Sciences is an instrumental part of the organization's efforts to protect the creative and financial interests of artists and songwriters. Among the measures he's working to push through Congress is the Songwriter Equity Act, which would allow significant changes to mechanical and performance royalty rates, and the Fair Play for Fair Pay Act, which would pay artists and labels when their songs are performed on terrestrial radio. The latter of these may not seem relevant to songwriters, as songwriters and publishers are already compensated for terrestrial radio play. However, says Poppo, this bill would minimize the financial squeeze on artists, which would have a direct effect on the earning potential of songwriters.

"Artists are already taking a huge hit in terms of record sales, but if they were at least being paid their fair performance royalties by terrestrial radio when their records are being played on the air, as the songwriters are, perhaps they would be more inclined to accept more outside songs written exclusively by songwriters rather than feel compelled to write them on their own," says Poppo.

Herbison further explains the impact of increased artist co-writes: "In Nashville, we've gone from needing 12,000–13,000 songs a year in the late nineties—that many songs were actually released on records—to 300 or 400 that the artist is not involved in writing," he says. "We've gone from 3,000 or 4,000 publishing deals, to 300 or 400. So it's awfully hard to breakin to the professional ranks as a songwriter."

Still, this refers to the traditional songwriting model of placing songs with major label acts, a model that can certainly yield lucrative returns but is also increasingly difficult to follow. If we're thinking outside the box and taking a Borchetta-like approach to career building, we know that the obvious path may not be the most lucrative or fulfilling.

"Revenue streams are constantly changing with a rapidly changing world, especially as it relates to technology, because these changes bring about new opportunities and demands for music, while making others obsolete," says Poppo. "If we consider a timespan as large as fifteen years, those changes become more significant. Consider the decrease in mechanical royalties from recording sales versus the new revenue streams resulting from digital streaming, Internet and satellite radio, online services, ringtones, etc. Consider, too, the growth in the video gaming and app industries, both of which utilize synchronized music, along with the many independent cable TV and movie channels, etc. And even the growth of Google and YouTube, which now monetizes video views, is one of the many examples of the changing landscape when it comes to monetizing music for songwriters. The good news is there has never been a greater demand for music and great songs."

Even if you don't think you know much about how Nashville's songwriting and recording process works, if you've seen the show *Nashville*, ABC's soapy ode to Music City, you know more than you think. Those studio sessions in which the producer (Jonathan Jackson's Avery Barkley) is directing a room full of musicians in harmoniously crafting the perfect sound is how records have been cut in Nashville for decades. Now, though, as bro-country and other subgenres adopt more pop influences, including digitally programmed tracks with synthesized bass lines and infectious drum loops, things are beginning to shift. And, in cases like this, publishers and labels would much rather pay one songwriter/producer with a knack for digitally programming backing tracks than a room full of session musicians under union contracts.

"I feel like there are some big advantages to where we've gone with technology and people doing tracks and demos at their house," says BJ Hill, Senior Director of A&R at Warner/Chappell Nashville. "With everybody being able to build tracks nowadays and get stuff to sound cool, I think it kind of levels the playing field a little bit, and guys are getting pub deals who maybe aren't great lyricists and who maybe used to have to be in order to contribute to the songwriting community.

"There are arguments for that being a good thing or a bad thing, and whether somebody who's just putting music down on a track is really a songwriter," adds Hill. "But regardless of what your opinion is, there are plenty of those guys who are getting pub deals and getting cuts, and who are having a ton of success right now, and that doesn't seem like it's going anywhere anytime soon."

Traditionally speaking, publishing deals are less than favorable for new writers. However, if songwriters can parlay additional skills or social media buzz that make them an especially attractive signee, Hill believes a publishing deal is still one of the best ways to get a foot in the door with artists and labels, and to experience the biggest potential career growth, even in a slumping industry.

"You want somebody that's going to work hard to make sure that every day you're writing with the best possible person for you, in your [position] right now," says Hill, of the ideal songwriter/publisher relationship. "Maybe you don't need to be writing with the blue-chip writer yet, because maybe your skills aren't completely honed. Maybe you need to be writing with some peers that will help you develop, so that the first time you get in that blue-chip room, you don't make a bad impression. And the information part of being tied into a publisher is important, too—just knowing there's a new band on Warner Brothers that's cutting a new record next week and knowing exactly what kinds of songs they're looking for is huge."

If [new songwriters] can parlay additional skills or social media buzz that make them an especially attractive signee, [BJ] Hill believes a publishing deal is still one of the best ways to get a foot in the door with artists and labels ...

Truly, the right publishing deal can be career-breaking huge, and, as Poppo points out, publishers can't operate without signing talented songwriters. "They need hit songs; their business model is predicated upon that one fact," he says. But there's a caveat.

"Naturally, everyone in business wants to hedge his or her bets and invest in the most sure things, and publishers are no different," explains Poppo. "Publishers need to be very mindful of the initial investment and likeliness and potential size of return on their investment, with far less room for error in today's profit margins, so anytime or any way a songwriter can help demonstrate more favorable odds for the publisher's business investment, it will help. There are innumerable avenues to self-market yourself and your songs today. Use them. If you get a buzz, you will get noticed and have more to sell, and with more leverage to negotiate."

The beauty of the Internet is that a laptop, wireless connection, and free social media account can turn any songwriter into a full-service marketing machine. Even if you're not Taylor Swift, with a legion of Swifties and a "big machine" turning gears in your favor, you can still get the attention of some of the folks in need of your incredible music.

Maybe you're a songwriter in Indianapolis who knows his way around Pro Tools pretty well. That skill may not land you on the couch opposite Jimmy Fallon, a la Taylor, but it could very well land you a publishing deal, and that publishing deal may walk you into doors you never could have imagined opening. Or maybe you've come across a talented singer at a coffee house open mic night and notice that her songs pale in comparison to the power of her vocals. Strike up a conversation. Offer to write for her for free. Pledge to ride the roller coaster of this fickle music business together.

Whatever you do, and however you choose to do it, attack your career with boldness. Your opportunity awaits.

IN THE KNOW ABOUT PROs

....

Andrea Williams

Finally, you've written some songs that someone other than your mother and best friend will hear. Perhaps you've landed a cut on a hot new indie artist's album, or maybe you've taken up writing songs for a local band's revamped live show. It's exciting when someone is singing your songs on stages across the country or a new radio station is plugging your music into heavy rotation every day. However, for the first time, you'll have no way of knowing exactly when and where your songs are being played—or "performed," in industry speak. Consequently, that also means you have no way to track your earned royalties. That's where performing rights organizations come in.

Performing rights organizations, or PROs, serve three main purposes in their affiliated songwriters' careers. First, they track the performances of their songs, including those on domestic terrestrial radio (online radio royalties are paid by SoundExchange), at live venues, and other public performances/broadcasts and TV/film broadcasts. The PROs then collect the appropriate licensing fees from the users of the songs, and, finally, distribute royalties (minus administrative fees) to the songwriters. There are three PROs in the United States—the American Society of Composers, Authors and Publishers (ASCAP), Broadcast Music, Inc. (BMI), and the Society of European Stage Authors and Composers (SESAC)—and they each serve this basic function.

As a songwriter, you may have heard that affiliating with a PRO is your first step to becoming a professional, but that may not actually be the case. In fact, Tim Fink, SESAC's VP of writer/publisher relations at the organization's Nashville headquarters, discourages writers from signing on with a PRO too early. "If you're thirteen years old, you probably don't need to go buy a car," he says. "You don't have your driver's license yet, and there's just no need for it. And it's the same thing with performance rights organizations. Most people can't tell you why they joined, and they don't realize that they've actually entered into a contract with that organization."

Obviously, if you fit the above description and know that artists are recording or performing your songs, you also know that you need to sign with a PRO if you expect to get paid. If you're not at that point in your career, however, Fink suggests you really consider your goals and plans as a songwriter. Are you a hobbyist, or are you serious about writing songs professionally? If the latter is true, you may derive some value from a PRO, even before you land your first cut.

"We provide tools and services for up-and-coming songwriters to meet their evolving needs, including educational panels, workshops, networking opportunities, and more," says Nicole George-Middleton, ASCAP's VP of rhythm & soul/urban membership. "We teach about the business, how to manage your money, and the art of songwriting, so when you're a new writer and you join ASCAP, you have access to all of these resources."

Indeed, each of the PROs offers some level of career development to its member songwriters that extends beyond the main function of collecting and disseminating royalties. But *how* each organization interacts with its writers and helps to nurture their careers can vary substantially. SESAC, for example, may offer fewer workshops and conferences for budding writers than ASCAP, but Fink believes the main benefit of affiliation with his organization is the hands-on, personal attention offered to writers, which is made possible by the fact that SESAC is, by far, the smallest of the three PROs. "At SESAC, there are only 30,000 members [compared to ASCAP's and BMI's 525,000 and 650,000, respectively], and that's by design," he says. "The relationship comes first, and the contract comes later, and it's the relationship that helps you get in the door."

Ultimately, it's up to songwriters to research each PRO and choose the organization that best suits their needs. It's certainly not a decision you want to enter into blindly, nor should you automatically choose the PRO that your favorite artist or songwriter is affiliated with. With that in mind, we've done some of the legwork to help you determine whether ASCAP, BMI, or SESAC is right for you.

ASCAP

WEBSITE: www.ascap.com
YEAR LAUNCHED: 1914
NUMBER OF MEMBERS: 525,000
LOCATIONS: New York, Los Angeles, Nashville, Atlanta, Miami, London, Puerto Rico
HOW TO JOIN: Sign up online with your social security number. A one-time processing fee of fifty dollars is required.
NOTABLE MEMBERS: Alicia Keys, Katy Perry, Pharrell Williams, Bill Withers

NOTEWORTHY FACTS:

- ASCAP is the only PRO that offers a one-year contract term to members.
- The ASCAP board of directors consists solely of songwriters and publishers.
- The annual ASCAP EXPO is the organization's flagship event, which draws thousands of attendees and puts up-and-coming songwriters in the same room as high-profile, successful writers and composers, all in the name of education and networking.

BMI

WEBSITE: www.bmi.com
YEAR LAUNCHED: 1939
NUMBER OF MEMBERS: 650,000
LOCATIONS: New York, Los Angeles, Nashville, Atlanta, Miami, London, Puerto Rico
HOW TO JOIN: Sign up online for free.
NOTABLE MEMBERS: Taylor Swift, Lady Gaga, Eminem, Willie Nelson
NOTEWORTHY FACTS:

- BMI was initially established to compete against ASCAP, which, until that point, had full market dominance. BMI offered music users lower licensing fees and offered to pay new songwriters a fixed fee per performance, as opposed to ASCAP's two-tier structure that penalized less established writers.
- BMI became the first PRO to represent songwriters in marginalized or less popular genres, including jazz, gospel, country, R&B, and blues.

SESAC

WEBSITE: www.sesac.com
YEAR LAUNCHED: 1930
NUMBER OF MEMBERS: 30,000
LOCATIONS: New York, Los Angeles, Nashville, Atlanta, Miami, London
HOW TO JOIN: Fill out the free online form with introductory information about your life and songs, and submit music samples. A writer representative will review all materials before scheduling a meeting or conference call. At that point, the rep will decide whether to extend an offer for representation.
NOTABLE MEMBERS: Mariah Carey, Natalie Grant, Lady Antebellum, Rico Love

NOTEWORTHY FACTS:

- Because of the personal nature of SESAC representation, writer reps are often able to closely assist in the career development of songwriters, including helping to arrange meetings with co-writers and publishers.
- SESAC is the only PRO that pays songwriters monthly royalties for domestic terrestrial radio plays. Those twelve disbursements are in addition to the quarterly royalty payments for all other performances.
- SESAC was the first PRO to pay live performance royalties to songwriters.

FOR THE LOVE OF THE MONEY

....

Andrea Williams

Barry Shrum is an entertainment lawyer who has been practicing law in the intellectual property, music, entertainment, and business industries for more than twenty-five years.

On June 30, 1997, hip-hop mogul Sean "Diddy" Combs (then known as Puff Daddy) released "All About the Benjamins," a single from his debut album *No Way Out*. It was a slicked-out rap anthem professing love, not for Benjamin Franklin himself, but for the hundred-dollar bills that bear his image— and, of course, all the wonderful things they can buy. Then, the very next day, on July 1, Diddy's Bad Boy Records dropped the second single from rapper The Notorious B.I.G.'s posthumous *Life After Death* album. The title? "Mo Money Mo Problems."

Since the dawn of recorded music, there has been no shortage of songs dedicated to all things green, and, still, the contradiction that Bad Boy illuminated back in the late 1990s lives on. It's most evident, perhaps, in the careers of the very people behind the music, the songwriters who pour everything into their search for the elusive hit that will sell millions of copies and, presumably, bring lots and lots of cash. But those same songwriters have heard the horror stories of their predecessors who didn't understand the business of their craft and, as a result, could relate to The Notorious B.I.G.'s hit all too well.

As an entertainment attorney with more than twenty-five years' experience, Nashville's Barry Shrum is acutely aware of how important it is that songwriters understand the value of their intellectual property, as well as how to protect and leverage it. In fact, he's been lead counsel on major copyright infringement cases that ultimately won six-figure verdicts for his clients. Here, Shrum details everything you need to know about earning money as a songwriter so you can get paid—without going to court.

When a songwriter finishes a song or a collection of songs, the first thing to be done is to register the copyrights on the U.S. Copyright Office's eCo site (copyright.gov/eco).

Once a songwriter writes a song, how, exactly, does he get paid?

As they often say in Music City, "It all begins with a song." But while that may be true, the *value* of a song is only as much as someone is willing to pay for it. A songwriter receives royalties when he (or the publisher) *licenses* one or more of the first five exclusive rights granted by Section 106 of the Copyright Act: distribution, reproduction, adaptation, display, and performance.

A writer receives income from distribution and reproduction rights, for example, when a record label "mechanically reproduces" the song and distributes it for sale. That mechanical royalty is prescribed by law and is called a *statutory royalty*. Currently, that is 9.1 cents per record. The songwriter is also paid this mechanical royalty when a song is downloaded from the Internet on iTunes, Amazon Music, or Google Play. It is important to distinguish "streaming" from downloading, in that streaming implicates the payment of royalties for licensing the digital performance in a sound recording—not the mechanical royalty referenced above. The royalties for that activity are collected by SoundExchange and distributed to the owner of the sound recording copyright and the artists/musicians that performed on the track, and any implicated performance rights for those streams are paid to the songwriters by the traditional performance rights organizations (PROs): ASCAP, BMI, and SESAC.

The performance royalties paid to songwriters are less defined than statutory royalties paid under the Copyright Act. In the United States, the songwriters and publishers are generally affiliated with one of the performance rights organizations. Under the authority of nonexclusive agreements with the songwriters, these organizations license out their performance rights to various venues and organizations. Each organization has its own proprietary formula for calculating performance royalties that are due to each songwriter/publisher based on various factors. These formulas are generally defined on each PRO's website.

Finally, there are other royalties to which a songwriter may be entitled. When Don Schlitz licensed the rights to his Kenny Rogers hit, "The Gambler," to a television production company for the [TV] miniseries of the same name, he received a royalty payment for the adaptation rights, as the song was "adapted" [for TV]. If the lyrics to the song were subsequently used in a paperback book about the movie, the publisher of the book would obtain a license to "display" the lyrics, and pay Mr. Schlitz an additional royalty for that use. Finally, if the television company wanted to use a recording of the song in the movie (either Kenny's version or their own recorded version), that would require an additional license, commonly called a synchronization license, to "sync" the copyright with audiovisual content.

When a songwriter finishes a song, or a collection of songs, the first thing to be done is to register the copyrights on the U.S. Copyright Office's eCo site (copyright. gov/eco). Next, I would recommend that the songwriter investigate the offerings of ASCAP, BMI, and SESAC, and choose one with which to affiliate. That way, if the songwriter anticipates that the song will be used commercially, she can submit the appropriate forms to her selected PRO to notify the organization of the impending use. Once alerted to the possibility of performances, the PRO will collect the writer's royalties. Also, the PRO has people who are dedicated to helping writers find affiliated publishers, who may advocate for the songwriter and help her seek out other uses for the song.

Is it mandatory that a songwriter register his copyright?

The Copyright Act clearly states that a copyright exists from the moment that an original expression is fixed in a tangible format. For the songwriter, this means that a copyright exists from the moment the song is created and [recorded] in some way (paper, tape, CD, digital, etc.). This ownership of the copyright is distinct from registering the copyright with the Copyright Office, which is not a required step, but it is very beneficial because it gives the creator certain additional benefits, not the least of which is statutory damages up to $200,000 if a willful infringement occurs. This is well worth the small registration fee.

For years, there has been this folklore surrounding the infamous "poor man's copyright," where the songwriter mails a copy of the song to his address so that the postmark serves as proof of creation. The problem is, it's neither copyright nor proof. A good lawyer can easily disprove this kind of evidence. It is better for the songwriter to keep an accurate journal of his activity, including dates and times when possible. This kind of evidence is more useful when it comes to proving who created the song.

What if there is more than one writer on a song? How do the co-writers ensure that they are both (or all) paid fairly?

A *split sheet* is a very rudimentary written document pertaining to one specific song. It can be completed by collaborating songwriters before, during, or immediately after a writing session. The document identifies the song and the percentages of revenues agreed to by each of the songwriters. Remember that, in the eyes of the law, each songwriter is said to have an equal and undivided 100 percent interest in the copyright itself, regardless of [the writers'] respective perceived contributions. Therefore, if there are two songwriters, the typical split of revenue would be 50/50. However, if the songwriters feel that the original creator of the melody and lyrics should get a higher percentage of revenues, say 70 percent, then the splits would be identified as 70/30. Often, split sheets will also contain additional information, such as the names of publishers and performance rights affiliation.

Examples of these documents are abundant on the Internet, but [it is important] to understand the legal implications. Having a signature on a split sheet is a good start toward a written collaboration agreement, but the songwriter should be careful: Signing off on a split sheet for less than an equal share of the revenues may have significant implications on a songwriter's future income. [Any concerns should be discussed in consultation] with a qualified attorney. In one case involving the writer of the hook in the Garth Brooks song "Two of a Kind, Workin' on a Full House," there was not a written split sheet, and the publisher ended up giving the contributor a lesser share. He had to file a lawsuit in order to enforce his rights.

Aside from a split sheet, what are the most common contracts that a songwriter would encounter, and the key terms and conditions of each?

A songwriter who is lucky enough to land a deal with a successful publishing company that has active writers will generally encounter two basic types of contracts: the single-song agreement (SSA) and the exclusive writing agreement. The exclusive agreement may be one of two kinds, depending on a number of factors.

The first thing a songwriter should know about these agreements is that *all of them* transfer some or all of the ownership in their copyrights to the music publisher, depending on the type of deal. Remember, ownership of the copyright is distinct from the revenues received from the copyright. Think of the revenues generated by the copyright as a pie that is split in half, with one side being the "publisher's half" and the other being the "songwriter's half." This will aid in visualizing the royalties a songwriter will receive from each deal.

The single-song agreement is just that—an agreement that transfers the copyright to *one song* to the music publisher. In exchange for that transfer, the songwriter receives the support of the publisher in exploiting that composition. Generally, all single-song agreements transfer 100 percent of the copyright to the publisher, although a successful songwriter may be able to negotiate different terms. As for revenues, the songwriter will receive 50 percent of everything the publisher receives, minus certain deductions, such as any demo expenses and advances. Typically, these types of agreements are used when a publisher has an interest in the writer but still has some reservations. For the publisher, it locks down the song without tying up resources.

The exclusive songwriting agreement involves more of a commitment from the publisher. Like the name says, the songwriter is agreeing to write "exclusively" for the publisher for a period of time, usually in exchange for a monthly salary. Like the single-song agreement, with the exclusive songwriting agreement, the songwriter is transferring 100 percent of all copyrights to the music publisher, often including songs written *before* the contract in addition to all of those written during the term. Although all copyrights are transferred, there are usually additional requirements that the songwriter deliver a minimum number of commercially viable songs during the term, usually twelve to fifteen. Similar to the single-song agreement, the writer is paid 50 percent of revenue after the typical deductions; in this case, that would definitely include the salary.

The co-publishing agreement is another type of exclusive agreement [stipulating that] the songwriter only transfers 50 percent of the copyright to the music publisher. Obviously, these kinds of agreements are typically reserved for the songwriters who have a track record of producing hits. Since the songwriter is only transferring half of the copyright, she receives 75 percent of the royalties after deduction of expenses (50 percent of the so-called "publisher's half" and 100 percent of the "songwriter's half" of the royalties). The critical term to consider in this type of agreement is who administers the copyright; i.e., who is entitled to license and collect the royalties. A songwriter should seek to obtain a portion of the administration rights, or at least have them revert back after the term.

Finally, once a songwriter has an established catalog of material, he may encounter what is called an "administration deal" in which a company only *administers* the copyrights for a fee, which ranges from 10 percent of gross on up. For this, the administration company generally collects and distributes the royalty streams from existing copyrights, and nothing more.

In today's entertainment environment, there are many variations on these types of agreements. Sometimes publishers will want to start with some sort of development deal to work with the songwriter to hone their talents before committing to something more serious. I have also seen hybrid publishing and recording agreements that not only transfer song copyrights to the publisher but also include some recording commitments so that the music publisher can essentially pitch the songwriter to the recording labels as an artist.

How much can a songwriter earn in today's industry?

Revenues in the songwriting industry have decreased over the last decade as a result of the decline in sales of physical product. However, a songwriter can certainly still establish an incredible income stream from the creation of songs. If a new songwriter enters into a writing agreement with an independent or small music publisher, a conservative salary would be in the range of $15,000–30,000 per year. The salary is, by definition in the agreement, a recoupable advance against royalties, meaning that the publisher will deduct the salary from future earnings paid to the songwriter, but the songwriter will not have to repay the advance if there aren't any earnings.

The salary is small potatoes compared to revenue streams, however. If the stars align and lightning strikes, and the music publisher successfully places a song with Taylor Swift, for example, the game changes entirely. Let's say, optimistically, that the songwriter's cut is on Swift's *1989* album that sold more than one million copies when released. In mechanical royalties alone, the songwriter's music publisher would receive a check for $91,000 (based on the mechanical royalty of 9.1 cents per record) from Big Machine Records during the next accounting period, of which the songwriter would be entitled to her $45,500 (in a traditional exclusive songwriting agreement that transfers 50 percent of all royalties to the publisher). Since the album ultimately went double platinum, the publisher would receive another check for $91,000 to split with the artist.

Now, let's say that a songwriter or music publisher is affiliated with SESAC. The performance royalties for a double-platinum song will likely be around the half-million mark, if not double that, depending on a number of factors. Of course, the songwriter would only receive half of that because of his publishing deal, so let's conservatively say that he will receive $300,000 in performance royalties. That money is paid directly to the songwriter and music publisher, respectively, so songwriters often refer to it as "mailbox money."

Now for the fun part. A song this successful is a likely candidate for inclusion in movies and advertisements, so if the publisher does her job correctly and has an in with several music supervisors, the real money can begin to pour in. Use of the full song as an opening theme in a movie can bring six figures. As the use becomes more obscure, the number goes down dramatically. Synchronization royalties are negotiated on an *ad hoc* basis, so there are no standards. For example, let's imagine that the song is placed in two movies at $750,000 each and one commercial for $500,000. The songwriter would receive half of the total, or $1 million.

So, our dream number now has risen to $1,391,000 for one song ($1 million in synch royalties for the movies and commercial; $300,000 in performance royalties for any time the song is played or performed in a public venue, including radio spins; and $91,000 for mechanical royalties). These numbers are, of course, based on speculation, and your results may vary.

Find a receptive music supervisor and submit relevant material for consideration. There is no requirement that the submissions come from a music publisher ...

What are some nontraditional revenue streams that songwriters should consider besides traditional album cuts, and what is the earning potential of those?

I'll answer this with an example. Gavin Heaney is a singer/songwriter known professionally as Latch Key Kid. Gavin creates his own style of music, in his basement, by playing all of the instruments on his recordings. In 2008, he wrote a song called "Good Times," which was picked up by DreamWorks Pictures for the opening scene of its movie *I Love You, Man*. It was also included as a song on the soundtrack. His Australian publisher then pitched the song to be used in commercials for the Australian TV show *Packed to the Rafters*. The song was seemingly on a snowball's run downhill at that point, because its next synchronization was in a commercial for Coca-Cola called "Jinx," which aired during Super Bowl XLII. The commercial exposed the already popular song to more than 97 million viewers. The song was also featured in trailers for other movies, television commercials for Liberty Mutual, inflight radio shows for Continental Airlines, and a one-minute short film titled *Dave Knoll Finds His Soul*.

I use this song as an example of nontraditional revenue streams. Heaney started this journey with a clever collaboration with a publishing company, Experience Records, and his love for action sports. The collaborative effort landed him licensing deals and credits on television shows such as *The Amazing Race* and *Survivor*, which in turn led to the aforementioned string of successes.

If there is one arena that a songwriter can exploit independently, it would be that of licensing out rights for these types of uses. Find a receptive music supervisor and submit relevant material for consideration. There is no requirement that the submissions come from a music publisher, and these types of individuals often scout YouTube for resources when looking for material for particular scenes. Do your research. If you have a favorite nighttime drama, research the genre and style of songs used in the show and attempt to replicate [the sound]. Someone out there may be looking for his next big find.

What do songwriters need to know about paying taxes on their earnings?

Like any other small business, a songwriter pays income tax on the revenues she receives after deducting allowable expenses and credits. As soon as practical and affordable, a songwriter should consider, with qualified legal counsel, what kind of entity to use to operate the business: sole proprietorship, limited liability company, or some type of corporation. This decision should also involve the opinion of a qualified accountant who specializes in the entertainment industry and has a working familiarity with songwriter splits and copyrights. By doing this early on, the songwriter can have a team in place to handle and distribute any revenues that come rolling in.

CAREER SONGWRITERS

Andrea Williams

These days, when American divorce rates hover around 50 percent, and social media seems to crown—and then dethrone—a new celebrity every few days, longevity in any pursuit seems less attainable than ever. This is especially true in music. The music industry and all its components—the styles, the major players, how those players earn a living—are in constant flux. One decade, the cool kids are rocking out to Seattle grunge in dank basements; the next, they're converging at coffee houses for acoustic open-mic nights.

That makes it all the more remarkable when songwriters are able to navigate these changes and maintain a successful career. And that's exactly the case for the following men and women. They are "career songwriters" because they've adapted, shifted, diversified, and reinvented themselves, refusing to be one-hit wonders. Here's how they do it.

BILLY STEINBERG

CITY: Los Angeles
YEARS ACTIVE: 36
BIO: If you've watched your share of television singing competitions, you're likely familiar with Billy Steinberg's work. He co-wrote the perennial reality show favorite and No. 1 hit "Alone" that was recorded by Heart in 1987 and later covered by Celine Dion. Other chart toppers in his repertoire include "Like A Virgin" (Madonna), "True Colors" (Cyndi Lauper), "So Emotional" (Whitney Houston), and "Eternal Flame" (The Bangles). Additionally, Billy co-wrote other well-known Top

10 U.S. pop hits, including "I'll Stand by You" (Pretenders, Carrie Underwood), "I Touch Myself" (the Divinyls), "How Do I Make You" (Linda Ronstadt), "I Drove All Night" (Roy Orbison, Cyndi Lauper, Celine Dion), and "In Your Room" (The Bangles).

I think it is absolutely important to find the right collaborator or collaborators if you need them. ... and that takes luck and determination.

As proof that Steinberg's career hasn't been on the decline since hitting its peak decades ago, he recently formed a new writing partnership, the results of which include "Too Little Too Late" (JoJo) and "Give Your Heart a Break" (Demi Lovato). Steinberg was inducted into the Songwriters Hall of Fame in 2011.

ON COLLABORATION: If I had only written songs by myself, and had not met Tom Kelly, I don't think I ever would have quit the grape business. I'd still be in agriculture. So I think it is absolutely important to find the right collaborator or collaborators if you need them. There are a few people who write songs by themselves, and they don't seem to need another party. But it's very important to find the right person, and that takes luck and determination. I think with Tom Kelly I got lucky, because he's the first person I asked to co-write with, and it worked out so brilliantly. But it's important to find somebody who really complements what you do.

For example, I was good at writing song lyrics, and Tom was a really good musician and great at writing melodies, so we got together and we had all the bases covered. We could write melodies and lyrics and chords, and it's important, I think, when you seek out a collaborator, that you look for somebody that's good at something you're not.

ON STAYING FRESH: Tom and I had a fabulous songwriting chemistry, and that sort of endured for about fifteen years, then I started to work with another really great songwriter named Rick Nowels, and we won the Grammy for a song that we wrote for Celine Dion. Then, after that, I met Josh Alexander. And the thing that made the meeting with Josh very good for me was that, while I've been writing songs for a very long time and my interest in music goes back to the fifties and the sixties, Josh is about thirty-five years younger than I am. So his production instincts and skills are contemporary, and I think meeting him allowed me to stay in the game, to stay relevant.

BRIAN WHITE

CITY: Nashville

YEARS ACTIVE: 30

BIO: As one of Music City's most sought after song-writers, Brian White has written fourteen No. 1 hits for Christian artists that include Mandisa, Karyn Williams, Brian Littrel, Point of Grace, 7th Time Down, Avalon, and Kutless. White's songs have also earned him two Dove Awards: one for Inspirational Song of the Year in 1994 for Michael English's "Holding Out Hope to You" and the other for 2004 Southern Gospel Song of the Year for "The Promise," recorded by The Martins.

White has also seen success in the country market, writing for superstar artists that include Rascal Flatts, Jason Aldean, Trace Adkins, Gary Allan, and Neal McCoy. His 2006 smash hit "Watching You," by Rodney Atkins, was named SESAC Country Song of the Year in 2007 and *Billboard* magazine's Most Played Country Song of 2007, while also being nominated for Song of the Year at the 2008 Academy of Country Music Awards.

....

As a songwriter, you are one day away from bankruptcy, and one hit away from retirement. The truth is, when it's in you to write, you don't do it for the money.

....

ON PERSISTENCE: No one ever said it would be easy, and, for sure, there are days when it can be extremely frustrating. But it's like this: As a songwriter, you are one day away from bankruptcy, and one hit away from retirement. The truth is, when it's in you to write, you don't do it for the money. It's just something that you have to do—the songs stir in your soul, and you have to get them out. I toured as an artist for about fifteen years and while writing for my own albums I also wrote for other artists. So you might say I was bi-vocational at that time, but my career was totally immersed in music and the creative process, whether it was in the writing room or taking those songs into the studio and producing them. I think it's important to know all angles of the business—the publishing and licensing side, how a PRO works for you, the recording process and how to run your own sessions, co-writing, and how to get your songs in front of the right people. The more you know, the less frustrated you will be because you didn't know.

KEYS TO SUCCESS: One of the keys to being successful in any kind of career is to build relationships. Another key is to remember that there is always an opportunity to be kind and help someone else. Don't always be out to make it about you. I have found in my years in the industry that artists and careers come and go and rise and fall, but the friends and relationships last. Never burn a bridge, because you never know when you might need to walk back across it. It's a smaller circle than you think, so build people up and help build their fire. When people gather 'round to see what's burning, they will see you in the glow. Also, never stop learning and never stop asking questions. I've been in the business thirty years, and I'm still learning every day. One last thing: Be a person of your word. Do what you say you're going to do, be on time, and be prepared. Sometimes the doors only open once. You want them to continue to open after you leave, and that will depend on what you did once you got in the first time.

LINDY ROBBINS

CITY: Los Angeles
YEARS ACTIVE: 21
BIO: Staying in the songwriting game for more than a decade is one thing—staying on the top of the charts for that period of time is a completely different story. Some of Robbins's most recent hits include the multiformat, worldwide No. 1 smash and ASCAP Pop Award winner "Want to Want Me" by Jason Derulo, David Guetta's worldwide No. 1 hit single "Dangerous" (featuring Sam Martin), Selena Gomez's "Slow Down," and "Miss Movin' On" by Fifth Harmony. The multiplatinum-selling songwriter has also written songs for notable artists that include One Direction, 5 Seconds of Summer, Leona Lewis (featuring OneRepublic), R5, Faith Hill, Anastasia, Brandy, Jason Mraz, Jordin Sparks, Lucy Hale, Toni Braxton, Monica, and many others.

ON BUILDING A TEAM: Being a topliner means you write melody and lyrics, rather than [produce] the music. And in pop songwriting, there's no such thing as just writing a song on the guitar. You write with a producer, and I think that's what I've really excelled at—always finding great producers who have a current sound. I could go back in my catalog and pick ten songs that are fifteen years old and have them reproduced, and they would sound current. A lot of times, it's just about the sound of the demo, which really needs to sound like a finished record now.

I also think I have always picked really good co-writers. I always co-write with other topliners or artists that are great singers, because having a great vocal on the song is also a big part of selling it. I've been able to pick really strong co-writers who are fresh and can add something, and the vast majority of the time, they're a lot younger than I am.

THE CASE FOR EXCELLENCE: The music industry has changed drastically because of streaming. Drastically. And for the vast majority of people, it's become a much more difficult profession to make a living in. 2000 was when my career really took off, and before then, records would easily sell twenty or thirty million. Even shortly after I got started, there were still records that were easily selling five or seven million, so you could make a good living on album tracks. But now album tracks pay virtually nothing, so the only way you can really make money is to either have singles—and they have to be successful singles—or you have to think outside the box. Maybe that's jingles, or TV and film, or being a singer-songwriter so you can make money performing.

But, of course, if songwriting is what you want to do in your heart, and that's what you love more than anything, if you're talented enough, you'll find a way. It used to be that even people with moderate talent could get by, but now I think that people have to be exceptionally talented in order to thrive in the music business.

STEVE DEAN

CITY: Nashville

YEARS ACTIVE: 34

BIO: Nashville songwriter Steve Dean has co-written seven No. 1 hits, including "Watching You" by Rodney Atkins, the most played song on country radio in 2007; the Grammy-nominated "It Takes a Little Rain" by The Oak Ridge Boys; Alabama's "Southern Star"; George Strait's "Round About Way"; Reba McEntire's "Walk On"; "Hearts Aren't Made to Break" by Lee Greenwood; and "No More Lonely" for The Roys.

In addition to his biggest hits, Dean has also written songs for The LoCash Cowboys, Joe Nichols, Dierks Bentley, Lee Ann Womack, Waylon Jennings, Sister Hazel, Pure Prairie League, and other artists, earning eight BMI Songwriter Awards and two BMI Publisher Awards along the way.

ON LOCATION: I moved to Nashville in 1980 to pursue a songwriting career. My dad suggested the move. He said if I went to where the action was I could get established artists to record my songs. That sounded like a great idea, so I got in my '74 Toyota and headed east on I-40 from Little Rock to Nashville.

I got involved in the music scene. I treated and still treat songwriting as a job, even though it doesn't feel like a job-job, or a real job. I write every day. It is a process that is constantly unfolding before my eyes, and it is something I try to improve on constantly. I am not in it for the money, but when my co-writers and I finish what we believe to be a great song, I feel successful beyond success. My goal, however, is that every time I sit down to write, I am swinging for the fences!

You have got to adapt to change for longevity.

ABOUT DIVERSIFICATION: At one time in my career, Music Row was my "one-stop shop." Over the years I have had three different publishing deals and went down to the Row everyday to write songs. I still go to the Row to write, but now, along with songwriting, I do singer/songwriter shows around the country with my trio Hits & Grins, I mentor new songwriters through Global Songwriters Connection and I perform at corporate events. The music industry is constantly changing, and it is totally different today than it was when I got my first break in 1982. My point is, you have got to adapt to change for longevity.

This past year I had my first No. 1 on the bluegrass chart with a song titled "No More Lonely" that was co-written and recorded by The Roys. For years I have made an effort to expand my horizons by exploring other genres of music, as I love them all. I am currently writing with a Mississippi blues artist and a New York rock artist, and my latest cut is a song called "Run Highway Run" recorded by the country rock band Sister Hazel.

PAM SHEYNE

CITY: Los Angeles

YEARS ACTIVE: 24

BIO: Pam Sheyne may be best known for the global smash "Genie in a Bottle," which became Christina Aguilera's debut single and was number one in twenty-one countries while selling seven million copies, but her success goes much deeper. In addition to co-writing the debut hit "He Loves U Not" for pop group Dream (USA No. 2 Hot 100/No. 1 Sound Scan) and Jessica Simpson's "Irresistible" (No. 15 USA Hot 100), Sheyne has also penned songs for Demi Lovato, Seal, Corrine Bailey Rae, The Saturdays, Casey Abrams, CeCe Winans, Tina Arena, Point of Grace, The Backstreet Boys, O Town, Nick Lachey, and Kristinia DeBarge.

Sheyne has spent much of her career writing outside the pop charts and has found a home for many of her songs with television and film projects. She has written end titles for Disney's *The Princess Diaries* and *Confessions of a Teenage Drama Queen*, as well as the Golden Globe-nominated film *The Young Victoria*. Other songs have been featured in films that include *Hannah Montana*, *Jump In*, *Camp Rock*, and *Camp Rock 2*, and the TV shows *Sonny With a Chance*, *Lizzie Maguire*, *Beverly Hills 90210*, *Roswell*, and *American Idol*.

ON GOING GLOBAL: It's really important to look at other markets in the world, as you may find you connect with a specific market like Japan, France, Germany, or the UK. If you have a worldwide publishing deal, it's crucial to get to know your subpublishers in each territory if possible and get on their radar. Find out what they are looking for, and if it makes sense financially, travel there and set up some co-writes with some of their local writers. This is what I've done for a number of years, and it definitely helped get my songs to different markets and get my name around. It's a fantastic experience making friends overseas and a learning curve seeing the difference in music and what people connect with in other places. I was fascinated when I first came to the U.S. and had some A&R guys say my lyrics were "too European." They explained that American women were more kick-ass and tough, and I learned and got better at my craft by coming to the U.S. a lot. If you [are] going to the UK, study the market before you go and figure out where you fit in, who you would be suited to working with, and always try to work with people better than you so you can "up" your game and learn!

ON WORK/LIFE BALANCE: It's always difficult to strike a balance with work and family life, and I've struggled with it, especially when traveling overseas for weeks at a time. You either feel guilty you're not working enough, or you feel guilty for not being with your child and being there for those really special moments. My son is now in middle school so it's a little easier, but I am grateful I have an amazing husband who takes care of everything while I'm away. My husband is also my business manager, so he understands how important it is for my career to travel and get out there. Also, I have always had a studio at home so I can see my son when he comes home from school, but I also work out at studios in and around LA. I guess you just have to do what works for you and try to find a comfortable balance. We have a routine, so I make a rule that I don't work weekends or super late nights unless it's absolutely necessary.

I'd advise anyone in the early stages of their careers to master their craft and specialize. Be the best at something; don't be good at everything.

SAM HOLLANDER

CITY: Los Angeles

YEARS ACTIVE: 24

BIO: Sam Hollander is one of the most talented and diverse songwriter/producers in the music industry, having achieved multiplatinum success writing and producing for major artists that include One Direction, Train, Daughtry, Katy Perry, The Fray, Carole King, Fitz and the Tantrums, Neon Trees, Cobra Starship, and Gym Class Heroes.

In 2008, *Rolling Stone* honored Hollander with its Hot List Producer of the Year award, and in 2012, he was selected as the music producer for the second season of NBC's Steven Spielberg-produced series *SMASH*, for which he wrote the Emmy-nominated song "Voice in a Dream." Along the way, Hollander has written and produced twenty U.S. Top 40 pop hits. Most recently, he co-wrote Fitz and the Tantrum's hit single "HandClap," along with five songs on the new Panic at the Disco album, which was one of the top-ten selling albums of 2015.

ON GETTING STARTED: There were many false starts in the beginning of my career. In that sense, I always felt like an overeager Olympic sprinter who jumped the gun and then slunk back home sans medal. From failed record deals to songs that rushed out of the gate only to disappear into the ether, it was all bad. The moment my career began to feel like something real was when I started writing with Carole King. This collaboration resulted in the title track and first single on her 2001 release "Love Makes the World." It brought a much needed morale boost and opened up doors to many other greats. Carole introduced me to Paul Williams. Paul introduced me to Jeff Barry. Suddenly, I was in an accelerated school absorbing lessons that trumped all the previous years of special education failings. The fact that she still performs the song live and it has become a valued part of her song-book is mind-blowing. That was really my early calling card.

WORDS OF WISDOM: I'd advise anyone in the early stages of their careers to master their craft and specialize. Be the best at something; don't be good at everything. It's just too competitive! And network. Network to a freakish extent, actually. These people you meet early on will cross your path both directly or indirectly numerous times throughout the years. Build a movement with them. My career has been full of serendipitous moments with people I rose with who drastically altered my future. When you are eventually blessed with opportunities, make a creative wish list. Ask yourself what you would do if you actually had the keys to the castle. What songs would you write? What acts would you work with? There will be a moment when the gates open. That's when you pounce and actualize! Long-term success is still a marriage of art and calculation.

FOR THE SAKE OF THE SONG

Advice from Next Gen Songwriters

....

David McPherson

Get a trio of rising award-winning songwriters to talk about their craft, and you'll hear a variety of advice. Just like asking someone the secret to being a successful lawyer or an inspiring teacher, there are some universal, timeless tips to each profession; yet, each individual must discover what works and what doesn't. Some scribble words and phrases on bar napkins or in tattered old journals. These song fragments and ideas might not make it into a until years later. Sleepless nights and a poem written from a phrase stuck in an artist's head in the early hours is as likely a seed for a hit song as a melody that pops unexpectedly into the mind while following a highway's white line. Some songwriters are lucky and these melodies come fast and often from unknown realms in the recesses of the brain.

One of my favorite songwriters, the late Texan Townes Van Zandt, penned the classic "For the Sake of the Song." In the chorus of this cut crammed with emotion, he warbles, "Maybe she just has to sing for the sake of the song/Who do I think I am to decide that she's wrong." That philosophy espoused in these two poetic lines is the ethos of good songwriters. No matter the words or the music, be true to you; write for the sake of your creation. Successful songwriters also write compositions where the words or the melody linger long in the listener's mind. To achieve this, an artist must be a good listener. For some songwriters, there is a bit of the lightning strikes (the muse). Those who are so lucky to create art via this stream of conscious technique have to be ready to grab hold of these a-ha moments when they come.

For this edition of *Songwriter's Market*, I chatted with three young rising songwriters (Simon Wilcox, Francesco Yates, and Scott Helman) to get their take on this unique art form and have them reflect on their craft.

SIMON WILCOX WRITES AWAY THE DAY

Simon Wilcox is just hitting her stride as a songwriter, coming up on two decades in the business. She started writing songs from a very early age, creating her first compositions when she was eight years old. Since then, the singer-songwriter has worked on more than fifty albums as a writer, co-producer and/or vocalist, many of which have achieved platinum, double platinum, and gold sales status, including the No. 1 singles "Home" by Three Days Grace (Jive/Zomba) and "Jealous" by Nick Jonas, which sold more than two million copies. Wilcox's songs have also appeared in numerous films, such as *Brothers* and *Raise Your Voice*. And a few of her TV credits include *CSI Miami*, *Desperate Housewives*, and *Beverly Hills 90210*. Though she started her music career as a solo artist with her 1999 release *Mongrel of Love*, these days you're more likely to find her collaborating with other songwriters and musicians at some studio in LA.

Born in Canada, Wilcox now calls the City of Angels home. Her regular writing routine includes arriving at a studio, usually by noon. Sometimes the artist who will record the song is there, and other times, it's just other songwriters. "We hang out for five to seven hours and try to come up with something that doesn't suck!" says Wilcox with a laugh.

Taking up residence in Los Angeles was part of her growth as a songwriter; it allowed her to mature without the expectations stemming from her parents' songwriting pedigree. (Her biological father is musician David Wilcox.) It also put her in a location where many of the collaborators and producers reside.

"I always felt driven to write songs," says Wilcox. "In some ways, it was the worst career path for me, because you hope that you can do something different from what your parents do. You can have more anonymity and freedom, which is what I found in the U.S. I live here to some degree because I'm not known as someone's daughter. I've made it completely on my own merit, which I had to do in Canada, too, but I feel there was some judgment involved. I wish I could have been an accountant or a banker or real estate mogul, but this is what I feel drawn to, and it's inescapable."

For Wilcox, that tug to write and express her feelings through songs was always there. She recalls a time in her early twenties feeling like there would be no life without music, without songwriting. "I really had no choice in the matter," she says. "It keeps me out of a psychiatric hospital every day! It's a wonderful, therapeutic tool … what a gift."

After she released *Mongrel of Love*, other artists approached Wilcox to work on their material, hoping she would share her gift, based on the songwriting they had heard on that debut. Suddenly, people started to ask the budding artist to co-write with them. "I loved co-writing so much but hadn't thought of it as a job. It had never occurred to me, but I really fell in love with it," says Wilcox.

In some ways, according to Wilcox, you expand your brainpower when you collaborate. "As human beings, and especially as songwriters, we have the tendency to travel the same narrow pathways," she explains. "How that manifests itself, as a writer, is you have the tendency to choose the same chord changes or some of the same subjects or similar melodies."

"When there is someone else there to push you, it can get really exciting," she adds. "Your brain goes to places it's never been before, and sometimes the songs really benefit from that."

Wilcox shares an example. When she co-wrote a pair of songs for the band 5 Seconds of Summer ("Vapor" and "Outer Space/Carry On") on its last album (*Sounds Good Feels Good*), record producer John Feldman was an incredible influence, shaping the direction on those songs. "He really steered the ship," she says. "He took the band and myself to new places … places we never would have gone without him there."

Chords, Cars, & Conversation

Sometimes, that songwriting seed—and inspiration for Wilcox—starts with chords strummed on the guitar or notes played on the piano. "I just hear melodies," she says. "I was working with Blink 182 recently, and in the car on the way to the session, the entire melody for the song came to me. I walked into the session and sang them the melody top to bottom, which thank goodness they liked. They tweaked it a bit to make it their own, but it started out with this complete melody that came to me."

Wilcox cites another way inspiration can come. The song in question is "Lowlife," which was recorded in 2016 by artist That Poppy. The concept for the song came from a real conversation with her husband. "I said to him, 'You are the highlight of my low life,' and I realized right after I said it that it was a really good idea for a song, even though I was feeling sorry for myself at the time."

As Wilcox shows, song ideas can appear in so many ways. The key: You have to be listening to hear them. That's her best advice. "Be aware and observant of the world around you, as you are never sure when ideas and inspiration for songs will come," she says. "There are so many songs out there now that you really have to be original in terms of what you write about. It's an exciting opportunity for people to write about things that haven't been written about before."

"It's hard to avoid writing about love or any of the basics: heartbreak, desire, and revenge, but I think that truth is the way to do it," says Wilcox. "If you really look for what is true when you are writing, that's always compelling … the truth is always original because everyone's truth is distinct."

Two of Wilcox's writing heroes, whose songs always shared nuggets of truth, are Elvis Costello (2016 inductee into the Songwriters Hall of Fame) and the late David Bowie. "I love the power that a record like *Ziggy Stardust* had to make me feel less alone," she says. "That's what I strive to do when I write … let people know that there are other people out there who feel the way they do."

The songwriter leaves readers with the final, simple piece of advice to not give up. "Never ever stop, because you never know when that song is going to come," she says. "If you get joy from the process of songwriting, then you should never ever stop writing songs. You just never know. It might take you twenty years. It might take you forty years, but it can still happen."

YOUNG SONGWRITING GENIUS FRANCESCO YATES

When Francesco Yates was eleven-years-old, he penned his first song, "Jaguars." He was inspired by Jack Black's character in *School of Rock*. It all spiralled from there.

"That is what ignited the whole movement I took towards music," says Yates. "I've never stopped writing since. Music was a passion for me that happened all at once. I just wanted to do it all the time. Something clicked in my head, and that was it."

Yates signed with Chris Smith Management and 21 Music by the time he was fourteen. At sixteen, an age where most teens are thinking of getting their driver's license, the songwriter inked a deal with Atlantic Records. After spending a few years experimenting with his sound and writing constantly, the singer released his debut, self-titled EP in late 2015, co-produced by Pharrell Williams. The collection features the radio-friendly hits "Call" and "Better to Be Loved."

"I've had the real privilege of working with a lot of great people," says Yates. "A lot of them symbolized what Jack Black was trying to teach the kids in that movie."

When there is someone else there to push you, it can get really exciting. Your brain goes to places it's never been before, and sometimes the songs really benefit from that.

Today, the twenty-year-old's life sometimes feels like a movie. He is writing away the days, building a following and honing his skills as a songwriter, learning from industry veterans such as Paul McCartney and Williams, the latter an experience he won't soon forget.

"Pharrell is the sensei ... the minister of the funk," says Yates. "He was very instrumental in shifting the way I thought about and the way I see music. I was just trying to soak up as much as I could during those sessions. He taught me to not be as afraid. He is very good at taking things that don't seem like they work with pop music and putting them into pop music.

"With me, it was the electric guitar," he continues. "He was very instrumental in encouraging me to be that guy on the guitar, which I always was in my basement but wasn't otherwise. He taught me to put that in the forefront. I didn't know where to position it. That was nice of him to impart his wisdom."

Yates knows there is so much more to learn. His debut, self-titled EP was a chance to showcase his songwriting muscles and the diversity of his knowledge, but he says a taste of his talents is all it was ever intended to be. "I just wanted to show all of the things that I can do," he says. "It was more a showcase, a sketch, if you can call it that, rather than a completed painted picture."

Like most songwriters, Yates says all it takes for a song to come to fruition is one moment of inspiration. As soon as you capture that idea, you've got to run with it. "Catch that moment where something flicks in your brain [and] go for it," he advises. "Technically, you can write a song, plan it, and have it sound decent, but the real stuff that is natural comes from a place ... out of thin air. My iPhone helps me with capturing vocal ideas and melodies that come to me from time to time."

Yates writes new material constantly. "It comes and goes, ebbs and flows, like everything else in life," he says. "I don't even want to try and understand it. Let it be magical that way."

SCOTT HELMAN ON HONESTY AND DEVELOPING HIS ART

When Scott Helman and I connect, he's hanging out in Montreal, Quebec, where he's rented an apartment to hunker down in and write some new songs, hoping to be inspired in this locale, away from his Toronto home. Sometimes a change of scenery is inspiring for a songwriter.

Like Yates, the twenty-year-old Helman caught the ears of the music industry as a teen. Certain people took the songwriter under their wings and groomed him until they felt he was ready to release some of his original songs. The wait was worth it. Last fall, he released his debut EP, *Augusta*. Two JUNO nominations followed (Canada's equivalent of the Grammys), along with heavy radio rotation for a pair of his compositions, "That Sweater" and "Bungalow."

Flash back five years. Warner Music Group signed Helman, who was then fifteen. While Yates's inspiration to make music and write songs came from a movie, Helman's passion was sparked after he got his first guitar. "I liked music class and liked playing music and listening to music, but it wasn't a huge part of my life in the sense that it swallowed me whole," the songwriter recalls. "I wasn't that good at anything. I was a handful in school. I didn't pay attention in class, and I was a troublemaker. I tried every hobby, all the sports, photography ... Then I was like, 'I want a guitar,' and my parents were like, 'It's just another thing,' but from the second I had it and learned to play, I couldn't stop playing."

The more Helman started to play the guitar and the piano, the more music became a huge part of his life. Like Wilcox, he cites David Bowie (the first artist's record he bought after he started playing guitar) as an early influence. "I remember thinking, 'If I could ever pick a dream, it would be to sit back as a seventy-year-old man and say I changed the world with my music."

....

Technically, you can write a song, plan it, and have it sound decent, but the real stuff that is natural comes from a place ... out of thin air.

....

While Helman is a long way from that goal, it was a motivating factor and a big inspiration for him to start writing songs. "That's where my songwriting started to come in," he says. "At first, I was just trying to match the amazingness I heard in those legendary musicians in my own art. The more I made songs, the more I wanted too, and it just never stopped."

While Helman started writing his first song sketches when he was thirteen, it wasn't until he was fifteen when the songs started to really come. That's when the artist started posting his creations online. The next thing you know, he gets a call from Warner Music. A couple of meetings later and he had a development deal. "They told me, 'We are not going to put out a record for four years. We just want you to write songs ... we want to work with you as an artist.' Had it not been for that process of development that was provided to me by the label I got signed to, I would be a totally different writer."

Neil Young—and specifically his classic *Live at Massey Hall 1971*—is another touchstone for Helman, and a writer that influenced his approach to songwriting. He admits the first songs he wrote were horrible. "I would learn tunes, play along with a record, fool around with some chords, hear a song on radio and try to play it," he recalls. "I wrote mostly about my life, trying to capture a feeling. I also loved ambiguous lyrics."

Helman's A&R representative heard some of these early compositions and gave the songwriter some advice that has stuck with him. "You need to write songs that have meaning. I was avoiding that because I didn't know how to do it and it scared me. When I got a bit older, I fell in love with songs that are dense with meaning. The first time I wrote a song like that, it was so rewarding."

Writing a song with meaning is about capturing a universal feeling that others can relate to in some way. These days, writing a song that achieves this is really important to Helman. "When you are younger, you are just trying to be a writer, and being ambiguous is great, because you can hide behind your lyrics and it's up to interpretation," he explains. "Also, when you are young, you do not want to be so vulnerable. Now I'm a bit older, I don't care as much what people think about me. That comes with age."

On the Power of Collaboration

Already in his young songwriting career, Helman has had the opportunity to work with some seasoned musicians, including Simon Wilcox and Thomas "Tawgs" Salter. He recalls his first co-writing writing session with KAI (Warner).

"I don't remember the song anymore but remember being 'wowed' and thinking everybody has their way of writing and their process, and it is so magical because of that. To write a song with someone is very intense, because you get to watch them write a song and steal all their ideas," says Helman. "I can't think of the last time I wrote a song where I didn't say, 'What would this writer do here?' or 'What would they think about this bridge?' It's very postmodern in that sense because it is this mish-mash of other people's styles. It can also be frightening because it can be like, 'I can't remember who I am anymore!'"

For Helman, co-writing with Wilcox is a magical experience. He's learned so much from this fellow crafter of songs. She was his third writing session. The pair convened on a blistering summer day. "The second she sat down and said hi to me, I could feel this energy from her that was like, no matter what you say, we are here to write and I respect you," he recalls. "I thought that was so cool. The second we started writing, I fell in love with her as a person and as a writer."

Most of the songs on *Augusta* were co-written with Wilcox and Salter during some late-night writing sessions. There was so much to figure out.

"That's the weird thing about songwriting. I say this all the time now because of the fact that it's my job; I'm financially and emotionally dependent on a process that I really don't understand, which in itself is both beautiful and horrifying. Sometimes you see a song and it is this thing right in front of you. Then, you have to sculpt it out. You already know what you want, and you just have to get the work done."

Other times the song begins with a certain feeling. "Somewhere Sweet" was one of those songs. "I just sat down from this shitty day at work and just knew that there was this feeling, and I just wrote it," he says. "It just happened. But that experience is rare."

More common, he says, are the times when you just have to write and you don't have anything to say. "Simon explained that feeling to me. She said it's like you are standing at the top of a cliff and you have to get down this cliff, and you have no idea how to, and then all of a sudden you are down there and you don't know how you got there," he says. "There's no reason or rhyme to it, but just like that, you have a song."

Helman says it is a scary feeling when you are trying to write a song when you have nothing. In those moments, the music usually comes first, and that melody then inspires and guides the rest of the creative process. That said, like every songwriter will tell you, there is no one way songs come. To illustrate, Helman shares a story of a recent composition that came from a bout of insomnia.

"I woke up in the middle of the night and couldn't sleep because I had this phrase in my head that kept repeating," he recalls. "The only way I could make it go away was if I started writing a poem with that phrase so I could get it out of my head and go to bed. This poem came out of me and I wrote a song with it. There are so many different ways songs can come."

Helman's final advice to young, aspiring songwriters is simply to write.

"I know that is a cop-out answer, but I would never have had these experiences of co-writing if I didn't call myself a writer," he says. "Early on, when I was a teen, I just wanted to be a songwriter so badly. It's not the greatest feeling … being a songwriter is not easy. Sometimes it's really hard and it can suck. It's the truth. A lot of people have taken those experiences and had a hard time. Even John Lennon I'm sure had times where he felt it hard to write something that he felt was good art.

"You just know, though, when you want to be a songwriter … it's your orientation," Helman adds. "When you decide you want to be one, it's important to just write a lot of songs, because they are going to suck. I remember watching this thing with Ed Sheeran before I put out *Augusta*, and he said, 'Writing songs is like turning on a tap. All the water that comes out initially is going to be brown and gross, and you have to just leave it on and continue to write songs. Then, one day, the water is going to look a little clearer, and it's going to happen."

DAVID MCPHERSON, a Canadian writer and editor, believes music is the elixir of life. For years, he's written poetry on bar napkins, but he's yet to pen a song. In the interim, he lives vicariously through the award-winning songwriters he's been fortunate enough to interview over the past twenty years as a music writer. With more than 17,000 songs on his iPod, and an ever-growing vintage vinyl collection, it's a joy for him to discover new music, and he loves sharing these discoveries with his wife and two children. David is a regular contributor to *Words + Music*, *Hamilton Magazine*, *No Depression*, and *Penguin Eggs*. Over the years, his writing on music has also appeared in *Paste*, *Performing Songwriter*, *American Songwriter*, *Bluegrass Unlimited*, *Exclaim*, *Canadian Musician*, and *Chart*. Reach him at david@mcphersoncommunications.com and follow him on Twitter (@mcphersoncomm).

TWENTY-FIRST CENTURY SONGWRITER

The Four Must-Haves for Your Home Studio

....

Andrea Williams

If your dream is to become a hit songwriter, writing a great song is only half the battle. At some point, you have to get your song in the hands of other people, whether it's an artist who may record it, a manager or label head, or a publisher who may sign you to a deal. And, unfortunately, you can't just send out a page of written lyrics, no matter how well-crafted they may be. The only way people can grasp the full scope of your song is if they have a full song to listen to, and that includes vocals and a backing track.

Don't worry if you can't play an instrument and are less than savvy when it comes to the latest gear. Today's technology has made it relatively easy for any songwriter to produce a professional-quality demo right in his bedroom. That's a good thing, because today's uber-competitive music industry demands pretty much that. You can probably get by with less than what's listed here, but working with these tools will ensure that you are operating on a professional level, and that alone could give you a much-needed advantage over other songwriters.

Here's what you'll need to get started.

THE COMPUTER: APPLE MACBOOK PRO

There are tons of different computers on the market at every price point imaginable, but in the music industry, there is only one computer that counts. Walk into any studio or songwriting room, and you'll find a Mac. This Apple allegiance isn't just about aesthetics or keeping up with the Joneses; working on a Mac ensures that the songwriter is working on the same operating system, or platform, as everyone else in the industry. Conversely, if you're working on a PC, you may have issues sending files to someone else or to a studio, and they may have to be converted to be fully compatible before than can be edited, mixed, and mastered.

Certainly, Macs are not cheap, but you don't need to buy the latest model available. Try searching for refurbished ones online. Just make sure that it has the most current features (like a thunderbolt port, for example). At the end of the day, consider it an investment and a tax write-off. It's still cheaper than paying for eight hours of studio time.

THE SOFTWARE: AVID PRO TOOLS 12

Like computers, there is an industry standard when it comes to recording software, and Pro Tools is the name of the game. Every studio runs Pro Tools, and if you want your music to be considered by labels and publishers, and produced professionally, at some point it will need to be converted into a Pro Tools file. Save time and energy by recording with this software from the very beginning.

For just under $600 (or $25 per month on subscription), you'll have the capability to compose, record, edit, and mix your music, in addition to sharing it easily with collaborators or decision makers. And for noninstrumentalists, Pro Tools includes more than sixty virtual instruments, effects, and sound processing plug-ins in a variety of styles, as well as factory loops that will make assembling your own backing track relatively easy.

THE INTERFACE: PRESONUS FIRESTUDIO PROJECT

Once you have your recording software, you'll need a recording interface. Simply put, an interface is a device that allows you to record music directly to your computer and communicate with the recording software. If you record yourself singing and playing acoustic guitar, that is an analog sound that must be converted to digital audio so that you can edit, save, or otherwise manipulate the file. The interface makes this possible.

At around $400, the PreSonus FireStudio Project interface is affordable and ideal for a small home studio, but it also has the capabilities to record a fully-produced demo if you choose. With eight mic inputs, you can cut live vocals, drums, guitar, bass, key, and more—all simultaneously. Typically, this price point dictates a much smaller interface with fewer capabilities, making the FireStudio Project a must-have for songwriters.

THE MICROPHONE: RODE NT1A

When it comes to recording basics, a high-quality microphone is paramount. Whether you're singing yourself or bringing in someone else to record your demos, you'll need to capture a crisp vocal that clearly displays the lyric and the emotion of the song. With a 1" cardioid condenser, the industry-standard RODE NT1A is warm and clear, with a sound quality that belies its under $300 price tag. Additionally, with a self-noise level of 5dBA, the NT1A is considered one of the quietest mics, making it ideal for cutting both vocals and guitar.

CROWDFUNDING FOR SONGWRITERS

Using Patreon to Go Beyond Project-Based Donations

Charlene Oldham

Fans fund ambitious albums and titanic tours through crowdfunding projects on platforms like Kickstarter and Indiegogo. But singers and songwriters can't exactly launch an inspiring online campaign to cover rent. Everyday expenses don't stop between big projects, and paltry payouts from AdSense, iTunes, and other digitally driven sources often earn artists pennies per video view or audio download.

The challenge of funding a continuous career prompted Patreon founder and chief executive Jack Conte to devise a different crowdfunding model. Conte was producing elaborate videos that would sometimes garner millions of views but typically translated into a check for a few hundred dollars from AdSense, says Taryn Arnold, community happiness representative at Patreon.

"Clearly, the machine that turns art into money was broken, so Jack set out to fix it, running with an idea of asking his fans to pledge one dollar per video," Arnold says. "If he had two thousand fans commit to pledging a few dollars a month, he could get a salary straight from his fans. And, just like that, Patreon was born."

Project-specific sites still have their place, especially if artists need a sizable sum up front to fund major endeavors. But those crowdfunding campaigns are often all-or-nothing propositions that have to be completely funded for the artist to receive any of the money pledged. The model means artists are often scrambling to drum up contributions before deadline and may spend months working to raise money for a campaign that goes unfunded in the end.

Striking a balance between risk and reward is difficult even when a project-based crowdfunding campaign is successful, says Michael Zeligs, founder of StartMotionMEDIA, a California company that helps artists and entrepreneurs develop and implement crowdfunding strategies. Fundraising efforts often leave little time for writing songs and making music in the heat of a campaign. One-shot contributions can also leave fans feeling left out of an artist's creative process once a particular project is over.

Patreon's model encourages copious creativity because patrons' contributions are triggered by a content creation goal the artist sets.

"You can spend two months campaigning and get 250 fans to pledge and you get your $10,000 or $80,000. You have to deliver the project and it's all over. With Patreon, all that work in enrolling a backer is lasting," he says. "Once those fans get in, they are in it for the long run. It's just a lot more sustainable in terms of the amount of time spent campaigning as an artist versus how much time you get to be funded to produce your art."

Patreon's model encourages copious creativity because patrons' contributions are triggered by a content creation goal the artist sets. On his personal Patreon page, Zeligs, a singer and songwriter, offers free audio downloads of his songs but requests contributions for original music videos. This structure is useful because it gives the fundraising a sense of purpose without a hard-and-fast deadline that determines whether creators make any money at all.

"The deadline pressure with standard crowdfunding platforms is really useful—it motivates the project creator and it motivates the fans. But there are ways to create urgency outside a ticking clock on a page," says Zeligs. "My goal is to create one new video a month, but if I need to take a month off, my patrons don't get charged. So there's a lot of freedom for me to take the time I need."

Patreon also offers an electronic alternative to touring, a process that can leave little time and energy for writing and recording new songs, particularly if you are serving as your own support staff, says singer, songwriter, and poet Amy Obenski.

"It's really exhausting, especially when you're an independent artist and you're driving and you're booking all the shows, and you're playing all the shows sleeping on friends' couches," she says. "Patreon gives you a way to fund your career through something other than touring."

Crowdfunding and concerts can also complement one another to diversify both a songwriter's fan base and income stream. Touring helps build the roster of fans who might be eager to support artists both at home and on the road. Zeligs plans to go on two or three tours a year. His goal is to add around five hundred names to his email list on each tour and give fans the option to find out more about what they can get through his Patreon page.

"Live performance is a way to build the community, but it feels crazy that most artists stop there. They got sixty people to a show. Ten of those people bought a CD and that's it," he says. "At each show, I'll have a call to action that says, 'You can buy a CD now, but here's the only way you can get access to the latest videos, to the latest music I'm making.'"

In addition to regularly released content, Patreon campaigns offer contributors exclusive incentives from the artists. Among other rewards, Obenski offers her patrons live footage from shows. Patreon also encourages artists to set motivational milestones letting donors know exactly how their money is being spent. The exclusive rewards help her feel like she's giving something back to patrons.

"I am offering a way for my biggest fans and supporters to be there in a way that other people can't," she says. "So, on Patreon, we create this discussion. I put up posts that only they can see. I create things that only they can have. For me, to think of it that way makes it easier for me to share, announce, and promote. So it's not just about the money. It feels like a little community."

TIPS FOR CREATING A WINNING PATREON PAGE:

"Let people into your process," says Taryn Arnold, community happiness representative at Patreon. "The people who support you on Patreon are fans that want a relationship with you. They want to see rough draft lyrics scribbled on a napkin. They want to see photos of the band on the road."

"Release new songs as they're ready," Arnold advises. "Many people are incredibly tied to the album release model of music. It's totally cool to do alongside Patreon—many people fund albums here. But your supporters on Patreon are hoping for new content as often as you've got it."

Keep it simple and intimate. "On your page, don't make it so businesslike," says singer, songwriter, and artist Julia Westlin. "Make it personal."

But not too personal—when she started her Patreon page, Westlin wanted to make some of her rewards hands on, offering to paint donors a picture or send them some other one-of-a-kind incentive. She found those types of rewards were too difficult to deliver. Now, she sticks to incentives that can be electronically disseminated, such as adding donors' names to the credits of a video.

"People really like that because they feel like they are part of the production, which they are."

Don't be afraid to ask patrons to pay a premium. When "David MeShow" started his page, he played around with price points, asking contributors for $4.99 rather than $5, for example. He also found patrons are just as likely to pay $5 as they are $2, even if digital downloads are available for 99 cents these days.

"It's not only that they want to get the song, it's that they want to support you and they are willing to pay a little more to do that."

Put some thought and effort into the main video on your Patreon page, show yourself in action, and try to limit it to about three minutes long, advises StartMotionMEDIA's Michael Zeligs.

"It's got to look like you've invested in it. So it's not putting an iPhone on your window sill and rambling for five minutes."

The video should be very specific about the content you're offering for contributions and how patrons can participate.

"Explain the process for making a pledge," says Zeligs. "You have to say, 'Here's where I'm going with this and here's how you can help.'"

Increase interest in your work through free giveaways before launching your Patreon page.

"A content strategy precedes a campaign," says Zeligs. "It's always important to give first and ask later."

When it's time for the ask, make the pitch personal. Zeligs sends e-mails directly to fans on his mailing list rather than relying on newsletter announcements.

"Those personal direct messages have ten times the success rate of a newsletter. It's got to be a high-touch fundraising approach to get traction these days," he says. "Persistence in communication, direct one-to-one e-mails, that's what does it. In three weeks of campaigning, I got sixty patrons."

CHARLENE OLDHAM is a teacher who currently focuses on college-level journalism courses, a music promoter who has helped clients attract media attention from newspapers and radio stations around the country, and a freelance writer whose recent work has appeared in national print and online outlets, including *SUCCESS* and Catster.com. She blogs about writing and life at www.charleneoldham.com.

A LITTLE BIRD TOLD ME

The Short & Sweet of Promoting on Twitter

....

Kelly Henkins

In my experience, I have found Twitter to be the best online source for networking. That little bird of happiness can brighten my day in the most unsuspecting moments.

Twitter is a friendly zone that is more like talking to someone at a conference than actual promotion. I have made 98 percent of my business connections through Twitter. As an entertainment writer and a street team promoter for over two hundred artists, I know what to look for when making connections. What do users post that encourages me to delve further into what they are offering? What are they doing to gain followers? Are they missing anything?

Whenever I look for someone to follow on Twitter, I start with their profile picture. I do not (nor should anyone using the platform) follow "eggs": the default icon prior to uploading a profile picture. You can choose any picture you want, but until you get more comfortable with your audience, I recommend a good headshot or logo, something that brands you. Upload this when you create your account. Then identify a username, also called a Twitter handle. Choose carefully, as this is who you will be known as. Try to stay as close to your name, company, or brand as possible. Sometimes, you have to use a variation because your "name" is already taken. As an example, there are a lot of Kellys out there. As a variation, I extended my name to be my blog name, "kellyscountry." My handle says exactly who I am: @kellyscountry.

Whether you choose to record your own songs or offer them up in a catalog for someone else to take to the charts, you still need to market yourself as a songwriter. You need to promote your name and build a reputation with artists and fans alike. With the onslaught of various social media platforms available today, you should find the one(s) that will work best for you and use them to your full potential. In her book, *Get Twitter-Pated: A Writer's Handbook to Twitter*, author Jen Nipps says, "All social media is about making connections." Twitter is networking at its core.

The first step is to have a website or blog—not a Facebook account, but an actual website or blog. (Reverbnation, www.reverbnation.com, is also a good option for musicians and songwriters.) Your website is a landing pad where you want potential clients to come—a place where they can find out more about who you are and what you have to offer.

From this point on, think of Twitter as a virtual conference and your homepage (on Twitter) as your business card. If you are at a conference or a local bar at a songwriter's showcase event, you give a potential audience a taste of what you offer, then hand them a card with details about where to find more information. This is Twitter's purpose for songwriters.

To keep from spamming your Twitter followers and getting ignored before you have even begun, think of your posts this way: 80 percent general information, 10 percent promoting others, 10 percent promoting yourself.

When I see a post on Twitter that catches my attention, I click on the username to check out their homepage. I look for professionalism: a nice header, a brief description of who they are, and a Web address. An example of a great homepage is @scotttaylorband. Their page is consistent with the design on their website.

My biggest turnoff on someone's homepage is the use of hashtags (#) in their description. These are great for showing you how to locate them on Twitter, but if you already have their name, hashtags in this context, to me, seem unprofessional. Save hashtags for your tweets. Take the time to write a brief sentence of who you are. In the novel world, we call these tag lines. Mine is "supporting artists one word at a time."

When you choose a conference, you probably look for ones that will have other songwriters, artists, and producers in attendance. You should do the same on Twitter. This is where hashtags come in. Type #songwriters, #music #producers, #(insert your genre) into the search bar and see what comes up. You can type in multiple hashtags at once. When the results come up, look at the top where there are several tabs, including TOP/LIVE/ACCOUNTS … Click on ACCOUNTS. For this example, I typed in #music #producers #country in the same search, which turned up a variety of accounts for music producers in the country music genre. Find ones that match your preferences and click FOLLOW. Also look for accounts of venues you play. Promoting these venues in your tweets is a nice thank you. If they are not on Twitter, encourage them to join you for easy, free promotion.

Don't go overboard; start with a few. Once you begin tweeting, you will have others following you, and you can return the courtesy.

What? You have to post? Well, yeah, that's the idea of a conference. You have to talk to people by either starting or offering something to a conversation. This is where the adage of the 80-10-10 Rule comes into play. People who seem to work this in reverse are often avoided or blocked. To keep from spamming your Twitter followers and getting ignored before you have even begun, think of your posts this way: 80 percent general information, 10 percent promoting others, 10 percent promoting yourself. And remember: You only have 140 characters to work with.

General information might be sharing links to news articles or blog posts that have something to do with the music business. You can also post things of interest to you. For example, I love big cats, as do many of my followers. Periodically, I will post cat pictures and tag a couple of those followers. I've provided general information while putting my followers' names out there.

Promoting others is important. This is the "You scratch my back, I'll scratch yours" philosophy. There is also a #FollowFriday, where you can post Twitter handles of some of your followers, encouraging anyone seeing the #FollowFriday groupings to make new friends by following them—one long conga line of networking. Also, when someone follows you, remember to thank them in a tweet. A simple "Thanks for the #Follow" (or #FollowBack if you followed them first) will suffice. Something more personal as "I look forward to networking with you" is also appropriate. Also, take a few minutes to Like or Retweet their tweets. What goes around comes around.

Then there is the final 10 percent: promoting yourself. This shameless self promotion is done via posting dates and venues you will be playing, as well as links and clips to works-in-progress. If you handle the first two percentage brackets well, you won't need to heavy-hand this one. Retweets and Likes will keep your name out there.

As with any other social media site, Twitter can become a time suck. Set a definitive "Twitter time," then get back to work. I use HootSuite (an application for pre-scheduling tweets to run at various dates and times) to schedule tweets in advance. TweetDeck is another option. Both work similarly in pre-scheduling tweets and are more about personal preference. As with any program, find the one that works best for you. This plan allows me to block out an hour to load tweets for the coming week about where artists are playing and posts remembering artists who have a birthday or have passed on. The rest of my time on Twitter is retweeting others—sharing what they post with my followers.

When I'm on the road visiting with artists or attending events, I always smile when they say they follow me on Twitter. I know in that instant the Twitter bird has been singing.

KELLY HENKINS is a full-time writer and artist. She is a trusted online voice for Texas music and spends most of her daytime networking with singers and songwriters all over the country. She lives in the rural Ozarks. She blogs at kellyscountry.blogspot.com, and you can also follow her on Twitter (@kellyscountry) or contact her at kellyscountry@missouri.usa.com.

BREAKING INTO NASHVILLE

A Conversation Between Jonathan Feist & Shane Adams

Jonathan Feist & Shane Adams

Jonathan Feist is editor in chief of Berklee Press, the book-publishing activity of Berklee College of Music. Shane Adams is president of Artist Accelerator, a Nashville-based artist development company. They are both authors, teachers at Berklee Online, and co-conspirators in many a madcap scheme, such as Shane's recent book, *The Singer-Songwriter's Guide to Recording in the Home Studio.*

Why is Nashville such a big deal for songwriters?

Nashville is the richest, most fertile environment for songwriters that I've ever seen—much more so than LA or New York. Many professional songwriters live here. It is a relatively small city, and so there are relatively few people, and everybody lives within about twenty minutes of each other.

There are lots of songwriting events going on all the time, such as writers nights and open mics. On any evening, there are probably four or five songwriter events happening in the city. So, songwriting is on the mind of Nashville constantly. You take a cab, and your cab driver is a songwriter. Everybody is a songwriter.

There's a section of town called Music Row: three to four square blocks of professional music publishing companies. The performance rights organizations (PROs) all have offices here. Then, there are record labels. There used to be more, but there are still around three big labels here.

Why do so many artists want to record in Nashville?

Nashville has tons of little recording studios. On my street, there are six recording studios! A couple of them have drum rooms, some have bigger rooms for larger ensembles, and two or three are small-project studios. There are also a lot of exceptional studio musicians.

The studios may be relatively small, but they are super high quality, capable of producing professional-grade demos and commercial recordings at a good value.

This proliferation of recording studios, great equipment, and amazing musicians attracts a lot of artists. While Nashville might be most known for country music, people are also recording Americana and rock and roll. Many alternative rock bands record here, and there's a lot of gospel/Christian music, too.

In addition, we have a tendency to work together, here, as a community. The result is exceptional quality, a spirit of creative collaboration, and relative affordability. Plus, there is the city's general cultural organization that supports and inspires songwriters and anyone who loves and values music: the Grand Ole Opry, the Country Music Hall of Fame, and the countless small performance venues and writers nights taking place all over the city. There's a lot here that musicians find inspiring.

The goal of a songwriter who wants to make a living should be to collaborate with others. You need to meet other artists, songwriters, and publishers, and get your songs in the hands of the people who can bring them to the largest possible market.

What is a "writers night"?

A writers night is a performance, usually at a bar, that features a series of songwriters playing their original tunes.

Writers nights started at the famous Bluebird Café in the mid-1970s when several famous songwriters started to do "writers in the round." This is where three or four writers set up their chairs in a circle in the middle of the club, facing each other, instead of on a stage. The tables and chairs for the audience were set up around the writers. Then, they'd play some famous songs and some other songs that weren't cut yet. This setup became a tradition, and it caught on at other clubs and venues.

A writers night is a little different from an open mic night, when an endless stream of performers each come up and play a couple songs, either originals or covers. Open night mics also abound in Nashville, but a writers night is a distinct form. Usually, for a writers night, three or four songwriters are up at the same time, playing longer sets, say four or five songs, and all the songs are originals.

A writers night might be set up in the traditional way, as a writers round, or the writers might just take turns going up on stage. But writers rounds/writers nights and open mic nights are both common, every night.

How do you play at these events?

On weekends, it's usually either by invitation or by audition. The top writers get invited to play. Other writers have to audition, often months in advance to play somewhere like the Bluebird.

For weeknight performances, each venue keeps a list. You can call and ask to be put on the list, even up to that same day. Last week, I went to a writers night during the week, and they had forty-five writers on the list! They started playing at around eight o'clock and went until two o'clock in the morning! That's common, for writers to play way into the wee hours.

For an open mic, you might be able to just show up with your guitar and have a chance to play a song, maybe two songs, without scheduling it in advance.

What's the relationship between Nashville's peforming artists and aongwriters?

The current stable of artists tends to write more of their own songs. Professional songwriters now tend to be writing with the artists, rather than writing themselves and then submitting their songs to artists who record their songs. Music Row used to be filled up with a greater number of small publishers, and there aren't as many today. So, it has become harder for independent songwriters to get publishing deals. We are all doing a lot of co-writing with artists.

What this means, strategically, is this: The goal of a songwriter who wants to make a living should be to collaborate with others. You need to meet other artists, songwriters, and publishers, and get your songs in the hands of the people who can bring them to the largest possible market.

Obviously, your songs have to be ready for the commercial market. There is another side to achieving success, though, besides honing your songwriting craft. You have to understand how to navigate through the industry that turns great songs into commercial hits. This means smart networking.

How do you meet others in the industry?

Musicians here meet each other everywhere. I just participated in a benefit concert for my daughters' parent-teacher organization. Of course, all the other kids' parents are also musicians! There were several phenomenal singer-songwriter parents who also participated, whom I'd never met before, and we all connected. This kind of chance event can lead to a professional collaboration. I don't know where else in the world that happens at such a high professional level.

We also meet each other at gigs and at writers nights. Everyone's always hustling here. I just went to a writers night and met a friend who is a terrific mastering engineer. It reminded me that I actually need a mastering engineer for one of my projects, so we talked, and I'll probably use him.

As you spend time here, you assemble a regular group of people that you like to work with. When you meet someone, you are also tapping into their connections.

What's the most likely path to success?

There's the myth that if you keep playing enough writers' rounds, eventually you'll get discovered. I just don't see that happening.

What I see as being truly effective is this: You need to develop a relationship with a writer's rep at your PRO: ASCAP, BMI, or SESAC. Those reps seem to be the ones who hold the keys to the kingdom. They have connections to artists, publishers, and other songwriters, and they are the ones who can actually help you get a cut.

Singer-songwriter Lauren Marx (photo by Jonathan Feist) is the kind of current artist looking to break out in Nashville.

Virtually all my songwriter clients find the most success with this path: meeting regularly with their writers' representatives at the PROs.

The problem is that PRO reps are inundated with crazy and nontalented people, and they are initially wary of new songwriters, so it can be hard to get a meeting with them. But the good news is that they actually want to find gifted writers who will work hard and stick it out.

It's like dating, but they are looking for a long-term relationship. There isn't usually love at first sight with a PRO rep. But I don't think I've ever met a songwriter who was gifted, who worked hard, and who developed a long-term relationship with their PRO who hasn't found some kind of success from that relationship.

What happens after you request a meeting with the PRO?

The typical response is, "Yeah, you want a meeting, and so does everyone else on that bus!" It's hard to get a meeting. I know BMI has a monthly free-for-all cage match, where they just let everybody show up at the front door.

They will probably brush you off at first. But if you call incessantly and keep bugging them, eventually you'll get a meeting.

How do these meetings typically play out?

Play them two or three of your songs, either recordings or live on your guitar. The question to ask them is, what would you do to this song to get it to where you would give me a meeting with a publisher? Ideally, they will give you a specific answer. Then, the next time you see them, play them the song with the changes they suggested just to show that you are listening and that you are willing to work.

After a couple years of meeting with them regularly and working with them to improve your music as they suggest, they will realize that you are sticking around and start helping you make connections. This is a much more effective approach than waiting until you think your songs are perfect and then meeting with them one time. Instead, develop a relationship and establish that you're a good writer willing to work and take direction.

Remember, their goal is to generate income through performance royalties for their company. They are looking for hits so that they can be heroes to their companies. Usually, that is accomplished by connecting good songwriters to publishing companies, record labels, and artists. Their challenge is always to meet someone with a good enough song.

Do many songwriters give up too soon?

I think so. I find one of the most important qualities for a new songwriter coming to town is not their ability to write; it's their ability to work and to stick around. I've seen incredibly gifted songwriters and musicians fail to gain traction here just because they didn't have the gumption to stay and actually do the work, making connections and getting their songs in front of the people who can actually help them in their careers.

Many artists seem to feel that success will just get handed to them because they are gifted and talented. But the process takes much longer than people expect.

It can be done, though. If you are truly talented, work hard, and stick with it, you will eventually find a measure of success.

....

JONATHAN FEIST is the author of *Project Management for Musicians* (winner of the 2015 International Book Award for Performing Arts), several other books, and hundreds of articles about music. He is editor in chief of Berklee Press, the book publishing department of Berklee College of Music, and teaches for Berklee Online.
....

....
SHANE ADAMS is a twice-GRAMMY-nominated music educator, award-winning producer, and songwriter. Shane is president of Artist Accelerator and is a founding instructor for Berklee Online, where he has taught lyric writing and songwriting since 2003.
....

CO-WRITE LIKE A PRO

Keys to Working Successfully with Another Songwriter

Andrea Williams

Today's music industry is all about co-writing. Whether it's an artist wanting to be more involved in the writing of his own songs or a veteran songwriter who excels at melody but needs help crafting the perfect lyric, collaboration is the name of the game. This may be good news for up-and-coming songwriters who aren't yet sure of their own skills or are looking to learn from someone more experienced—but only if they learn the ins and outs of co-writing like a pro. Here's what you need to know.

SHOW UP WITH SOME GREAT IDEAS...

While the saying goes that two heads are better than one, and one of the main benefits of co-writing is the ability to attack the blank page with the combined power of two or more, a dreaded touch of writer's block is still prone to strike a co-writing session, making ideas hard to come by.

"[An] established writer also needs to feel that their partner is helping them get better, not loving all the mediocre ideas."

For that reason, one of the best ways to co-write like a pro is to show up to the writing session with a few ideas in tow. Nothing gets creative juices flowing like not having to start from scratch, and, says Sheree Spoltore, founder and president of the Global Songwriter's Connection, a great jumping off point is often a catchy or otherwise unique song title. This is especially true if your session is with a writer who is more experienced than you. It shows that you're willing to bring new ideas to the table while also giving her a fresh take on the same topics she's likely been writing about for years. "My friend Bryan White, who is a highly sought after hit songwriter in Nashville, often says, 'Dare to suck,'" Spoltore says. "In other words, even if it's a stupid idea, just shoot it out there, because you never know—it may spur the thought of something else."

This can be tough advice, especially for a newbie writer who's so nervous she can barely put pen to paper. But the reality is that, while it can be frustrating when doors don't open as soon as you'd like, the months or years that you spend below the radar of publishers and labels are a valuable time for honing your skills. You can trust, then, that once opportunities arise, you are prepared. So if you've found yourself in a songwriting room with other professionals, it's likely because you've earned your way there. Turn that truth into the confidence you need to speak up during the writing session. And try not to be intimidated.

"A young writer who is so eager to work with an established writer that he loves everything that comes out of the established writer's mouth is a huge red flag," says Suzan Koc, a former executive with Warner/Chappell, BMG, and Hit & Run Music who now teaches music publishing at the Musician's Institute in Hollywood. "The established writer also needs to feel that their partner is helping them get better, not loving all the mediocre ideas."

But the converse is also true, and up-and-coming writers can actually speak up too much, says songwriter Michelle Bell, who's written for Jennifer Lopez, Britney Spears, Mary J. Blige, and others. "I think sometimes people get insecure or scared that they're not offering enough to the session, so they throw out too many ideas," she says. "It's better to share quality over quantity—but don't be afraid to share. If you have established your publishing splits and how you will handle the business before you start writing, then you will feel more open to make mistakes or not share until you have the right ideas to improve the song."

For more detailed advice on how to craft a song title that publishers and labels will love, email sheree@globalsongwriters.com and put Songwriter's Market Title Tips in the subject line.

BE WILLING TO LEARN

Songwriting is a lot like yoga, medicine, or the legal profession—you're always practicing, continually learning, and trying to improve upon your craft. And in that sense, every songwriting session has the potential to morph into a music master class in which you can glean tips from your co-writer(s) that will help establish the very foundation your career is built upon. Be open to this education and absorb everything you can.

"I can still remember the lessons that I learned from Pat Pattison," Spoltore says. "In a co-write, I learned the importance of putting my melody emphasis on emotional words or important words, rather than words like *and* or *that*. From John Schweers, who wrote 'I Left Something Turned on at Home,' I learned the importance of including a smile factor in a song. From co-writes with Jim Collins, I learned the value and importance in including inner rhyme in my songs—not just rhyming lines on the end, but creating inner rhyme that didn't show."

Spoltore's advice to new songwriters? Get a notebook. "And after every co-writing session, if I were you, I'd take notes," she says. "Ask yourself what you learned from that writer and then begin to incorporate those lessons into your own songwriting."

WORK FROM A PLACE OF GENEROSITY

So you've pushed aside all the butterflies, and you're excited that this songwriting session could very well pave the way to your first No. 1 hit and riches beyond your wildest imagination. But that doesn't mean you should kill the creative vibe or anger the music-making gods with petty conflicts about who wrote what.

Spoltore notes that this is a nonissue in Nashville writers rooms, as there is an unwritten rule that all writers present in a room will share equally in the final product regarding credit and earnings. It eliminates tension and shifts the focus to where it belongs: songwriting. "The reason we use this method is that my idea that I share may not actually wind up in the song, but if I didn't share that with you, we might not have gotten to the great idea that you thought of," explains Spoltore.

For New York or LA writers, who may typically count lines written or rely on some other more exact method for determining credit, Spoltore encourages them to use the Music City method of splits. "Honestly, the universe is very abundant," she says, "but you've got to give to receive. I believe that when we remain in a state of abundance, abundance comes to us. And I've found this to be so true in my own life. When you just say, 'Hey, let's all share in this equally,' you open the door for more, so much more, to come into your life."

That generosity goes for creative ideas as well, says Koc. When you hit an impasse with another writer regarding a certain lyric or melody that you can't agree on, she suggests erring on the side of compromise. "It doesn't matter whose line it is; the song is created together no matter what," says Koc. "It's like a child. A mother is not going to like her child less because he or she looks like the dad. You do what's right for the kid, and you do what's right for the song. If you truly believe your idea is better, try to articulate it based on the song, not based on ego. The ego is an important part of being a creator; however, put the ego on the result, not the process."

BE WILLING TO SPEAK UP FOR YOURSELF

Unfortunately, no matter how willing you are to compromise or equally split songwriting credit, that won't always be possible. You may never have a songwriting session in Nashville, so it will be important for you to address the business of your songwriting to protect your earning interests. And the best approach is to have the discussion up front, says Koc. "If you are one of three writers, and there are two topliners and one producer, ask before the session starts if it's an even one-third split or if the producer takes 50 percent," she says. "This will allow you to know where you stand and if you want to be part of the session."

Like Spoltore, Bell is in favor of equal splits, but when this is not possible, and you plan to work with the same co-writer(s) in the future, she suggests determining "a consistent split you will always use to avoid any conflicts in the future." And in those cases, says Koc, try to have a signed split sheet when you walk out of the room.

"I do realize sometimes it's not possible, but as much as it is possible, have a little sheet everyone signs," Koch says, "because here is what a lot of people forget: The law says it's all equal shares unless it's in writing."

Being brave enough to speak up doesn't just apply to matters of finance. Songwriting, like all creative endeavors, is an extremely emotional process. And sometimes emotions will transcend the music and lead to conflict. When this happens, the only way to keep the situation from exploding into something bigger is to discuss it immediately. "I have on my desk a little acorn," Spoltore says. "And the reason it's there is to remind me to address any conflict, or potential conflicts, while [it's] an acorn, rather than when they become an oak tree."

But don't mistake this admonition as an excuse to call someone else in to clean up the messes you'd rather avoid, says Koc. "Be a grown up and talk to your collaborators. Don't send your manager or publisher to have the uncomfortable talk. They were not in the room; you were."

Spoltore agrees. "Things can get bonky-wonky between songwriters, and when they do, recognize it," she says. "Don't try to pretend like it doesn't exist, because when you confess it, you disperse it. Say, 'For whatever the reason, this isn't feeling right for me, and I'm not going to let this happen.'"

Often, though, the best cure for songwriting conflict is prevention. Completely avoiding problems before they occur is never an exact science, but there are some common warning signs that can at least help you steer clear of disaster very early in the process. Namely, Koc advises songwriters to write with others who share the same tastes and sensibilities, as opposed to gravitating toward others in your genre who may be polar opposites. As an example, if you are a staunch Christian conservative, you may be signing up for trouble by co-writing with a left-wing atheist. "If songwriters like different things, it's a huge red flag, because they are going to conflict on the aesthetics of the song they are writing together," says Koc.

Meanwhile, Bell recommends avoiding "challengers," or people who object to every single component of the song, from the melodies to the chords, even the ones they first suggested themselves. "While challenging is a good thing if you want to make sure you're choosing the best ideas, you want to make sure you're not overthinking it and killing the vibe," she says. "It's a picture, not a pixel. Sometimes you have to get the idea or sketch outline first; then you go back and fill in the details and specifics."

Walking away from a songwriting session you fought so hard to get into may seem like a step in the wrong direction, but any time you spend avoiding headaches or tension of any kind simply means that you'll have more time for what matters most—writing songs.

TRUE TO YOUR VOICE

Advice from Some Seasoned Songwriters

....

David McPherson

Take a country-loving songwriter from Yonkers, New York, a veteran musician with dyslexia from Toronto, Ontario, and a songsmith who lives in the woods far from the maddening crowds—and who answers to the nickname "Tawgs"—and what do you get? A trio of seasoned songwriters: Chip Taylor, Marc Jordan, and Thomas "Tawgs" Salter. Among them the hits are numerous. Their musical creations include such memorable songs as "Try (Just a Little Bit Harder)," "Rhythm of My Heart," and "You Are Loved (Don't Give Up)" that have been recorded by Janis Joplin, Rod Stewart, and Josh Groban.

When I wrote songs, I never really wrote them thinking, I want to write a song about this or that. I just picked up a guitar at some point during the day and just let the chordal things flow. I sang nonsense.

For many, writing songs is better than any therapy. As one songwriter I interviewed joked, "It keeps me out of a psychiatric ward!" There is no magic method to writing songs. After spending time chatting with this trio of songwriters, though, a few common pieces of advice emerged. Listen to your voice and be true to yourself. Sometimes, the simplest words and phrases, reworked in your own unique way, turn into a hit. Other times, learning a new chord sparks your imagination.

All three artists subscribe to the "never quit" philosophy. There's no denying songwriting is hard work. The desire to throw in the towel and find a "real" job is a constant, unwanted voice, nagging and needling you. As an artist, you need to silence that inner critic, that voice that tells you your songs are not worthy of an audience. Imagine if Taylor had not won the war against the self-defeating demon that lurks inside his mind. The world would never have heard the sing-a-long party anthem "Wild Thing" or the beautiful ballad "Angel of the Morning"—a 1981 single that sold a million copies for country-pop singer Juice Newton.

Davey Wilson

CHIP TAYLOR: FROM YONKERS TO THE SONGWRITERS HALL OF FAME

In June 2016, Chip Taylor joined the latest group of inductees into the Songwriters Hall of Fame that also included Tom Petty, Elvis Costello, and Marvin Gaye. That's fine company indeed, but it's a well-deserved, and overdue, honor for the 76-year-old. For five decades, he's added to a deep and rich song catalog brimming with a menagerie of creations from cult classics to mega selling hits. Taylor was born and raised in Yonkers, New York, a town of approximately 200,000 that borders the Bronx, a couple of miles north of Manhattan. The artist's homage to his hometown, the Grammy-nominated *Yonkers NY* (2009), shows his storytelling talent.

When I congratulate Taylor on his induction into the Songwriters Hall of Fame, the ever humble artist references his first guitar teacher. "Where would I be without him? He taught me my first three chords," he says. "Where would I be without the guitar player who played on my demos that I sent to Chet Atkins? I'm sure one of the reasons he liked my songs was because they were authentic. I owe so much to so many people.

"Songwriting doesn't just come because you are brilliant," he adds. "You use your spirit and then all the blessings you have, people who are kind and who listen to you. Never pat yourself on the back for all of that. I take a lot of people with me when I get such a nice honor handed to me."

To understand where this songwriting journey began and learn from this master at his craft, one needs to first take a trip back to Taylor's formative years in Yonkers. Born James Wesley Voight, Taylor is the brother of Oscar-winning actor Jon Voight (*Midnight Cowboy, Coming Home, Deliverance* et al). From a young age, he developed a passion for country music thanks to a tube Motorola radio, which his parents let him listen to into the wee hours.

"One night, when I was around nine years old, I found a station in Wheeling, West Virginia," recalls Taylor. "It totally changed my life." Later, on the same radio, he discovered the blues. "I just got lost in something that meant a lot to me."

I've Got Chills, They're Multiplying

When it comes to music, Taylor has always been moved, not by brainy stuff, but instead by the physical reaction he has to certain sounds. "I get chills," he says. The first time this happened for the songwriter was when his parents, unable to find a babysitter, took six-year-old Taylor to a Broadway show. "When I heard that orchestra start to play, my body was on fire," he says. "I remember when we left the theater, I did not want to talk to my mother or father. I pretended I was sleeping in the car, but I wasn't. I just wanted to keep that feeling I felt from that orchestra."

That sensation happens every time Taylor's muse blesses him with a song. At 16, the New Yorker was lucky to get his foot into the music business, signing with King Records. Initially, he wasn't selling enough records to make a living, so he was lucky that a couple of small publishers in Manhattan gave him a chance. The next thing you know, one of his compositions ended up in the hands of Chet Atkins, a musician and record producer for RCA Victor's Nashville division.

"My publisher called me in and read the note from Chet that said, 'I'm getting that song you sent down. I have no idea who Chip Taylor is. It's very hard for me to believe that he is from New York, but wherever he's from, I want to hear every song he writes!'

"That was it," says Taylor. "That's how I really got into the business. All of a sudden, I started writing songs, and every one this publisher sent to Chet Atkins."

Before long, the boy from Yonkers was having his songs recorded by some of Nashville's top acts, such as The Brown Family, Eddy Arnold, Bobby Bare, and later, Willie Nelson and Waylon Jennings. A publishing deal soon followed that included a $30 advance per song. Later, Taylor received a staff writing job.

"I was always following a spirit," he says of his songwriting process. "When I wrote songs, I never really wrote them thinking, *I want to write a song about this or that.* I just picked up a guitar at some point during the day and just let chordal things flow. I sang nonsense. I didn't want to think about anything. I just wanted to let a spirit come out of me ... something that gave me that chill. Sometimes I didn't even know what it was."

Taylor recalls the genesis of one of his biggest hits, "Angel of the Morning," and how it took a while for these chills to come. "After about forty-five minutes of nothing coming, the melody came out, along with the line 'There'll be no strings to bind your hands/Not if my love can't bind your heart.'

"I had no idea what it meant, but I knew that it gave me such a chill … I was just on fire," he continues. "I wrote it down, sang it again, and then another line came: 'And there's no need to take a stand/For it was I who chose to start.' It gave me such a chill. I didn't know where I was going or who I was."

Listen Up!

Even though he sometimes doesn't know where the song is going, the one constant Taylor knows is that when he pens a song, he's writing as a listener. "That's what I do," he says. "I don't continue songs as a listener unless something happens to me. That's the way I write everything. I'm always looking to feel that chill."

Good songwriting is about the listener. You have to involve the listener even though you don't know who that listener is going to be. The concept has to be one that everybody can identify with.

Another piece of advice Taylor always gives songwriters is to find what they love. "When I was a kid I couldn't wait to hear Johnny Cash, The Brown Family, and Lefty Frizzell," he says. "I had real passion for this stuff. I didn't like everything, but the stuff I liked, I really liked. So, if I phrase a little bit like Willie Nelson, it's because I loved listening to Willie when I was a kid. There was always something in the spirit of what I wrote that was attached to the music I loved."

For Taylor, getting that spirit to come is not so much about where he is or his frame of mind as it is about being open to the experience. He does suggest going someplace that has soothing music to help facilitate your muse.

"When I pick up the guitar, I may not know what is underneath me at the time," he says. "I'm trying to let something inside of me come out. The mood may come only because I gave it a channel to come, whereas other times I may be walking down the street and all of a sudden I'll start to sing a little something."

Five decades on, thankfully for Taylor, and for music lovers, he still gets the chills, and the songs continue to come. A final nugget he leaves songwriters with is to be true to themselves.

"When you are writing something, you shouldn't write so other people will like it," he says. "Write in your own feeling, in your own words. Your words will be different than somebody else's words. That's the voice a songwriter should write in, his or her own voice. Write so it means something to you. Let your spirit carry you. That's my best advice."

MARC JORDAN: A UNIQUE WRITING STYLE

When it comes to songwriting, Marc Jordan has put in his 20,000 hours. He says there is not a day that goes by that he doesn't write. While the Canadian is best known for the worldwide hit "Rhythm of My Heart," which has sold more than 15 million units globally for Rod Stewart, over the years he's also collaborated with a roster of who's who in the music industry, including David Foster, Graham Nash, Jon Anderson (Yes), and Bruce Hornsby. The list of artists who've covered his compositions is just as impressive: everyone from Diana Ross and Cher to Joe Cocker and Kenny Loggins. The Torontonian has a unique writing style he chocks up to dyslexia, which he only discovered he had after his daughter was tested.

"When I was in school, they didn't know what dyslexia was," he says. "I never thought of it, but when I look back, while it was not great for my schoolwork, it didn't seem to hamper me in music. It made me unique, because, in a way, it informed my writing style. I never developed a sense of linear story in my writing—a beginning, middle, and an end—but it actually works in songwriting because you have three minutes to write something that people perceive as a story, so you have to leave a lot of gaps in the logic.

"Songwriting allows you to make leaps that you couldn't do in a novel or even a poem," he says. "It's a unique art form."

Make It Universal & The Language of Melody

Write songs that are universal, advises Jordan. He recalls going out on tour after releasing his first record. People came up to him and said what particular songs they loved meant to them. "Invariably, it was never what I had set out to write about," says Jordan. "I realized that everybody interprets songs in their own way and you have to leave gaps for people to jump in with their own life. You want people to be involved in your songs, so you can't make it about you.

"That is a mistake young songwriters make," he says. "They write about themselves or something in their life in a blow-by-blow assessment. That's not what good songwriting is about. Good songwriting is about the listener. You have to involve the listener even though you don't know who that listener is going to be. The concept has to be one that everybody can identify with. It's like the tree in the forest. If a song is never heard, what good is it?"

When Jordan first started, he would find inspiration in something he read or saw in the newspaper, or maybe on the back of a bus. These stories or images would tweak his imagination. Today, he realizes that melody is also a language.

"Melody predates our written language," says Jordan. "The first way we communicated was with rhythm. People would beat on trees and make drums and then we started chanting and singing, and melody became a form of communication, and then we had words. The challenge of great songwriting—listen to Jimmy Webb and he nails it almost every time—is that the lyric has to be saying the same thing that the melody is saying because the melody is saying something. If you are saying something different than the melody, you've got a wagon with two horses pulling in different directions."

Like Taylor, Jordan believes in the importance of listening. "I always jam a melody out first," he says. "When I have a rough melody, I know what the song is about, because the melody tells me. Then I have to make sure the words are saying the same thing. I understand melody now in a way I never did when I was young."

These well-chosen words also need to fit the writer's voice. "Joni Mitchell said an interesting thing to me once," recalls Jordan. "She said, 'I don't trust singers and songwriters that don't sing and write in their own voice.' What she was saying was that the cadence of what you write, wordwise, has to fit the cadence of your conversation."

Jordan would describe his approach as image-driven combined with a lot of metaphor. "I don't really spell stuff out," he says. "I try to create a feeling that is universal, that everybody can identify with. We are all human beings. We all love. We all fight. We all hate. We all get angry. We all get sad. We all seek love and affection. You have to find interesting ways to communicate that, and you don't have to spell it out."

And your brain helps create those patterns, solving problems and connecting the dots. "When you look up into the sky, and you look at the clouds, you don't see clouds," he says. "You see, oh, that looks like a horse or that looks like Santa Claus's beard ... your brain always tries to create order out of chaos and tries to see something familiar in the unfamiliar. So don't spell things out in your songs. The listener's brain will do it automatically."

These days Jordan mainly co-writes with others, finding collaborative sessions less lonely. Whether writing on your own or with others, there's no magic formula, though. It comes down to hard work and regular practice.

"There is this fantasy that art just comes through you," he says. "In a way, it does come through you, but you've got to build the highway. Some people have a dirt road, and some people have a superhighway. When I was young, I would wait for inspiration. I didn't write that much, and sometimes that will work, but you can't rely on it. You need to really build that road between you and the universe."

THOMAS "TAWGS" SALTER ON CAR RIDES & COLLABORATION

Thomas Salter, better known in the industry by his nickname "Tawgs," still gets goose bumps every time he writes a song. He wrote his first tune on the guitar when he was sixteen years old. He captured the composition on a four-track with a cassette tape, along with a drum machine, in the makeshift studio he created in his bedroom. "That was the first time I ever recorded one of the songs I had written and played it back, and I just fell in love with that whole process," says Salter.

Since then, Salter has co-written hit songs for Josh Groban, and his music, production, and collaborations have been featured on such television shows as *Vampire Diaries*, *Grey's Anatomy*, *American Idol*, and *The Simpsons*. He admits that over the years his approach to songwriting hasn't changed much. Usually, it begins by hearing a melody in his head, and then there's no stopping. "Hopefully you can get it down quick enough," he says. "Today it's a little easier with iPhones and stuff, as you can record your ideas right away."

Tawgs does a lot of his writing in the car on his commutes to and from Toronto. "I'll start hearing an idea in my head, and the next thing you know I've got the record function out on my phone and I just record idea after idea," he says. "Driving gives me time to think about song ideas. The ones that are really good, I can hear the whole thing. I hear the drum parts, the bass parts, and the melodies. When it happens, it's like, *Whoa, that's a good one!*, and it gets me really excited."

Usually, if he's set to work with an artist and they are getting ready to write a song together, he'll get some jolt of inspiration a couple of days or a day before. "Sometimes it can come from a long day of work as my brain just opens up to new ideas," he says. "It's definitely cyclical, though. I'm not creative all the time, so when it happens, you have to be there and ready to capture it."

Being self-aware of what is happening inside you is extremely important just so you can maximize the writing experience. Be aware of what your role is and how you can help make the situation successful.

Collaboration is the key to Salter's success. When you collaborate with another songwriter or musician, he says the process either involves getting together with ideas or starting from scratch; usually, it's the former. "For example, I'll come in with an idea, which hopefully will be one of those good ones I was talking about, and the artist or other songwriter will also come in with an idea," he says. "Everyone plays his or her ideas, and then you say, let's go with that one. That's usually how it works. We all lay our cards on the table and then we decide which way to go."

Salter says he's been lucky to collaborate with some amazing writers who have great ideas in spades. Once you find a writing partner that clicks, and where the chemistry is right, stick with him. For Tawgs, Josh Groban is one of these long-time collaborators. The pair first started working together in 2006. "I've been able to work with really talented people that can deliver a song," he says. "When you find that relationship, you have to hold onto it, but first, you have to look for where the talent is."

"You could have a collaboration partner that doesn't come up with the lion's share of ideas but directs in a certain way that really helps the situation," says Salter. "Everybody plays a part. When you find that magic connection with people, you have to stick with it."

Another key, says Salter, is to know your limitations. For example, writing lyrics is not his forte. "There is a lot of ego involved and at play when working with people and other songwriters," he says. "Being self-aware of what is happening inside you is extremely important just so you can maximize the writing experience. Be aware of what your role is and how you can help make the situation successful."

Salter also pays a lot of attention to the body language of the artist he's collaborating with. "A lot of the time people just don't pay attention to that stuff, but that's where a lot of the good songs come from," he says. "When everyone is aware in the room and knows the cues, great things happen."

Tawgs's final advice is to quiet those little voices inside your head telling you that you, or your songs, are not good enough. "I would be lying if I told you that still doesn't happen to me," he says. "It's the people who learn to silence those voices who succeed."

PHIL CODY

An Interview with the Two-Time ASCAP Song of the Year Winner

....

John Anderson

Phil Cody began his songwriting career in the 1960s and became famous as the lyricist for Neil Sedaka, penning such 1970s hits as "Laughter in the Rain," "Solitaire," and "Bad Blood." The two-time ASCAP Song of the Year winner has gold and platinum records to his name, with songs recorded by Elvis, The Carpenters, Huey Lewis and the News, ABBA, and Sheryl Crow. He continues to write and perform, and currently teaches a lyric writing class at the Songwriting School of Los Angeles.

How long have you been a songwriter?
I think I wrote my first song in 1965. I met a bunch of guys in college and put a band together, and we all left school in our sophomore years and went to work in Greenwich Village, and ultimately got a gig in a really important club down there. We came down there as just a regular cover band and over the course of a year grew up into a band that was writing its own stuff. It wasn't really good. People thought what we were doing was good enough to offer us a recording contract [with Columbia Records], but over time, most of the guys in the band went back to school. I decided to stay in New York City, and pitch songs to publishers.

How has the industry changed since then for aspiring songwriters?
It's almost impossible to be an aspiring traditional songwriter these days. You have to have an enormous amount of energy. You have to have the will to go out there and

socialize, or use social media constantly, do all these things. Back in the day, people threw money at us to help us develop and waited around for us to grow into something, or grow into a tax write-off. So there was a willingness to invest that way in talent. And that's not around anymore. People are pretty much left to their own devices. There aren't really any record labels left. There's a monolithic central core, and then there are all these outliers of indie stuff that goes on.

As a songwriter, do you keep to a regular writing schedule, or do you tend to wait for inspiration?

When I'm working … the important part for me is to just get my hands on the piano. It all starts with getting up in the morning and sitting down at the piano for a bunch of hours—and not with any intent in mind other than to be there and see what happens. I also teach songwriting, so I occasionally get together with other people and find out what their processes are. I enjoy that collaborative aspect of getting out of my own comfort zone and working with other people.

When you actually get a song going, an idea going, what is your process then?

Maybe it's my experiences early on in my creative life as a jingle writer, but I always seem to do choruses first. I always find myself writing melodies that lend themselves to being the chorus part of the song and always seem to come up with really good choruses. And then I have to spend the next two weeks scouring around to knock whatever square pegs of verses I can into the round holes of choruses. I tell my students I don't set out to write anything that means anything, because I'm into music and sounds, and, to me, how a song sounds is as important as what it means. Sort of the notes and music and melody dictate me.

Do you tend to create the music first and then write the lyrics, or is it the other way around?

Well, if I get lucky and I write a chorus and everything happens at the same time, that's really a good day. And I have those days. I have those days where I sit down and everything's clicking, I have a good amount of energy going, and all of a sudden, I'll just sit there and I'll hear something and go, 'Oh yeah, I know what that is,' and I can visualize it. I can see it from beginning to end. And that happens with complete songs. One of my hits that I wrote with Neil Sedaka was like that, a song called "Laughter in the Rain." I didn't want to write the song. I wasn't interested in even being at the piano that day. I went out, took a walk, came back, sat down at [Sedaka's] elbow, picked up my yellow pad of paper, and the song just finished from beginning to end in about ten minutes.

Did you use Sedaka's music for that, or how did that song come about?

[Sedaka] would always present me with almost a completed melody and chords and chart. We would sit down, and I would always sit at his right elbow with my little yellow pad, and he would play. And if I needed to have him repeat a line, he was very good at just being able to go over and over a line and melodically give me back that line verbatim. We'd get that line and then we'd move on. He was very patient. It was a really cool gig. It was almost like working with a human tape recorder.

I tell my students I don't set out to write anything that means anything, because I'm into music and sounds, and, to me, how a song sounds is as important as what it means.

When you work in tandem with someone, how is the approach different from writing for yourself?

I think every moment is different. I don't try to impose my will upon a songwriting session. I go in [to the session and] I want to see what's there, who the person I'm working with is, what their temperament is like, what they like to do, what their interests are. I'm creating a temporary partnership rather than saying, 'You will do this or we're not writing.' I never take that approach. I tend to treat songwriting as an exploration rather than a discipline. I go in and just try to find out what the environment is, and then we'll proceed from there. And if I come away without a song, it's not a tragedy. I used to feel that if I went into a session and we didn't write anything, it would be awful. And these days, I don't care. It's really great if you have a song, and if you don't have a song, there are other days when you'll have songs.

When you're writing songs for yourself at your home studio, how does that differ?

For so long I had written songs for other people that it took me a little while to learn how to write songs for myself again and express, solely, what's going on in my consciousness and my bloodstream and all that. I had to relearn how to write for myself. I realized that what I was relying on was memory—and not in a sentimental way, not in a nostalgic way. But memory would spark the creative process. So I've gotten to a place where I'm bored with doing the memory thing. I've tried to find where I stand at the present time and how I can bring my current experiences of the person I am, seventy years old, [with] plenty of creative energy left, lots of juju. How do I get that out in a way that's relevant, if not for public consumption, just at least for me to feel good about bringing stuff to my peers and have them hear what I'm doing?

When you first started out, did you have songwriting mentors?

I hung around with a bunch of other young songwriters, and we would talk to each other. And I signed a deal with Don Kirshner. He signed me to a publishing and production deal, and I got to meet the Tokens—remember "The Lion Sleeps Tonight"? They were signed to the company, and they had offices right next to me. And we would go through this thing where everybody would meet in the Tokens' office every once and a while, and we'd tear our demos to shreds. I've been teaching some workshops now where I bring part of that experience of being in the room with the Tokens.

I'm trying to get [students] to have that moment that Bob Dylan talks about where spirits talk to him. Where you can find that moment where you relax your analytical process and voices talk to you.

How important is it for a young songwriter to be in a community of other songwriters and musicians?

Well, I think it's really important. I work in a place called the Songwriting School of Los Angeles, and it basically provides a first stepping stone to being able to network with other songwriters and people who've been there already. So you have a balance: You have mentorship and a group of peers to hang your work on and get feedback.

How do you find your inspiration for song ideas?

Ah, man, just wake up in the morning. No, it's true. I've had a really long and interesting life, so there's always material there, always material. And I have a really active imagination, so I can pick those two things and just go.

For the class you teach at the songwriting school, what are some of the lessons you try to impress upon your students?

I'm teaching a lyric-writing class, and I'm realizing there's a lot to the learning process. I come from the university of trial and error, never went to school to be a songwriter. But I looked at what was going on, and there's an awful lot of analysis going on in learning how to write songs. They spend a lot of time memorizing stuff, thinking about things, and I'm trying to get them to the point where they can put the analysis aside for a while. I'm trying to get them to have that moment that Bob Dylan talks about where spirits talk to him, where you can find that moment where you relax your analytical process and voices talk to you. Some of them get it. The thing that strikes me with lyric writing is that you don't necessarily have to do it just one way. I mean some of them are very didactic in their approach, very much like you have to go from A to B to C to D and make sense of everything, and everything has to mean something and has to be tied together in a nice little package. Those at the other end are people who want to write from wild flights of inspiration. So I try to find a way to include both ends of that, and it's not often easy. But again, we have this five-minute window to tell a story. And so I try to make them aware of what the implications are as far as our word choices and how to get maybe one word to paint a picture that stands for thousands of words.

Who are some of the songwriters and lyricists that you admire?

I'm a huge Joni Mitchell fan. I'm a singer/songwriter person. I love Paul Simon. I like what he represents as far as an intellectual and a poet. I like James Taylor and Leonard Cohen, that group of people. In my capacities as a teacher, I hear a lot of young songwriters that no one's ever heard of yet, and some of the signs are very hopeful. I have a great deal of optimism for some of them.

JOHN ANDERSON has written extensively on the South Florida music scene for various publications, including the *Miami New Times* and *Miami Herald*.

A MUSICAL LEGEND IN THE MAKING

An Interview with Erik Blu2th Griggs

....

Vanessa Herron

Till Bronner

Erik Blu2th Griggs was a musician before he was potty trained. The Grammy-nominated songwriter, who won the BMI "Song of the Year," has enjoyed a lifelong love affair with music that has taken him around the world and into studios with some of the greatest artists of our time. Here, he shared how he became an in-demand songwriter, how he develops ideas, and much more.

How did you first get into music?

I didn't have a playpen at eighteen months old. My mom could just sit me at the piano and do whatever she wanted to do, because she knew I wasn't going anywhere.

Did you take lessons?

For a few months when I was a kid. Then I went to college for three months before I dropped out. I don't really believe in Plan Bs, and my Plan A didn't require college, so it didn't make sense for me. I did great, but I was preparing for something I wasn't interested in. If you want to be a concert pianist, the orchestra has about sixty violins, but how many pianos does it have?

One?

One! Maybe two. [laughs] ... And as far as knowledge is concerned, a self-motivated person can go online and learn whatever they want these days.

Yes, my daughter calls it YouTube University.

> It's one of the best schools in the world! If I was going to be a doctor or a lawyer, I would've aced school because it's required. But for me, there were no degrees needed—just skill. I was taking time away from developing my skills to learn things I already knew, didn't need to know, or could've learned without paying thousands of dollars.

Don't meet people at a level that's below what they need. Be better than what's necessary, because they're already dealing with people who can at least do what's needed. ... You have to underpromise and overdeliver, be a lot better than whatever a project calls for.

I know you do R&B and pop. Any other genres?

> I know when most people say this, it's not true—but I do everything.

Scottish dance?

> [laughs] Yeah, I can do that! ... I've done jazz in Berlin, pop in Sweden, gospel in Alabama, country in Nashville ... I played on the *Dreamgirls* soundtrack ... I also played on *Straight Outta Compton*.

What are you doing now with Dr. Dre?

> I'm working with some of his artists, TV and film stuff ...

What was your big break?

> My first placement was "One" for Tyrese.

How did that come about?

> I came to LA with nothing but a guitar and a suitcase. I didn't know anybody. I just knew it was time to come, and I played everywhere I could. I'd only played guitar for six years before coming here, but guitars are portable. Keyboards, not so much.

Did you play on street corners?

> I never did the street corner thing. I couldn't afford the amplifier then. But I played for Robert Napoleon and became his musical director two weeks after meeting him. He introduced me to the Underdogs [music producers].

Who's that?

Damon Thomas and Harvey Mason, Jr. They're called the Underdogs because they were from other camps under other people when they formed a new team. My second song placement was "No Air" for Chris Brown and Jordin Sparks. I didn't get a publishing deal until about a year later.

Do you still work with the Underdogs?

Yeah! I always tell young people, "Every door you walk out of, you should be able to walk into."

What's your advice for an aspiring songwriter/producer?

Get really good. Don't meet people at a level that's below what they need. Be better than what's necessary because they're already dealing with people who can at least do what's needed. How do you get the gig if you're fresh off the banana boat and they already have "go-to" people? You have to underpromise and overdeliver, be a lot better than whatever a project calls for. I moved to LA at twenty-seven and [did] a lot to prepare myself. I was overqualified for anything someone could ask me to do in music, because I'd spent my entire life working towards that. I knew how to build and operate a studio, engineer, cut vocals, sing, play four instruments … then I came to California.

You sing, too. Any plans to release an album?

It's more of a "have to" than a "want to," because if I don't, I feel like I'll have wasted that part of me and robbed the world of what I have to offer as an artist.

You also teach at the Songwriting School of Los Angeles.

Yes. It's owned by Rob Seals. I developed a six-week songwriting curriculum for them.

Some say you're on your way to being a legend. Who have you worked with?

Babyface … currently, with Dr. Dre. That's how I know I'm not a legend; I work *with* them.

What was Babyface like?

Incredible. Babyface has about 126 Top 10 records, but when we're writing, I'm writing with "Kenny." We're just two dudes trying to get a song right, and he has no ego. Working with these people helps you realize why they're "them." People with the most ego usually don't get to the top.

Where will your career be in five years?

I apply creativity to music more than anything else. That's what has grown, because I've been watering it. But there's other things I do, like stand-up comedy. It's the biggest rush! Music is my first love, but comedy and other outlets let me be a novice again. The whole process of learning is what I fell in love with in the first place.

I heard that if you cut a starfish, it regrows the missing part of its body. That's how I make songs. I start with anything—it could be a guitar lick, a concept, a melody, a chord progression, anything. Then, at some point, it starts writing itself.

Earlier, you suggested being around people who have reached the place you want to go.

Yes! And they can provide confirmation! I knew I was good at music, but for Babyface to come into the studio and say, "Yo, man, this lyric may sound corny. What do you think?" What do *I* think? Later on I thought, *Do you know you're Babyface, dude?* But then I was like, "Yeah, that line's corny, but I see what you're trying to do. This is how we can get it done." The reason he asked me was it sounded corny to him. If I had been a suck-up, it would've messed up the whole thing. That's the art of co-writing, and he understands that. That's how he got to where he is ... Dre's the same way. There's a sign in Dre's studio that says, "Your ego is not your amigo." He's a billionaire, one of the most important producers ever, and he's like, "I think it's dope. What do *you* think?" He's not like, "If I like it, that's it."

How long does it take you to come up with a track or a song?

Usually, I can do an entire record in a day and be ready to mix the next day.

Where do you find inspiration?

Everywhere! I heard that if you cut a starfish, it regrows the missing part of its body. That's how I make songs. I start with anything—it could be a guitar lick, a concept, a melody, a chord progression, anything. Then, at some point, it starts writing itself.

Do you pull lyrics from personal experiences?

Here's the thing. I think I'd be good at acting, because I put myself in character to do different kinds of music. When I play jazz, I don't play what I'd play. I study people who did it and try to think like they might think.

What's next for you?

I'm working on a project for my partner, Shawn Stockman, of Boyz II Men. We just opened a studio together. He and I can do two songs a day, because he has a lot of pent-up creativity just bursting out. It's crazy. As for my own project, I only need one or two more songs.

Are you going to sign with a label?

I'm thinking about Hidden Beach Records, but I may put it out there myself. My greater purpose isn't to go platinum or tour. I don't tour now, because it's hard. It's good for a kid who wants to see the world.

You look young enough.

That's because I don't tour. [laughs] It's hard to stay healthy, work out, and eat right on tour.

It's hard to do that when you're stationary.

Right! But it's also hard to sleep or do anything required for good health. A lot of people who tour their whole lives end up in really bad shape. Touring is good money, but there are no residuals. It's cool, but how do you budget? I'd rather do something where profits gain momentum.

When you were starting out, how'd you make ends meet?

It wasn't easy. Look, I was flat broke with the biggest song in the world on the radio. Publishing takes nine months to generate.

What do you do while you're waiting?

The best you can! [laughs] It takes nine months after you have a hit before you get paid.

Even with a publishing deal?

From a songwriter standpoint, you'd like to be paid based on your future. But publishers base calculations on what you've done in the past. I'd like deals to be more incentivized, but that's how the game works.

To contact Erik Blu2th Griggs, visit his website, www.blu2th.net/.

VANESSA HERRON is an optioned screenwriter with fifteen years of professional experience. She has several film and television projects in various stages of development. Vanessa was a 2012 Guy Hanks and Marvin Miller Fellow and ranked in the top 20 percent of the 2012 Nicholl Fellowship. She is a freelance journalist, and works as an executive producer and news editor for iHeart Media in Los Angeles. Vanessa lives with her family in Thousand Oaks, California.

MORGAN TAYLOR

On All-Ages Songwriting & Dark Pie Concerns

....

Mark Bacino

Described by *The New York Times* as "A cross between 'Yellow Submarine' and Dr. Seuss," the work of singer-songwriter-illustrator Morgan Taylor is super-catchy, literate, and whimsical—a slightly trippy, pop art confection for both the eyes and the ears.

Beginning his musical career as a teen in the eighties, Taylor has had a long and varied sonic history, playing in various bands, working as a solo artist and sharing bills with the likes of Bob Dylan, Wilco, The Polyphonic Spree, and many more.

In 2004, Morgan, a self-taught illustrator, casually began drawing a picture book project that would later serve as inspiration for the visual side of his Gustafer Yellowgold all-ages music video series.

I caught up with the talented Ohio-born, New York-based Taylor to discuss songwriting and his Grammy-nominated, multimedia release *Dark Pie Concerns*, the latest installment in the Yellowgold DVD/CD cycle, featuring words, music, and moving images all crafted by Taylor himself. Morgan and I also talk all-ages music and, of course, pie.

From a songwriting standpoint, do you think there's much of a difference between crafting straight-up, "adult" pop music and writing for the all-ages genre? It seems like you've successfully blurred the line between the two worlds.

My foremost mission is to prove that you don't have to sacrifice your own musical tastes to enjoy music with your children. I find it aggravating, but understandable, that the moment you say the C-word [meaning children's], a huge gate slams down because the instant, mainstream associations are so negative for so many. I really hope I can change that, or at least help.

What I've been doing is creating music for parents who grew up on late seventies pop, eighties MTV, and the alternative music revolution, then spent the nineties in bars going to see original alternative pop music. Most of those folks have children now but still have the same tastes in music. Just because you choose to procreate doesn't suddenly mean you have to bring music into your home that you wouldn't have otherwise enjoyed. There are way more options now. For me, the only difference is the lyrics. And sometimes, barely so.

Here's the great irony: It wasn't until I started putting my cartoon illustrations with my alt-pop music that I got to do things like open for Wilco or The Polyphonic Spree. What happened was, I accidentally found a newer, truer voice. As soon as I started thinking of things from the angle of guys like Jim Henson or Dr. Seuss, as opposed to Radiohead or The Strokes, my career actually began, all the ingredients: true pop songwriting, humor, and now the element of adding my offbeat colored-pencil videos. It made me stand out enough that people started reacting very positively. My lyrics were still referencing mortality and things that people hadn't heard in the genre before.

Obviously, your Gustafer Yellowgold work has a very strong visual component—character illustrations, animation, etc. Does the visual aspect of things influence the songwriting, or is it the other way around?

Well, when I created my first album/DVD, I was strictly using the songs I'd written during my first couple of years in the downtown New York City music scene (1999–2001). I worked as a sound engineer at a small club on the Lower East Side. I had an amazing outpouring of creativity stimulated by this songwriter scene immersion, and I had a surplus of material I wasn't using in my band at the time. Those particularly whimsical songs got sifted out and became the basis for the Gustafer Yellowgold project. There was no pretense of an audience, demographic, or anything. I was really writing them to get a giggle out of my bandmates and to take liberty with my own freak flag, I guess.

Essencewise, you could say along the lines of Ween, They Might Be Giants, or XTC, there was an oddness lyrically, but the music and craft was taken seriously, just not as dark perhaps as the tunes I was using for my "real band." Songs like "I'm from the Sun," "Pterodactyl Tuxedo," and "Tiny Purple Moon" just set the stage for these characters. Going forward from that point, I began writing with the characters in mind.

When you're not on the road touring your live show or at the drafting table illustrating the visual end of the work, what does a typical songwriting session of yours look like? Can you walk us through your process?

Much of the time when I'm writing, I do have a vague notion of what might be happening in the animated video that will accompany it. It usually starts with either a song title that inspires a concept or a kernel of a guitar progression/melody that comes around.

What will usually happen is I'll begin noodling, improvising a guitar figure on my acoustic guitar, and if I feel any intrigue, a melody will sort of just appear and I'll sing some mumbly words, and it starts building. I record it onto my voice memo on my phone as soon as possible, because usually the kids are in the house and I know I could be distracted away at any moment. So in a way, I feel I'm stealing a bit of time for this moment, and the pressure sometimes adds to the urgency in a useful way. So many of my voice memos in the past seven years have the boys' voices in the background, playing, talking, yelling ... I've accumulated these throughout the years, and it's fun to listen back and hear how young the sounds are from the kids in the background. It makes a little time capsule out of the song's inception in a way.

If I have what I feel are strong parts, at least verse/chorus, I'll keep recording new voice memos as the song grows. Maybe a bridge will pop out later, and I'll record that on its own and label it accordingly. If the song shows itself as worth finishing, then I'll make a word document and type out the lyrics like a piece of poetry, trimming fat out, removing unnecessary personal pronouns, and making sure the turns of phrase seem fresh ... stuff like that. Somehow, seeing it laid out on the page in an "official" state helps me with this polishing process.

Lastly, I think we've all had a few dark pies in our lives, but for the uninitiated, what exactly is "Dark Pie," and should they be concerned?

Ha! Yes, they should. The song "Dark Pie" can be taken literally or metaphorically. The protagonist in this song is trapped in a *Groundhog Day* loop of pie burning, and the music is definitely inspired by some late seventies disco era with a little ELO. and Bee Gees thrown in.

It's also about knowing when to ask for help. On a deeper level, you could say it's ultimately a song about suffering in the sense that sometimes being able to help yourself is the actual problem, and what or whom you burn in the process is the trouble you've caused, the cause for concern!

I named the CD/DVD *Dark Pie Concerns* because I generally enjoy wordplay and confusing-sounding titles. This one has an oddness of tracing the syllabic and vowel form from *Dark Knight Returns.* I love titles that make you have to look twice and think *What the hell does that mean?*

Gustafer Yellowgold's *Dark Pie Concerns* is available now. To learn more about Morgan Taylor and his work, visit www.gustaferyellowgold.com.

MARK BACINO is a singer-songwriter based in New York with three album releases to his credit as an artist. When not crafting his own melodic brand of retro-pop, Mark can be found producing fellow artists or composing for television/advertising via his Queens English Recording Co. Mark is also a contributing writer for *Guitar World*, as well as the founder-curator of intro.verse. chorus, a website dedicated to exploring the art of songwriting. For more information, visit www.markbacino.com.

MUSIC PUBLISHERS

///

Music publishers work with songwriters the same way literary agents work with authors: they find and review songs, represent artists, and find ways for artists to make money from their songs by plugging the songs to recording artists and entertainment firms. In return for a share of the money made from your songs, they take care of paperwork and accounting, help you vet new songs, seek out foreign licensing deals, set you up with co-writers (recording artists or other songwriters), fund demo productions, give advances against future royalties, and so on.

HOW DO MUSIC PUBLISHERS MAKE MONEY FROM SONGS?

Music publishers make money by getting songs recorded onto albums, film and television soundtracks, commercials, etc. and other areas. While this is their primary function, music publishers also handle administrative tasks such as copyrighting songs; collecting royalties for the songwriter; negotiating and issuing synchronization licenses for use of music in films, television programs and commercials; arranging and administering foreign rights; auditing record companies and other music users; suing infringers; and producing new demos of new songs. In a small, independent publishing company, one or two people may handle all these jobs. Larger publishing companies are more likely to be divided into the following departments: creative (or professional), copyright, licensing, legal affairs, business affairs, royalty, accounting, and foreign.

HOW DO MUSIC PUBLISHERS FIND SONGS?

The *creative department* is responsible for finding talented writers and signing them to the company. Once a writer is signed, it is up to the creative department to develop and nurture the writer so he will write songs that create income for the company. Staff members often put writers together to form collaborative teams. And, perhaps most important, the creative department is responsible for securing commercial recordings of songs and pitching them for use in film and other media. The head of the creative department—usually called the "professional manager"—is charged with locating talented writers for the company.

HOW DO MUSIC PUBLISHERS GET SONGS RECORDED?

Once a writer is signed, the professional manager arranges for a demo to be made of the writer's songs. Even though a writer may already have recorded his own demo, the publisher will often re-demo the songs using established studio musicians in an effort to produce the highest-quality demo possible.

Once a demo is produced, the professional manager begins shopping the song to various outlets. He may try to get the song recorded by a top artist on his or her next album or get the song used in an upcoming film. The professional manager uses all the contacts and leads he has to get the writer's songs recorded by as many artists as possible. Therefore, he must be able to deal efficiently and effectively with people in other segments of the music industry, including A&R (artists and repertoire) personnel, recording artists, producers, distributors, managers, and lawyers. Through these contacts, he can find out what artists are looking for new material, and who may be interested in recording one of the writer's songs.

HOW IS A PUBLISHING COMPANY ORGANIZED?

After a writer's songs are recorded, the other departments at the publishing company come into play.

- The **LICENSING AND COPYRIGHT DEPARTMENTS** are responsible for issuing any licenses for use of the writer's songs in film or television and for filing various forms with the copyright office.
- The **LEGAL AFFAIRS DEPARTMENT** and **BUSINESS AFFAIRS DEPARTMENT** work with the professional department in negotiating contracts with writers.
- The **ROYALTY AND ACCOUNTING DEPARTMENTS** are responsible for making sure that users of music are paying correct royalties to the publisher and ensuring the writer is receiving the proper royalty rate as specified in the contract and that statements are mailed to the writer promptly.

- Finally, the **FOREIGN DEPARTMENT**'s role is to oversee any publishing activities outside of the U.S., to notify sub-publishers of the proper writer and ownership information of songs in the catalog and update all activity and new releases, and to make sure a writer is being paid for any uses of his material in foreign countries.

FINDING THE RIGHT MUSIC PUBLISHER FOR YOU

How do you go about finding a music publisher that will work well for you? First, you must find a publisher suited to the type of music you write. If a particular publisher works mostly with alternative music and you're a country songwriter, the contacts he has within the industry will hardly be beneficial to you.

Each listing in this section details, in order of importance, the type of music that publisher is most interested in; the music types appear in **boldface** to make them easier to locate. It's also very important to submit only to companies interested in your level of experience (refer to "A Sample Listing Decoded" in the article "Where Should I Send My Songs?"). You will also want to refer to the Category Indexes, which list companies by the type of music with which they work. Publishers placing music in film or television will be preceded by a ✪ (see the Film & TV Index for a complete list of these companies).

Do Your Research!

It's important to study the market and do research to identify to which companies you should submit.

- Many record producers have publishing companies or have joint ventures with major publishers who fund the signing of songwriters and who provide administrative services. Because producers have an influence over what is recorded in a session, targeting the producer/publisher can be a useful avenue.
- Because most publishers don't open unsolicited material, try to meet the publishing representative in person (at conferences, speaking engagements, etc.) or try to have an intermediary intercede on your behalf (for example, an entertainment attorney, a manager, an agent, etc.).
- As to demos, submit no more than three songs unless that publisher makes it clear they want more songs.
- As to publishing deals, co-publishing deals (where a writer owns part of the publishing share through his or her own company) are relatively common if the writer has a well-established track record.
- Are you targeting a specific artist to sing your songs? If so, find out if that artist even considers outside material. Get a copy of the artist's latest album, and see who wrote most of the songs. If the artist wrote them all, he's probably not interested in hearing material from outside writers. If the songs were written by a variety of different

writers, however, he may be open to hearing new songs.

- Check the album liner notes, which will list the names of the publishers of each writer. These publishers obviously have had luck pitching songs to the artist, and they may be able to get your songs to that artist, as well.
- If the artist you're interested in has a recent hit on the *Billboard* charts, the publisher of that song will be listed in the "Hot 100 A-Z" index. Carefully choosing which publishers will work best for the material you write may take time, but it will only increase your chances of getting your songs heard. "Shotgunning" your demo packages (sending out many packages without regard for music preference or submission policy) is a waste of time and money and will hurt, rather than help, your songwriting career.

Once you've found some companies that may be interested in your work, learn what songs those publishers have handled successfully. Most publishers are happy to provide you with this information in order to attract high-quality material. As you're researching music publishers, keep in mind how you get along with them personally. If you can't work with a publisher on a personal level, chances are your material won't be represented as you would like it to be. A publisher can become your most valuable connection to all other segments of the music industry, so it's important to find someone you can trust and with whom you feel comfortable.

Independent or Major Company?

Also consider the size of the publishing company. The publishing affiliates of the major music conglomerates are huge, handling catalogs of thousands of songs by hundreds of songwriters. Unless you are an established songwriter, your songs probably won't receive enough attention from such large companies. Smaller, independent publishers offer several advantages. First, independent music publishers are located all over the country, making it easier for you to work face-to-face rather than by mail or phone. Smaller companies usually aren't affiliated with a particular record company and are, therefore, able to pitch your songs to different labels and acts. Independent music publishers are usually interested in a smaller range of music, allowing you to target your submissions more accurately. The most obvious advantage to working with a smaller publisher is the personal attention they can bring to you and your songs. With a smaller roster of artists to work with, the independent music publisher is able to concentrate more time and effort on each particular project.

SUBMITTING MATERIAL TO PUBLISHERS

When submitting material to a publisher, always keep in mind that a professional, courteous manner goes a long way in making a good impression. When you submit a demo through the mail, make sure your package is neat and meets the particular needs of the publisher. Review each publisher's submission policy carefully, and follow it to the letter. Disregarding this information will only make you look like an amateur in the eyes of the company to which you're submitting.

Listings of companies in Canada are preceded by a ☺, and international markets are designated with a ☽. You will find an alphabetical list of these companies at the back of the book, along with an index of publishers by state in the Geographic Index.

PUBLISHING CONTRACTS

Once you've located a publisher you like and he's interested in shopping your work, it's time to consider the publishing contract—an agreement in which a songwriter grants certain rights to a publisher for one or more songs. The contract specifies any advances offered to the writer, the rights that will be transferred to the publisher, the royalties a songwriter is to receive, and the length of time the contract is valid.

- When a contract is signed, a publisher will ask for a 50-50 split with the writer. *This is standard industry practice*; the publisher is taking that 50 percent to cover the overhead costs of running his business and for the work he's doing to get your songs recorded.
- It is always a good idea to have a publishing contract (or any music business contract) reviewed by a competent entertainment lawyer.
- There is no "standard" publishing contract, and each company offers different provisions for its writers.

Make sure you ask questions about anything you don't understand, especially if you're new in the business. Songwriter organizations such as the Songwriters Guild of America (SGA) provide contract review services, and can help you learn about music business language and what constitutes a fair music publishing contract. See the Organizations section for more information on the SGA and other songwriting groups.

When signing a contract, it's important to be aware of the music industry's unethical practitioners. The "song shark," as he's called, makes his living by asking a songwriter to pay to have a song published. The shark will ask for money to demo a song and promote it to radio stations; he also may ask for more than the standard 50 percent publisher's share or ask you to give up all rights to a song in order to have it published. Although none of these practices is illegal, it's certainly not ethical, and no successful publisher uses these methods. *Songwriter's Market* works to list only honest companies interested in hearing new material.

Please read the article "Avoiding the Rip-Offs" for more information.

ADDITIONAL PUBLISHERS

There are **more publishers** located in other sections of the book! Use the Index to find listings within other sections who are also music publishers.

Icons

For more instructional information on the listings in this book, including explanations of symbols that coincide with certain listings, read the article "How To Use *Songwriter's Market*."

ABET PUBLISHING

411 E. Huntington Dr., Suite 107-372, Arcadia CA 91006. (866)574-0275. **Website:** www.abetpublishing.com. "Abet Publishing offers a very unique and eclectic variety of genres. From world music, classical to cutting-edge electronica, acoustic, ambient, chill mood, rock, and alternative. We are highly driven by passion for exceptional quality music. Abet Publishing is proud to be the launching pad for many talented and diverse artists. We are committed to supporting artists who are looking to create a body of musical work intended to be listened to and experienced as an album and to find ways for our artists' music to be heard and experienced."

HOW TO CONTACT Contact via form on website. Include with a link to music or website.

MUSIC **Easy listening**, **chill**, **rock**, **world music**, **alternative**.

ALL ROCK MUSIC

United States. **E-mail:** info@collectorrecords.nl. **Website:** www.collectorrecords.nl. **Contact:** Cees Klop, president. Music publisher, record company (Collector Records) and record producer. Publishes 40 songs/year; publishes several new songwriters/year. Staff size: 3. Pays standard royalty.

Also see the listings for Collector Records in the Record Companies and Record Producers sections of this book.

AFFILIATES All Rock Music (United Kingdom).

HOW TO CONTACT Submit demo package by mail. Unsolicited submissions are OK. SAE and International Reply Coupons. Responds in 2 months.

MUSIC Mostly **'50s rock**, **rockabilly** and **country rock**; also **piano boogie woogie**. Published *Rock Crazy Baby* (album), written and recorded by Art Adams (1950s rockabilly), released 2004; *Marvin Jackson* (album), by Marvin Jackson (1950s rockers), released 2005; *Western Australian Snake Pit R&R* (album), recorded by various (1950s rockers), released 2005, all on Collector Records.

TIPS "Send only the kind of material we issue/produce as listed."

ATTACK MEDIA GROUP

141 Spadina Ave., Suite 204, Toronto, Ontario M5V 2K8 Canada. **E-mail:** info@attackmediagroup.com. **Website:** www.attackmediagroup.com. A Toronto-based, privately owned media and entertainment company. Already the owner of an extensive music publishing catalog, Attack Media Group's mission is to target potential acquisitions in the music, film and TV industries ranging from independent record labels, artists, DVD acquisitions, feature-length films to purchases in the music publishing sector, along with acquiring children's and extreme sports content.

BAITSTRING MUSIC

2622 Kirtland Rd., Brewton AL 36426. **E-mail:** bolivia.records@yahoo.com. **Contact:** Roy Edwards, president.

Also the listings for Cheavroia Music in this section, Bolivia Records in the Record Companies section, and Known Artist Productions in the Record Producers section of this book.

AFFILIATES Cheavoria Music Co. (BMI).

HOW TO CONTACT Submit only one song by e-mail. Unsolicited submissions are OK.

MUSIC Mostly **R&B**, **pop** and **easy listening**; also **country** and **gospel**. Published "Forever and Always," written and recorded by Jim Portwood (pop); and "Make Me Forget" (by Horace Linsley) and "Never Let Me Go" (by Cheavoria Edwards), both recorded by Bobbie Roberson (country), all on Bolivia Records.

BEARSONGS

Box 944, Edgbaston, Birmingham B16 8UTT United Kingdom. +(44)0121-454-7020. **Website:** www.bigbearmusic.com. **Contact:** Jim Simpson, managing director; Russell Fletcher, professional manager. Music publisher and record company (Big Bear Records). Member PRS, MCPS. Publishes 25 songs/year; publishes 15-20 new songwriters/year. Pays standard royalty.

Also see the listings for Big Bear Records in the Record Companies section and Big Bear in the Record Producers section of this book.

HOW TO CONTACT Submit demo by mail. Unsolicited submissions are OK. Prefers CD. Does not return material. Responds in 3 months.

MUSIC Mostly **blues**, **swing**, and **jazz**. Published *Blowing With Bruce* and *Cool Heights* (by Alan Barnes), recorded by Bruce Adams/Alan Barnes Quintet; and *Blues For My Baby* (by Charles Brown), recorded by King Pleasure & The Biscuit Boys, all on Big Bear Records.

TIPS "Have a real interest in jazz, blues, swing."

⊘ BEST BUILT SONGS

1317 16th Ave. S., Nashville TN 37212. (615)385-4466. **Fax:** (615)383-4216. **Website:** www.bestbuiltsongs.com. **Contact:** Larry Sheridan, owner/producer. Larry Sheridan and Robin Ruddy are the owners and driving force behind Best Built Songs. Larry is involved in signing new songs and writers and pitching material for the company. Robin is an in-demand session player and live performer in Nashville. She sings, plays pedal steel, banjo, dobro, guitar, and mandolin. She also is a staff writer for Best Built. Artists/songwriters include: Amanda Martin, Doug Forshey, Marc-Alan Barnette, Robin Ruddy, and Wade Trammell.

HOW TO CONTACT *Does not accept unsolicited material.*

⊘ THE BICYCLE MUSIC CO.

Concord Bicycle Music, 100 N. Crescent Dr., Suite 323, Beverly Hills CA 90210. (310)286-6600. **Fax:** (310)286-6622. **E-mail:** info@bicyclemusic.com. **Website:** www.bicyclemusic.com. The Bicycle Music Co. is a globally influential independent music publisher, record label, and rights manager. "We are committed to innovative marketing, creative and administrative practices, promoting exceptional growth on behalf of our songwriters, recording artists, and investor partners."

HOW TO CONTACT *The Bicycle Music Co. does not accept unsolicited material.*

MUSIC Has published music by AFI, Alanis Morissette, Cyndi Lauper, Dave Matthews Band, Johnny Cash, Michael Jackson, Nine Inch Nails, Survivor, Willie Nelson, and more.

BIG FISH MUSIC PUBLISHING GROUP

12720 Burbank Blvd., Suite 124, Valley Village CA 91607. (818) 508-9777. **E-mail:** clisag21@yahoo.com. **Website:** See their Facebook page for more information. **Contact:** Chuck Tennin. Producer: Gary Black (country, pop, adult contemporary, rock, crossover songs, other styles). Professional Music Manager: Lora Sprague (jazz, New Age, instrumental, pop rock, R&B). Professional Music Manager: B.J. (pop, TV, film, and special projects). Professional Music and Vocal Consultant: Zell Black (country, pop, gospel, rock, blues). Producer, Independent Artists: Darryl Harrelson, Major Label Entertainment (country, pop and other genres). Managing Director: James Ziegler. Marketing Director: Claire Applewhite. Songwriter/

Consultant: Jerry Zanandrea (Z Best Muzic). Staff Songwriters: Billy O'Hara, Joe Rull, Lisa Faye. Music Publisher, record company (California Sun Records) and production company. Publishes 10-30 songs/year; publishes 10 new songwriters/year. Staff size: 10. Pays standard royalty. "We also license songs and music copyrights to users of music, especially TV and film, commercials, and recording projects." Member: BMI, ASCAP, CMA and ACM.

AFFILIATES Big Fish Music (BMI) and California Sun Music (ASCAP).

HOW TO CONTACT *Write first and obtain permission to submit.* Include SASE for reply. "**Please do not call or e-mail submissions.** After permission to submit is confirmed, we will assign and forward to you a submission code number allowing you to submit up to 4 songs maximum, preferably on CD. Include a properly addressed cover letter, signed and dated, with your source of referral (*Songwriter's Market*) with your assigned submission code number and an SASE for reply and/or return of material. Include lyrics. *Unsolicited material will not be accepted.* This is our submission policy to review outside and new material." Responds in 2 weeks.

FILM & TV Places 6 songs in TV/year. Recently published "Even the Angels Knew" (by Cathy Carlson/Craig Lackey/Marty Axelrod); "Stop Before We Start" (by J.D. Grieco); "Oh Santa" (by Christine Bridges/John Deaver), all recorded by The Black River Girls in *Passions* (NBC); licensed "A Christmas Wish" (by Ed Fry/Eddie Max), used in *Passions* (NBC); "Girls Will Be Girls" (by Cathy Carlson/John LeGrande), recorded by The Black River Girls, used in *All My Children* (ABC); "The Way You're Drivin' Me" and "Ain't No Love 'Round Here" (by Jerry Zanandrea), both recorded by The Black River Girls, used in *Passions* (NBC); "Since You Stole My Heart"(by Rick Colmbra/Jamey Whiting), used in *Passions* (NBC); "Good Time To Fly," "All I Need Is A Highway," and "Eyes Of The Children" (by Wendy Martin), used in *Passions* (NBC); "It's An Almost Perfect Christmas" (by Michael Martin), used in *Passions* (NBC); "Dear Santa" (by James Ziegler), used in *The Young and The Restless*.

MUSIC Country, including **country pop, country A/C** and **country crossover** with "a cutting edge"; also **pop, rock, pop ballads, adult contemporary, uplifting, praise, worship, spiritual,** and **inspirational adult contemporary gospel** "with a powerful message," **instrumental background and theme mu-**

sic for TV, film, and commercials, **New Age/instrumental jazz** and **novelty**, **orchestral classical**, **R&B** and **children's music**, for all kinds of commercial use. Published "If Wishes Were Horses" (single by Billy O'Hara); "Purple Bunny Honey" (single by Robert Lloyd/Jim Love); "Leavin' You For Me" (single by J.D. Grieco); "Imagine Us" (by Claire Applewhite); "Heroes to Us" and "I Thank You" (by Joe Rull).

TIPS "Demo should be professional, high quality, clean, simple, dynamic, and must get the song across on the first listen. Good clear vocals, a nice melody, a good musical feel, good musical arrangement, strong lyrics and chorus—a unique, catchy, clever song that sticks with you. Looking for unique country and pop songs with a different edge that can cross over to the mainstream market for ongoing Nashville music projects and songs for hot female country acts that can cross over to adult contemporary and pop with great lush harmonies. Also, catchy, up-tempo songs with an attitude and a groove, preferably rock, that can be marketed to today's youth."

⊘ BIG LOUD SHIRT

1111 16th Ave. S., Suite 201, Nashville TN 37212. (615)329-1929. **Fax:** (615)329-1930. **E-mail:** info@ bigloudshirt.com. **Website:** www.bigloudshirt.com. Big Loud Shirt is an independently owned and operated music publishing company that was established by multiple award-winning songwriter and producer, Craig Wiseman. Boasts 36 No. 1 hits, over 60 singles, and countless awards. (ASCAP, BMI)

HOW TO CONTACT *Big Loud Shirt does not accept unsolicited material.*

MUSIC Country. Published "Live Like You Were Dying" (Tim McGraw), "Before He Cheats" and "Blown Away" (Carrie Underwood), "I Saw God Today" (George Strait), "Cruise" (Florida Georgia Line), and more.

⊘ BIXIO MUSIC GROUP & ASSOCIATES/ IDM MUSIC

111 E. 14th St., Suite 140, New York NY 10003. (212)695-3911. **E-mail:** info@bixio.com. **Website:** www.bixio.com. (ASCAP) Music publisher, record company and rights clearances. Estab. 1985. Publishes a few hundred songs/year; publishes 2 new songwriters/year. Staff size: 6. Pays standard royalty.

HOW TO CONTACT *Does not accept unsolicited material.*

MUSIC Mostly **soundtracks**. Published "La Strada Nel Bosco," included in the TV show *Ed* (NBC); "La Beguine Du Mac," included in the TV show *The Chris Isaac Show* (Showtime); and "Alfonsina Delle Camelie," included in the TV show *UC: Undercover* (NBC).

⊘ BLUEWATER MUSIC

P.O. Box 120904, Nashville TN 37212. (615)327-0808. **Fax:** (615)327-0809. **E-mail:** info@bluewatermusic. com. **Website:** www.bluewatermusic.com. **Contact:** Bennet Davidson, assistant, creative department. Bluewater Music is an independent music publisher, copyright administrator and artist management company. No. 1's include "Believe Me Baby, I Lied" by Trisha Yearwood, "Unbelievable" by Diamond Rio and "Big Deal" by LeAnn Rimes. Songs also have been featured in various TV and film projects, including *The Simpsons*, *Family Guy*, *Nashville* and *One Tree Hill*.

◗ *Bluewater is not currently accepting unsolicited submissions.*

⊘ BMG CHRYSALIS US

BMG Chrysalis US, 29 Music Square E., Nashville TN 37203. **Website:** www.bmgchrysalis.com. BMG offers a new digital-age service alternative to songwriters, artists, and rights owners in the music industry. It is a rights management company equally representing music publishing and recording rights. (ASCAP, BMI) Estab. 1968.

HOW TO CONTACT *BMG Chrysalis does not accept any unsolicited submissions.*

MUSIC BMG Chrysalis is a global music giant that has published songs by artists including Blink-182, Kylie Minogue, Blake Shelton and many others.

⊘ BOURNE CO. MUSIC PUBLISHERS

5 W. 37th St., New York NY 10018. (212)391-4300. **Fax:** (212)391-4306. **E-mail:** bourne@bournemusic. com; info@bournemusic.com. **Website:** www.bournemusic.com. Publishes educational material and popular music.

AFFILIATES ABC Music, Ben Bloom, Better Half, Bogat, Burke & Van Heusen, Goldmine, Harborn, Lady Mac and Murbo Music.

HOW TO CONTACT *Does not accept unsolicited submissions.*

MUSIC **Piano/vocal**, **band pieces** and **choral pieces**. Published "Amen" and "Mary's Little Boy Child" (singles by Hairston); "When You Wish Upon a Star" (single by Washington/Harline); and "San Antonio Rose" (single by Bob Willis, arranged John Cacavas).

◯ BRANDON HILLS MUSIC, LLC (BMI)

N. 3425 Searle County Line Rd., Brandon WI 53919. (920)570-1076 or (920)398-3729. **E-mail:** martab@ centurytel.net. **Website:** www.brandonhillsmusic. com. **Contact:** Marsha L. Brown. Publishes 4 new songwriters/year. Staff size: 2. Pays standard royalty of 50 %.

HOW TO CONTACT Submit demo package by mail. Unsolicited submissions are OK. Prefers CD with 1-4 songs and cover letter. Does not return submissions. Responds only if interested.

MUSIC Mostly **country (traditional, modern, country rock)**, **contemporary Christian**, **blues**; also **children's** and **bluegrass** and **rap**. Published "Let It Rain," recorded by Steff Nevers, written by Larry Migliore and Kevin Gallarello (Universal Records, Norway); "Do You Like My Body," recorded by Ginger-Ly, written by Nisa McCall (SEI Corp and Big Daddy G Music, CA); "Did I Ever Thank You Lord," recorded by Jacob Garcia, written by Eletta Sias (TRW Records); "Honky Tonk In Heaven," recorded by Buddy Lewis, written by Mike Heath and Bob Alexander (Ozark Records).

TIPS "We prefer studio-produced CDs. The lyrics and the CD must match. Cover letter, lyrics, and CD should have a professional look. Demos should have vocals up front and every word should be distinguishable. Please make sure your lyrics match your song. Submit only your best. The better the demo, the better the chance of getting your music published and recorded."

⊘ CAPITOL CHRISTIAN MUSIC GROUP

101 Winners Circle, Brentwood TN 37027. (615)371-4300. **Website:** www.capitolcmgpublishing.com. (ASCAP, BMI, SESAC) Music publisher. Publishes more than 100 songs/year. Represents more than 35,000 songs and over 300 writers. Hires staff songwriters. Pays standard royalty.

AFFILIATES Birdwing Music (ASCAP), Sparrow Song (BMI), His Eye Music (SESAC), Ariose Music (ASCAP), Straightway Music (ASCAP), Shepherd's Fold Music (BMI), Songs of Promise (SESAC), Dawn Treader Music (SESAC), Meadowgreen Music Co. (ASCAP), River Oaks Music Co. (BMI), Stonebrook Music Co. (SESAC), Bud John Songs, Inc. (ASCAP), Bud John Music, Inc. (BMI), Bud John Tunes, Inc. (SESAC), Worship Together Songs, Thank You Music, Thirst Moon River.

HOW TO CONTACT Capitol Christian Music Group does not accept unsolicited submissions, but it does recommend interested writers submit songs via GospelMusic.org and ChristianMusicSummit.com as a way to have songs reviewed and critiqued by execs at Capitol and other top Christian publishers.

MUSIC Published Chris Tomlin, Toby Mac, David Crowder, Jeremy Camp, Stephen Curtis Chapman, Delirious, Tim Hughes, Matt Redman, Demon Hunter, Underoath, Switchfoot, Third Day, Casting Crowns, and many others.

TIPS "Do what you do with passion and excellence and success will follow; just be open to new and potentially more satisfying definitions of what 'success' means."

⊘ CARLIN AMERICA

126 E. 38th St., New York NY 10016. (212)779-7977. **Website:** www.carlinamerica.com. Carlin America is among the largest of the few remaining independent music publishers in the US, and is still owned by the family of its founder, music industry icon Freddy Bienstock. Carlin's catalog spans 100 years of popular and classical music history. Vintage ballads, No. 1 hits from the rock 'n' roll years, numerous rock and pop bestsellers, great song standards, Broadway showtunes and significant classical works are among the vast range of Carlin titles that have been recorded by virtually every major recording artist.

AFFILIATES Alley Music Corp.; Bienstock Publishing Co.; Bro 'n Sis Music, Inc.; Carbert Music, Inc.; Carlin America, Inc.; Elvis Music, Inc.; Family Style Publishing, Inc.; Fort Knox Music, Inc.; Frank & Nancy Music, Inc.; Freddy Bienstock Music Co.; Herald Square Music, Inc.; Johnny Bienstock Music, Inc.; Mandy Music; Edward B. Marks Music Co.; Piedmont Music Co.; Range Road Music, Inc.; Sis 'n Bro Music, Inc.; White Haven Music Inc.

HOW TO CONTACT Carlin America does not accept unsolicited material.

MUSIC Every conceivable genre: **jazz**, **country**, **R&B**, **soul**, **pop**, **rock**, **the great American songbook**, **classic music**, etc. Published "Back in Black" (AC/DC), "I Got You (I Feel Good)" by James Brown, "Owner of a Lonely Heart" by Yes, "Total Eclipse of the Heart" by James Steinman, "Sky Pilot" (by the Animals), and more.

CARNIVAL MUSIC

Carnival Music, 24 Music Square W., #2, Nashville TN 37203. (615)259-0841. **Fax:** (615)259-0843. **Website:** www.carnivalmusic.net. Carnival Music isn't a publishing company, or a record label, though it does the work of both. It's a music company, front to back, founded by industry veterans Frank Liddell and Travis Hill in 1997, not with the intent of using music to prop up a business, but to build a business that could find and nurture compelling, lasting music, and set the stage for compelling, lasting careers.

MUSIC Carnival's current roster includes country voices David Nail, Brent Cobb and Hailey Whitters, roots-rooted talents Stoney LaRue, Rob Baird, and Mando Saenz, and the style-blending Logan Brill and Derik Hultquist. Each Carnival writer puts forth his or her own stylistic stamp; all possess that undeniable talent.

CASABLANCA MEDIA PUBLISHING

249 Lawrence Ave. E., Toronto, Ontario M4N 1T5 Canada. (416)921-9214. **E-mail:** info@casablancamediapublishing.com. **E-mail:** agilbert@casaent. com. **Website:** www.casablancamediapublishing.com. **Contact:** Jennifer Mitchell, president; Jana Cleland, vice president. Casablanca is the largest independent music publisher in Canada. Provides domestic and foreign music publishing administration services to copyright owners around the globe.

HOW TO CONTACT E-mail a SoundCloud or Bandcamp streaming link for review. Do not send any attachments or CDs.

CHRISTMAS & HOLIDAY MUSIC

26642 Via Noveno, Mission Viejo CA 92691. (949)859-1615. **E-mail:** justinwilde@christmassongs.com. **Website:** www.christmassongs.com. **Contact:** Justin Wilde. Publishes 8-12 songs/year; publishes 8-12 new songwriters/year. Staff size: 1. "All submissions must be complete songs (i.e., music and lyrics)." Pays standard royalty.

AFFILIATES Songcastle Music (ASCAP).

HOW TO CONTACT Submit MP3 with attached lyric sheet or demo CD by mail. Unsolicited submissions are OK. *Do not call. MP3 with attached lyric sheets okay, but only attach one MP3 per e-mail and put song title in ALL CAPS in subject line.* See website for submission guidelines. "First Class mail only. Registered or certified mail not accepted. Prefers CD

with no more than 5 songs with lyric sheets. Do not send lead sheets or promotional material, bios, etc." Include SASE. Does not return material out of the US. Responds only if interested.

FILM & TV Places 10-15 songs in TV/year. Published Barbara Streisand's "It Must Have Been the Mistletoe."

MUSIC Strictly **Christmas, Halloween, Hanukkah, Mother's Day, Thanksgiving, Father's Day** and **New Year's Eve music** in every style imaginable: easy listening, rock, pop, blues, jazz, country, reggae, rap, children's secular or religious. *Please do not send anything that isn't a holiday song.* Published "It Must Have Been the Mistletoe" (single by Justin Wilde/Doug Konecky) from *Christmas Memories* (album), recorded by Barbra Streisand (pop Christmas), by Columbia; "What Made the Baby Cry?" (single by Toby Keith) and "Mr. Santa Claus" (single by James Golseth) from *Casper's Haunted Christmas* soundtrack (album), recorded by Scotty Blevins (Christmas) on Koch International.

TIPS "We only sign one out of every 200 submissions. Please be selective. If a stranger can hum your melody back to you after hearing it twice, it has 'standard' potential. Couple that with a lyric filled with unique, inventive imagery, that stands on its own, even without music. Combine the two elements, and workshop the finished result thoroughly to identify weak points. Submit to us only when the song is polished to perfection. Submit positive lyrics only. Avoid negative themes like 'Blue Christmas.'"

CLEOPATRA RECORDS

11041 Santa Monica Blvd., Suite 703, Los Angeles CA 90025. (310)477-4000. **Website:** www.cleopatrarecords.com. **Contact:** Brian Perera. Cleopatra Records is a Los Angeles-based independent record label founded in 1992 by entrepreneur and music fan Brian Perera. It has since grown into a family of labels, including Hypnotic Records, Goldenlane, Stardust, Purple Pyramid, Deadline and X-Ray Records, encompassing a variety of genres with emphasis on unique and experimental artists.

HOW TO CONTACT Submit music submissions via mail to above address. Or use the form on the website (preferred method). *Do not call.* All submissions must have a link to music (Soundcloud, Beatport, etc.), your website, your social media accounts, current tour dates, biography, photos, and contact information.

MUSIC Gothic rock, **hard rock**, **heavy metal**, **electronic**, and **dubstep**. Also reissues of out-of-print music.

⊘ COMBUSTION MUSIC

1004 18th Ave. S., Nashville TN 37212. (615)515-5490. **Website:** www.combustionmusic.com. Since opening, Combustion Music has become one of Nashville's most successful independent publishing companies, earning a multitude of platinum LPs & No. 1 singles, both domestically and internationally, and across several genres. Partnered with Atlas Music Publishing.

HOW TO CONTACT *Combustion Music does not accept unsolicited material.*

MUSIC All genres. Published "Jesus, Take the Wheel," "Use Somebody," "You're Gonna Miss This," and more.

⊘ COPPERFIELD MUSIC GROUP

1400 South St., Nashville TN 37212. (615)726-3100. **Fax:** (615)726-3172 fax. **E-mail:** ken@copperfield-music.com. **Website:** www.copperfieldmusic.com. **Contact:** Ken Biddy. Music Publishing & Indie Label.

HOW TO CONTACT Contact ken@copperfieldmu-sic.com first and obtain permission to submit a demo by e-mail. Company does not return submissions or accept phone calls. Responds only if interested.

MUSIC Country only. Does not want rap or heavy/metal/rock. Recently published "Daddy Won't Sell the Farm" from *Tattoos and Scars* (album), recorded by Montgomery Gentry (country).

◑ THE CORNELIUS COMPANIES/ GATEWAY ENTERTAINMENT, INC.

Gateway Entertainment, Inc., Dept. SM, 118 16th Ave. S. Suite 4-92, Nashville TN 37203 United States. **E-mail:** corneliuscompanies@bellsouth.net. **E-mail:** corneliuscompanies@bellsouth.net. **Website:** www.corneliuscompanies.com. **Contact:** Ron Cornelius or Terry Bell. Over the past several years, The Cornelius Companies has published hundreds of great songs that have been recorded by major label artists. Among them have been triple-platinum and gold albums by Alabama (RCA), Faith Hill (Warner Bros.), Confederate Railroad (Atlantic), and David Allen Coe (Columbia and recently got the title cut of The Little River Band's last album, *Cuts Like a Diamond*. Gateway Entertainment, Inc. has also had success in film/TV song placements with HBO, the Steven Seagal movie *Force of Execution*, and *My Best Friend* for Lions Gate, just to mention a few. (BMI, ASCAP, SESAC) Music pub-

lisher and record producer (Ron Cornelius). Publishes 60-80 songs/year; publishes 2-3 new songwriters/year. Occasionally hires staff writers. Pays standard royalty.

AFFILIATES Robin Sparrow Music (BMI), Strummin' Bird Music (ASCAP) and Bridgeway Music (SESAC).

HOW TO CONTACT Contact by e-mail for permission to submit material. Prefers songs links but will accept up to 3 MP3's max. No CDs submissions will be accepted. Will respond as soon as possible.

FILM & TV Active in film/TV song placement.

MUSIC Mostly mainstream country/country pop. Other genres include pop, R&B, alternative rock and old-school country, rock original masters from 1960s 1970s , 1980s, 1990s suitable for film/TV placement.

TIPS Old-school and retro songs are now in high demand for film/TV.

⊖ CRINGE MUSIC (PRS, MCPS)

The Cedars, Elvington Lane, Hawkinge, Kent CT18 7AD United Kingdom. (01)(303)893-472. **E-mail:** info@cringemusic.co.uk. **Website:** www.cringemu-sic.co.uk. **Contact:** Christopher Ashman. Music publisher and record company (Red Admiral Records). Estab. 1979. Staff size: 2.

HOW TO CONTACT Submit demo package by e-mail. Unsolicited submissions are OK. Submission materials are not returned. Responds if interested.

MUSIC All styles.

CUPIT MUSIC

P.O. Box 121904, Attn: Artist/Writer Submission, Nashville TN 37212. (615)731-0100. **Website:** www.cupitmusic.com. "Cupit Music Group is a complete entertainment company that was established in 1980 by industry veteran Jerry Cupit. Jerry has worked with such artists as John Anderson, George Jones, Hank Williams Jr., Lonestar, Tim McGraw, Ken Mellons, Kevin Sharp, Jo-El Sonnier and many others. Jerry has enjoyed a successful career in the entertainment industry as an accomplished songwriter, musician, author, producer, publisher, and manager. Jerry has won awards for his songwriting talent from BMI and ASCAP, including the millionaire award for his writing contribution to *Jukebox Junkie*, as well as the Tennessee Songwriter's Association Hallmark Award." (ASCAP, BMI) Part of a growing catalog of more than 1,200 songs, Cupit Music Publishing has had many songs recorded by dozens of recording artists.

HOW TO CONTACT Clearly mark package with "ARTIST" or "WRITER." Include a SASE. Include 1 or more recent photographs. Print out and complete the Artist Submission form from the website. Allow a minimum of 8 weeks for a response.

⊘ CURB MUSIC

49 Music Square E., Nashville TN 37203. (615)321-5080. **Website:** www.curb.com. (ASCAP, BMI, SESAC)

○ *Curb Music only accepts submissions through reputable industry sources and does not accept unsolicited demos.*

AFFILIATES Mike Curb Music (BMI); Curb Songs (ASCAP); and Curb Congregation Songs (SESAC).

◐ DAYWIND MUSIC PUBLISHING

114A Commerce Ave., Hendersonville TN 37075. (615)826-8101. **E-mail:** info@daywindpublishing.com. **Website:** www.daywindpublishing.com. **Contact:** Rick Shelton, vice president. Since its inception in 1995, Daywind Music Publishing has emerged as the premier source of new songs for the Southern Gospel and Church Print/Choral markets. DMP boasts of an exclusive staff of 13 prestigious songwriters. Daywind Music Publishing has been blessed with more than 75 Singing News Song of the Year and Gospel Music Association (Dove) nominations, as well as 37 radio singles hitting the top position on the charts. BMI awarded DMP's Christian Taylor Music, Christian Music Publisher of the Year in both 2002 and 2004.

MUSIC Daywind Music Publishing remains committed to the exhortation and encouragement of the church through the advancement of quality Christian music.

DEFINE SOMETHING IN NOTHING MUSIC

202 N. Baker St., Mount Vernon WA 98273. (360)421-9225. **Website:** http://dsinm.weebly.com. **Contact:** Jaime Reynolds. Music agency. Staff Size: 5. Pays 75% of gross revenue.

HOW TO CONTACT Prefers MP3s. Contact for permission first. Contact via Facebook message at: http://www.facebook.com/1967band. Does not return submissions. Responds in 2 weeks if interested.

MUSIC Interested in all styles. "We welcome everything all over the world."

TIPS "Please e-mail a zip file via yousendit.com. No phone calls or mail, no CDs or cassettes."

⊘ DELLA MUSIC PUBLISHING

Della Music Publishing LLC, 509 Mandeville St., New Orleans LA 70117. (917)517-0357. **Fax:** (504)304-4754. **E-mail:** deborahevansmusic@gmail.com. **Website:** https://sites.google.com/site/dellamusicpublishingllc/. **Contact:** Deborah Evans. Deborah Evans started Della Music Publishing in August 2007 and represents both domestic and foreign catalogs. Maintains and promotes the catalogs of many rap and hip hop artists such as Reggie Noble (pka Redman) and Erick Sermon, the Keep On Kicking Music classic reggae catalog, Sweet River Music, and professional artists and songwriters such as Randy Klein and Anya Singleton. She represents several overseas publishers such as Cee Dee Music from the United Kingdom and Editions Ozella from Germany. She is a member of the Association of Independent Music Publishers (AIMP), the Copyright Society of the USA (CSUSA), and the National Music Publishers' Association (NMPA).

DE WALDEN MUSIC INTERNATIONAL

5507 Carpenter Ave., Valley Village CA 91607. (818)763-6995. **E-mail:** zigwal@pacbell.net. **Website:** www.dewaldenmusic.com. **Contact:** Christian de Walden. "We believe in musical excellence. With nominations and awards from all over the world, DMI strives to publish the highest-quality music product. Our years of experience and knowledge help to keep us on top in the music industry. During the past 25 years, de Walden Music has collaborated with several international TV networks and/or promoters from Europe to Southeast Asia to Latin and South America."

HOW TO CONTACT E-mail and request permission to submit before submitting.

MUSIC Pop rock, **Latin pop**, **Eurodance**.

⊘ DISNEY MUSIC PUBLISHING

500 S. Buena Vista St., Burbank CA 91521. (818)569-3241. **Fax:** (818)845-9705. **Website:** http://music.disney.com. (ASCAP, BMI) Affiliate(s) Seven Peaks Music and Seven Summits Music.

○ Part of the Buena Vista Music Group.

HOW TO CONTACT *"We cannot accept any unsolicited material."*

⊘ DOWNTOWN MUSIC PUBLISHING

485 Broadway, 3rd Floor, New York NY 10013. **Website:** www.dmpgroup.com. Established in 2007, Downtown Music Publishing is a leading independent music publisher. Over the past six years, Downtown's

catalog has grown to include over 60,000 copyrights, including the works of John Lennon and Yoko Ono, hard rock legends Mötley Crüe, renowned film composer Hans Zimmer, influential punk rockers Social Distortion, pop songstress Ellie Goulding and the critically acclaimed artist and actor Mos Def. Downtown writers have penned hit singles for artists such as Beyoncé, Bruno Mars, Carrie Underwood, Katy Perry, Keith Urban, and Rihanna. Managed by a team of executives with backgrounds in music supervision, advertising, and licensing, Downtown works to match its clients' interests with a broad range of media. In addition to traditional placement in film, TV, advertising, and video games, Downtown excels in digital and mobile licensing, product placement, merchandising, and integrated brand partnerships. Affiliates include Songtrust and MAS: Music and Strategy.

DUANE MUSIC, INC.

382 Clarence Ave., Sunnyvale CA 94086. (408)739-6133. Music publisher and record producer. Publishes 10-20 songs/year; publishes 1 new songwriter/year. Pays standard royalty.

AFFILIATES Morhits Publishing (BMI).

HOW TO CONTACT Submit demo by mail. Unsolicited submissions are OK. Prefers CD with 1-2 songs. Include SASE. Responds in 2 months.

MUSIC Mostly **blues**, **country**, **disco** and easy listening; also **rock**, **soul** and **top 40/pop**. Published "Little Girl" (single), recorded by The Syndicate of Sound & Ban (rock); "Warm Tender Love" (single), recorded by Percy Sledge (soul); and "My Adorable One" (single), recorded by Joe Simon (blues).

ELECTRIC MULE PUBLISHING CO. (BMI)/NEON MULE MUSIC (ASCAP)

1019 17th Ave. S., Nashville TN 37212. (615)321-4455. **E-mail:** emuleme@aol.com.

MUSIC Country, pop.

EMSTONE MUSIC PUBLISHING

P.O. Box 398, Hallandale FL 33008. **E-mail:** webmaster@emstonemusicpublishing.com. **Website:** www.emstonemusicpublishing.com. **Contact:** Mitchell Stone; Madeline Stone. (BMI)

HOW TO CONTACT Submit demo by mail or e-mail with any number of songs. Include a lyric sheet for each song. Unsolicited submissions are OK. Does not return material and responds only if interested.

MUSIC All types. Published *Greetings from Texas* (2009) (album), by Greetings From Texas; "Gonna Recall My Heart" (written by Dan Jury) from *No Tears* (album), recorded by Cole Seaver and Tammie Darlene, released on CountryStock Records; and "I Love What I've Got" (single by Heather and Paul Turner) from *The Best of Talented Kids* (compilation album) recorded by Gypsy; "My Christmas Card to You" (words and music by Madeline and Mitchell Stone); and "Your Turn to Shine" (words and music by Mitchell Stone).

TIPS "Keep the materials inside your demo package as simple as possible. Just include a brief cover letter (with your contact information) and lyric sheets. Avoid written explanations of the songs; if your music is great, it'll speak for itself. We only offer publishing contracts to writers whose songs exhibit a spark of genius. Anything less can't compete in the music industry."

EXPERIENCE MUSIC GROUP

P.O. Box 15158, Beverly Hills CA 90209. **E-mail:** info@experiencemusicgroup.com. **Website:** http://experiencerecords.com/. **Contact:** Evan Stein. Experience Music Group is a boutique music licensing, audio branding and artist management agency based in Beverly Hills, California. Founded in January 2003 by Evan Stein and Martin Weiner, Experience Music Group specializes in creating the perfect synthesis of music and message for brands, film, TV and advertising. With an extensive catalog of eclectic music from around the world, Experience Music Group serves as a bridge connecting independent musicians to media and brands.

HOW TO CONTACT E-mail streaming links ONLY to info@experiencemusicgroup.com (no MP3s, no downloads). See full submission instructions online.

FAME PUBLISHING

603 E. Avalon Ave., Music Shoals AL 35661. (256)381-0801. **E-mail:** info@fame2.com. **Website:** www.fame2.com. FAME Publishing was started in 1959 as Florence Alabama Music Enterprises, which was shortened to FAME. The company was started by Rick Hall, Billy Sherill and Tom Stafford over the City Drug Store in Florence, Alabama. Hall and Sherill had gotten a couple cuts working with publisher James Joiner and his Tune Publishing Company when they were approached by Stafford to start their own com-

pany. After a few cuts Sherrill and Stafford left Hall with Sherill going to Nashville to become one of the most successful Producers/Songwriters/Executives in Nashville in the 1970's & 1980's. Today the company has a catalog of over 3,000 songs with multiple top 10 singles, ASCAP awards and Song of the Year awards. The catalog boosts the writing of Jason Isbell, Walt Aldridge, James LeBlanc, Dylan LeBlanc Brad Crisler, Gary Nichols, Angela Hakcer, Robert Byrne, Gary Baker, Russell Smith, Tony Colton and many more.

HOW TO CONTACT Contact via email for more information on publishing.

MUSIC Country.

◐◐ FIRST TIME MUSIC (PUBLISHING) U.K.

Ebrel House, 2a Penlee Close, Praa Sands, Penzance, Cornwall TR20 9SR England, United Kingdom. +44(01736)762826. **E-mail:** panamus@aol.com. **Website:** www.panamamusic.co.uk; www.songwriters-guild.co.uk; www.digimixrecords.com. **Contact:** Jack Golding, (Head of A&R development). Music publisher, record company (Digimix Records Ltd. www.digimixrecords.com, Rainy Day Records, Mohock Records, Pure Gold Records). Estab. 1986. Publishes 500-750 songs/year; 20-50 new songwriters/year. Staff size: 6. Hires staff writers. Pays standard royalty; "50-60% to established and up-and-coming writers with the right attitude."

AFFILIATES Scamp Music Publishing, Panama Music Library, Musik Image Library, Caribbean Music Library, PSI Music Library, ADN Creation Music Library, Promo Sonor International, Eventide Music, Melody First Music Library, Piano Bar Music Library, Corelia Music Library, Panama Music Ltd., Panama Music Productions, Digimix Worldwide Digital Publishing.

HOW TO CONTACT Submit demo package by mail. Unsolicited submissions are OK. Submit on CD only, "of professional quality" with unlimited number of songs/instrumentals and lyric or lead sheets. Responds in 1 month. SAE and IRC required for reply.

FILM & TV Places 200 songs in film and TV/year. "Copyrights and phonographic rights of Panama Music Ltd. and its associated catalog idents have been used and subsist in many production broadcasts and adverts produced by major and independent production companies, TV, film/video companies, radio broadcasters (not just in the UK, but in various countries worldwide) and by commercial record companies for general release and sale. In the UK and Republic of Ireland they include the BBC networks of national/regional TV and radio, ITV network programs and promotions (Channel 4, Border TV, Granada TV, Tyne Tees TV, Scottish TV, Yorkshire TV, HTV, Central TV, Channel TV, LWT, Meridian TV, Grampian TV, GMTV, Ulster TV, Westcountry TV, Channel TV, Carlton TV, Anglia TV, TV3, RTE (Ireland), Planet TV, Rapido TV, VT4 TV, BBC Worldwide, etc.), independent radio stations, satellite Sky Television (BskyB), Discovery Channel, Learning Channel, National Geographic, Living Channel, Sony, Trouble TV, UK Style Channel, Hon Cyf, CSI, etc., and cable companies, GWR Creative, Premier, Spectrum FM, Local Radio Partnership, Fox, Manx, Swansea Sound, Mercury, 2CRFM, Broadland, BBC Radio Collection, etc. Some credits include copyrights in programs, films/videos, broadcasts, trailers and promotions such as *Desmond's, One Foot in the Grave, EastEnders, Hale and Pace, Holidays from Hell, A Touch of Frost, 999 International,* and *Get Away.*"

MUSIC All styles. Published "I Get Stoned" (hardcore dance), recorded by AudioJunkie & Stylus, released by EMI records (2009) on *Hardcore Nation 2009*; "Long Way to Go" (country/MOR) on *Under Blue Skies*, recorded by Charlie Landsborough, released on Rosette Records (2008); "Mr Wilson" (folk) from *Only the Willows are Weeping*, released on Digimix Records (2014); "Born to be Free" (progressive rock/goth rock), recorded by Bram Stoker on *Heavy Rock Spectacular*, released by Belle–Marquee Inc., Japan, and many more.

TIPS "Have a professional approach—present well-produced demos. First impressions are important and may be the only chance you get. Writers are advised to join the Guild of International Songwriters and Composers in England (www.songwriters-guild.co.uk)."

⊘ FOX MUSIC

Website: www.foxmusic.com. The contributions of Fox Music over the last 70 years transcend the field of film and TV music. Introduced by this department are such monuments of modern culture as "Love is a Many Splendored Thing," "On the Good Ship Lollipop," the score from *Laura* and the theme from *M*A*S*H.*

MUSIC *Fox Music does not accept unsolicited materials.*

⬤ FRICON MUSIC CO.

11 Music Square E., Nashville TN 37203. (615)826-2288. **Fax:** (615)826-0500. **E-mail:** fricon@comcast.net. **Contact:** Terri Fricon, president; Madge Benson, professional manager. Publishes 25 songs/year; publishes 1-2 new songwriters/year. Staff size: 6. Pays standard royalty.

AFFILIATES Fricout Music Co. (ASCAP) and Now and Forever Songs (SESAC).

HOW TO CONTACT *Contact first and obtain permission to submit.* Prefers CD with 3-4 songs and lyric or lead sheet. "Prior permission must be obtained or packages will be returned." Include SASE. Responds in 2 months.

MUSIC Mostly **country**.

○ GLAD MUSIC CO.

14340 Torrey Chase, Suite 380, Houston TX 77014. (281)397-7300. **E-mail:** hwesdaily@gladmusicco.com. **Website:** www.gladmusicco.com. **Contact:** Wes Daily. Music publisher, record company and record producer. Publishes 3 songs/year; publishes 2 new songwriters/year. Staff size: 2. Pays standard royalty.

AFFILIATES Bud-Don (ASCAP), Rayde (SESAC), and Glad Music (BMI).

HOW TO CONTACT Submit 1-3 songs via CD, with lyric sheet and cover letter. Lyric sheet should be folded around CD and submitted in a rigid case and secured with rubber band. Does not return material. Include SASE or e-mail address for reply. To submit MP3s via e-mail, e-mail first to request permission from Wes Daily.

MUSIC Mostly **country**. Does not want weak songs. Published *Love Bug* (album by C. Wayne/W. Kemp), recorded by George Strait, released 1995 on MCA and again in 2014 on his live CD, DVD, and CMT; *Walk Through This World With Me* (album), recorded by George Jones; *Race Is On* (album by D. Rollins), recorded by George Jones, both released 1999 on Asylum; "Party's Over," "What A Way To Live," and "Night Life" by Willie Nelson.

⬤ GOODNIGHT KISS MUSIC

10153 1/2 Riverside Dr. #239, Toluca Lake CA 91602. (831)479-9993 or (808)331-0707. **Website:** www.goodnightkiss.com; www.smalluses.com. **Contact:** Janet Fisher. (BMI, ASCAP) Publishes 6-8 songs/year; publishes 4-5 new songwriters/year. Pays standard royalty.

Goodnight Kiss Music specializes in placing music in movies and TV.

AFFILIATES Scene Stealer Music (ASCAP).

HOW TO CONTACT "Check our website or subscribe to newsletter (www.goodnightkiss.com) to see what we are looking for and to obtain codes. Packages must have proper submission codes, or they are discarded." Only accepts material that is requested on the website. Does not return material. Responds in 6 months.

FILM & TV Places 3-5 songs in film/year. Published "I Do, I Do, Love You" (by Joe David Curtis), recorded by Ricky Kershaw in Road Ends; "Bee Charmer's Charmer" (by Marc Tilson) for the MTV movie *Love Song*; "Right When I Left" (by B. Turner/J. Fisher) in the movie *Knight Club*.

MUSIC **All modern styles.** Published and produced Addiction: *Highs & Lows* (CD), written and recorded by various artists (all styles), released 2004; *Tall Tales of Osama Bin Laden* (CD), written and recorded by various artists (all styles parody), released 2004; and *Rythm of Honor* (CD), written and recorded by various artists (all styles), slated release 2005, all on Goodnight Kiss Records.

TIPS "The absolute best way to keep apprised of the company's needs is to subscribe to the online newsletter. Only specifically requested material is accepted, as listed in the newsletter (what the industry calls us for is what we request from writers). We basically use an SGA contract, and there are never fees to be considered for specific projects or albums. However, we are a real music company, and the competition is just as fierce as with the majors."

⊘ GREEN HILLS MUSIC GROUP

P.O. Box 159298, Nashville TN 37215. **Website:** www.greenhillsmusicgroup.com. Green Hills Music Group, a boutique-style home for exceptional songwriters, represents the music of such hitmakers as Bob Regan, Bonnie Baker, Georgia Middleman, Rick Giles, Steve Williams, and Paul Duncan. Green Hills has had songs recorded by numerous artists, including Rascal Flatts, George Strait, Bomshel, Hunter Hayes, Bucky Covington, Luke Bryan, Jake Owen, Jimmy Wayne, Claire Lynch, Edens Edge, Mark Chesnutt and The Derailers.

HOW TO CONTACT *Green Hills Music Group is not currently accepting unsolicited material.*

MUSIC Country.

HACATE ENTERTAINMENT GROUP

245 Eight Ave., #869, New York NY 10011. (212)586-4229. **Website:** www.hacate.com. Hacate Entertainment Group (HEG) was founded in 1989 by songwriter and artist Sarah-Chanderia, who made a promise to herself that she would never offer deals which she, as a writer and artist, would feel uncomfortable signing. The company includes several different publishing entities, including Hacate Music (ASCAP-estab. 1989), Vinkona Music (BMI-estab. 1997), KittiKami Music (SESAC-estab. 2001) and Hacate Entertainment (TONO -estab. 2002). "We represent the rights of a select group of writers; some of which we represent for multiple songs worldwide, and some for one song in one territory. Our goal isn't to control music, but rather to work as partners with committed professionals who are as serious about their careers as we are, to make sure that they get all the money they're entitled to."

HOW TO CONTACT *Does not accept unsolicited material.*

MUSIC Has placed music with MGM, 20th Century Fox, New Line Cinema, Disney, HBO, ABC, WB Network, David Lynch, Lions Gate, Discovery Channel, Microsoft, EA Games, Bold Ogilvy, Leo Burnett, McCann Erickson, Footcombe Belding, The World Bank, AT&T, Kraft, and Johnson & Johnson.

⊘ R L HAMMEL ASSOCIATES, INC.

P.O. Box 531, Alexandria IN 46001. **Website:** www.rl-hammel.com. "Consultants to the Music, Recording & Entertainment Industries." Music publisher, record producer and consultant. Estab. 1974. Staff size: 3-5. Pays standard royalty.

AFFILIATES LADNAR Music (ASCAP) and LEMMAH Music (BMI).

HOW TO CONTACT *Not accepting unsolicited submissions at this time.*

MUSIC Mostly **pop**, **R&B** and **Christian**; also **MOR**, **light rock**, **pop country** and **feature film title cuts**. Produced/arranged *The Wedding Collection Series* for WORD Records. Published *Lessons For Life* (album by Kelly Hubbell/Jim Boedicker) and *I Just Want Jesus* (album by Mark Condon), both recorded by Kelly Connor, released on iMPACT Records. Produced major oratorio "Testament" written by David Featherstone.

◯ HIP SON MUSIC

Boston MA **E-mail:** info@hipsonmusic.com. **Website:** www.hipsonmusic.com. Hip Son Music is a music publishing, music production and record company based in Boston. "Both Hip Son Music and Hip Son Publishing (BMI) work with talented music artists, producers, songwriters and performers involved in electronic, world, alternative and pop music. Our vocal and instrumental music catalog has been licensed for various movies, documentaries and TV shows on the networks including MTV, VH1, Fox TV, BBC, and ITV UK."

MUSIC Hip Son Music offers instrumental and vocal electronic and pop music for use in TV, film, TV commercials, Flash presentations, ring tones and other digital media. Our vocal and instrumental music catalog has been licensed for various movies and TV shows including: independent movies *Exploring Love*, *Road To Victory*, *Ghost In Cabin*, MTV shows (*The Real World*, *Road Rules*, *MADE*, *RR/RW Challenge*, *Pimp My Ride*, *Making the Band*, *Undressed*), VH1 (*Band Reunited*, *Born To Diva*), Fox TV (*Girl Next Door* - Playboy special), BBC (*The World*), featured in the documentary *Picture Me Enemy* (the winner of Philadelphia's Film Festival), on Flash movies. DVD products and promo campaigns produced by Berkleemusic.

◯ HITSBURGH MUSIC CO.

P.O. Box 1431, 233 N. Electra, Gallatin TN 37066. (615)452-0324. **Contact:** Harold Gilbert. Publishes 12 songs/year. Staff size: 4. Pays standard royalty.

AFFILIATES 7th Day Music (BMI).

HOW TO CONTACT Submit demo by mail. Unsolicited submissions are OK. Submit 2-3 songs on CD with lead sheet. Prefers studio produced demos. Include SASE. Responds in 6 weeks.

MUSIC Mostly **country gospel** and **MOR**. Published "That Kind'a Love" (single by Kimolin Crutchet and Dan Serafini), from *Here's Cissy* (album), recorded by Cissy Crutcher (MOR), released 2005 on Vivaton; "Disorder at the Border" (single), written and recorded by Donald Layne, released 2001 on Southern City; and "Blue Tears" (single by Harold Gilbert/Elaine Harmon), recorded by Hal, released 2006 (reissue) on Southern City.

⊘ HORIPRO ENTERTAINMENT GROUP

818 18th Ave. S., Nashville TN 37203. (615)255-9837. **Website:** www.horipro.com. HoriPro Entertainment Group, Inc. (H.E.G.) is a full-service, independent music publisher. Offering songwriter development, song pitching/plugging, music licensing, record production and first-class administration services, Hori-Pro Entertainment Group provides a total publishing solution for its valued clients. "While able to provide the same services found at major publishing conglomerates, HoriPro is rooted in a hands-on approach to music publishing and songwriter development, operating under a true passion for music and the musicians who create it. Working individually with each songwriter, producer, and artist from its two offices located in Nashville, Tennessee, and Los Angeles, California, HoriPro develops a unique roadmap to success for each of its clients. An independent publisher with global reach, HoriPro's network provides for opportunities to take music beyond the scope of most traditional music publishers. The independent nature of HoriPro allows for an uncluttered corporate structure and a willingness to endeavor projects that other publishers simply cannot. With over 20 years of experience in the U.S., HoriPro's devoted staff has worked tirelessly to create value for its deep catalog of songs - not only placing existing hits in traditional and emerging outlets, but working with its roster of songwriters to create new successes."

HOW TO CONTACT *Does not accept unsolicited material.*

MUSIC Works with such artists as REO Speedwagon, Jerry Reed, Marilyn Manson, Ryan Beaver, Sonia Leigh, George Strait, Sophie B. Hawkins, and KISS.

⊘ IMAGEM MUSIC

229 W. 28th St., Floor 11, New York NY 10001. (212)699-6588. **Fax:** (212)358-5309. **E-mail:** us@imagem.com. **Website:** us.imagemmusic.com. "In a publishing world where quantity seems to trump quality, where rollups, mergers and cost-cutting dominate headlines, Imagem Music stands alone as a true independent publishing home for great talent. We are a place where creativity meets proactivity, where works of art meet worth ethic."

HOW TO CONTACT *Imagem Music does not accept unsolicited material.*

MUSIC Any genre. Has worked with artists such as Phil Collins, Genesis, M.I.A., Pink Floyd, Vampire Weekend, Daft Punk, and more.

⊘ INGROOVES

55 Francisco St., #710, San Francisco CA 94113. (415)489-7000. **E-mail:** info@ingrooves.com. **Website:** www.ingrooves.com. "INgrooves Music Group is committed to powering creativity in today's dynamic music marketplace by providing the best distribution, marketing and rights management tools and services to content creators and owners. We develop state-of-the-art, cost-efficient and scalable technology platforms, and our partners benefit from our experienced, knowledgeable people, our unparalleled commitment to customer service and our thoughtful marketing solutions that drive results. We aspire to be the most transparent and solution-driven partner for all of the labels and artists we work with. We believe this approach helps us and our partners succeed today and for years to come."

HOW TO CONTACT "If you are interested in partnering with INgrooves, fill out the online form at www.ingrooves.com. A representative will get back to you ASAP."

INTENSE MUSIC CO.

19360 Rinaldi St., Suite 217, Porter Ranch CA 91326. (818)700-9655. **E-mail:** sr@intensemusic.com. **Website:** www.intensemusic.com. **Contact:** Sylvester Rivers. "Exciting, inspiring, sensual and intense—the music we publish and provide lifts you higher and higher. Take an excursion, indulge your sense. Hear our music."

HOW TO CONTACT *Does not accept unsolicited material.*

◐○ ISLAND CULTURE MUSIC PUBLISHERS

E-mail: islandking@islandkingrecords.com. **Website:** www.islandkingrecords.com. (BMI) Music publisher and record company (Island King Records). Estab. 1996. Publishes 10 songs/year; publishes 3 new songwriters/year. Hires staff songwriters. Staff size: 3. Pays standard royalty.

HOW TO CONTACT Submit demo package by mail. Unsolicited submissions are OK. Prefers CD with 8 songs and lyric sheet. Send bio and 8×10 glossy. Does not return material. Responds in 1 month.

MUSIC Mostly **reggae**, **calypso**, and **zouk**; also **house**. Published *De Paris a Bohicon* (album), recorded by Rasbawa (reggae), released 2006 on Island King Records; "Jah Give Me Life" (single by Chubby) from *Best of Island King* (album), recorded by Chubby (reggae), released 2003 on Island King Records; "When People Mix Up" (single by Lady Lex/L. Monsanto/Chubby) and "I Am Real" (single by L. Monsanto) from *Best of Island King* (album), recorded by Lady Lex (reggae), released 2003 on Island King Records.

⬤⭘ JA/NEIN MUSIKVERLAG GMBH

Oberstr. 14 A, D - 20144, Hamburg, Germany. (GEMA) Oberstr. 14 A, D - 20144, Hamburg Germany. **Fax:** (49)(40)448 850. **E-mail:** janeinmv@aol.com. General Manager: Mary Dostal. Music publisher, record company and record producer. Member of GEMA. Publishes 50 songs/year; publishes 5 new songwriters/year. Staff size: 3. Pays 50-66% royalty.

AFFILIATES Pinorrekk Mv., Star-Club Mv. (GEMA).

HOW TO CONTACT Submit audio (visual) carrier by mail. Unsolicited submissions are OK. "We do not download unsolicited material, but visit known websites." Prefers CD or DVD. Enclose e-mail address. Responds in 2 months maximum.

MUSIC Mostly **jazz**, **world** (**klezmer**), **pop**, **rap** and **rock**.

TIPS "We do not return submitted material. Send your best A-Side works only, please. Indicate all rights owners, like possible co-composer/lyricist, publisher, sample owner. Write what you expect from collaboration. If artist, enclose photo. Enclose lyrics. Be extraordinary! Be fantastic!"

⊘ QUINCY JONES MUSIC

6671 W. Sunset Blvd., #1574A, Los Angeles CA 90028. (323)957-6601. **Fax:** (323)962-5231. **Website:** www.quincyjones.com. (ASCAP)

HOW TO CONTACT *Quincy Jones Music does not accept unsolicited submissions.*

MUSIC The Quincy Jones Music Publishing catalog is home to over 1,600 titles spanning five decades of music covering numerous musical genres including jazz, R&B, pop, rock 'n' roll, Brazilian, alternative and hip-hop. Over the years, such legendary performers as Frank Sinatra, Count Basie, Sarah Vaughan, Louis Jordan, Lesley Gore, Barbra Streisand, Billy Eckstine and Tony Bennett have recorded our songs. We remain a presence in today's market by way of such

artists as 98°, Tevin Campbell, K-Ci & Jo Jo, George Benson, Ivan Lins, S.W.V., Vanessa Williams, Patti Austin, The Manhattan Transfer, James Ingram, Barry White and Ray Charles. Our current roster of talent includes lyricists, composers, musicians, performers and producers.

⭘ PATRICK JOSEPH MUSIC

1012 18th Ave. S., Nashville TN 37125. **E-mail:** pat@pjmsongs.com. **Website:** www.songspub.com/PJM. **Contact:** Pat Higdon. In August of 2013, music publishing veteran Pat Higdon re-launched his Patrick Joseph Music brand in the Nashville marketplace. The renewal of this successful publishing company marks a new partnership with New York- and Los Angeles-based SONGS Music Publishing. Patrick Joseph Music will be dedicated to writer service, actively signing new writers, as well as developing the reach for existing catalogs and songs.

⊘ LAUREN KEISER MUSIC PUBLISHING

St. Louis MO (203)560-9436. **E-mail:** info@laurenkeisermusic.com. **Website:** www.laurenkeisermusic.com. **Contact:** Lauren Keiser. Veteran music publisher Lauren Keiser, started Lauren Keiser Music Publishing (ASCAP) and Keiser Classical (BMI) from the purchase of MMB Music's assets of St. Louis and is joining it with new deals and editions he is creating and developing. His almost 40 years of being involved with Alfred, Cherry Lane and Carl Fischer Music publishing companies has provided a basis and foundation for a new music publishing company based on his experience. The firm publishes performance and music copyrights of gifted concert and symphonic composers in addition to producing publications of talented writers and artists.

MUSIC Classical composers represented include Claude Baker, David Baker, Daniel Dorff, Peng-Peng Gong, Sheila Silver, David Schiff, David Stock, George Walker, and many more.

⭘ KIRSTI MANNA SONGS

P.O. Box 167, Old Hickory TN 37138. (615)473-1031. **E-mail:** info@kirstimannasongs.com. **Website:** http://www.kirstimannasongs.com. **Contact:** Kirsti Manna. Featuring several hundred titles including a radio gold standard No. 1 song that launched the career of country superstar, Blake Shelton, "Austin." Also has many, many songs written by hit writers responsible for cuts by Tim McGraw, Brittany Spears,

Kenny Chesney, Lil' Jon, Jason Aldean, George Strait, and many more.

HOW TO CONTACT Send an email before submitting.

⊘ KOBALT

8201 Beverly Blvd., 4th Floor, Suite 400, Los Angeles CA 90048. (310)967-3087. **Fax:** (310)967-3089. **E-mail:** info@kobaltmusic.com. **Website:** www.kobaltmusic. com. "Kobalt Music Publishing, Kobalt Label Services and Kobalt Neighbouring Rights divisions each offer a modern alternative to the traditional music business model, empowering creators with flexible contracts, ownership, control, and total transparency. We represent over 8,000 artists and songwriters, 600,000 songs and 500 publishing companies, servicing our clients with global licensing management, works and rights distribution, royalty collection and processing, online data and royalty statements, creative services, synch and brand partnerships, record release management and marketing."

HOW TO CONTACT *Kobalt does not accept unsolicited material.*

MUSIC All genres. Published music by Big and Rich, Busta Rhymes, Eddie Vedder, Gotye, Kelly Clarkson, Kid Cudi, LMFAO, Maroon 5, Paul McCartney, and more.

◑ LAKE TRANSFER MUSIC

Lake Transfer Artist & Tour Management, Lake Transfer Productions, 12400 Ventura Blvd., Suite 346, Studio City CA 91604. (818) 508-7158. **E-mail:** info@laketransfer.com. **E-mail:** info@laketransfer.com. **Website:** www.laketransfer.com; www.laketransfermgmt.com. **Contact:** Jim Holvay, professional manager (pop, R&B, soul); Tina Antoine (hip-hop, rap); Steven Barry Cohen (alternative rock, R&B). The creation of music and musical performances as they are relevant to the particular artist at that time. Music publisher and record producer (Steve Barri Cohen). Estab. 1989. Publishes 11 songs/year; publishes 3 new songwriters/year. Staff size: 6. Pay "depends on agreement, usually 50% split."

◖ The landscape of the music business has changed very rapidly via new innovations in technology and the way the listener gets his or her music. One thing that has never changed is a great song will write its own ticket.

AFFILIATES Lake Transfer Music (ASCAP) and Transfer Lake Music (BMI).

HOW TO CONTACT Accepting unsolicited submissions through 2016.

MUSIC Mostly **alternative pop**, **R&B/hip-hop** and **dance**. Does not want country and western, classical, New Age, jazz or swing. Published "Tu Sabes Que Te Amo (Will You Still Be There)" (single by Steve Barri Cohen/Rico) from *Rico: The Movement II* (album), recorded by Rico (rap/hip-hop), released 2004 on Lost Empire/Epic-Sony; "When Water Flows" (single by Steve Barri Cohen/Sheree Brown/Terry Dennis) from *Sheree Brown "83"* (album), recorded by Sheree Brown (urban pop), released 2004 on BBEG Records (a division of Saravels, LLC); and "Fair Game" (single by LaTocha Scott/Steve Barri Cohen) *Soundtrack from the movie Fair Game* (album), recorded by LaTocha Scott (R&B/hip-hop), released 2004 on Raw Deal Records, College Park, Georgia. "All our staff are songwriters/producers. Jim Holvay has written hits like 'Kind of a Drag' and 'Hey Baby They're Playin our Song' for the Buckinghams. Steve Barri Cohen has worked with everyone from Evelyn 'Champagne' King (RCA), Phantom Planets (Epic), Meredith Brooks (Capitol) and Dre (Aftermath/Interscope)."

TIPS "Trends change, but it's still about the song. Make sure your music and lyrics have a strong (POV) point of view."

◔ LEVY MUSIC PUBLISHING

22509 Carbon Mesa Road, Malibu CA 90265. (310)571-5389. **E-mail:** info@levymusic.tv. **Website:** http://levymusic.tv. Levy Music Publishing, LLC is a companion entity to the Levy Entertainment Group. With over 400 artists and composers, our clients are given the option to easily license all types of music from our exclusive publishing catalog. Long-standing relationships with major and indie record labels and music publishers, ensuring the most excellent and affordable results.

HOW TO CONTACT Submit songs online through 1-800-PLAY.com.

MUSIC "Levy Entertainment Group & Levy Music Publishing are based from The Studio Malibu Estate. Many of the biggest names in entertainment have recently utilized our studio & other services provided. Including James Cameron, Ron Howard, Nicki Minaj, Britney Spears & Sean Combs just to name a few."

LOVECAT MUSIC

P.O. Box 548, Ansonia Station, New York NY 10023-0548. **E-mail:** license@lovecatmusic.com. **Website:**

www.lovecatmusic.com. "LoveCat Music is an independent record label and music publisher, founded in 1999. We license original songs for use in films, TV, advertisement, trailers and games. All our songs are available one-stop easy license for filmmakers for all types of projects. Our songs come from great artists from over 50 different countries. Listen for our songs in great films and TV shows like *True Blood*, *N.C.I.S. L.A.*, *Spongebob Squarepants*, *C.S.I.* and many more."

HOW TO CONTACT E-mail to request permission before submitting.

MUSIC All genres.

LYRIC HOUSE PUBLISHING

6266 Sunset Blvd., Suite B, Hollywood CA 90028. (323)505-6339. **E-mail:** info@lyrichouseco.com. **Website:** www.lyrichouseco.com. Lyric House is a full-service music publishing and licensing company. Offers creative and administrative publishing services for bands, artists, and songwriters, both nationally and internationally.

HOW TO CONTACT Send music via e-mail, download or streaming links only. Do not send MP3s. Does NOT accept lyric-only submissions.

MUSIC All genres. Catalog available online.

⃝ M&T WALDOCH PUBLISHING, INC.

4803 S. Seventh St., Milwaukee WI 53221. **Contact:** Timothy J. Waldoch, creative management (rockabilly, pop, country), vice president; Mark T. Waldoch, professional manager (country, top 40). (BMI) Publishes 2-3 songs/year; publishes 2-3 new songwriters/year. Staff size: 2. Pays standard royalty.

HOW TO CONTACT Submit demo package by mail. Unsolicited submissions are OK. Prefers CD with 3-6 songs and lyric or lead sheet. Include SASE. Responds in 3 months.

MUSIC Mostly **country/pop**, **rock**, **top 40 pop**; also **melodic metal**, **dance**, **R&B**. Does not want rap. Published "It's Only Me" and "Let Peace Rule the World" (by Kenny LePrix), recorded by Brigade on SBD Records (rock).

TIPS "Study the classic pop songs from the 1950s through the present time. There is a reason why good songs stand the test of time. Today's hits will be tomorrow's classics. Send your best well-crafted, polished song material."

⊘ ⃝ MAJOR BOB MUSIC

1111 17th Ave. S., Nashville TN 37212. (615)329-4150. **Fax:** (615)329-1021. **Website:** www.majorbob.com. **Contact:** Tina Crawford, director of A&R. "Bob Doyle began his music publishing company with a firm belief in his heart that the American dream could still be realized. So he left a safe, comfortable job as director of member relations at ASCAP where he had seven years' tenure and mortgaged his home for the start-up funds to pursue his dream. Armed with a deep conviction in a then-unknown songwriter named Garth Brooks, Doyle began to build a collection of musical copyrights that he believed in. Today those copyrights have been recorded by country, R&B, soul and pop artists and heard in movies, TV and videos throughout the world. Systematically, Doyle chose songwriters who he could nurture and teach the intricacies of the craft of songwriting. Choosing not to join the wave of today's corporate consolidation mentality, Doyle has chosen not to sell his independent publishing group. He continues to carefully build his publishing interests and partner with both new and seasoned songwriters. The publishing group has accumulated over 50 awards from performing rights organizations including Song of the Year for 'The Fool,' a song penned by three struggling songwriters who had never had a hit previously. Doyle's songs have been on over 30 platinum and gold certified albums in the U.S., representing units sold on over 130 million records."

MUSIC Music: Kenny Chesney's "There Goes My Life," Rascal Flatts' "I Melt," "Take Me There," and "Fast Cars & Freedom," and cuts ranging from The Plain White T's to Carrie Underwood. Garth Brooks has written 14 of his 25 No. 1 singles for Doyle's publishing company.

◑ MCCLURE & TROWBRIDGE PUBLISHING, LTD. (ASCAP, BMI)

P.O. Box 148548, Nashville TN 37214. (615)504-8435. **E-mail:** manager@trowbridgeplanetearth.com. **Website:** http://trowbridgeplanetearth.com. Music publisher and record label (JIP Records) and production company (George McClure, producer). Publishes 35 songs/year. Publishes 5 new songwriters/year. Staff size: 8. Pays standard royalty of 50%.

HOW TO CONTACT *Follow directions ONLINE ONLY—obtain control number to submit a demo via US Mail. Requires CD with 1-5 songs, lyric sheet, and* cover letter. Does not return submissions. Responds in 3 weeks if interested.

MUSIC Country, **gospel**, **roots** and **swing**. Publisher of Women in Country and Band of Writers (BOW) series. Published *Experience (Should Have Taught Me)* album 2010 on JIP Records; *The Lights Of Christmas* album; "Playboy Swing," released 2008 on JIP Records; "Miles Away" (single) on Discovery Channel's *The Deadliest Catch*; and "Playboy Swing," released 2008 on JIP Records.

⊘ MCJAMES MUSIC INC.

1724 Stanford St., Suite B, Santa Monica CA 90404. (310)712-1916. **Fax:** (419)781-6644. **E-mail:** tim@mcjamesmusic.com; steven@mcjamesmusic.com. **Website:** www.mcjamesmusic.com. **Contact:** Tim James; Steven McClintock. (BMI) Writers include: Kevin Fisher, Franki Love, Pamela Phillips Oland, Stephen Petree, Jeremy Dawson, Chad Petree, Brian Stoner, Cathy-Anne McClintock, Tim James, Steven McClintock, Ryan Lawhon. Publishes 50 songs/year. Staff size: 4. Pays standard royalty. Does administration and collection for all foreign markets for publishers and writers.

AFFILIATES 37 Songs (ASCAP) and McJames Music, Inc. (BMI) (Sequence 37 SESAC)

HOW TO CONTACT *Only accepts material referred by a reputable industry source.* Prefers CD with 2 songs and cover letter. Does not return material. Responds in 6 months.

FILM & TV Places two songs in film and three songs in TV/year. Music Supervisor: Tim James/Steven McClintock. *Blood and Chocolate, 3 Day Weekend, Dirty Sexy Money, Brothers and Sisters, Dancing with the Stars, Dexter, Always Sunny in Philadelphia, America's Top Model.* Commercials include Honda Australia, Scion California, Motorola Razr 2 worldwide.

MUSIC Mostly **modern rock, country, pop, jazz** and **euro dance**; also **bluegrass** and **alternative**. Will accept some mainstream rap but no classical. Published "Le Disko," "You are the One," "Rainy Monday" (singles from Shiny Toy Guns on Universal), "Be Sure," "What It Is" (singles from Cris Barber), "Keeps Bringing Me Back" (from Victoria Shaw on Taffita), "Christmas Needs Love to be Christmas" (single by Andy Williams on Delta), recent cover by ATC on BMG/Universal with "If Love is Blind," single by new Warner Bros. act Sixwire called "Look at me Now."

TIPS "Write a song we don't have in our catalog or write an undeniable hit. We will know it when we hear it."

⊘ MIDI TRACK PUBLISHING (BMI)

P.O. Box B, Milford PA 18337. (718)767-8995. **E-mail:** info@allrsmusic.com. **Website:** www.allrsmusic.com. **Contact:** Renee Silvestri-Bushey, president; F. John Silvestri, founder, vice president, A&R; Leslie Migliorelli, director of operations. Music publisher, record company (MIDI Track Records), music consultant, artist management, record producer. Voting member of NARAS / National Academy of Recording Arts and Sciences (The Grammy Awards), voting member of the Country Music Association (The CMA Awards); SGMA/Southern Gospel Music Association, SGA/Songwriters Guild of America (Diamond Member). Staff size: 6. Publishes 3 songs/year; publishes 2 new songwriters/year. Pays standard royalty. Affiliate(s) ALLRS Music Publishing Co. (ASCAP).

HOW TO CONTACT "Call or e-mail first to obtain permission to submit. We do not accept unsolicited submissions." If permission is granted, you will be given additional submission instructions. Does not return material. Responds within 8 months, only if interested.

FILM & TV Places one song in film/year. Published "Why Can't You Hear My Prayer" (single by F. John Silvestri/Leslie Silvestri), recorded by Iliana Medina in a documentary by Silvermine Films.

MUSIC Mostly **country, gospel, top 40, R&B, MOR** and **pop**. Does not want show tunes, jazz, classical or rap. Published "Why Can't You Hear My Prayer" (single by F. John Silvestri/Leslie Silvestri), recorded by Tent-time Grammy nominee Huey Dunbar of the group DLG (Dark Latin Groove), released on MIDI Track Records (including other multiple releases); "Chasing Rainbows" (single by F. John Silvestri/Leslie Silvestri/Darin Kelly), recorded by Tommy Cash (country), released on MMT Records (including other multiple releases); "Because of You" (single by F. John Silvestri/Leslie Silvestri), recorded by Iliana Medina, released 2002 on MIDI Track Records (including other multiple releases also recorded by Grammy nominee Terri Williams, of Always, Patsy Cline, Grand Ole Opry member Ernie Ashworth), released on KMA Records, MMT Records, MIDI Track Records, including other multiple releases; "My Coney Island Love" (single by F. John Silvestri/Leslie Silvestri), recorded by ten-time Grammy nominee Huey Dunbar, released 2005-2009 on MIDI Track Records. "It's Over" (single by F John Silvestri/Leslie Silvestri) recorded by Randy Albright released on Midi Track Records including other multiple releases, "Chasing Rainbows" (single by F John Silvestri/Leslie Silvestri) recorded by Jackie, Mustang Sally, Doreen Lee released on Midi Track Records 2005-2015 including other multiple releases

TIPS "Attend workshops and music seminars. Have your song critiqued, and visit our website for advice, tips, and info on the music industry."

⊘ MORAINE MUSIC GROUP

500 E. Iris, Nashville TN 37204. (615)383-0400. **Website:** www.morainemusic.com. Moraine Music Group is one of Nashville's leading independent publishing and production companies with decades of hits spanning various genres. Over the years, Moraine has gained a reputation for representing unique songwriters, delivering breakthrough singles and songs that have been included on numerous Grammy-winning records. Superstars such as Kelly Clarkson, Taylor Swift, The Dixie Chicks, Garth Brooks, Kenny Wayne Shepherd, Kenny Chesney, Tim McGraw, Lee Brice, Justin Moore, Alan Jackson, Lee Ann Womack, The Judds, Trisha Yearwood, Tina Turner and many more have recorded Moraine's songs. Moraine's songs have been included in numerous films, soundtracks, TV shows and commercials. Recent commercials include Subaru, Splenda, Glade and Tourism Ireland. A continuously growing group of TV shows and films have featured Moraine's songs including *Parenthood*, *House*, *Nashville*, *Private Practice*, *One Tree Hill* and *Safe Haven*. Several of the company's songs have become milestone moments: from The Judds' ACM Song of the Year and #1 hit, "Why Not Me" to Jo Dee Messina's No. 1 country and AC single, "Bring on the Rain," and Sara Evan's chart-topping smash "Suds in the Bucket." Moraine has given the first No. 1 singles for many artists including, "There's Your Trouble" for the Dixie Chicks and Justin Moore's first No. 1, "Small Town USA." Moraine is equally as proud to have record-breaking singles that range from Garth Brooks' single, "More Than A Memory," which entered the charts at No. 1. Kenny Wayne Shepherd's hit "Blue on Black" which was named Billboard's Rock Song of the Year and spent a record 17 consecutive weeks as No. 1. In addition, Moraine's long-time dedication to Americana and Folk Music formats resulted in the

company being named SESAC Publisher of the Year. With these varied success, Moraine has received over 50 publishing country and pop awards from ASCAP, BMI, and SESAC.

HOW TO CONTACT *Does not accept unsolicited material.*

MUSIC Country.

MORGAN MUSIC GROUP

1800 Grand Ave., Nashville TN 37212. (615)321-9029. **E-mail:** songmerch@aol.com. **Website:** www.dennismorgansongwriter.com. **Contact:** Dennis Morgan. "With the sole idea of publishing other writers' songs, Dennis Morgan set up the following companies in 1985: Morganactive Songs, Inc. (ASCAP), Dennis Morgan Music (BMI), Cottagehouse Music (SESAC) and several other related companies. This includes record labels and recording studios all based in Nashville, Tennessee, with satellite offices in Santa Monica, California, and Minneapolis, Minnesota. Since the company's first signing, which was songwriter great Frank Myers, the Morgan Music Group has developed and published some of the biggest hits in the world, including 'I Swear,' written by Frank Myers and Gary Baker and published by Morganactive Songs, Inc. Recorded by John Michael Montgomery and All-4-One, it is one of the biggest songs of all time. It's in over 300 compilation albums around the world and, as we speak, is being used in a worldwide cologne commercial. Other classic songs published by Morganactive include 'The Dance,' written by Tony Arata and recorded by Garth Brooks. Also, five more Morganactive songs recorded by Garth and written by Tony (these six songs alone have been on 50 million records). 'Here I Am,' written again by Tony and a No. 1 on Patty Loveless. 'Saved By Love,' written by Chris Smith and published by Dennis Morgan Music, was recorded by Amy Grant and was No. 1 for 13 weeks. Hundreds more have been recorded, as Morgan Music Group, Inc. really is a company that nurtures talent and energizes dreams—with much more to come."

HOW TO CONTACT *Does not accept unsolicited material.*

MUSIC Pop, country, rock.

MPL MUSIC PUBLISHING

41 W. 54th St., New York NY 10019. (212)246-5881. **Fax:** (212)246-7852. **E-mail:** contact@mplcommunications.com. **Website:** www.mplcommunications.com. Founded by Paul McCartney, MPL's music

publishing business has been marked by considered acquisitions and sensitive, honest handling of copyrights.

HOW TO CONTACT E-mail a link to your song. "Don't call us. If we like what we hear, we'll be in touch."

MUSIC Published classics such as "Ac-Cent-Tchu-Ate The Positive," "Autumn Leaves," "Baby, It's Cold Outside," "Big Girls Don't Cry," "The Christmas Song," "One for My Baby," "It's So Easy," "Blue Suede Shoes," "Sentimental Journey," "Tenderly," and more.

MPL MUSIC PUBLISHING

41 W. 54th St., New York NY 10019. (212)246-5881. **Website:** www.mplcommunications.com.

HOW TO CONTACT *Does not accept unsolicited material.*

MUSIC All genres. Has placed songs with *New Girl, Penny Dreadful, Deadpool, Joy, Family Guy, The Flash, American Horror Story, The Finest Hours, Sleepy Hollow*, and more.

⊘ THE MUSIC ROOM PUBLISHING GROUP

525 S. Francisca Ave., Redondo Beach CA 90277 United States. (310)316-4551. **E-mail:** mrp@aol.com. **Website:** http://musicroomonline.com; www.musicroom.us. **Contact:** John Reed. (ASCAP)/MRP MUSIC (BMI) Music publisher and record producer. Pays standard royalty.

AFFILIATES MRP Music (BMI).

HOW TO CONTACT *Not accepting unsolicited material.*

MUSIC Mostly **pop/rock/R&B** and **crossover**. Published "That Little Tattoo," "Mona Lisa" and "Sleepin' with an Angel" (singles by John E. Reed) from *Rock With An Attitude* (album), recorded by Rawk Dawg (rock), released 2002; "Over the Rainbow" and "Are You Still My Lover" (singles) from *We Only Came to Rock* (album), recorded by Rawk Dawg, released 2004 on Music Room Productions[[PIRg]].

⦿⊙ NERVOUS PUBLISHING

5 Sussex Crescent, Northolt, Middlesex UB5 4DL United Kingdom. +44(20) 8423 7373. **Fax:** +44(20) 8423 7773. **E-mail:** info@nervous.co.uk. **Website:** www.nervous.co.uk. **Contact:** Roy Williams, owner. Music publisher, record company (Nervous Records) and record producer. MCPS, PRS and Phonographic Performance Ltd. Publishes 100 songs/year; publishes

25 new songwriters/year. Pays standard royalty; royalties paid directly to US songwriters.

⊙ Nervous Publishing's record label, Nervous Records, is listed in the Record Companies section.

HOW TO CONTACT Submit demo by mail. Unsolicited submissions are OK. Prefers CD with 3-10 songs and lyric sheet. "Include letter giving your age and mentioning any previously published material." SAE and IRC. Responds in 3 weeks.

MUSIC Mostly **psychobilly, rockabilly** and **rock** (impossibly fast music—e.g.: Stray Cats but twice as fast); also **blues, country, R&B** and **rock** (1950s style). Published *Trouble* (album), recorded by Dido Bonneville (rockabilly); *Rockabilly Comp* (album), recorded by various artists; and *Nervous Singles Collection* (album), recorded by various artists, all on Nervous Records.

TIPS "Submit *no* rap, soul, funk—we want *rockabilly*."

⊘ NEW HEIGHTS ENTERTAINMENT

Website: www.newheightsent.com. New Heights Entertainment is a privately held personal management and consulting firm with its core business focusing on music producers, songwriters, record label management, music publishing, brand development and strategic guidance for entertainment content and IP creators.

HOW TO CONTACT *Does not accept unsolicited materials.*

MUSIC All genres and styles.

⦿ A NEW RAP JAM PUBLISHING

New Experience Rec/Wealth Nation Universal Music Group/Rick Ross Music Group/Universal Music Group UMG., New Experience Records, 1017 Myrtle St., Marks MS 38646. 662-388-1716 or 567-712-2861. **E-mail:** newexperiencerecords@yahoo.com. **E-mail:** jamesjrmilligan@yahoo.com. **Website:** newexperiencerecordsmusic.com. **Contact:** A&R Department James Milligan or William Roach. "We have been in the music publishing business over 25 years now and are always looking for great songs. If you got a hit send it for review now with contact info. With our new partners, we plan to make even greater things happen with great artist and songs. Welcome to the family: Rick Ross Universal Music Group, Wealth Nation Music Group, UMG Universal Music Group, Sony/Red Distribution." Professional Managers:

William Roach (rap, clean); James Milligan (country, 1970s music, pop). Music publisher and record company (New Experience/Faze 4 Records, Pump It Up Records, and Rough Edge Records). Publishes 50-100 songs/year; Grind Blocc Records and Touch Tone Digital International Records publishes 5-10 new songwriters/year. Hires staff songwriters. Pays standard royalty.

AFFILIATES Songwriters Party House Publishing (BMI), Creative Star Management, and Rough Edge Records. Distribution through KVZ Distribution and States 51 Distribution.

HOW TO CONTACT *Write first to arrange personal interview or submit demo CD by mail.* Unsolicited submissions are OK. Prefers CD with 3-5 songs and lyric or lead sheet. Include SASE. Responds in 6-8 weeks. "Visit www.myspace.com/newexperiencerecords2 for more information."

MUSIC Mostly **R&B**, **pop**, **blues**, and **rock/rap** (clean); also **contemporary**, **gospel**, **country** and **soul**. Published "Lets Go Dancing" (single by Dion Mikel), recorded and released 2006 on Faze 4 Records/New Experience Records; "The Broken Hearted" (single) from The Final Chapter (album), recorded by T.M.C. the milligan connection (R&B/gospel); James Jr.; "Girl Like You" feat. Terry Zapp Troutman, additional appearances by Kurtis Blow, King MC, Sugarfoot Lead Singer (Ohio Players) Lavel Jackson 2009/10 on New Experience/Pump It Up Records. Other artists include singer-songwriter James, Jr. on Faze 4 Records/Rough Edge Records Grind Blocc Records.

TIPS "We are seeking hit artists from the 1970s, 1980s, and 1990s who would like to be signed, as well as new talent and female solo artists. Send any available information supporting the group or act. We are a label that does not promote violence, drugs, or anything that we feel is a bad example for our youth. Establish music industry contacts, write and keep writing, and most of all, believe in yourself. Use a good recording studio but be very professional. Just take your time and produce the best music possible. Sometimes you only get one chance. Make sure you place your best song on your demo first. This will increase your chances greatly. If you're the owner of your own small label and have a finished product, please send it. And if there is interest, we will contact you. Also, be on the lookout for new artists on Rough Edge Records and Touch Tone Records. Now reviewing blues and soul music. If you have a developing record label and would like distribution send us your artist listing record label information to be considered and thank you for considering us for your next project."

◑ NEXT DECADE ENTERTAINMENT

65 W. 55th St., Suite 4F, New York NY 10019. (212)583-1887, ext. 10. **Fax:** (212)813-9788. **E-mail:** info@next-decade-ent.com. **Website:** www.nextdecade-ent.com. **Contact:** Stu Cantor, president. "Next Decade is more than just a music publisher. We're experts with years of experience and knowledge about music and licensing. Our approach is hands-on and service oriented. We work with clients closely to make sure their copyrights are not only protected and properly exploited, but that opportunities for growth and development are identified and that we are involved with the newest companies and people for licensing opportunities."

MUSIC Represents such artists as Boston, Harry Belafonte, Millie Jackson, Ray Griff, Eric Lindell, Vic Mizzy, and more.

◓ NORTH STAR MEDIA

40900 Woodward Ave., Suite 350, Bloomfield Hills MI 48304. (818)766-2100. **Website:** www.northstarmedia.com. Founded in 2001, North Star Media is a boutique music publisher offering a personalized, full-service approach to publishing and rights management solutions for artists, film and TV production companies, ad agencies, and new media outlets. North Star Media proudly represents a diverse roster of recording artists, ranging from brand-new indies to multi-platinum superstars, and works closely with some of today's top composers and producers who specialize in the creation of custom scores and production cues. To achieve its goals, North Star Media maintains a highly curated catalog, uses catalog management and distribution systems from SynchTank and Soundminer (to assist in matching music to placement opportunities), and employs the use of Counterpoint's industry-leading Music Maestro accounting and royalty reporting system (to provide accurate and timely payments to its artists and other rightsholders). For its artists, North Star Media offers the following services: pursuing synch placement opportunities across all media in the US and international markets through its vast network of music supervisors and sub-publishers, advising and handling of worldwide copyright administration, and artist development.

HOW TO CONTACT *Does not accept unsolicited materials.*

⊘ NOTTING HILL MUSIC

8961 Sunset Blvd., Suite 2E, West Hollywood CA 90069. (310)273-4230. **Fax:** (310)273-4237. **Website:** www.nottinghillmusic.com. "The Notting Hill Music Group Ltd. is a truly international music publishing operation, based in London and Los Angeles, with first-class representation in every corner of the globe."

HOW TO CONTACT *Notting Hill Music does not accept unsolicited material.*

MUSIC Any genre. Published music by 50 Cent, Aretha Franklin, Black Eyed Peas, Bob Dylan, Calvin Harris, Elton John, Jay Z, Lionel Richie, Madonna, and more.

⊘ OLE

266 King St. W., Suite 500, Toronto ON M5V 1H8 Canada. **E-mail:** majorlyindie@olemm.com. **Website:** www.majorlyindie.com. Ole is the world's fastest growing rights management company. Founded in 2004, and with offices in Toronto, Nashville, New York, and Los Angeles, Ole boasts a team of 45 experienced industry professionals focused on acquisitions, creative development and worldwide copyright administration. Ole has recently entered the production music space with the acquisition of MusicBox and Auracle, which have operations in New York, Toronto and Los Angeles. Ole is committed to the creative development of its 60-plus staff songwriters, legacy writers and composers and the cultivation of our catalogs and client catalogs. Ole has ongoing co-ventures with Last Gang Publishing (Alt Rock), Roots Three Music (Country), and tanjola (Pop/Rock/Urban).

HOW TO CONTACT *Does not accept unsolicited submissions.*

MUSIC Notable copyrights with Ole include those by Taylor Swift, Rascal Flatts, Justin Timberlake, Jay-Z, Eric, Church, Kelly Clarkson, Pink, Aerosmith, Tim McGraw, and many more.

⊘ PEERMUSIC

2397 Shattuck Ave., Suite 202, Berkeley CA 94704. (510)848-7337. **Fax:** (510)848-7355. **E-mail:** sfcorp@peermusic.com. **Website:** www.peermusic.com. Music publisher and artist development promotional label. Hires staff songwriters. "All deals negotiable." Affiliate(s) Songs of Peer Ltd. (ASCAP) and Peermusic III Ltd. (BMI).

HOW TO CONTACT "We do NOT accept unsolicited submissions. We only accept material through agents, attorneys and managers."

MUSIC Mostly **pop**, **rock** and **R&B**. Published music by David Foster (writer/producer, pop); Andrew Williams (writer/producer, pop); Christopher "Tricky" Stewart (R&B, writer/producer).

⊘ PEERMUSIC

901 W. Alameda Ave., Suite 108, Burbank CA 91506. (818)480-7000. **Website:** www.peermusic.com. peermusic was founded over 85 years ago by renowned visionary Ralph S. Peer, and is the largest independent music publisher in the world, with 32 offices in 28 countries and over a quarter of a million copyrights. Since 2010, peermusic has celebrated a string of huge hits, including "Firework" by Katy Perry, "Umbrella" and "What's My Name" by Rihanna, "Single Ladies (Put A Ring On It)" by Beyoncé, "Banjo" by Rascal Flatts, "Jealous" by Nick Jonas, "Night Train" by Jason Aldean, and "Darte Un Beso" by Prince Royce.

HOW TO CONTACT *Does not accept unsolicited materials.*

⊘ PERLA MUSIC

134 Parker Ave., Easton PA 18042. (212)957-9509. **Fax:** (917)338-7596. **E-mail:** PM@PMRecords.org. **Website:** www.pmrecords.org. **Contact:** Gene Perla. (ASCAP) Music publisher, record company (PMRecords.org), record producer (Perla.org), studio production (TheSystemMSP.com) and Internet Design (CCINYC.com). Publishes 5 songs/year. Staff size: 5.

HOW TO CONTACT *E-mail first and obtain permission to submit.*

MUSIC Mostly **jazz** and **rock**.

◑ POLLYBYRD PUBLICATIONS LTD.

468 N. Camden Dr., Suite 200, Beverly Hills CA 90210. 310 860-7499. **Fax:** (310)860-7400. **E-mail:** pplzmi@aol.com. **Website:** www.pplzmi.com. **Contact:** Dakota Hawk, vice president. Professional managers: Cisco Blue (country, pop, rock); Tedford Steele (hip-hop, R&B). Music publisher, record company (PPL Entertainment) and management firm (Sa'mall Management). Publishes 100 songs/year; publishes 25-40 new songwriters/year. Hires staff writers. Pays standard royalty.

AFFILIATES Kellijai Music (ASCAP), Pollyann Music (ASCAP), Ja'Nikki Songs (BMI), Velma Songs International (BMI), Lonnvanness Songs (SESEC), PPL

Music (ASCAP), Zettitalia Music, Butternut Music (BMI), Zett Two Music (ASCAP), Plus Publishing and Zett One Songs (BMI).

HOW TO CONTACT *Write first and obtain permission to submit.* No phone calls. Prefers CD with 4 songs and lyric and lead sheet. Include SASE. Responds in 2 months.

MUSIC Published *Return of the Players* (album) by Juz-Cuz 2004 on PPL; "Believe" (single by J. Jarrett/S. Cuseo) from *Time* (album), recorded by Lejenz (pop), released 2001 on PRL/Credence; *Rainbow Gypsy Child* (album), written and recorded by Riki Hendrix (rock), released 2001 on PRL/Sony; and "What's Up With That" (single by Brandon James/Patrick Bouvier) from *Outcast* (album), recorded by Condottieré; (hip-hop), released 2001 on Bouvier.

TIPS "Make those decisions—are you really a songwriter? Are you prepared to starve for your craft? Do you believe in delayed gratification? Are you commercial or do you write only for yourself? Can you take rejection? Do you want to be the best? If so, contact us."

⊙ QUARK MUSIC GROUP

Quark Inc., P.O. Box 452, Newtown CT 06470. (917)687-9988. **E-mail:** Submission details on website at http://www.quarkmusicgroup.com/about-quark/. **Website:** www.quarkmusicgroup.com. Music publisher, record company (Quark Records) and record producer (Curtis Urbina). Estab. 1984. Publishes 12 songs/year; 2 new songwriters/year. Staff size: 4. Pays standard royalty.

AFFILIATES Quarkette Music (BMI), Freedurb Music (ASCAP), and Quark Records.

HOW TO CONTACT Contact details available on website.

FILM & TV Places 10 songs in film/year. Music Supervisor: Curtis Urbina.

MUSIC Pop. Does not want anything short of a hit.

RAZOR & TIE ENTERTAINMENT

214 Sullivan St., Suite 5, New York NY 10012. (212)598-2259. **Fax:** (212)473-9173. **E-mail:** bprimont@razorandtie.com. **Website:** www.razorandtiemusicpublishing.com. **Contact:** Brooke Primont, senior vice president, music placement, and licensing.

HOW TO CONTACT *Does not accept unsolicited material.*

MUSIC Songwriters and groups represented include Dar Williams, Bad Books, David Ford, Finch, Brand New, Emerson Lake & Palmer, BeBe Winans, Joe Jackson, Joan Baez, Nonpoint, Yellowcard, Foreigner, HIM, Saves the Day, Suzanne Vega, and many more.

⊘ RONDOR MUSIC INTERNATIONAL/ ALMO/IRVING MUSIC

Part of Universal Music Publishing Group, 2440 Sepulveda Blvd., Suite 119, Los Angeles CA 90064. (310)235-4800. **Fax:** (310)235-4801. **E-mail:** rondor-la@umusic.com. **Website:** www.universalmusicpublishing.com. The Rondor catalog embodies the works of such important songwriters as The Beach Boys, Al Green, Otis Redding, Peter Frampton, Isaac Hayes, Supertramp, Tom Petty and Leon Russell. Rondor also represents many significant songwriters and artists including Rod Temperton, Mark Knopfler, Emmylou Harris, William Orbit, Saliva, Will Jennings, Garbage, Jurassic 5, Shep Crawford, and Steven Van Zandt. (ASCAP, BMI)

AFFILIATES Almo Music Corp. (ASCAP) and Irving Music, Inc. (BMI).

HOW TO CONTACT *Does not accept unsolicited submissions.*

⊘ ROUND HILL MUSIC

400 Madison Ave., 18th Floor, New York NY 10017. (212)380-0080. **E-mail:** info@roundhillmusic.com. **Website:** www.roundhillmusic.com. Round Hill Music is a full-service, creative music company with a core focus on music publishing. "We take a thoughtful, long-term approach to building both a stellar song catalog and a roster of talented active writers that our team is proud to work so closely with on a daily basis. Our ultimate goal is to deliver value from every single song in our catalog, while simultaneously providing all of our writers with the individualized attention they need to succeed. The Round Hill team achieves this goal through everything from synch licensing and song placements to setting up co-writes and performing international song registration, all while maintaining one of the most transparent and accurate royalty accounting systems in the music publishing marketplace. We're on a mission to bring back the kind of personalized creative attention that was so inherent to the initial heyday of music publishing, and our boutique size gives us the agility we need to realize that mission. From the iconic hits of yesterday, to the future chart toppers of tomorrow, our love for our music is at the center of everything we do."

⊜○ R.T.L. MUSIC

Perthy Farm, The Perthy, Shropshire SY12 9HR United Kingdom. **E-mail:** info@rltmusic.co.uk. **Website:** www.rtlmusic.co.uk. **Contact:** Tanya Woof, international A&R manager. Music publisher, record company (Le Matt Music) and record producer. Publishes approximately 30 songs/year. Pays standard royalty.

AFFILIATES Lee Music (publishing), Swoop Records, Grenouille Records, Check Records, Zarg Records, Pogo Records, R.T.F.M. (all independent companies).

HOW TO CONTACT Submit demo by mail. Unsolicited submissions are OK. Prefers CD or DVD with 1-3 songs and lyric and lead sheets; include still photos and bios. "Make sure name and address are on CD." Send IRC. Responds in 6 weeks.

MUSIC All types. Published "The Old Days" (single by Ron Dickson) from *Groucho* (album), recorded by Groucho (pop); "Orphan in the Storm" (single by M.J. Lawson) from *Emmit Till* (album), recorded by Emmit Till (blues); "Donna" (single by Mike Sheriden) from *Donna* (album), recorded by Mike Sheriden (pop), all released 2006 on Swoop.

○ RUSTIC RECORDS, INC. PUBLISHING

6337 Murray Lane, Brentwood TN 37027. (615)371-0646. **E-mail:** info@rusticrecordsinc.com. **Website:** www.rusticrecordsinc.com. **Contact:** Jack Schneider, president; Nell Schneider, executive vice president, office manager.. (ASCAP, BMI, SESAC) Music publisher, record company (Rustic Records Inc.) and record producer. Publishes 20 songs/year. Pays standard royalty.

AFFILIATES Covered Bridge Music (BMI), Town Square Music (SESAC), Iron Skillet Music (ASCAP). Submit demo by mail. Unsolicited submissions are OK. Prefers CD with no more than 5 songs and lyric sheet for each song, publish contact info for songwriter.

MUSIC Mostly **country**. Published "In Their Eyes" (single by Jamie Champa); "Take Me As I Am" (single by Bambi Barrett/Paul Huffman); and "Yesterday's Memories" (single by Jack Schneider), recorded by Colte Bradley (country), released 2003.

TIPS "Send 3 or 4 traditional country songs, novelty songs, 'foot-tapping, hand-clapping' gospel songs with strong hook for male or female artist or duet. Enclose SASE (manila envelope)."

○ SANDALPHON MUSIC PUBLISHING

P.O. Box 18197, Panama City Beach FL 32417. **E-mail:** sandalphonmusic@yahoo.com. **Contact:** Ruth Otey. Music publisher, record company (Sandalphon Records), and management agency (Sandalphon Management). Staff size: 2. Pays standard royalty of 50%.

HOW TO CONTACT Submit demo by mail. Unsolicited submissions are fine. Prefers CD with 1-5 songs, lyric sheet, and cover letter. Include SASE or SAE and IRC for outside United States. Responds in 6-8 weeks.

MUSIC Mostly **rock**, **country**, and **alternative**; also **pop**, **blues**, and **gospel**.

⊙ SB21 MUSIC PUBLISHING

1610 16th Ave. S., 2nd Floor, Nashville TN 37212. (615)775-0254. **E-mail:** info@sb21music.com. **Website:** www.sb21music.com. SB21 Music is an independent music publishing company started by Steve Pasch. Writers with SB21 have had country cuts with major artists, such as Tim McGraw, Wynonna, John Michael Montgomery, and Clay Walker, including 2006 Billboard Country's Most Played Song of the Year Rodney Adkins' "Watching You."

⊙ SHAWNEE PRESS, INC.

P.O. Box 13819, Milwaukee WI 53213 United States. **E-mail:** info@shawneepress.com. **Website:** www.ShawneePress.com. Music publisher. Publishes 150 songs/year. Staff size: 12. Pays negotiable royalty.

AFFILIATES GlorySound, Harold Flammer Music, Mark Foster Music, Wide World Music, Concert Works.

HOW TO CONTACT *Does not accept unsolicited submissions.*

MUSIC Mostly **church/liturgical**, **educational choral** and **instrumental**.

○ SILICON MUSIC PUBLISHING CO.

222 Tulane St., Garland TX 75043. **E-mail:** support@siliconmusic.us. **Website:** http://siliconmusic.us. **Contact:** Steve Summers, public relations. Music publisher and record company (Front Row Records). Publishes 10-20 songs/year; publishes 2-3 new songwriters/year. Pays standard royalty.

    Also see the listing for Front Row Records in the Record Companies section of this book.

HOW TO CONTACT Submit demo package by mail. Unsolicited submissions are OK. Prefers CD with 1-2 songs. Does not return material. Responds ASAP.

MUSIC Mostly **rockabilly** and **1950s material**; also **old-time blues/country** and **MOR**. Published "Rockaboogie Shake" (single by James McClung) from *Rebels and More* (album), recorded by Lennerockers (rockabilly), released 2002 on Lenne (Germany); "Be-Bop City" (single by Dan Edwards), "So" (single by Dea Summers/Gene Summers), and "Little Lu Ann" (single by James McClung) from *Do Right Daddy* (album), recorded by Gene Summers (rockabilly/1950s rock 'n' roll), released 2004 on Enviken (Sweden).

TIPS "We are very interested in 1950s rock and rockabilly original masters for release through overseas affiliates. If you are the owner of any 1950s masters, contact us first! We have releases in Holland, Switzerland, United Kingdom, Belgium, France, Sweden, Norway and Australia. We have the market if you have the tapes! Our staff writers include James McClung, Gary Mears (original Casuals), Robert Clark, Dea Summers, Shawn Summers, Joe Hardin Brown, Bill Becker and Dan Edwards."

⊘ SILVER BLUE MUSIC/OCEANS BLUE MUSIC

3940 Laurel Canyon Blvd., Suite 441, Studio City CA 91604. (818)980-9588. **E-mail:** jdiamond20@aol.com. **Website:** www.joeldiamond.com. **Contact:** Joel Diamond. (ASCAP, BMI) Music publisher and record producer (Joel Diamond Entertainment). Publishes 50 songs/year. Pays standard royalty.

HOW TO CONTACT *Does not accept unsolicited material.* "No CDs returned."

FILM & TV Places 4 songs in film and 6 songs in TV/year.

MUSIC Mostly **pop** and **R&B**; also **rap** and **classical**. Produced and managed The 5 Browns' 3 No. 1 CDs on Sony. Published "After the Lovin" (by Bernstein/Adams), recorded by Engelbert Humperdinck; "This Moment in Time" (by Alan Bernstein/Ritchie Adams), recorded by Engelbert Humperdinck. Other artists include David Hasselhoff, Kaci (Curb Records), Ike Turner, Andrew Dice Clay, Gloria Gaynor, Tony Orlando, Katie Cassidy, and Vaneza.

⦿◐ SINUS MUSIK PRODUKTION, ULLI WEIGEL

Geitnerweg 30a, D-12209, Berlin Germany. **Website:** www.ulli-weigel.de. **Contact:** Ulli Weigel, owner.

Music publisher, record producer and screenwriter. Wrote German lyrics for more than 500 records. Member: GEMA, GVL. Publishes 20 songs/year; publishes 6 new songwriters/year. Staff size: 3. Pays standard royalty.

AFFILIATES Sinus Musikverlag H.U. Weigel GmbH.

HOW TO CONTACT Submit demo package by mail. Prefers CD with up to 10 songs and lyric sheets. If you want to send MP3 attachments, you should contact before. Attachments from unknown senders will not be opened. Responds in 2 months by e-mail. "If material should be returned, please send 3 International Reply Coupons (IRC) for a CD. No stamps."

MUSIC Mostly **rock**, **pop** and **New Age**; also **background music for movies and audio books**. Published "Simple Story" (single), recorded by MAANAM on RCA (Polish rock); *Die Musik Maschine* (album by Klaus Lage), recorded by CWN Productions on Hansa Records (pop/German), "Villa Woodstock" (film music/comedy) Gebrueder Blattschuss, Juergen Von Der Lippe, Hans Werner Olm (2005).

TIPS "Take more time working on the melody than on the instrumentation. I am also looking for master-quality recordings for non-exclusive release on my label (and to use them as soundtracks for multimedia projects, TV and movie scripts I am working on)."

⦿ SONGS FOR THE PLANET, INC.

P.O. Box 40251, Nashville TN 37204. (615)269-8682. **Fax:** (615)269-8929. **E-mail:** justinpeters@songsfortheplanet.com; songsfortheplanet@songsfortheplanet.com. **E-mail:** newwritersubmission@songsfortheplanet.com. **Website:** http://songsfortheplanet.com. **Contact:** Justin Peters. (ASCAP)

AFFILIATES Justin Peters Music, Platinum Planet Music and Tourmaline (BMI).

HOW TO CONTACT Contact via e-mail, and a detailed submission policy will be sent.

MUSIC Mostly **country, classic rock, Southern rock, inspirational AC Pop, Southern gospel/Christian** and **worship songs**. Published "The Bottom Line" recorded by Charley Pride on Music City Records (written by Art Craig, Drew Bourke, and Justin Peters); "No Less Than Faithful" (single by Don Pardoe/Joel Lyndsey), recorded by Ann Downing on Daywind Records, Jim Bullard on Genesis Records and Melody Beizer (No. 1 song) on Covenant Records; "No Other Like You" (single by Mark Comden/Paula Carpenter), recorded by Twila Paris and Tony Melendez

(No. 5 song) on Starsong Records; "Making A New Start" and "Invincible Faith" (singles by Gayle Cox), recorded by Kingdom Heirs on Sonlite Records; "I Don't Want To Go Back" (single by Gayle Cox), recorded by Greater Vision on Benson Records; and "HE HAD MERCY ON ME" (by Constance and Justin Peters) recorded by Shining Grace.

⊘ SONY/ATV MUSIC PUBLISHING

8 Music Square W., Nashville TN 37203 United States. (615)726-8300. **Fax:** (615)726-8329. **E-mail:** info@sonyatv.com. **Website:** www.sonyatv.com. ASCAP, BMI, SESAC.

HOW TO CONTACT *Sony/ATV Music does not accept unsolicited submissions.*

⊘ STILL WORKING MUSIC GROUP

1625 Broadway, Suite 200, Nashville TN 37203. (615)242-4201. **Website:** http://stillworkingmusicgroup.com. (ASCAP, BMI, SESAC) Music publisher and record company (Orby Records, Inc.).

AFFILIATES Still Working for the Woman Music (ASCAP), Still Working for the Man Music (BMI) and Still Working for All Music (SESAC).

HOW TO CONTACT *Does not accept unsolicited submissions.*

FILM & TV Published "First Noel," recorded by The Kelions in Felicity.

MUSIC Mostly **rock**, **country** and **pop**; also **dance** and **R&B**. Published "If You See Him/If You See Her" (by Tommy Lee James), recorded by Reba McIntire/Brooks & Dunn; "Round About Way" (by Wil Nance), recorded by George Strait on MCA; and "Wrong Again" (by Tommy Lee James), recorded by Martina McBride on RCA (country).

TIPS "If you want to be a country songwriter you need to be in Nashville where the business is. Write what is in your heart."

⊘ TEN TEN MUSIC GROUP

33 Music Square W., Suite 110, Nashville TN 37203. (615)255-9955. **Fax:** (615)255-1209. **E-mail:** info@tentenmusic.com. **Website:** www.tentenmusicgroup.com. **Contact:** Barry Coburn, president; Nathan Nicholson, vice president and creative director. "Ten Ten Music Group, Inc. has established itself as one of the most successful independent music publishing companies in Nashville. Appearing on Billboard's list of Top Song Publishers from 2004 to 2006, Ten Ten Music continues to expand its footprint across

multiple genres. With cuts by major rock groups like Papa Roach, Shinedown, Halestorm, and Cavo, as well as other superstars, including One Direction, Bonnie Raitt and Selena Gomez, the diverse talent of Ten Ten Music's writing staff has ventured far beyond Nashville."

MUSIC "The writing staff at Ten Ten has also enjoyed recent success with cuts by country artists such as Tim McGraw, Miranda Lambert, Pistol Annie's, Reba McEntire, David Nail and many others. Continuing a tradition of developing and nurturing the careers of such superstars as Alan Jackson and Keith Urban, Ten Ten has also been working to shape the careers of up-and-coming artists Clare Dunn and Femke Weidema."

◯ TINDERBOX MUSIC

3148 Bryant Ave. S., Minneapolis MN 55408. (612)375-1113. **Fax:** (612)341-3330. **E-mail:** brady@tinderboxmusic.com; patrick@tinderboxmusic.com; staff@tinderboxmusic.com. **Website:** www.tinderboxmusic.com. Tinderbox is a music promotions and distribution company. "We work with unsigned, indie-label, and major-label artists across the country by obtaining press and radio airplay in appropriate markets and formats. We specialize in college radio and the artists that fit the CMJ (*College Music Journal*) and secondary FM and community formats. We also provide local and national distribution for artists, as well as publishing and music licensing opportunities."

HOW TO CONTACT "There are 2 ways to submit: physically or digitally. As we live in a digital age, it is probably easier for you to submit your music to us via Bandcamp, Facebook, Reverbnation, Soundcloud, or Sonicbids. Got links? We'll take them! Just e-mail them to us. If you are a hip-hop or electronic artist, please submit your music to jordan@tinderboxmusic.com." Do not send songs as an attachment. Links only. Include a short bio. "If you have a one-sheet that is less than 7MB in size, you may attach that. If you like to do things old-school, you can also send us physical submissions. Your CD must be radio ready. By this we mean that it should have been professionally recorded, mixed, and mastered. Watch out for profanity. When sending a physical submission, please send us 2 or 3 copies of your CD (depending on which departments you're interested in). More than one person will probably want to review your CD. We do promise that we will get back to everyone who submits material via phone, e-mail, or snail mail regarding your submission and you can typically expect to hear from us within 48 hours." More details available at the website.

MUSIC "We specialize in **indie, pop/alternative, modern rock, triple-A, rock,** and **acoustic-based rock, hip-hop** and **electronic music**. Although we love jazz, we don't regularly promote jazz, sorry. Featured artists include Imagine Dragons, Gentleman Hall, Twenty One Pilots, Stars Go Dim, others."

TRANSITION MUSIC CORP.

P.O. Box 2586, Toluca Lake CA 91610. (323)860-7074. **E-mail:** submissions@transitionmusic.com; info@ transitionmusic.com. **Website:** www.transitionmusic.com. Publishes 250 songs/year; publishes 50 new songwriters/year. Variable royalty based on song placement and writer.

AFFILIATES Pushy Publishing (ASCAP), Creative Entertainment Music (BMI) and One Stop Shop Music (SESAC).

HOW TO CONTACT Submit no more than two songs, online only, to submissions@transitionmusic. com. Accepts all genres and unsolicited music. See additional submission instructions online.

FILM & TV "TMC provides music for all forms of visual media. Mainly TV." Music-all styles.

MUSIC "TMC has become an industry leader with more than 120,000 domestic TV performances this year alone, and 23 TV series and 8 networks rely exclusively on Transition Music Corp. (TMC) for comprehensive music solutions for 'ALL' things music, including: our digital online production music library, composers, clearance & licensing, connecting to new and indie artists, music supervision, IP management, administration and creation of music-driven revenue streams. Ultimate Exposure is TMC's way of giving the independent artist individual attention and gets your music in the hands of the decision makers. Ultimate Exposure is a specialty brand focusing on your success in the visual media world. Our team brings precision and efficiency to your artistic journey."

TIPS "Supply master-quality material with great songs."

TRF MUSIC LIBRARIES

106 Apple St., Suite 302, Tinton Falls NJ 07724. **E-mail:** info@trfmusic.com. **Website:** www.trfmusic. com. **Contact:** Michael Nurko, music publisher. Pays standard royalty.

AFFILIATES Dorian Music Publishers, Inc. (BMI) and TRF Music, Inc.

○ Also see listing for TRF Production Music Libraries in the Advertising, Audiovisual & Commercial Music Firms section of this book.

HOW TO CONTACT "We accept submissions of new compositions."

MUSIC All categories, mainly **instrumental** and **acoustic** suitable for use as **production music**, including **theme** and **background music for TV and film**. "Have published more than 50,000 titles since 1931."

TRIO PRODUCTIONS, INC.

SONGSCAPE MUSIC, LLC, Trio Productions, Inc, 1026 15th Ave. S., Nashville TN 37212. (615)726-5810. **E-mail:** Robyn@trioproductions.com. **Website:** www. trioproductions.com. **Contact:** Robyn Taylor-Drake. "We are a publishing, consulting, and artist development company for singers and songwriters. Our mentoring program is designed to help songwriters and singers realize their potential and understand how the music business works."

AFFILIATES ASCAP, BMI, SESAC, AIMP, CMA, IPA

HOW TO CONTACT Visit the site to submit online via MusicXray.

MUSIC **Country, pop,** and **Americana**.

UNIVERSAL MUSIC PUBLISHING

2100 Colorado Ave., Santa Monica CA 90404. (310)235-4700. **Fax:** (310)235-4900. **Website:** www. umusicpub.com. (ASCAP, BMI,SESAC)

HOW TO CONTACT *Does not accept unsolicited submissions.*

VAAM MUSIC GROUP

P.O. Box 29550, Hollywood CA 90029. **E-mail:** pmarti3636@aol.com. **Website:** www.vaammusic.com. **Contact:** Pete Martin, president. (BMI) Music publisher and record producer (Pete Martin/Vaam Productions). Estab. 1967. Publishes 9-24 new songs/year. Pays standard royalty.

AFFILIATES Pete Martin Music (ASCAP).

MUSIC "Please visit the website for up-to-date current 'song requests.' We mostly work with **country, Top 40,** and **R&B**. Submitted material must have potential of reaching top 5 on charts."

TIPS "Study the top 10 charts in the style you write. Stay current and up-to-date with today's market."

○ WALKERBOUT MUSIC GROUP

P.O. Box 24454, Nashville TN 37202. (615)269-7074. **Fax:** (888)894-4934. **E-mail:** matt@walkerboutmusic.com; info@aristomedia.com. **Website:** www.walkerboutmusic.com. **Contact:** Matt Watkins, director of operations. (ASCAP, BMI, SESAC) Publishes 50 songs/year; 5-10 new songwriters/year. Pays standard royalty.

AFFILIATES Goodland Publishing Co. (ASCAP), Marc Isle Music (BMI), Gulf Bay Publishing (SESAC), Con Brio Music (BMI), Wiljex Publishing (ASCAP), Concorde Publishing (SESAC).

HOW TO CONTACT "Please see website for submission information."

MUSIC Mostly **country/Christian** and **adult contemporary.**

⊘ WARNER/CHAPPELL MUSIC, INC.

10585 Santa Monica Blvd., Los Angeles CA 90025. (310)441-8600. **Fax:** (310)470-8780. **Website:** www. warnerchappell.com.

HOW TO CONTACT *Warner/Chappell does not accept unsolicited material.*

◐ WEAVER OF WORDS MUSIC

2239 Bank St., Baltimore MD 21231. (276)970-1583. **E-mail:** weaverofwordsmusic@gmail.com. **Website:** www.weaverofwordsmusic.com. **Contact:** H.R. Cook, president. (BMI) Music publisher and record company (Fireball Records). Publishes 12 songs/year. Pays standard royalty.

AFFILIATES Weaver of Melodies Music (ASCAP).

HOW TO CONTACT Submit demo by mail. Unsolicited submissions are OK. Prefers CD with 3 songs and lyric or lead sheets. "We prefer CD submissions but will accept MP3s—limit 2." Include SASE. Responds in 3 weeks.

MUSIC Mostly **country**, **pop**, **bluegrass**, **R&B**, **film and TV** and **rock**. Published "Zero To Love" (single by H. Cook/Brian James Deskins/Rick Tiger) from *It's Just The Night* (album), recorded by Del McCoury Band (bluegrass), released 2003 on McCoury Music; "Muddy Water" (Alan Johnston) from *The Midnight Call* (album), recorded by Don Rigsby (bluegrass), re-

leased 2003 on Sugar Hill; "Ol Brown Suitcase" (H.R. Cook) from *Lonesome Highway* (album), recorded by Josh Williams (bluegrass), released 2004 on Pinecastle; and "Mansions of Kings" from *Cherry Holmes II* (album), recorded by IBMA 2005 Entertainer of the Year Cherry Holmes (bluegrass), released 2007 on Skaggs Family Records.

WORDS WEST

661 N. Harper Ave., Suite 205, Los Angeles CA 90048. (323)966-4433. **Website:** wordswest.com. Words West LLC is an independent, boutique music publishing company based in Los Angeles, California. The catalog includes many popular standards from a variety of genres dating from the 1950s to the present day. Words West, though it publishes a variety of writers, is primarily built around the song catalog of the renowned lyricist Norman Gimbel, an inductee to the Songwriters Hall of Fame, a multiple Oscar nominee and Oscar winner, and a Grammy-winning songwriter. The catalog contains many some of the greatest-performed songs of all time and international standard hits that are very current and active today throughout the licensing to film, TV, advertising, new media and the recording industry.

HOW TO CONTACT *Does not accept unsolicited submissions.*

MUSIC All genres.

⊘ WRENSONG/REYNSONG

1229 17th Ave. S., Nashville TN 37212. (615)321-4487. **Fax:** (615)327-7917. **E-mail:** christina.wrensong@ gmail.com. **Website:** www.reynsong.com. **Contact:** Christina Mitchell. Wrensong/Reynsong is an independent music publishing company with offices in Nashville and Minneapolis. Conceived by father/daughter team, Reyn Guyer and Ree Guyer Buchanan, the company began with only 20 songs and is now home to over 3,000. "Our current writer roster consists of Jon Randall, Ashely Monroe, John Wiggins, Clint & Bob Moffatt (Like Strangers), Trevor Rosen, Jacob Davis amd Shelley Skidmore." "Wrensong/Reynsong offers full in-house administration services for our writers and the catalogs we represent, as well as outside writers and catalogs."

HOW TO CONTACT *Does not accept unsolicited material.*

RECORD COMPANIES

//

Record companies release and distribute records, cassettes and CDs—the tangible products of the music industry. They sign artists to recording contracts, decide what songs those artists will record, and determine which songs to release. They also are responsible for providing recording facilities, securing producers and musicians, and overseeing the manufacture, distribution and promotion of new releases.

MAJOR LABELS & INDEPENDENT LABELS

Major labels and independent labels—what's the difference between the two?

The Majors

As of this writing, there are three major record labels, commonly referred to as the "Big 3":

- **SONY BMG** (Columbia Records, Epic Records, RCA Records, Arista Records, J Records, Provident Label Group, etc.)
- **UNIVERSAL MUSIC GROUP** (Universal Records, Interscope/Geffen/A&M, Island/Def Jam, Dreamworks Records, MCA Nashville Records, Verve Music Group, etc.)
- **WARNER MUSIC GROUP** (Atlantic Records, Bad Boy, Asylum Records, Warner Bros. Records, Maverick Records, Sub Pop, etc.)

Each of the "Big 3" is a large, publicly traded corporation beholden to shareholders and quarterly profit expectations. This means the major labels have greater financial resources and promotional muscle than a smaller "indie" label, but it's also harder to get signed to a major. A big major label may also expect more contractual control over an artist's or band's sound and image.

As shown in the above list, they also each act as umbrella organizations for numerous other well-known labels—former major labels in their own right, well-respected former independent/boutique labels, as well as subsidiary "vanity" labels fronted by successful major label recording artists. Each major label also has its own related worldwide product distribution system, and many independent labels will contract with the majors for distribution into stores.

If a label is distributed by one of these major companies, you can be assured any release coming out on that label has a large distribution network behind it. It will most likely be sent to most major retail stores in the United States.

The Independents

Independent labels go through smaller distribution companies to distribute their product. They usually don't have the ability to deliver records in massive quantities as the major distributors do. However, that doesn't mean independent labels aren't able to have hit records just like their major counterparts. A record label's distributors are found in the listings after the **DISTRIBUTED BY** heading.

Which Do I Submit To?

Many of the companies listed in this section are independent labels. They usually are the most receptive to receiving material from new artists. Major labels spend more money than most other segments of the music industry; the music publisher, for instance, pays only for items such as salaries and the costs of making demos. Record companies, at great financial risk, pay for many more services, including production, manufacturing and promotion. Therefore, they must be very selective when signing new talent. Also, the continuing fear of copyright infringement suits has closed avenues to getting new material heard by the majors. Most don't listen to unsolicited submissions, period. Only songs recommended by attorneys, managers, and producers who record company employees trust and respect are being heard by A&R people at major labels (companies with a referral policy have a ⊘ preceding their listing). But that doesn't mean all major labels are closed to new artists. With a combination of a strong local following, success on an independent label (or strong sales of an independently produced and released album) and the right connections, you could conceivably get an attentive audience at a major label.

But the competition is fierce at the majors, so you shouldn't overlook independent labels. Since they're located all over the country, indie labels are easier to contact and can be important in building a local base of support for your music (consult the Geographic Index at the back of the book to find out which companies are located near you).

Independent labels usually concentrate on a specific type of music, which will help you target companies to send your submissions. And since the staff at an indie label is smaller, there are fewer channels to go through to get your music heard by the decision makers in the company.

HOW RECORD COMPANIES WORK

Independent record labels can run on a small staff, with only a handful of people running the day-to-day business. Major record labels are more likely to be divided into the following departments: A&R, sales, marketing, promotion, product management, artist development, production, finance, business/legal and international.

- The **A&R DEPARTMENT** is staffed with A&R representatives who seek out new talent. They go out and see new bands, listen to demo tapes, and decide which artists to sign. They also look for new material for already-signed acts, match producers with artists and oversee recording projects. Once an artist is signed by an A&R rep and a record is recorded, the rest of the departments at the company come into play.
- The **SALES DEPARTMENT** is responsible for getting a record into stores. They make sure record stores and other outlets receive enough copies of a record to meet consumer demand.
- The **MARKETING DEPARTMENT** is in charge of publicity, advertising in magazines and other media, promotional videos, album cover artwork, in-store displays, and any other means of getting the name and image of an artist to the public.
- The **PROMOTION DEPARTMENT**'s main objective is to get songs from a new album played on the radio. They work with radio programmers to make sure a product gets airplay.
- The **PRODUCT MANAGEMENT DEPARTMENT** is the ringmaster of the sales, marketing and promotion departments, assuring that they're all going in the same direction when promoting a new release.
- The **ARTIST DEVELOPMENT DEPARTMENT** is responsible for taking care of things while an artist is on tour, such as setting up promotional opportunities in cities where an act is performing.
- The **PRODUCTION DEPARTMENT** handles the actual manufacturing and pressing of the record and makes sure it gets shipped to distributors in a timely manner.
- People in the **FINANCE DEPARTMENT** compute and distribute royalties, as well as keep track of expenses and income at the company.
- The **BUSINESS/LEGAL DEPARTMENT** handles and oversees any and all contracts for the company, not only between the record company and artists but with foreign distributors, record clubs, etc.
- And finally, the **INTERNATIONAL DEPARTMENT** is responsible for working with international companies for the release of records in other countries.

LOCATING A RECORD LABEL

With the abundance of record labels out there, how do you go about finding one that's right for the music you create? First, it helps to know exactly what kind of music a record label releases. Become familiar with the records a company has released, and see if they fit in with what you're doing. Each listing in this section details the type of music a particular record company is interested in releasing. You will want to refer to the Category Index to help you find those companies most receptive to the type of music you write. You should only approach companies open to your level of experience (see "A Sample Listing Decoded" in the article "How to Use *Songwriter's Market*"). Visiting a company's website also can provide valuable information about a company's philosophy, the artists on the label and the music with which they work.

NETWORKING

Recommendations by key music industry people are an important part of making contacts with record companies. Songwriters must remember that talent alone does not guarantee success in the music business. You must be recognized through contacts, and the only way to make contacts is through networking. Networking is the process of building an interconnecting web of acquaintances within the music business. The more industry people you meet, the larger your contact base becomes, and the better your chances are of meeting someone with the clout to get your demo into the hands of the right people. If you want to get your music heard by key A&R representatives, networking is imperative.

Networking opportunities can be found anywhere industry people gather. A good place to meet key industry people is at regional and national music conferences and workshops. There are many held all over the country for all types of music (see the Workshops and Conferences section for more information). You should try to attend at least one or two of these events each year; it's a great way to increase the number and quality of your music industry contacts.

Creating a Buzz

Another good way to attract A&R people is to make a name for yourself as an artist. By starting your career on a local level and building it from there, you can start to cultivate a following and prove to labels that you can be a success. A&R people figure if an act can be successful locally, there's a good chance they could be successful nationally. Start getting booked at local clubs, and start a mailing list of fans and local media. Once you gain some success on a local level, branch out. All this attention you're slowly gathering, this "buzz" you're generating, will not only get to your fans but to influential people in the music industry, as well.

SUBMITTING TO RECORD COMPANIES

When submitting to a record company, major or independent, a professional attitude is imperative. Be specific about what you are submitting and what your goals are. If you are strictly a songwriter and the label carries a band you believe would properly present your song, state that in your cover letter. If you are an artist looking for a contract, showcase your strong points as a performer. Whatever your goals are, follow submission guidelines closely, be as neat as possible and include a top-notch demo. If you need more information concerning a company's requirements, write or call for more details. (For more information on submitting your material, see the articles "Where Should I Send My Songs?" and "Demo Recordings.")

RECORD COMPANY CONTRACTS

Once you've found a record company that is interested in your work, the next step is signing a contract. Independent label contracts are usually not as long and complicated as major label ones, but they are still binding, legal contracts. Make sure the terms are in the best interest of both you and the label. Avoid anything in your contract that you feel is too restrictive. It's important to have your contract reviewed by a competent entertainment lawyer. A basic recording contract can run from 40-100 pages, and you need a lawyer to help you understand it. A lawyer also will be essential in helping you negotiate a deal that is in your best interest.

Recording contracts cover many areas, and just a few of the things you will be asked to consider are: What royalty rate is the record label willing to pay? What kind of advance are they offering? How many records will the company commit to? Will they offer tour support? Will they provide a budget for video? What sort of a recording budget are they offering? Are they asking you to give up any publishing rights? Are they offering you a publishing advance? For more information on contracts, lawyers, and payment, please see the interview with entertainment lawyer Barry Shrum—"For the Love of the Money."

ADDITIONAL RECORD COMPANIES

There are **more record companies** located in other sections of the book! Use the Index to find additional record companies within other sections.

The Case for Independents

If you're interested in getting a major label deal, it makes sense to look to independent record labels to get your start. Independent labels are seen by many as a stepping stone to a major recording contract. Very few artists are signed to a major label at the start of their careers; usually, they've had a few independent releases that helped build their reputation in the industry. Major labels watch independent labels closely to locate up-and-coming bands and new trends. In the current economic atmosphere at major labels—with extremely high overhead costs for developing new bands and the fact that only 10 percent of acts on major labels actually make any profit—they're not willing to risk everything on an unknown act. Most major labels won't even consider signing a new act that hasn't had some indie success.

But independents aren't just farming grounds for future major label acts; many bands have long-term relationships with indies and prefer it that way. While they may not be able to provide the extensive distribution and promotion that a major label can (though there are exceptions), indie labels can help an artist become a regional success, and may even help the performer to see a profit, as well. With the lower overhead and smaller production costs an independent label operates on, it's much easier to "succeed" on an indie label than on a major.

Icons

For more instructional information on the listings in this book, including explanations of symbols, read the article "How To Use *Songwriter's Market*."

4AD

17-19 Alma Rd., London SW18 1AA United Kingdom. **E-mail:** 4AD@4AD.com. **Website:** www.4ad.com. **HOW TO CONTACT** Send an e-mail to request permission to submit. "Sadly, there just aren't enough hours in the day to respond to everything that comes in. We'll only get in touch if we really like something." **MUSIC** Mostly **rock, indie/alternative**. Current artists include Blonde Redhead, Bon Iver, Camera Obscura, The Breeders, The National, TV On The Radio, and more.

ALBANY RECORDS

915 Broadway, Albany NY 12207. **E-mail:** infoalbany@aol.com. **Website:** www.albanyrecords.com. "Do you enjoy classical music that is off the beaten path? Are you frustrated by the lack of imaginative releases by the major classical labels? Albany Records is where you should look. Albany Records is devoted to music by American composers (with a few notable exceptions) performed by the best of America's artists. From premiere recordings of orchestral music by Roy Harris, Morton Gould and Don Gillis to music by George Lloyd and Andrei Eshpai, there is something for everyone on Albany Records––provided your interests are just a bit out of the ordinary."
MUSIC **Choral, chamber, opera, instrumental, organ, wind & brass, percussion, classical, world**, etc.

ARKADIA ENTERTAINMENT CORP.

P.O. Box 77, Saugerties NY 12477. (845)246-9955. **Fax:** (845)246-9966. **E-mail:** info@view.com. **E-mail:** acquisitions@view.com. **Website:** www.view.com/arkadia.aspx. Labels include Arkadia Jazz and Arkadia Chansons. Record company, music publisher (Arkadia Music), record producer (Arkadia Productions), and Arkadia Video. Estab. 1995.
HOW TO CONTACT *Write or call first and obtain permission to submit.*
MUSIC Mostly **jazz, classical**, and **pop/R&B**; also **world**.

ASTRALWERKS

101 Avenue of the Americas, 10th Floor, New York NY 10013. **E-mail:** astralwerks.astralwerks@gmail.com. **Website:** www.astralwerks.com.

- Astralwerks is a subsidiary of the EMI Group, one of the "Big 4" major labels. EMI is a British-based company.

HOW TO CONTACT *Does not accept unsolicited submisisons.*
MUSIC Mostly **alternative/indie/electronic**. Artists include VHS or BETA, Badly Drawn Boy, The Beta Band, Chemical Brothers, Turin Breaks, and Fatboy Slim.

ATLAN-DEC/GROOVELINE RECORDS

2529 Green Forest Court, Snellville GA 30078-4183. (877)751-5169. **E-mail:** atlandec@prodigy.net. **Website:** www.atlan-dec.com. **Contact:** James Hatcher A&R. This company has grown to boast a roster of artists representing different genres of music. "Our artists' diversity brings a unique quality of musicianship. This uniqueness excites our listeners and has gained us the reputation of releasing only the very best in recorded music." Atlan-Dec/Grooveline Records CDs are distributed worldwide through traditional and virtual online retail stores. Record company, music publisher and record producer. Staff size: 2. Releases 3-4 singles, 3-4 LPs and 3-4 CDs/year. Pays 10-25% royalty to artists on contract; statutory rate to publisher per song on record.
DISTRIBUTED BY The Orchard & CD Baby.
HOW TO CONTACT Submit demo package by mail. Unsolicited submissions are OK. Prefers CD with lyric sheet. Does not return material. Responds in 3 months.
MUSIC Mostly **R&B/urban, hip-hop/rap**, and **contemporary jazz**; also **soft rock, gospel, dance**, and **new country**. Released "Temptation" by Shawree, released 2004 on Atlan-Dec/Grooveline Records; *Enemy of the State* (album), recorded by Lowlife (rap/hip-hop); *I'm The Definition* (album), recorded by L.S. (rap/hip-hop), released 2007; "AHHW" (single), recorded by LeTebony Simmons (R&B), released 2007. Other artists include Furious D (rap/hip-hop), Mark Cocker (new country), and Looka, "From the Top" (rap/hip-hop) recorded in 2008.

ATLANTIC RECORDS

1290 Avenue of the Americas, New York NY 10104. (212)707-2000. **Fax:** (212)581-6414. **E-mail:** contact@atlanticrecords.com. **Website:** www.atlanticrecords.com. Labels include Big Beat Records, LAVA, Nonesuch Records, Atlantic Classics, and Rhino Records. Record company. Pays negotiable royalty to artists on contract; negotiable rate to publisher per song on record.

○ Atlantic Records is a subsidiary of Warner Music Group, one of the "Big 4" major labels.

DISTRIBUTED BY WEA.

HOW TO CONTACT *Does not accept unsolicited material.* "No phone calls please."

MUSIC Artists include Missy Elliott, Simple Plan, Lupe Fiasco, Phil Collins, B.O.B., Jason Mraz, and Death Cab For Cutie.

●○ AWAL

1019 17th Ave. S., Suite 201, Nashville TN 37212. **E-mail:** info@awal.com. **Website:** www.awal.com.

DISTRIBUTED BY AWAL, or Artists Without a Label, is a full-featured music services platform for independent artists. Sister company of Kobalt Music (listing in Music Publishers). Services include distribution, marketing, etc.

HOW TO CONTACT Click the "Join Us" link on the site to receive an e-mail with application and membership details.

MUSIC All genres.

⊘ AWARE RECORDS

800 18th Ave., Suite C, Nashville TN 37203. (615)864-8043. **E-mail:** info@awaremusic.com. **Website:** www. awaremusic.com.

HOW TO CONTACT *Does not accept unsolicited submissions.*

MUSIC Mostly **rock/pop**. Artists include Mat Kearney and Guster.

●○ BAD TASTE RECORDS

Box 1243, S - 221 05 Lund, Sweden. **E-mail:** info@badtasterecords.se. **Website:** www.badtasteempire.com.

HOW TO CONTACT "We listen to everything we receive. It usually takes awhile because we receive a lot of demos, but eventually we always listen to it. Send CDs to the address above. Do not e-mail MP3s. With the amount of demos we receive there is rarely time to write back, unless of course we're interested in releasing your band or including a song on one of our compilations. Please don't be too disappointed by this. We would love to be able to write back to everyone, but we are already working days, nights and weekends to try and get things done." Just in case, though, please include your e-mail address. More details are posted on the website.

MUSIC Works with bands such as Danko Jones, Logh, Quit Your Dayjob, Embee, Lemonheads, Langhorns, and more.

◑ BIG COFFEE RECORDS

4867 Ashford Dunwoody Rd. #6202, Atlanta GA 30338. (404) 890-8724. **E-mail:** info@bigcoffeerecords.com. **Website:** www.bigcoffeerecords.com. Big Coffee Records is an independent record label located in Atlanta, Georgia, dedicated to releasing like-minded quality local music in many genres, including: rock, Southern rock, blues, R&B, Americana, contemporary jazz, smooth jazz, groove, club, as well as New Age, stress relief, meditation, healing, with music for film, TV, and advertising placement.

MUSIC Artists include Mose Jones, Steve McRay, Java Monkey, Cole/Taylor, Francine Reed, etc.

○ BIG FACE ENTERTAINMENT

100 State St., Suite 360, Albany NY 12207. **E-mail:** info@bigfaceonline.com. **Website:** www.bigfaceonline.com. Big Face Entertainment, your hybrid record label that offers multi-dimensional services that caters to the artists. "In other words, we are the house that creates the product and puts it out there! We focus on what is truly important at our company opposed to others; investing in the music and talented artists that create the content. We believe in creating a collaborative and innovative environment where our artist can thrive and reach their full capacity in a stress-free atmosphere."

MUSIC Artists include Legend, Island Boy, Daytona, and more. **Rap**, **hip-hop**, **pop**, etc.

◑ BIG HEAVY WORLD

P.O. Box 428, Burlington VT 05402-0428. (802) 865-1140. **E-mail:** info@bigheavyworld.com. **Website:** www.bigheavyworld.com. "Big Heavy World has been pulling together compilations of Vermont artists since 1996 with the release of Sonic Tonic, the indie-alt-core battle cry of our veteran scene-pimping phalanx. We've plowed lovingly through more than 15 titles and continue to unite regional musicians within projects that ultimately, we hope, bring recognition to Vermont's deserving music community and maybe make the world a better place in the process. Most Big Heavy World compilations and their release parties have created exposure and fiscal support for worthy humanitarian organizations like Spectrum Youth and Family Services, the Make A Wish Foundation, the Women's Rape Crisis Center, 242 Main, and Vietnam Assistance for the Handicapped."

❶ BLACKHEART RECORDS

636 Broadway, New York NY 10012. (212)353-9600. **Fax:** (212)353-8300. **E-mail:** blackheart@blackheart.com. **Website:** www.blackheart.com.

HOW TO CONTACT Unsolicited submissions are OK. E-mail before submitting. Responds only if interested.

MUSIC Mostly **rock**. Artists include Joan Jett & the Blackhearts, The Dollyrots, The Vacancies, Girl In A Coma, and The Eyeliners.

○ BLANK TAPE RECORDS

E-mail: blanktaperecords@gmail.com. **Website:** www.blanktaperecords.org. Blank Tape Records is a collectively owned and operated independent record label based in southern Colorado dedicated to creating and sharing music. "Our artists make up songs, wander and sing cross-country, conjure spirits and invent albums so that we might do the impossible and make a living out of our curiosities." Since 2008, Blank Tape has released over 20 albums, the majority featuring the diverse and talented music scene of the front range.

MUSIC Roster includes The Changing Colors, The Haunted Windchimes, Mike Clark & The Sugar Sounds, Grant Sabin, Desirae Garcia, and more.

TIPS "We are friends helping friends put out records, working through an organic process. We don't make our artists sign contracts, so our relationships are based on friendship, good work ethic and trust. We all contribute to the Blank Tape Family in some way, shape, or form; we are artists, designers, social media managers, photographers, envelope stuffers, web designers, audio engineers and videographers dedicated to each other's vision and dream. New bands and artists come into the fold when they have made a mark within our community and there is a mutual agreement that we can benefit from one another."

CAMBRIA RECORDS & PUBLISHING

P.O. Box 374, Lomita CA 90717. (310)831-1322. **Fax:** (310)833-7442. **E-mail:** cambriamus@aol.com. **Website:** cambriamus.com.

DISTRIBUTED BY Albany Distribution.

HOW TO CONTACT *Write first and obtain permission to submit.*

MUSIC Mostly **classical**. Released *Songs of Elinor Remick Warren* (album) on Cambria Records. Other artists include Marie Gibson (soprano), Leonard Pennario (piano), Thomas Hampson (voice), Mischa Leftkowitz (violin), Leigh Kaplan (piano), North Wind Quintet, and Sierra Wind Quintet.

❷ CAPITOL RECORDS

1750 N. Vine St., Hollywood CA 90028. (323)462-6252. **Fax:** (323)469-4542. **Website:** www.capitolrecords.com. Labels include Blue Note Records, Grand Royal Records, Pangaea Records, The Right Stuff Records and Capitol Nashville Records.

❍   Capitol Records is a subsidiary of the EMI Group, one of the "Big 4" major labels.

DISTRIBUTED BY EMD.

HOW TO CONTACT *Capitol Records does not accept unsolicited submissions.*

MUSIC Artists include Coldplay, The Decemberists, Beastie Boys, Katy Perry, Interpol, Lily Allen, and Depeche Mode.

❷❀ CAPP RECORDS, INC.

P.O. Box 150871, San Rafael CA 94915-0871. (415)457-8617. **E-mail:** tim@capprecords.com. **Website:** www.capprecords.com. **Contact:** Tim Davis. CAPP Records, Inc. is an American record label and synch licensing company based in the San Francisco Bay area of California which was founded in 1995 by Dominique C. Toulon & Marc J. Oshry.

HOW TO CONTACT Submit 1-3 best songs by e-mail only to Tim Davis/A&R. Unsolicited submissions are OK. Prefers MP3 (320k) files or direct-streaming links for listening. Only responds if interested.

FILM & TV Places 100-plus songs in TV, film, and advertising per year. Currently doing music placements: NBC/Universal, Arnold Advertising, *Keeping Up With the Kardashians*, MTV, VH1, A&E Network, Discovery Channel, and more.

MUSIC Represents all styles of premium-quality recordings only.

❷ COLUMBIA RECORDS

550 Madison Ave., 23rd Floor, New York NY 10022. (212)833-4000. **Fax:** (212)833-4389. **Website:** www.columbiarecords.com. Record company.

❍   Columbia Records is a subsidiary of Sony BMG, one of the "Big 4" major labels.

DISTRIBUTED BY Sony.

HOW TO CONTACT *Columbia Records does not accept unsolicited submissions.*

MUSIC Artists include Aerosmith, Marc Anthony, Beyonce, Bob Dylan, and Patti Smith.

⊘ COSMOTONE RECORDS

2951 Marina Bay Dr., Suite 130, PMB 501, League City TX 77573-2733. **E-mail:** marianland@earthlink.net. **Website:** www.marianland.com/music.html; www.cosmotonerecords.com. Record company, music publisher (Cosmotone Music, ASCAP), and record producer (Rafael Brom).

DISTRIBUTED BY marianland.com

HOW TO CONTACT *"Sorry, we do not accept material at this time."* Does not return materials.

MUSIC Mostly **Christian pop/rock**. Released *Rafael Brom I, Padre Pio, Lord Hamilton, Dance for Padre Pio, Peace of Heart, Music for Peace of Mind, The Sounds of Heaven, The Christmas Songs, Angelophany, The True Measure of Love, All My Love to You Jesus* (albums), and *Rafael Brom Unplugged* (live concert DVD), *Life is Good, Enjoy it While You Can, Change*, by Rafael Brom, *Refugee from Socialism* by Rafael Brom, and *Move Your Ass*, by Rafael Brom, *Peanut Regatta* by Rafael Brom, and *Best of Rafael Brom*, Volume I, II, III and IV.

CULT RECORDS

P.O. Box 25911, Brooklyn NY 11202. **E-mail:** info@cultrecords.com. **Website:** www.cultrecords.com. Founded and run by Julian Casablancas, Cult Records is an indie-record label. Focused on quality over quantity, Cult is pledged to the highest standard for every song on each record it puts out.

HOW TO CONTACT Submit demos through online form on the site.

MUSIC "Our current roster includes Julian Casablancas + The Voidz, Karen O, Har Mar Superstar, Nelson London (C O L O R), Rey Pila, Cerebral Ballzy and Albert Hammond, Jr." Previous releases include The Virgins, Exclamation Pony, and Reputante.

⊘ CURB RECORDS

48 Music Square E., Nashville TN 37203. (615)321-5080. **Fax:** (615)327-1964. **Website:** www.curb.com.

HOW TO CONTACT *Curb Records does not accept unsolicited submissions; accepts previously published material only. Do not submit without permission.*

MUSIC Released *Everywhere* (album), recorded by Tim McGraw; *Sittin' On Top of the World* (album), recorded by LeAnn Rimes; and *I'm Alright* (album), recorded by Jo Dee Messina, all on Curb Records. Other artists include Mary Black, Merle Haggard, David Kersh, Lyle Lovett, Tim McGraw, Wynonna, and Sawyer Brown.

O DENTAL RECORDS

P.O. Box 20058, New York NY 10017. **E-mail:** artvscommerce@dentalrecords.com. **Website:** www.dentalrecords.com.

HOW TO CONTACT "Check website to see if your material is appropriate." *Not currently accepting unsolicited submissions.*

MUSIC **Pop-derived structures**, **jazz-derived harmonies**, and **neo-classic-wannabee-pretenses**. Claims no expertise, nor interest, in urban, heavy metal, or hard core. Released *Perspectivism* (album), written and recorded by Rick Sanford (instrumental), released 2003 on Dental Records. Other artists include Les Izmor.

DIM MAK

Los Angeles CA **E-mail:** demos@dimmak.com. **Website:** www.dimmak.com. Dim Mak is an independent record label, events company, and lifestyle brand founded by Steve Aoki. The label has released music in **punk**, **indie rock**, **hardcore**, and **electronic dance**.

DIZZYBIRD RECORDS

Grand Rapids MI **Website:** dizzybirdrecords.com. Dizzybird Records was established "by a couple of kids who decided to ignore various reports claiming the music industry was unfit for dreamers. After years of putting a magnifying glass up to notes, giving into the addiction that compels one to not miss a show, swimming laps in an ocean of beer, programming community radio shows, curating jukebox playlists, and staring at the moon with a glorious mixture of confusion and excitement ... this bird has landed."

HOW TO CONTACT Contact via online form.

TIPS "There are two of us here. At any given moment, we are either texting each other about how we disagree on promo artwork or sharing dreamy-fuzzed-out songs we just discovered. It's like living in a snow globe. That said, feel free to reach out using those Internet windows over there. Maybe we can dream together?!!? Chirp."

DOMINO RECORDING CO.

P.O. Box 47029, London SW18 1EG United Kingdom. **Website:** www.dominorecordco.us. The Domino Record Co. was founded by Laurence Bell, and its first release was Sebadoh's "Soul and Fire." Since then, the label has developed a mix of lo-fi and experimental acts.

HOW TO CONTACT *Domino is no longer accepting postal submissions of demos.* "If you truly believe your music belongs on Domino, you can submit your recordings via a message through our environmentally friendly Soundcloud. Log in to your Soundcloud account and then click on the Send a Message icon below our logo."

DOUBLE DOUBLE WHAMMY

338 W. Ridgewood Ave., Ridgewood NJ **E-mail:** hello@dbldblwhmmy.com. **Website:** dbldblwhmmy.com.

HOW TO CONTACT Currently not accepting demo submissions. Check website for updates.

MUSIC Currently releasing records and tapes from LVL UP, Crying, Frankie Cosmos, Free Cake For Every Creature, QUARTERBACKS, Radiator Hospital, Flashlight O, Mitski, and Liam Betson.

EARACHE RECORDS

4402 11th St., #400A, Long Island City NY 11101. (347)507-1402. **Website:** www.earache.com.

MUSIC Rock, industrial, heavy metal techno, death metal, grindcore. Artists include Municipal Waste, Dillinger Escape Plan, Bring Me the Horizon, Deicide, Oceano, and more.

⊘ ELEKTRA RECORDS

75 Rockefeller Plaza, 17th Floor, New York NY 10019. **Website:** www.elektra.com.

Elektra Records is a subsidiary of Warner Music Group, one of the "Big 4" major labels.

DISTRIBUTED BY WEA.

HOW TO CONTACT *Elektra does not accept unsolicited submissions.*

MUSIC Mostly **alternative/modern rock.** Artists include Bruno Mars, Cee Lo, Justice, Little Boots, and *True Blood.*

⊘ EPIC RECORDS

550 Madison Ave., 23rd Floor, New York NY 10022. (212)833-8000. **Fax:** (212)833-4054. **Website:** www.epicrecords.com. Labels include Beluga Heights, Daylight Records and E1 Music. Record company.

Epic Records is a subsidiary of Sony BMG, one of the "Big 4" major labels.

DISTRIBUTED BY Sony Music Distribution.

HOW TO CONTACT *Write or call first and obtain permission to submit* (New York office only). Does not return material. Responds only if interested. *Santa Monica and Nashville offices do not accept unsolicited submissions.*

MUSIC Artists include Sade, Shakira, Modest Mouse, The Fray, Natasha Bedingfield, Sean Kingston, Incubus, The Script.

TIPS "Do an internship if you don't have experience or work as someone's assistant. Learn the business and work hard while you figure out what your talents are and where you fit in. Once you figure out which area of the record company you're suited for, focus on that, work hard at it, and it shall be yours."

⊘ EPITAPH RECORDS

2798 Sunset Blvd., Los Angeles CA 90026. (213)355-5000. **E-mail:** publicity@epitaph.com. **Website:** www.epitaph.com. Record company. Contains imprints Hellcat Records and Anti. "Epitaph Records was founded by Bad Religion guitarist Brett Gurewitz with the aim of starting an artist-friendly label from a musician's point of view. Perhaps most well known for being the little indie from Los Angeles that spawned the 1990s punk explosion."

HOW TO CONTACT "Post your demos online at one of the many free music portals, then simply fill out the Demo Submission form on website."

MUSIC Artists include Social Distortion, Alkaline Trio, Rancid, The Weakerthans, Weezer, Bad Religion, Every Time I Die.

○ EQUAL VISION RECORDS

P.O. Box 38202, Albany NY 12203-8202. (518)458-8250. **E-mail:** info@equalvision.com. **E-mail:** music@equalvision.com. **Website:** equalvision.com. "We're an independent record label entirely owned and operated with no outside financial support. We are, however, distributed by the Alternative Distribution Alliance (ADA Music), which is a subsidiary of Warner Music Group. ADA also distributes some of our favorite independent labels, such as Sub Pop, Epitaph, Saddle Creek, Atlantic, Doghouse, Fearless, Hopeless, Matador, Merge, Polyvinyl, and more."

HOW TO CONTACT In an effort to become more environmentally friendly, Equal Vision Records no longer accepts unsolicited physical demos. Instead, please e-mail music@equalvision.com with a link to your songs on the Web. It's much faster, cheaper, and easier to listen to music online. "If we like your tunes, we'll request a CD or demo package."

TIPS "We love talking about music, but, unfortunately, we can't respond or give tips to every band that sends in a submission; there just aren't enough hours in the day, and we need to devote our time to our current artists. Instead, spend your time writing the best music you can. Travel, tour, flyer, and build your band on your own. The harder you work, the more likely we are to notice."

❶ ETERNAL OTTER RECORDS

8 Mayo St. #2, Portland ME 04101. **Website:** www.eternalotterrecords.com. Eternal Otter Records is an online music label devoted to limited-edition recordings of exceptional musical talents, drawn primarily from the Portland, Maine, area. The criterion for all Eternal Otter releases is not simply the talent of the individual artist; it is, to a larger extent, defined by the enduring, timeless nature of the music itself.

HOW TO CONTACT Contact via online form.

MUSIC Artists include Cerebus Soul, Lady Lamb and Beekeeper, The Milkman's Union, Jesse Pilgrim & the Bonfire, Panda Bandits, and more.

FATHER/DAUGHTER RECORDS

San Francisco CA **E-mail:** daughter@fatherdaughterrecords.com. **Website:** www.fatherdaughterrecords.com. Father/Daughter are 2 folks, bound by blood but years apart. Run out of 2 homes in San Francisco and Miami, the love of music brings this long-distance family just that much closer.

HOW TO CONTACT "Got some tunes to send our way or just want to say hi? E-mail us at daughter@fatherdaughterrecords.com."

⊘ FAT POSSUM RECORDS

Oxford MS **Website:** www.fatpossum.com. Fat Possum Records is an independent record label that was originally focused on recording previously unknown Mississippi blues artists but has recently signed some younger acts to its roster.

⊘ FAT WRECK CHORDS

2196 Palon Ave., San Francisco CA 94124. **E-mail:** mailbag@fatwreck.com. **Website:** www.fatwreck.com.

MUSIC **Punk**, **rock**, **alternative**. Artists include NOFX, Rise Against, The Lawrence Arms, Anti-Flag, Me First and the Gimme Gimmes, Propagandhi, Dillinger Four, Against Me!, and more.

FEARLESS RECORDS

13772 Goldenwest St. #545, Westminster CA 92683. **E-mail:** demos@fearlessrecords.com. **Website:** www.fearlessrecords.com.

HOW TO CONTACT Send all demos to mailing address. "Do not e-mail us about demos or with links to MP3s."

MUSIC **Alternative, pop, indie, rock, metal**. Artists include Plain White T's, Mayday Parade, Blessthefall, Breathe Carolina, The Summer Set, Forever The Sickest Kids, The Downtown Fiction, Real Friends, Jason Lancaster (Go Radio), Motionless In White, and more.

◯ FIREANT

2009 Ashland Ave., Charlotte NC 28205. (704)335-1400. **E-mail:** lewh@fireantmusic.com. **Website:** www.fireantmusic.com.

DISTRIBUTED BY The Orchard, City Hall Records, and eMusic.com.

HOW TO CONTACT Submit demo by mail. Unsolicited submissions are OK. Does not return material.

MUSIC Mostly **progressive**, **traditional**, and **musical hybrids**. "Anything except New Age and MOR." Released *Loving the Alien: Athens Georgia Salutes David Bowie* (album), recorded by various artists (rock/alternative/electronic); and *Good Enough* (album), recorded by Zen Frisbee. Other artists include Mr. Peters' Belizean Boom and Chime Band.

◯ FLYING HEART RECORDS

4015 NE 12th Ave., Portland OR 97212. **E-mail:** flyheart@teleport.com. **Website:** http://home.teleport.com/~flyheart.

DISTRIBUTED BY Burnside Distribution Co.

HOW TO CONTACT Submit demo by mail. Unsolicited submissions are OK. Prefers CD with 1-10 songs and lyric sheets. Does not return material. "SASE required for *any* response." Responds in 3 months.

MUSIC Mostly **R&B**, **blues**, and **jazz**; also **rock**. Released *Vexatious Progr.* (album), written and recorded by Eddie Harris (jazz); *Juke Music* (album), written and recorded by Thara Memory (jazz); and *Lookie Tookie* (album), written and recorded by Jan Celt (blues), all on Flying Heart Records. Other artists include Janice Scroggins, Tom McFarland, Thara Memory, and Snow Bud & The Flower People.

FOOL'S GOLD

536 Metropolitan Ave., Brooklyn NY 11211. **E-mail:** info@foolsgoldrecs.com. **E-mail:** demos@foolsgold-recs.com. **Website:** www.foolsgoldrecs.com. Fool's Gold was founded by DJs A-Trak and Nick Catchdubs and quickly established itself with a non-stop series of releases bridging the worlds of hip hop and electronic music.

○ FORGED ARTIFACTS

5000 Lyndale Ave. S., Unit 1, Minneapolis MN 55419. **E-mail:** forgedartifacts@gmail.com. **Website:** www.forgedartifacts.com. **Contact:** Matt Linden. An indie record company based in Minneapolis, Minnesota.

HOW TO CONTACT Feel free to send demos/sounds to forgedartifacts@gmail.com. Streamable links only. If you have physical demos, send them to the address above.

MUSIC Artists include Some Pulp, Baked, Gloss, France Camp, Nice Purse, and more.

FRENCHKISS RECORDS

111 E. 14th St., Suite 229, New York NY 10003. **E-mail:** info@frenchkissrecords.com. **Website:** www.french-kissrecords.com. Frenchkiss Records was founded by Syd Butler.

HOW TO CONTACT *Does not accept demo submissions via mail.* "Submit your 2 best songs (no downloads; e-mails with downloads get deleted) via e-mail with 'DEMO' in the subject line."

TIPS "We listen to everything we get; if we like what we hear, we will contact you."

○ FUELED BY RAMEN

1633 Broadway, 10th Floor, New York NY 10019. **Website:** www.fueledbyramen.com.

HOW TO CONTACT Send demos by mail to address above. Do not e-mail about demos. Make sure there's a bio, contact information, touring information, and more. "Your music will speak for itself, but the packaging is our first impression of your band. There is no bigger frustration than opening a package

and seeing a demo that looks like it was sent without even trying."

MUSIC Alternative, rock, indie. Artists include The Academy Is..., Cobra Starship, Gym Class Heroes, Panic! at the Disco, Paramore, Sublime with Rome, This Providence, and more.

TIPS "To be honest, each one of our bands has been signed for different reasons, and there are numerous things that we always look for—from your music, to your work ethic, to your personality, to everything in between. The most important thing you can do is work hard and accomplish as much as you can for your band before trying to get signed to a label. Develop a local following, tour the country, record an EP, start a street team, get interviewed by your local publications, etc.—we look for bands that are creating their own buzz and aren't depending on somebody else to do it for them. Putting all you can into your band will attract labels wishing to do the same."

◑ MARTY GARRETT ENTERTAINMENT

320 W. Utica Place, Broken Arrow OK 74011. (918) 451-6780. **E-mail:** martygarrett@earthlink.net. **Website:** http://martygarrettent.homestead.com; www.musicbusinessmoney.homestead.com. **Contact:** Marty R. Garrett, president. Labels include Lonesome Wind Records. Record company, record producer, music publisher, and entertainment consultant. Authorized agent for Christian music artist David Ingles. Releases 1 CD/year. Pays negotiable royalty to artists on contract; statutory rate to publisher per song on record.

HOW TO CONTACT Call or check website to review submission instructions and if submissions are currently being accepted. Prefers CD only and lyric or lead sheets with chord progressions listed. Does not return material. Do not send press packs or bios unless specifically instructed to do so. Responds in 4-6 weeks.

MUSIC Mostly **scripture-based Christian** and **gospel**, **honky tonk**, and **traditional country**. Released "Somebody Somewhere" by Marty Garrett on Lonesome Wind Records. Co-produced and released The Very Best Of David Ingles on DIP Records.

TIPS "We help artists record and release major-label quality CD products to the public for sale through any number of methods, including Radio and 1-800 TV. Although we do submit finished products to major record companies for review, our main focus is to establish and surround each artist with his or her own long-term production, promotion and distribution organization. Professional studio demos are not required, but make sure vocals are distinct, up-front, and up-to-date. I personally listen to each submission received, so call or check website FIRST to see if I am conducting reviews."

GLASSNOTE RECORDS

770 Lexington Ave., 16th Floor, New York NY 10065. (646)214-6000. **Fax:** (646)237-2711. **E-mail:** demos@ glassnotemusic.com. **Website:** www.glassnotemusic. com. Glassnote Entertainment Group is a full-service independent music company founded by Daniel Glass, one of the most accomplished and respected music people in the industry. His devotion to music and the artists that create this magic is what drove him to create the new company.

HOW TO CONTACT Send submissions by post or e-mail. However, do not e-mail MP3s to all e-mail addresses—only to the demos e-mail address.

TIPS "We do receive a lot of submissions, but someone will listen to it. We understand you've worked hard on your music, and we think you've earned at least that. However, submissions that come from managers, lawyers, agents or other people that we know or would like to know do receive priority."

O GRAVEFACE

5 West 40th St., Savannah GA 31401. **E-mail:** mail@ graveface.com. **Website:** www.graveface.com. Graveface is an extremely small recording label. "We are constantly searching for brilliant music to release to the world. If you are a fan of the music we already release, feel free to send us samples of your brilliance. We might reply back to you and we might not. We are happy with our little roster but if you really impress us, you will certainly be getting an e-mail."

MUSIC Artists include The Appleseed Cast, Creepoid, Dosh, The Loose Salute, The Casket Girls, The Stargazer Lilies, Hospital Ships, Gramma's Boyfriend, Dreamend, and many more.

O HACIENDA RECORDS & RECORDING STUDIO

1236 S. Staples St., Corpus Christi TX 78404. (361)882-7066. **Fax:** (361)882-3943. **E-mail:** sales@hac"endarecords.com. **Website:** http://hacienda-records. myshopify.com.

HOW TO CONTACT Submit demo package by mail. Unsolicited submissions are OK. Prefers CD with cover letter. Does not return material. Responds in 6 weeks.

MUSIC Mostly **tejano**, **regional Mexican**, **country** (Spanish or English), and **pop**. Released "Chica Bonita" (single), recorded by Albert Zamora and D.J. Cubanito; "Si Quieres Verme Llorar" (single) from *Lisa Lopez con Mariachi* (album), recorded by Lisa Lopez (mariachi); "Tartamudo" (single) from *Una Vez Mas* (album), recorded by Peligro (norteno); and "Miento" (single) from *Si Tu Te Vas* (album), recorded by Traizion (tejano). Other artists include, Gary Hobbs, Steve Jordan, Grammy Award nominees Mingo Saldivar and David Lee Garza, Michelle, Victoria Y Sus Chikos, La Traizion.

◑ HARDROC RECORDS

Website: www.hardrocrecords.com. HardRoc Records is an independent record label based out of Newark, New Jersey. With its deep connection to street music and support of mainstream flair, Hardroc has made itself the base for the most relevant and promising artists from New Jersey and the Tristate area.

HOW TO CONTACT Use online form to contact.

MUSIC Artists include Nice and Ill, Roky Reign, Chad B., 22 McGraw, Aitch, and more. **Hip-hop**, **rap**, **pop**, **trance**, etc.

⊘ HEADS UP INT., LTD.

Concord Music Group, 100 N. Crescent Dr., Garden Level, Beverly Hills CA 90210. **Website:** www.concordmusicgroup.com/labels/Heads-Up/.

MUSIC Mostly **jazz**, **R&B**, **pop** and **world**. Does not want anything else. Released *Long Walk to Freedom* (album), recorded by Ladysmith Black Mambazo (world); *Pilgrimage* (album), recorded by Michael Brecker (contemporary jazz); *Rizing Sun* (album), recorded by Najee (contemporary jazz). Other artists include Diane Schuur, Mateo Parker, Victor Wooten, Esperanza Spalding, Incognito, George Doke, Take 6, Fourplay.

◑ HOPELESS RECORDS

P.O. Box 7495, Van Nuys CA 91409. **E-mail:** information@hopelessrecords.com. **E-mail:** ar@hopelessrecords.com. **Website:** www.hopelessrecords.com. Founded in 1993, Hopeless Records is a southern

California independent record label home to Yellow-card, All Time Low, Silverstein, Bayside, Enter Shikari, The Wonder Years, Taking Back Sunday, The Used, and many more. Throughout the 20-year history of Hopeless Records, the label has released over 100 albums and launched the careers of Avenged Sevenfold, Thrice, and Melee. In 1999, Hopeless Records formally started supporting nonprofit organizations under the Sub City name with charitable albums, tours, and events. Now a registered 501(c)(3) nonprofit organization, Sub City continues this mission of raising funds and awareness for worthy causes and to-date has raised over $2 million dollars for over 50 nonprofit organizations.

HOW TO CONTACT E-mail ar@hopelessrecords. com with your band name in the subject. Send your bio, YouTube videos, EPKs, etc. If you attach MP3s, do not attach more than 1-2 of your best songs to the e-mail. No longer accepting physical submissions.

MUSIC Works with such artists as Divided by Friday, Bayside, Driver Friendly, New Found Glory, The Used, Taking Back Sunday, Neck Deep, and more.

IDOL RECORDS

P.O. Box 140344, Dallas TX 75214. (214)370-5417. **E-mail:** info@idolrecords.com. **Website:** www.idolrecords.com. **Contact:** Erv Karwelis, president. Releases 30 singles, 80 LPs, 20 EPs and 10-15 CDs/year. Pays negotiable royalty to artists on contract; negotiable rate to publisher per song on record.

DISTRIBUTED BY MVD Entertainment Group.

HOW TO CONTACT Mail to: Idol Records P.O. Box 140344 Dallas, TX 75214. No phone calls or e-mail follow-ups.

FILM & TV Erv Karwelis: erv@idolrecords.com.

MUSIC Mostly **rock**, **pop**, and **alternative**; also some **hip-hop**. *The O's - Between The Two* (album), *Here Holy Spain - Division* (album), *Calhoun - Heavy Sugar* (album), *Little Black Dress - Snow in June* (album), all released 2009-12 on Idol Records. Other artists include Flickerstick, DARYL, Centro-matic, The Deathray Davies, GBH, PPT, The Crash that Took Me, Shibboleth, Trey Johnson, Black Tie Dynasty, Old 97's.

IMAGEN RECORDS

3905 National Dr., Suite 440, Burtonsville MD 20866. **E-mail:** info@imagenrecords.com. **Website:** www. imagenrecords.com. Imagen Records is a full-service indie label based in the Washington, D.C., area. Ima-

gen artists represent the best in rock, pop, hip-hop and R&B. With a growing roster of innovative artists, Imagen Records has significant resources and experience that supports its artists to maximize success. Founded by a musician and businessperson, Imagen artists enjoy a fully collaborative artist development process with a 360-degree perspective. In the current market environment, Imagen has the ability to make significant investments in new talent, which gives it a strong competitive edge in the marketplace. As a label that was founded in 2007, Imagen employs the newest, most innovative methods to maximize use of new media and technologies, including new fan base management and content delivery methods.

HOW TO CONTACT Contact via online form.

MUSIC **Rock**, **pop**, **hip-hop**, and **R&B**. Artists include Framing & Hanley, New Medicine, 3 Years Hollow, Separation, and Candlelight Red.

INTERSCOPE/GEFFEN/A&M RECORDS

2220 Colorado Ave., Santa Monica CA 90404. (310)865-1000. **Fax:** (310)865-7908. **Website:** www. interscope.com. Labels include Blackground Records, Cherrytree Records, will.i.am music group and Aftermath Records. Record company.

Interscope/Geffen/A&M is a subsidiary of Universal Music Group, one of the "Big 4" major labels.

HOW TO CONTACT *Does not accept unsolicited submissions.*

MUSIC Artists include Beck, U2, M.I.A, Keane, Lady Gaga, and ...And You Will Know Us By The Trail Of Dead.

ISLAND/DEF JAM MUSIC GROUP

1755 Broadway, New York NY 10019. (212)333-8000. **Fax:** (212)603-7654. **Website:** www.islanddefjam.com.

Island/Def Jam is a subsidiary of Universal Music Group, one of the "Big 4" major labels.

HOW TO CONTACT *Island/Def Jam Music Group does not accept unsolicited submissions. Do not send material unless requested.*

MUSIC Artists include Bon Jovi, Rick Ross, Fall Out Boy, The Gaslight Anthem, Kanye West, Rihanna, The Killers, Jay-Z, Babyface, Snow Patrol, and Ludacris.

JAGJAGUWAR

1499 W. Second St., Bloomington IN 47403. **E-mail:** info@jagjaguwar.com. **E-mail:** demos@jagjaguwar.

com. **Website:** www.jagjaguwar.com. Jagjaguwar is an independent indie-rock record label.

HOW TO CONTACT "We do accept links to properly labeled, high-quality MP3s or streams as demos; please direct these to demos@jagjaguwar.com. Please do not e-mail MP3s directly, as we will not accept them as such."

TIPS "Please include all your contact information along with your electronic demo submissions; we will contact you if we are interested in what you have sent."

KILL ROCK STARS

107 SE Washington St., Suite 155, Portland OR 97214. **Website:** www.killrockstars.com.

DISTRIBUTED BY Redeye Distribution.

HOW TO CONTACT *Does not accept or listen to demos sent by mail.* Will listen to links online only if in a touring band coming through Portland. "If you are not touring through Portland, don't send us anything." Prefers link to web page or EPK. Does not return material.

MUSIC Mostly **punk rock**, **neo-folk**, or **anti-folk** and **spoken word**. Artists include Deerhoof, The Decemberists, Boats, Xiu Xiu, The Gossip, Horse Feathers, Erase Errata, The Thermals, Kinski, Marnie Stern, and Two Ton Boa.

TIPS "We will only work with touring acts, so let us know if you are playing Portland. Particularly interested in young artists with indie-rock background."

KORDA RECORDS

P.O. Box 2346, Minneapolis MN 55402. **E-mail:** info@kordarecords.com; allison@kordarecords.com. **Website:** www.kordarecords.com. **Contact:** Allison LaBonne. Korda Records is a Minneapolis-based record label cooperative launched by Allison LaBonne (Typsy Panthre, The Starfolk, The Owls), David Schelzel (The Ocean Blue), Brian Tighe (The Starfolk, The Hang Ups, The Owls) and the Legendary Jim Ruiz (Jim Ruiz Set).

MAD DECENT

Los Angeles CA **E-mail:** info@maddecent.com. **E-mail:** demos@maddecent.com. **Website:** www.maddecent.com. Mad Decent is the name of the Los Angeles-based record label spearheaded by Wesley Pentz, better known as Diplo. As an influential label, Mad Decent aims to bring new genres and cultures to light in the ever-diversifying music community. Aside from the music released, Mad Decent is also known for its annual Block Parties, a series of outdoor party/concerts in select cities across the US and Canada.

MAGNA CARTA RECORDS

A-1 Country Club Rd., East Rochester NY 14445. (585)381-5224. **E-mail:** info@magnacarta.net. **Website:** www.magnacarta.net.

HOW TO CONTACT Submit physical demo CD to the address above. Requirements: Artist must be touring. Artist must be established in his or her local scene. Artist must have a Web presence: Facebook, Twitter, YouTube, etc. When sending a physical demo, please take time and effort to package it properly. Include all relevant materials.

MUSIC Mostly **progressive metal**, **progressive rock**, and **progressive jazz**.

MATADOR RECORDS

304 Hudson St., 7th Floor, New York NY 10013. (212)995-5882. **Fax:** (212)995-5883. **E-mail:** info@matadorrecords.com. **Website:** www.matadorrecords.com.

HOW TO CONTACT "We are sorry to say that we *no longer accept unsolicited demo submissions.*"

MUSIC **Alternative rock**. Artists include Lou Reed, Pavement, Belle and Sebastian, Cat Power, Jay Reatard, Sonic Youth, Yo La Tengo, Mogwai, The New Pornographers, and more.

MCA NASHVILLE

1904 Adelicia St., Nashville TN 37212. (615)340-5400. **Fax:** (615)340-5491. **Website:** www.umgnashville.com.

MCA Nashville is a subsidiary of Universal Music Group, one of the "Big 4" major labels.

HOW TO CONTACT *MCA Nashville cannot accept unsolicited submissions.*

MUSIC Artists include Tracy Byrd, George Strait, Vince Gill, Sugarland, The Mavericks, and Shania Twain.

MEGAFORCE RECORDS

P.O. Box 63584, Philadelphia PA 19147. (215)922-4612. **Fax:** (509)757-8602. **Website:** www.megaforcerecords.com.

DISTRIBUTED BY Red/Sony Distribution.

HOW TO CONTACT *Contact first and obtain permission to submit.* Submissions go to the Philadelphia office.

MUSIC Mostly **rock**. Artists include Truth and Salvage, The Meat Puppets, and The Disco Biscuits.

MERGE RECORDS

Durham NC **E-mail:** merge@mergerecords.com. **Website:** www.mergerecords.com. Merge Records is an independent record label founded by Laura Ballance and Mac McCaughan. Started as a way to release music from its band Superchunk, Merge Records now releases music by world-famous artists, including Arcade Fire and Robert Pollard.

◑ METAL BLADE RECORDS

5737 Kanan Rd. #143, Agoura Hills CA 91301. (805)522-9111. **Fax:** (805)522-9380. **E-mail:** metalblade@metalblade.com. **Website:** www.metalblade.com.

HOW TO CONTACT Submit demo through website form. Does not accept physical copies of demos. Unsolicited submissions are OK. Response time varies, but "be patient."

MUSIC Mostly **heavy metal** and **industrial**; also **hardcore**, **gothic** and **noise**. Released "Gallery of Suicide," recorded by Cannibal Corpse; "Voo Doo," recorded by King Diamond; and "A Pleasant Shade of Gray," recorded by Fates Warning, all on Metal Blade Records. Other artists include As I Lay Dying, The Red Chord, The Black Dahlia Murder, and Unearth.

TIPS "Metal Blade is known throughout the underground for quality metal-oriented acts."

MEXICAN SUMMER

87 Guernsey St., Brooklyn NY 11222. **Website:** www.mexicansummer.com. Founded by Kemado Records, Mexican Summer is an independent record label that started out by releasing limited-edition, ornately packaged vinyl pieces. Mexican Summer has since expanded its catalog to more than 100 releases across multiple formats.

◑ MINT 400 RECORDS

E-mail: mint400recs@yahoo.com. **Website:** www.fairmontmusic.com/1/m4r.html. **Contact:** Neil Sabatino, owner. A northern New Jersey indie-rock record label focusing on the digital marketplace.

HOW TO CONTACT Send links to streaming music.

MUSIC Acts include Fairmont, Any Day Parade, The Trashpickers, Dave Charles, Jack Skuller, Ladybirds, Depression State Troopers, Sink Tapes, and many more.

TIPS "I like a lot of different kinds of music and on the label we have everything from old timey country to surf to indie rock to 1960s motown. What I am most interested in is great songwriting and an original singing voice. We do digital distro, recording, producing, engineering, mastering, video editing, Web design, art and graphic design, music licensing, radio promotion and a little PR. Some bands need all of our services and some do not, but we are more than willing to help with every aspect of your music career. We do not give cash advances or tour support. Also, we deal only in digital records and do not press anything. However, for bands who foot the bill for pressings of vinyl we do have distro."

○ MODAL MUSIC, INC.

P.O. Box 6473, Evanston IL 60204-6473. (847)864-1022. **E-mail:** info@modalmusic.com. **E-mail:** modalmusic@juno.com. **Website:** www.modalmusic.com.

HOW TO CONTACT Submit demo package by mail. Unsolicited submissions are OK. Prefers CD with bio, PR, brochures, any info about artist and music. Does not return material. Responds in 4 months.

MUSIC Mostly **ethnic** and **world**. Released "St. James Vet Clinic" (single by T. Doehrer/Z. Doehrer) from *Wolfpak Den Recordings* (album), recorded by Wolfpak; "Dance The Night Away" (single by T. Doehrer) from *Dance The Night Away* (album), recorded by Balkan Rhythm Band™; "Sid Beckerman's Rumanian" (single by D. Jacobs) from *Meet Your Neighbor's Folk Music*™ (album), recorded by Jutta & The Hi-Dukes™; and *Hold Whatcha Got* (album), recorded by Razzemetazz™, all on Modal Music Records. Other artists include Ensemble M'chaiya™, Nordland Band™ and Terran's Greek Band™.

TIPS "Please note our focus is primarily traditional and traditionally based ethnic, which is a very limited, non-mainstream market niche. You waste your time and money by sending us any other type of music. If you are unsure of your music fitting our focus, please call us before sending anything. Put your name and contact info on every item you send!"

MOM + POP MUSIC

New York NY **Website:** www.momandpopmusic.com. Mom + Pop Music is an independent record label launched by Michael Goldstone.

MUSIC Indie and **alternative** music. Mom + Pop Music hosts a total of 22 active artists, including Andrew Bird, Metric, Ingrid Michaelson, and Flume.

○ MTS RECORDS

750 Cedarwood Dr., Pittsburgh PA 15235. **E-mail:** michael@mtsmanagementgroup.com. **Website:** www.mtsrecords.net. "Our artists' releases have received worldwide airplay and have charted on some of the most recognized airplay charts in the industry, including Music Row, New Music Weekly, Mediabase, Roots Music Report, Americana Music Association and more!"

HOW TO CONTACT "Send a link to your website, so we can take a listen. If you want to submit demos, please send no more than 2 MP3s. If we want to hear more, we will ask."

MUTE RECORDS

E-mail: mute@mute.com; demos@mute.com. **Website:** www.mute.com. Mute was founded by Daniel Miller and has since signed and developed some of the world's most influential recording artists, including Depeche Mode, Goldfrapp, and Erasure. The label has always been a champion of electronic music.

HOW TO CONTACT "We love to receive your demos. Please don't send too much material to begin with—3 or 4 of your best tracks is a great start. We're not able to reply individually to everyone, but we can assure you that all demos are reviewed, and we'll be in touch if we like what we hear." Submit no more than 4 streaming links by e-mail.

TIPS *"We no longer accept demos submitted by post."*

NEON GOLD

New York NY **Website:** www.neongoldrecords.com. Neon Gold Records is a boutique record label founded by Derek Davies and Lizzy Plapinger. Initially operating as a vinyl-only singles label, Neon Gold has launched the debut releases of many acts, including Passion Pit, Ellie Goulding, Gotye, and Icona Pop. In 2014, Neon Gold teamed up with Atlantic Records to make Neon Gold an imprint under Atlantic.

●○ NERVOUS RECORDS

5 Sussex Crescent, Northolt, Middx UB5 4DL United Kingdom. 44(020)8423 7373. **Fax:** 44(020)8423 7713. **E-mail:** info@nervous.co.uk. **Website:** www.nervous.co.uk. **Contact:** R. Williams. Record company (Nervous Records), record producer and music publisher (Nervous Publishing and Zorch Music). Member: MCPS, PRS, PPL, ASCAP, NCB. Releases 2 albums/year. Pays 8-12% royalty to artists on contract; statutory rate to publisher per song on records. Royalties paid directly to US songwriters and artists or through US publishing or recording affiliate.

○ Nervous Records' publishing company, Nervous Publishing, is listed in the Music Publishers section.

HOW TO CONTACT Unsolicited submissions are OK. Prefers CD with 4-15 songs and lyric sheet. SAE and IRC. Responds in 3 weeks.

MUSIC Mostly **psychobilly** and **rockabilly**. "No heavy rock, AOR, stadium rock, disco, soul, pop—only wild rockabilly and psychobilly." Released *Extra Chrome*, written and recorded by Johnny Black; *It's Still Rock 'N' Roll to Me*, written and recorded by The Jime. Other artists include Restless Wild and Taggy Tones.

● NIGHT SLUGS

London United Kingdom. **Website:** www.nightslugs.net. Night Slugs is an electronic music label established by Alex Sushon (aka Bok Bok) and James Connolly (aka L-Vis 1990). It was started in response to artists featured at their club nights being unsigned.

OGLIO RECORDS

3540 W. Sahara Ave. #308, Las Vegas NV 89102. (702)800-5500. **Website:** http://oglio.com.

HOW TO CONTACT *No unsolicited demos. Use online form to contact.*

MUSIC Mostly **alternative rock** and **comedy**. Released *Shine* (album), recorded by Cyndi Lauper (pop); *Live At The Roxy* (album), recorded by Brian Wilson (rock); *Team Leader* (album), recorded by George Lopez (comedy).

ORCHID TAPES

Brooklyn NY **E-mail:** orchidtapes@gmail.com. **Website:** orchidtapes.com. Orchid Tapes is a vinyl and free download-based record label run by Warren Hildebrand and Brian Vu, a couple with a shared interest in the creation and curation of music and artwork that breaks free of the established norm, disregards trends, reflects the dedication of its creator and provokes a strong emotional resonance with whomever experiences it. The overall goal of Orchid Tapes is to share and explore music that reflects these ideals with those who are willing and able to listen, and also to unite and expose like-minded artists from all over the world under a collective-style label.

HOW TO CONTACT "While we do accept demo e-mails from bands and musicians, we'd encourage you to read a link on our website, which clarifies our position on demo submissions a bit."

◐◑ THE PANAMA MUSIC GROUP OF COMPANIES

Ebrel House, 2a Penlee Close, Praa Sands, Penzance, Cornwall TR20 9SR England, United Kingdom. +44 (0)1736 762826. **E-mail:** panamus@aol.com. **Website:** www.panamamusic.co.uk, www.songwriters-guild.co.uk, www.digimixrecords.com. **Contact:** R. Jones, CEO; Jack Golding, A&R. Labels include Pure Gold Records, Panama Music Library, Rainy Day Records, Panama Records, Mohock Records, Digimix Records Ltd. (www.digimixrecords.com). Registered members of Phonographic Performance Ltd. (PPL). Record company, music publisher, production and development company (Panama Music Library, Melody First Music Library, Eventide Music Library, Musik Image Music Library, Promo Sonor International Music Library, Caribbean Music Library, ADN Creation Music Library, Piano Bar Music Library, Corelia Music Library, PSI Music Library, Scamp Music, First Time Music Publishing U.K.), Digimix Music Publishing, registered members of the Mechanical Copyright Protection Society (MCPS) and the Performing Right Society (PRS) (London, England UK), management firm and record producer (First Time Management & Production Co.). Staff size: 6. Pays variable royalty to artists on contract; statutory rate to publisher per song on record subject to deal.

DISTRIBUTED BY Media U.K. Distributors and Digimix Worldwide Digital Distribution.

HOW TO CONTACT Submit demo package by mail. Unsolicited submissions are OK. CD or MP3 only with unlimited number of songs/instrumentals and lyric or lead sheets where necessary. "We do not return material so there is no need to send return postage. We will, due to volume of material received, only respond to you if we have any interest. Please note: no MP3 submissions, attachments, downloads, or referrals to websites in the first instance via e-mail. Do not send anything by recorded delivery or courier as it will not be signed for. If we are interested, we will follow up for further requests and offers as necessary."

MUSIC All styles. Published by Scamp Music: "F*ck Me I'm Famous" written by Paul Clarke and Matthew Dick (film/DVD [Universal Films, Hollywood] and single and album track [Universal Records]), released worldwide in *Get Him to the Greek*, Universal films Hollywood, starring Russell Brand, recorded by Dougal & Gammer, "We Killed The Rave" (voted best hardcore track of 2013), recorded by Dougal & Gammer, released as an album track on Clubland Xtreme Hardcore 9 by Universal Records in 2013, published by Scamp Music. Also published "Get Your Lovekicks" (soul/R&B), recorded by Leonie Parker, released by Digimix Records Ltd.; "Country Blues" (country), recorded by The Glen Kirton Country Band on Digimix Records Ltd., published by Scamp Music; "Guitar Hero" (hardcore), recorded by Dougal & Gammer, released by Universal Records/All Around the World; published by Scamp Music: "I Get Stoned" (hardcore dance) recorded by AudioJunkie & Stylus, released by EMI records on *Hardcore Nation 2009*, published by Panama Music Library; "Everytime I Hear Your Name" (pop dance), recorded by Cascada, released by All Around The World/Universal Records, published by Scamp Music; "Illumination—Deep Skies 5" 7 track album (Holistic, mind, body, & soul) by Kevin Kendle release 2015 by Eventide Music and Digimix Records Ltd, published by Panama Music Library; "Heavy Rock Spectacular" Progressive Rock, recorded by Bram Stoker released by Digimix Records Ltd. 2015, published by Scamp Music, and many more.

PAPER + PLASTICK

E-mail: e.customer@paperandplastick.com. **Website:** http://paperandplastick.com.

MUSIC Rock, punk, and more. Artists include: Dopamines, Andrew Dost, Coffee Project, Foundation, Gatorface, Blacklist Royals, Landmines, We are the Union, and more.

PAPER GARDEN RECORDS

170 Tillary St., Apt. 608, Brooklyn NY 11201. **E-mail:** info@papergardenrecords.com. **E-mail:** demos@papergardenrecords.com. **Website:** www.papergardenrecords.com. "Paper Garden Records is a boutique record label in Brooklyn run by 2 lovers, 2 cats, and their friends."

◑ PARLIAMENT RECORDS

Parliament Record Group, Parliament Records, 357 S. Fairfax Ave. #430, Los Angeles CA 90036. (323)653-

0693. **Fax:** (323)653-7670. **E-mail:** parlirec@aol.com. **E-mail:** Parlirec@aol.com. **Website:** www.parliamentrecords.com. **Contact:** Benny Weisman.

HOW TO CONTACT Submit demo package by mail. Unsolicited submissions are OK. Prefers CD with 3-10 songs and lyric sheet. Include SASE. "Mention *Songwriter's Market*. Please make return envelope the same size as the envelopes you send material in, otherwise we cannot send everything back." Responds in 6 weeks.

MUSIC Mostly **R&B**, **soul**, **dance**, and **top 40/pop**; also **gospel** and **blues**. Arists include Rapture 7 (male gospel group), Wisdom Gospel Singers (male gospel group), Chosen Gospel Recovery (female gospel group), Jewel With Love (female gospel group), Apostle J. Dancy (gospel), TooMiraqulas (rap), The Mighty Voices of Joy (male gospel group) L'Nee (hip hop/soul).

TIPS "Parliament Records will also listen to 'tracks' only. If you send tracks, please include a letter stating what equipment you record on—CDs or MP3s."

PARTISAN RECORDS

281 N. 7th St., #2, Brooklyn NY 11211. **E-mail:** info@partisanrecords.com. **Website:** www.partisanrecords.com. **Contact:** Tim Putnam and Ian Wheeler. Partisan Records is a Brooklyn-based artist-run independent label dedicated to the unique visions of those we are so privileged to represent. We believe that artistry in its many forms essentially has a singular purpose: to create and share the next new story. At Partisan, our artists create the stories that others will tell.

MUSIC Current artists include Callers, Ages of Ages, Deer Tick, Amy Wells, Dolorean, Middle Brother, Heartless Bastards, Lumerians, Phox, Mountain Man, more.

PC MUSIC

London United Kingdom. **E-mail:** demos@pcmusic.info. **Website:** pcmusic.info. PC Music is a record label and music-making collective run by producer A.G. Cook. The label has an eccentric roster of artists who devise alternate personas often inspired by cyberculture. Its releases focus on dance music with pitch-shifted, feminine vocals.

PEAPOD RECORDINGS

P.O. BOX 2631, South Portland ME 04116. **E-mail:** info@peapodrecordings.com. **Website:** www.peapodrecordings.com. **Contact:** Ron Harrity. Peapod Recordings is a small label based out of Portland, Maine.

HOW TO CONTACT "At this time we're not looking for new artists. However, we do love to hear new music, so if you just feel like sharing what you've been up to, please e-mail us with MP3 or .zip file links only. Please no attached MP3s. Also keep in mind that we can't always return e-mails regarding your music. Thanks!"

MUSIC Artists include Dead End Armory, Foam Castles, Brown Bird, If and It, Olas, Dan Blakeslee, Hearts by Darts, Honey Clouds, and many more.

QUARK RECORDS

P.O. Box 452, Newtown CT 06470. (917)687-9988. **E-mail:** ar@quarkmusicgroup.com. **Website:** www.quarkrecordsusa.com. **Contact:** Curtis Urbina, CEO. Record company and music publisher (Quarkette Music/BMI and Freedurb Music/ASCAP). Releases 3 singles and 3 LPs/year. Pays negotiable royalty to artists on contract; $3/_4$ statutory rate to publisher per song on record.

HOW TO CONTACT Prefers CD with 2 songs (max). Include SASE. "Must be an absolute 'hit' song!" Responds in 6 weeks.

MUSIC **Pop** and **electronica** music only.

RADICAL RECORDS

222 Dean St. #1, Brooklyn NY 11217. (212)475-1111. **Fax:** (212)475-3676. **E-mail:** info@radicalrecords.com; keith@radicalrecords.com. **Website:** www.radicalrecords.com. **Contact:** Keith Masco, president; Bryan Mechutan, general manager/sales and marketing. "We do accept unsolicited demos, however, please allow ample time for a response. Also, please note that we deal almost exclusively with punk rock. Feel free to send us your hip-hop, folk, jazz fusion, demo but don't be surprised when we don't show up at your door with a contract. Please make sure you have an e-mail address clearly printed on the disc or case. Most importantly, don't call us, we'll call you."

DISTRIBUTED BY City Hall, Revelation, Select-O-Hits, Choke, Southern, Carrot Top, and other indie distributors.

HOW TO CONTACT *E-mail first for permission to submit demo.* Prefers CD. Does not return material. Responds in 1 month.

MUSIC Mostly **punk**, **hardcore**, **glam** and **rock**.

TIPS "Create the best possible demos you can and show a past of excellent self-promotion."

RAVE RECORDS, INC.

Attn: Production Dept., 13400 W. Seven Mile Rd., Detroit MI 48235. **Website:** www.raverecords.com. **Contact:** Carolyn and Derrick, production managers. Record company and music publisher (Magic Brain Music/ASCAP).

HOW TO CONTACT *"We do not accept unsolicited submissions."*

MUSIC Mostly **alternative rock** and **dance**. Artists include Cyber Cryst, Dorothy, Nicole, and Bukimi 3.

RCA RECORDS

550 Madison Ave., New York NY 10022. **Website:** www.rcarecords.com. Labels include RCA Records Nashville and RCA Victor. Record company.

- RCA Records is a subsidiary of Sony BMG, one of the "Big 4" major labels.

DISTRIBUTED BY BMG.

HOW TO CONTACT *RCA Records does not accept unsolicited submissions.*

MUSIC Artists include The Strokes, Dave Matthews Band, Christina Aguilera, and Foo Fighters.

REPRISE RECORDS

3300 Warner Blvd., 4th Floor, Burbank CA 91505. (818)846-9090. **Website:** www.warnerbrosrecords.com.

- Reprise Records is a subsidiary of Warner Music Group, one of the "Big 4" major labels.

DISTRIBUTED BY WEA.

HOW TO CONTACT *Reprise Records does not accept unsolicited submissions.*

MUSIC Artists include Eric Clapton, My Chemical Romance, Michael Bublé, The Used, Green Day, Alanis Morissette, Fleetwood Mac, and Neil Young.

RHYMESAYERS ENTERTAINMENT

Minneapolis MN **Website:** www.rhymesayers.com. Rhymesayers is an independent hip hop record label. Years after hip-hop began, it boast ones of independent hip-hop's strongest and most respected rosters.

RISE RECORDS

15455 NW Greenbrier Pkwy., Suite 115, Beaverton OR 97006. **E-mail:** matthew@riserecords.com. **Website:** www.riserecords.com. **Contact:** Matthew Gordner.

HOW TO CONTACT E-mail a link to your music (Facebook, Bandcamp, YouTube, or Purevolume) using the e-mail form on the website. "Please save your money and don't mail a press kit. Also, less is more;

just send the link to your music. If we need more information we'll let you know."

MUSIC **Rock, metal, alternative**. Artists include Bouncing Souls, Memphis May Fire, Of Mice & Men, Secrets, Poison The Well, Transit, Hot Water Music, and more.

ROADRUNNER RECORDS

1290 Avenue of the Americas, 28th Floor, New York NY 10104. **E-mail:** publicity@roadrunnerrecords.com. **Website:** www.roadrunnerrecords.com.

HOW TO CONTACT Submit demo by e-mail at signmeto@roadrunnerrecords.com. Submissions are currently open.

MUSIC **Rock**, **metal**, **alternative**. Artists include Korn, Killswitch Engage, Opeth, Nickelback, Lenny Kravitz, Lynyrd Skynyrd, Megadeth, Slipknot, and more.

ROBBINS ENTERTAINMENT LLC

35 Worth St., 4th Floor, New York NY 10013. (212)675-4321. **Fax:** (212)675-4441. **E-mail:** info@robbinsent.com. **Website:** www.robbinsent.com.

DISTRIBUTED BY Sony/BMG.

HOW TO CONTACT "If you're interested in submitting a demo to Robbins Entertainment, please follow these instructions: 1) Make sure that everything is labeled properly, from artist and title to your contact information; 2) Please send us no more than 3 tracks, and make sure they are representative of your very best; 3) Radio edits preferred. If you'd like to send a digital demo, please use download links only (YouSendit, SoundCloud, or FTP etc.) and write to info@robbinsent.com. Do not send MP3s attached to an e-mail. These will automatically be discarded. We do listen to everything that comes through, but please keep in mind that we get a lot of submissions every week. If we like what we hear, we will contact you."

MUSIC **Commercial dance** only. Released top 10 pop smashes: "Heaven" (single), recorded by DJ Sammy; "Everytime We Touch" (single), recorded by Cascada; "Listen To Your Heart" (single), recored by DHT; as well as Hot 100 records from Rockell, Lasgo, Reina and K5. Other artists include: September, Andain, Judy Torres, Jenna Drey, Marly, Dee Dee, Milky, Kreo and many others.

TIPS "Do not send your package 'Supreme-Overnight-Before-You-Wake-Up' delivery. Save yourself some money. Do not send material if you are going to state in your letter that, 'If I had more (fill in the blank) it would sound better.' We are interested in hearing your best and only your best. Do not call us and ask if you can send your package. The answer is yes. We are looking for dance music with crossover potential."

🔘 ROLL CALL RECORDS

Los Angeles CA **E-mail:** info@rollcallrecords.com. **Website:** www.rollcallrecords.com. Come download some music for free at our website.

MUSIC Released albums by such artists as Army Navy, Isbells, Royal Canoe, Typhoon, Wintersleep, and more.

ROTTEN RECORDS

P.O. Box 56, Upland CA 91786. (909)920-4567. **Fax:** (909)920-4577. **E-mail:** rotten@rottenrecords.com. **Website:** www.rottenrecords.com. **Contact:** Ron Peterson, president.

DISTRIBUTED BY RIOT (Australia), Sonic Rendezvous (NL), RED (US) and PHD (Canada).

HOW TO CONTACT Submit demo package by mail. Unsolicited submissions are OK. Prefers CD or MySpace link. Does not return material.

MUSIC Mostly **rock**, **alternative** and **commercial**; also **punk** and **heavy metal**. Released *Paegan Terrorism* (album), written and recorded by Acid Bath; *Kiss the Clown* (album by K. Donivon), recorded by Kiss the Clown; and *Full Speed Ahead* (album by Cassidy/Brecht), recorded by D.R.T., all on Rotten Records.

TIPS "Be patient."

🔘 ROUGH TRADE RECORDS

66 Golborne Rd., London W10 5PS United Kingdom. **E-mail:** demos@roughtraderecords.com. **Website:** www.roughtraderecords.com.

HOW TO CONTACT "Demo submissions are welcome; however, we are not entitled to return any materials submitted to us. Please make sure you keep copies for yourself. Demos should be marked for attention of Paul Jones. Due to the postal delays, you're advised to send MP3 demos online using our Soundcloud page (info on Website)." To e-mail, use online form on the website.

MUSIC Alternative. Artists include Super Furry Animals, Jarvis Cocker, The Hold Steady, Emiliana Torrini, British Sea Power, The Libertines, My Morning Jacket, Jenny Lewis, The Strokes, The Mystery Jets, The Decemberists, and more.

🔘 RUSTIC RECORDS

6337 Murray Lane, Brentwood TN 37027. (615)371-0646. **E-mail:** zach@rusticrecordsinc.com. **Website:** rusticrecordsinc.com. **Contact:** Jack Schneider, president and founder; Nell Schneider; Brien Fisher.

DISTRIBUTED BY CDBaby.com and available on iTunes, MSN Music, Rhapsody, and more.

HOW TO CONTACT Submit professional demo package by mail. Unsolicited submissions are OK. CD only; no MP3s or e-mails. Include no more than 4 songs with corresponding lyric sheets and cover letter. Include appropriately-sized SASE. Responds in 4 weeks.

MUSIC Good combination of traditional and modern **country**. Releases: *Ready to Ride* - debut album from Nikki Britt, featuring "C-O-W-B-O-Y," "Do I Look Like Him," "Star in My Car," and "You Happened;" *Hank Stuff* from DeAnna Cox - featuring "I'm a Long Gone Mama," and "I'm so Lonesome I Could Cry."

TIPS "Professional demo preferred."

SADDLE CREEK

P.O. Box 8554, Omaha NE 68108. **Website:** www.saddle-creek.com. Saddle Creek is an independent record label that supports musicians it believes have the authenticity and talent to captivate and transform culture at large. "We pride ourselves on creating an independent, artist-friendly environment by championing creative control and acting in the best interests of our partners."

HOW TO CONTACT "We don't listen to demos every day, but check them out periodically. If we're interested, we'll get back to you." Submit through online demo submission page.

TIPS "Please note, though, we have never signed a band based on a demo."

🔘 SECRET STASH RECORDS

1621 Hennepin Ave., #150A, Minneapolis MN 55403. **E-mail:** info@secretstashrecords.com. **Website:** www.secretstashrecords.com. Secret Stash Records is an independent record label owned and operated in Minneapolis, Minnesota. "We are dedicated to one thing: releasing great music in great collectible LP packages. Whether you are a DJ looking for rare grooves to sample, or just an average Joe looking for great music, we've got you covered."

HOW TO CONTACT Use online form to contact.

MUSIC Funk, soul, blues.

SILVER WAVE RECORDS

P.O. Box 7943, Boulder CO 80306. (303)443-5617. **Fax:** (303)443-0877. **E-mail:** info@silverwave.com. **Website:** www.silverwave.com. **Contact:** Valerie Sanford, art director.

MUSIC Mostly **Native American** and **world**.

SIMPLY GRAND MUSIC INC

P.O. Box 770208, Memphis TN 38177-0208. (901)763-4787 or (615)515-7772. **E-mail:** info@simplygrandmusic.com. **Website:** www.simplygrandmusic.com. **Contact:** Linda Lucchesi, president. Record company (Simply Grand Music) and music publisher (Beckie Publishing Company). Staff size: 5. Released 5 CDs last year. Royalties are negotiable. Distributed by The Orchard, Ace Records and various others.

HOW TO CONTACT Contact first and obtain permission to submit a demo. E-mail links to download MP3 with lyrics preferred. If sending physical mail, include CD and limit 3 songs per submission. Please give 2-4 weeks for a response. Please include lyrics and a SASE if you want any materials returned.

MUSIC Mostly interested in **country**, **soul/R&B**, **pop**; also interested in **top 40**, **soft rock**. Recent placements include the TV series *Sleepy Hollow*, *Forever*, *Public Morals*, *Graceland*, *Rookie Blues*, and films *The Diary of a Teenage Girl* and *Criminal Activity*. Recent releases include "More Lost Soul Gems From Sounds of Memphis" on Ace Records, "Sweet Talk" by Ciera Ouellette, and the Ciera Ouellette Collection.

◑ SMALL STONE RECORDS

P.O. Box 02007, Detroit MI 48202. (248)219-2613. **Fax:** (248)541-6536. **E-mail:** sstone@smallstone.com. **Website:** www.smallstone.com.

DISTRIBUTED BY ADA, Bertus, Cargo Records GmbH.

HOW TO CONTACT Submit CD/CD-ROM by mail. Unsolicited submissions are OK. Does not return material. Responds in 2 months.

MUSIC Mostly **alternative**, **rock** and **blues**; also **funk** (not R&B). Released *Fat Black Pussy Cat*, written and recorded by Five Horse Johnson (rock/blues); *Wrecked & Remixed*, written and recorded by Morsel (indie rock, electronica); and *Only One Division*, written and recorded by Soul Clique (electronica), all on Small Stone Records. Other artists include Acid King, Perplexa, and Novadriver.

TIPS "Looking for esoteric music along the lines of Bill Laswell to Touch & Go/Thrill Jockey records material. Only send along material if it makes sense with what we do. Perhaps owning some of our records would help."

◑ SMOG VEIL RECORDS

1093 A1A Beach Blvd. #343, St. Augustine Beach FL 32080. (904)547-1393. **E-mail:** franklisa@aol.com. **Website:** svrshop.myshopify.com. Smog Veil Records has been releasing records since 1991, most geared to the post-young, most of which are ridiculous, bombastic, and otherwise underappreciated rock 'n' roll from Northeastern Ohio.

HOW TO CONTACT Submit CD or CD-ROM to Frank Mauceri by mail. Does not accept submissions by e-mail or links to website. Submissions must include a contact, press kit, and plans for touring. Response time is slow. Demo submissions cannot be returned to the submitter.

MUSIC Artists include Batusis, David Thomas, Thor, This Moment in Black History, Butcher Boys, and Prisoners.

⊘ SONY BMG

550 Madison Ave., New York NY 10022. **Website:** www.sonymusic.com.

◐ Sony BMG is one of the primary "Big 4" major labels.

HOW TO CONTACT For specific contact information, see the listings in this section for Sony subsidiaries Columbia Records, Epic Records, Sony Nashville, RCA Records, J Records, Arista, and American Recordings.

⊘ SONY MUSIC NASHVILLE

1400 18th Ave. S., Nashville TN 37212-2809. Labels include Columbia Nashville, Arista Nashville, RCA, BNA, and Provident Music Group.

◐ Sony Music Nashville is a subsidiary of Sony BMG, one of the "Big 4" major labels.

HOW TO CONTACT *Sony Music Nashville does not accept unsolicited submissions.*

⊘ STAX RECORDS

Stax Records / Concord Music Group, 100 N. Crescent Dr., Beverly Hills CA 90210. **E-mail:** publicity@concordmusicgroup.com. **Website:** www.staxrecords.com. Stax Records is critical in American music history as it's one of the most popular soul music record labels of all time—second only to Motown in sales and influence, but first in gritty, raw, stripped-down soul music. In 15 years, Stax placed more than 167 hit songs in the Top 100 on the pop charts, and a staggering 243 hits in the Top 100 R&B charts. It launched the careers of such legendary artists as Otis Redding, Sam & Dave, Rufus & Carla Thomas, Booker T, & the MGs, and numerous others. Among the many artists who recorded on the various Stax Records labels were the Staple Singers, Luther Ingram, Wilson Pickett, Albert King, Big Star, Jesse Jackson, Bill Cosby, Richard Pryor, the Rance Allen Group, and Moms Mabley.

MUSIC Current Stax recording artists include Ben Harper, Booker T. Jones, and others.

STONES THROW RECORDS

2658 Griffith Park Blvd. #504, Los Angeles CA 90039. **E-mail:** losangeles@stonesthrow.com. **Website:** www. stonesthrow.com.

HOW TO CONTACT "Stones Throw receives a lot of unsolicited demos that we don't always have time to listen to, but don't let that discourage you from sending us your music. Please take the time to check the following points before sending anything. Acceptable formats are vinyl or CD. No MP3 files via e-mail. They will be blocked and unheard. We get a lot of Bandcamp, Soundcloud, and other links with music—too many to listen to, but we hear them, too. We receive hundreds of demos every year, so put your best track first. We cannot acknowledge receipt of your submission. Calling or e-mailing to make sure the package has been received will not improve your chances of it being heard."

MUSIC One of the leading names in underground hip-hop. Artists include 7 Days of Funk, Anika, J Rocc, The Stepkids, James Pants, Madvillain, Arabian Prince, Jonwayne, more.

SUB POP RECORDS

2013 Fourth Ave., Third Floor, Seattle WA 98121. (206)441-8441. **Fax:** (206)441-8245. **E-mail:** info@ subpop.com. **Website:** www.subpop.com. Sub Pop Records is a medium-sized independent record label that has released music by several well-known artists, including Nirvana, Soundgarden, Sebadoh, Hot Hot Heat, The Shins, Iron and Wine, Flight of the Conchords, Beach House, and others.

TIPS "It is our intent to market and sell the recorded music (and related merchandise) of artists whose music we really and truly love. We mean to represent these artists as faithfully and diligently as possible and hold out hope that this is enough for us to remain solvent in the face of the well-documented collapse of the music industry at large."

SUGAR HILL RECORDS

E-mail: info@sugarhillrecords.com. **Website:** www. sugarhillrecords.com.

Welk Music Group acquired Sugar Hill Records in 1998.

HOW TO CONTACT *No unsolicited submissions.* "If you are interested in having your music heard by Sugar Hill Records or the Welk Music Group, we suggest you establish a relationship with a manager, publisher, or attorney that has an ongoing relationship with our company. We do not have a list of such entities."

MUSIC Mostly **Americana**, **bluegrass**, and **country**. Artists include Nitty Gritty Dirt Band, Sarah Jarosz, Donna the Buffalo, The Infamous Stringdusters, Joey + Rory, and Sam Bush.

TEXAS ROSE RECORDS

1137 Seminary Ridge, Garland TX 75043. **E-mail:** txrr1@aol.com. **Website:** www.texasroserecords.com. **Contact:** Nancy Baxendale, president. Record company, music publisher (Yellow Rose of Texas Publishing) and record producer (Nancy Baxendale). Staff size: 1. Releases 3 CDs/year. Pays negotiable royalty to artists on contract; statutory rate to publisher per song on record.

DISTRIBUTED BY Self distribution.

HOW TO CONTACT *E-mail first for permission to submit.* Submit 1 song via MP3 file with copy of lyrics in Word format. Does not return material. Responds only if interested.

MUSIC Mostly **country**, **soft rock**, **pop**, and **R&B**. Does not want hip-hop, rap, heavy metal. Released *Flyin' High Over Texas* (album), recorded by Dusty Martin (country); *High On The Hog* (album), recorded by Steve Harr (country); *Time For Time to Pay* (album), recorded by Jeff Elliot (country); *Double XXposure* (album), recorded by Jeff Elliott and Kim Neeley (country), *Pendulum Dream* (album) recorded by Maureen Kelly (Americana) and "Cowboy Super Hero" (single) written and recorded by Robert Mauldin.

TIPS "We are interested in songs written for today's market with a strong musical hook and a great chorus. No home recordings, please."

TINY ENGINES

Charlotte NC **E-mail:** info@tinyengines.net. **E-mail:** submissions@tinyengines.net. **Website:** www.tinyengines.net. Tiny Engines is an indie record label based in the Carolinas. The label is an evolution of ideas and a gathering of like-minded people who dig inspiring music, a tight-knit community of friends and strong, independent DIY ethics.

HOW TO CONTACT "We do not accept physical submissions. But, you can e-mail submissions to submissions@tinyengines.net. Do not send submissions to any other e-mail address. Please include a streaming link and a download link if possible. Do not attach MP3 or zip files. Also, please do not follow up with us. We do our best to listen to everything and if we like it we will definitely be in touch."

⊘ TOMMY BOY ENTERTAINMENT LLC

120 Fifth Ave., 7th Floor, New York NY 10011. **E-mail:** info@tommyboy.com. **Website:** www.tommyboy.com.

DISTRIBUTED BY WEA, Subway Records.

HOW TO CONTACT E-mail to obtain current demo submission policy.

MUSIC Artists include Chavela Vargas, Afrika Bambaataa, Biz Markie, Kool Keith, and INXS.

◑ TOPCAT RECORDS

P.O. Box 670234, Dallas TX 75367. (972)484-4141. **E-mail:** info@topcatrecords.com. **Website:** www.topcatrecords.com.

DISTRIBUTED BY City Hall.

HOW TO CONTACT *Call first and obtain permission to submit.* Prefers CD. Does not return material. Responds in 1 month.

MUSIC Mostly **blues, swing, rockabilly, Americana, Texana** and **R&B**. Released *If You Need Me* (album), written and recorded by Robert Ealey (blues); *Texas Blueswomen* (album by 3 Female Singers), recorded by various (blues/R&B); and *Jungle Jane* (album), written and recorded by Holland K. Smith (blues/swing), all on Topcat. Released CDs: *Jim Suhler & Alan Haynes—Live*; Bob Kirkpatrick *Drive Across Texas*; *Rock My Blues to Sleep* by Johnny Nicholas; *Walking Heart Attack,* by Holland K. Smith; *Dirt Road* (album), recorded by Jim Suhler; *Josh Alan Band* (album), recorded by Josh Alan; *Bust Out* (album), recorded by Robin Sylar. Other artists include Grant Cook, Muddy Waters, Big Mama Thornton, Big Joe Turner, Geo. "Harmonica"

Smith, J.B. Hutto and Bee Houston. "View our website for an up-to-date listing of releases."

TIPS "Send me blues (fast, slow, happy, sad, etc.) or good blues-oriented R&B. No pop, hip-hop, or rap."

TOUCH AND GO/QUARTERSTICK RECORDS

P.O. Box 25520, Chicago IL 60625. (773)388-8888. **Fax:** (773)388-3888. **E-mail:** info@tgrec.com. **Website:** www.tgrec.com.

HOW TO CONTACT Mail to one or the other (staffed by same people no need to send to both labels). "Demos are listened to by any and all staffers who want to or have time to listen to them. Do not call or e-mail us about your demo." Do not e-mail MP3s or Web URLs.

MUSIC All Styles. Artists include Therapy?, TV on the Radio, Pinback, Naked Raygun, Blonde Redhead, Henry Rollins, Yeah Yeah Yeahs, Girls Against Boys, and more.

◑ TRANSDREAMER RECORDS

P.O. Box 1955, New York NY 10113. **Website:** www.transdreamer.com. Transdreamer Records started as a small alternative label with a vision to develop extremely high-quality artists. The name, Transdreamer, symbolizes artists and projects that attempt to transcend normal genre conventions. The Transdreamer logo does not subscribe to the typical "steady product flow, cram-as-many-releases-into-the-market-as-possible, hopefully-one-will-hit" mentality. Fewer releases hopefully means focus, and a high level of excellence and great music.

DISTRIBUTED BY Red/Sony.

HOW TO CONTACT "Feel free to send in your demo to the above address, but please don't call us asking if it's any good. If we are interested, we will harass you. Thanks."

MUSIC Mostly **alternative/rock**. Artists include The Delgados, Arab Strap, Dressy Bessy, The Dig, and Holly Golightly.

⊘ UNIVERSAL MOTWON RECORDS

1755 Broadway, #6, New York NY 10019. (212)373-0600. **Fax:** (212)373-0726. **Website:** www.universalmotown.com.

Universal Motown Records is a subsidiary of Universal Music Group, one of the "Big 4" major labels.

HOW TO CONTACT *Does not accept unsolicited submissions.*

MUSIC Artists include Lil' Wayne, Erykah Badu, Days Difference, Kem, Paper Route, and Kelly Rowland.

⊘ VAGRANT RECORDS

6351 Wilshire Blvd., Los Angeles CA 90048. **E-mail:** info@vagrant.com. **Website:** www.vagrant.com.

HOW TO CONTACT "We do not accept unsolicited demos."

MUSIC Rock, alternative. Artists include PJ Harvey, The 1975, Active Child, Bad Suns, Blitzen Trapper, California Wives, Eels, James Vincent McMorrow, Wake Owl, Bombay Bicycle Club, Benjamin Francis Leftwich, AlunaGeorge, Edward Sharpe and the Magnetic Zeros, Black Joe Lewis, Reptar, and more.

⊘ THE VERVE MUSIC GROUP

1755 Broadway, 3rd Floor, New York NY 10019. (212)331-2000. **E-mail:** contact@vervemusicgroup.com. **Website:** www.vervemusicgroup.com. Record company. Labels include Verve, GRP, and Impulse! Records.

○ Verve Music Group is a subsidiary of Universal Music Group, one of the "Big 4" major labels.

HOW TO CONTACT *The Verve Music Group does not accept unsolicited submissions.*

MUSIC Artists include Boney James, Diana Krall, Ledisi, Herbie Hancock, Queen Latifah, and Bruce Hornsby & The Noisemakers.

VICTORY RECORDS

346 N. Justine St., Suite #504, Chicago IL 60607. **E-mail:** contact@victoryrecords.com. **Website:** www.victoryrecords.com.

HOW TO CONTACT Submit demo using online submission manager.

MUSIC Alternative, **metal**, **rock**. Artists include The Audition, Bayside, Catch 22, Funeral For A Friend, Otep, Hawthorne Heights, Ringworm, Secret Lives of the Freemasons, Silverstein, The Tossers, Voodoo Glow Skulls, William Control, Streetlight Manifesto, and more.

⊘ VIRGIN MUSIC GROUP

5750 Wilshire Blvd., Los Angeles CA 90036. (323)462-6252. **Fax:** (310)278-6231. **Website:** www.virginrecords.com.

○ Virgin Records is a subsidiary of the EMI Group, one of the "Big 4" major labels.

DISTRIBUTED BY EMD.

HOW TO CONTACT *Virgin Music Group does not accept recorded material or lyrics unless submitted by a reputable industry source.* "If your act has received positive press or airplay on prior independent releases, we welcome your written query. Send a letter of introduction accompanied by all pertinent artist information. Do not send a tape until requested. All unsolicited materials will be returned unopened."

MUSIC Mostly **rock** and **pop**. Artists include Lenny Kravitz, Placebo, Joss Stone, Ben Harper, Iggy Pop, and Gorillaz.

WARNER BROS. RECORDS

3300 Warner Blvd., Burbank CA 91505. (818)953-3361; (818)846-9090. **Fax:** (818)953-3232. **Website:** www.wbr.com.

DISTRIBUTED BY WEA.

HOW TO CONTACT *Warner Bros. Records does not accept unsolicited material.* "All unsolicited material will be returned unopened. Those interested in having their tapes heard should establish a relationship with a manager, publisher or attorney that has an ongoing relationship with Warner Bros. Records."

MUSIC Released *Van Halen 3* (album), recorded by Van Halen; *Evita* (soundtrack); and *Dizzy Up the Girl* (album), recorded by Goo Goo Dolls, both on Warner Bros. Records. Other artists include Faith Hill, Tom Petty & the Heartbreakers, Jeff Foxworthy, Porno For Pyros, Travis Tritt, Yellowjackets, Bela Fleck and the Flecktones, Al Jarreau, Joshua Redmond, Little Texas, and Curtis Mayfield.

◐ WARP RECORDS

London United Kingdom. **Website:** www.warp.net. Warp was founded by Steve Beckett and the late Rob Mitchell and soon became home to artists who would be influential in electronic music. In 2013, Warp won Independent Label of the Year at the AIM Awards.

⊘ WIND-UP ENTERTAINMENT

72 Madison Ave., 7th Floor, New York NY 10016. **Website:** www.winduprecords.com. Wind-up Records is a privately owned, full-service music entertainment firm founded in 1997. The company has successfully launched numerous multi-platinum artists, including Evanescence, Creed, Seether, and Finger Eleven, and has further built on the successes

of Five for Fighting and O.A.R. In addition to these marquee acts, Wind-up has scouted and developed several award-winning, newer artists, such as Civil Twilight, Company of Thieves, and Thriving Ivory. Since its inception nearly 15 years ago, the company has shipped over 60 million units worldwide, generating over $700 million in gross revenue. Wind-up has garnered 7 multi-platinum albums (including one diamond—sales over 10 million) and 7 gold albums. The Company has licensed music to high-profile TV shows and motion pictures and has released several motion picture soundtracks, most notably, the platinum-selling, "Walk the Line" and "Daredevil," which went on to sell over 700,000 copies. Combining a team of creative A&R scouts, in-house writers, and engineers with its own recording studio and housing in New York, Wind-up cultivates a fluid and collaborative recording process with its artists, independent of points in their career.

DISTRIBUTED BY BMG.

HOW TO CONTACT *Write first and obtain permission to submit.* Use online form. Prefers CD or DVD. Does not return material or respond to submissions.

MUSIC Mostly **rock**, **folk** and **hard rock**. Artists include Seether, Evanescence, Finger Eleven, Creed, and People In Planes.

TIPS "We rarely look for songwriters as opposed to bands, so writing a big hit single would be the rule of the day."

◑ XEMU RECORDS

2 E. Broadway, Suite 901, New York NY 10038. (212)807-0290. **E-mail:** xemurecord@aol.com. **Website:** www.xemu.com. **Contact:** Cevin Solling. Xemu Records is an independent record label, founded in 1990 in New York by writer, filmmaker, philosopher, musician, music producer and artist Cevin Soling as a vehicle for his music and music production endeavors. Originally conceived as a "record label" nod to underground cult movements of the 1960s and 1970s the label has since grown to be a home to burgeoning young bands in the psychedelic music and independent music scenes.

DISTRIBUTED BY Redeye Distribution.

HOW TO CONTACT *Write first and obtain permission to submit.* Prefers CD with 3 songs. Does not return material. Responds in 2 months.

MUSIC Mostly **alternative**. Released *Happy Suicide, Jim!* (album) by The Love Kills Theory (alternative rock); *Howls From The Hills* (album) by Dead Meadow; *The Fall* (album), recorded by Mikki James (alternative rock); *A is for Alpha* (album), recorded by Alpha Bitch (alternative rock); *Hold the Mayo* (album), recorded by Death Sandwich (alternative rock); *Stockholm Syndrome* (album), recorded by Trigger Happy (alternative rock) all released on Xemu Records. Other artists include Morning After Girls, Spindrift, and Rumpleville.

RECORD PRODUCERS

The independent producer can best be described as a creative coordinator. He's often the one with the most creative control over a recording project and is ultimately responsible for the finished product. Some record companies have in-house producers who work with the acts on that label (although, in more recent years, such producer-label relationships are often non-exclusive). Today, most record companies contract out-of-house, independent record producers on a project-by-project basis.

WHAT RECORD PRODUCERS DO

Producers play a large role in deciding what songs will be recorded for a particular project and are always on the lookout for new songs for their clients. They can be valuable contacts for songwriters because they work so closely with the artists whose records they produce. They usually have a lot more freedom than others in executive positions and are known for having a good ear for potential hit songs. Many producers are songwriters and musicians themselves. Since they wield a great deal of influence, a good song in the hands of the right producer at the right time stands a good chance of being cut. And even if a producer is not working on a specific project, he is well acquainted with record company executives and artists and often can get material through doors not open to you.

SUBMITTING MATERIAL TO PRODUCERS

It can be difficult to get your tapes to the right producer at the right time. Many producers write their own songs and even if they don't write, they may be involved in their own publishing companies so they have instant access to all the songs in their catalogs. Also, some genres are more dependent on finding outside songs than others. A producer working with a rock group or a singer-songwriter will rarely take outside songs.

It's important to understand the intricacies of the producer/publisher situation. If you pitch your song directly to a producer first, before another publishing company publishes the song, the producer may ask you for the publishing rights (or a percentage thereof) to your song. You must decide whether the producer is really an active publisher who will try to get the song recorded again and again or whether he merely wants the publishing because it means extra income for him from the current recording project. You may be able to work out a co-publishing deal where you and the producer split the publishing of the song. That means he will still receive his percentage of the publishing income, even if you secure a cover recording of the song by other artists in the future. Even though you would be giving up a little bit initially, you may benefit in the future.

Some producers will offer to sign artists and songwriters to "development deals." These can range from a situation where a producer auditions singers and musicians with the intention of building a group from the ground up, to development deals where a producer signs a band or singer-songwriter to his production company with the intention of developing the act and producing an album to shop to labels (sometimes referred to as a "baby record deal").

You must carefully consider whether such a deal is right for you. In some cases, such a deal can open doors and propel an act to the next level. In other worst-case scenarios, such a deal can result in loss of artistic and career control, with some acts held in contractual bondage for years at a time. Before you consider any such deal, be clear about your goals, the producer's reputation, and the sort of compromises you are willing to make to reach those goals. If you have any reservations whatsoever, don't do it.

The listings that follow outline which aspects of the music industry each producer is involved in, what type of music he is looking for, and what records and artists he's recently produced. Study the listings carefully, noting the artists each producer works with, and consider if any of your songs might fit a particular artist's or producer's style. Then determine whether they are open to your level of experience (see "A Sample Listing Decoded" in the article "How to Use *Songwriter's Market*").

Consult the Category Index to find producers who work with the type of music you write, and the Geographic Index at the back of the book to locate producers in your area.

ADDITIONAL RECORD PRODUCERS

There are **more record producers** located in other sections of the book! Use the Index to find listings within other sections that are also record producers.

Icons

For more instructional information on the listings in this book, including explanations of symbols, read the article "How To Use *Songwriter's Market*."

WILLIAM ACKERMAN

P.O. Box 419, Bar Mills ME 04004. **E-mail:** will@williamackerman.com. **Website:** www.williamackerman.com.

MUSIC Has worked with George Winston, Michael Hedges, Heidi Anne Breyer, Fiona Joy Hawkins, Devon Rice, Erin Aas. **Music: acoustic, alternative, instrumental**.

⊘ADR STUDIOS

250 Taxter Rd., Irvington NY 10533. (914)591-5616. **Fax:** (914)591-5617. **E-mail:** adrstudios@adrinc.org. **Website:** www.adrinc.org. **Contact:** Stuart J. Allyn. Produces 6 singles and 3-6 CDs/year. Fee derived from sales royalty and outright fee from recording artist and record company.

○ *Does not accept unsolicited submissions.*

MUSIC Mostly **pop, rock, jazz**, and **theatrical**; also **R&B** and **country**. Produced *Thad Jones Legacy* (album), recorded by Vanguard Jazz Orchestra (jazz), released on New World Records. Other artists include Billy Joel, Aerosmith, Carole Demas, Michael Garin, The Magic Garden, Bob Stewart, The Dixie Peppers, Nora York, Buddy Barnes and various video and film scores.

ALLRS MUSIC PUBLISHING CO. (ASCAP)

P.O. Box B, Milford PA 18337. (718)767-8995. **E-mail:** info@allrsmusic.com. **Website:** www.allrsmusic.com. **Contact:** Renee Silvestri-Bushey, president. Music publisher, record company, music consultant, artist management, record producer. Voting member of NARAS / National Academy of Recording Arts and Sciences (The Grammy Awards), voting member of the Country Music Association (The CMA Awards); SGMA/Southern Gospel Music Association, SGA/Songwriters Guild of America (Diamond Member). Staff size: 6. Publishes 3 songs/year; publishes 2 new songwriters/year. Pays standard royalty.

AFFILIATES Midi-Track Publishing Co. (BMI).

HOW TO CONTACT "Call or e-mail first to obtain permission to submit. We do not accept unsolicited submissions." If permission is granted, you will be given additional submission instructions. Does not return material. Responds within 8 months, only if interested.

MUSIC Mostly **country, gospel, top 40, R&B, MOR**, and **pop**. Does not want show tunes, jazz, classical or rap. Published "Why Can't You Hear My Prayer" (single by F. John Silvestri/Leslie Silvestri), recorded by ten-time Grammy nominee Huey Dunbar of the group DLG (Dark Latin Groove), released on MIDI Track Records (including other multiple releases); "Chasing Rainbows" (single by F. John Silvestri/Leslie Silvestri/Darin Kelly), recorded by Tommy Cash (country), released on MMT Records (including other multiple releases); "Because of You" (single by F. John Silvestri/Leslie Silvestri), recorded by Iliana Medina, released 2002 on MIDI Track Records (including other multiple releases also recorded by Grammy nominee Terri Williams, of Always, Patsy Cline, Grand Ole Opry member Ernie Ashworth), released on KMA Records, MMT Records, MIDI Track Records, including other multiple releases; "My Coney Island Love" (single by F. John Silvestri/Leslie Silvestri), recorded by ten-time Grammy nominee Huey Dunbar, released 2005-2009 on MIDI Track Records. "It's Over" (single by F John Silvestri/Leslie Silvestri) recorded by Randy Albright released on Midi Track Records including other multiple releases, "Chasing Rainbows" (single by F John Silvestri/Leslie Silvestri) recorded by Jackie, Mustang Sally, Doreen Lee released on Midi Track Records 2005-2015 including other multiple releases.

TIPS "Attend workshops and music seminars. Have your song critiqued, and visit our website for advice, tips, and info on the music industry."

AMERICANA PRODUCTION

6566 Rolling Fork Dr., Nashville TN 37205. (615)974-5836. **E-mail:** tim@timlorsch.com. **Website:** www.timlorsch.com. **Contact:** Tim Lorsch. Tim Lorsch is a Nashville-based producer, session player, arranger and songwriter. He has produced critically acclaimed records and played on thousands of recordings covering a wide spectrum of musical styles. He has made contributions to Grammy- and Emmy Award-winning projects, performed on TV and scored for the theater. Artists he has performed and/or recorded with include Kris Kristofferson, Kenny Chesney, Keith Urban, Pat Green, Ray Price, Percy Sledge, Lorrie Morgan, Andrew Gold, Joy Lynn White, Goose Creek Symphony, Mel McDaniel, Mary Gauthier, Hank Thompson, Jo-El Sonnier, Allison Moorer, Danni Leigh, Townes Van Zandt, The Kinleys, Keith Gaddis, Lucinda Williams, Rodney Crowell, Kevin Welch and Sam Baker.

MUSIC Americana. Has worked with Amanda Pearcy, Sam Baker, and more.

TIM ANDERSEN

(651)271-0515. **E-mail:** tandersen2005@yahoo.com. **Website:** www.timandersenrecordingengineer.com. "Can offer all those techniques to make your project rise above 'the usual' to something extraordinary, the way real records are made." Producer, mix engineer, guitarist. Classic rock song composer.

○ Does not produce rock bands from pre-production to mix. Does not master. Does not market songs.

MUSIC Has worked with House of Pain, Shaq, Judgement Night, SDTRK, De Jef, Patti LaBelle, Temptations, Hiroshima, Krazy Bone, Snoop Dogg. **Music: rock, R&B, hip-hop, rap, acoustic.**

TIPS Produces in Minneapolis out of Taylor Arts, LLC in its new recording room. "Please do not ask me to get you a record deal. If you want production of your song, call me."

◑❀ ANDREW LANE

Atlanta GA (213) 400-4007. **E-mail:** andrewlanester@gmail.com. **Website:** www.drewrightmusic.com. **Contact:** Andrew Lane, Queen Throngkompol (executive assistant).

HOW TO CONTACT E-mail Andrew Lane or call his executive assistant, Queen Throngkompol, at the number above.

MUSIC Has produced such artists as The Backstreet Boys, Irene Cara, Keith Sweat, Kelly Rowland, Keana, The Clique Girls, and more. TV and film clients include Disney, Nikelodeon, MTV, BET, Country Music Network, HBO, ESPN, Freeform, etc.

◑ AUDIO 911

P.O. Box 212, Haddam CT 06438. **Website:** www.audio911.com. Produces 4-8 singles, 3 LPs, 3 EPs and 4 CDs/year. Fee derived from outright fee from recording artist or record company. Submit demo by mail. Unsolicited submissions are OK. Prefers CD or DVDs with several songs and lyric or lead sheet. "Include live material if possible." Does not return material. Responds in 3 months.

MUSIC Mostly **rock, pop, top 40** and **country/acoustic.** Produced *Already Home* (album), recorded by Hannah Cranna on Big Deal Records (rock); *Under the Rose* (album), recorded by Under the Rose on Utter Records (rock); and *Sickness & Health* (album), recorded by Legs Akimbo on Joyful Noise Records (rock). Other artists include King Hop!, The Shells,

The Gravel Pit, G'nu Fuz, Tuesday Welders and Toxic Field Mice.

WILLIE BASSE

Los Angeles CA (818)731-9116. **E-mail:** williebasse@gmail.com. **Website:** www.williebasse.com. **Contact:** To book Willie for music production or engineering services, contact Aggressive Management at the number listed.

MUSIC Has worked with Canned Heat, Finis Tasby, Frank Goldwasser, Paul Shortino, Jeff Nothrup, Black Sheep. **Music: rock, blues, heavy metal.**

EVAN BEIGEL

P.O. BOX 801556, Santa Clarita CA 91380. (818)321-5472. **E-mail:** mail@evanjbeigel.com. **Website:** www.evanjbeigel.com. Evan J. Beigel is a composer, producer, and recording engineer who learned his craft through a traditional music education and mentorships with world-class producers and engineers, such as Keith Olsen (Fleetwood Mac), Taavi Mote (U2, Madonna), and Pat Regan (Rainbow, Deep Purple).

MUSIC Has worked with Troup, Badi Assad, Ray Kurzweil, Gilli Moon, Michelle Featherstone, Killer Tracks. **Music: rock, indie, alternative, folk, dance/electronica.**

BLACK CROW MUSIC GROUP

1806 Division St., Nashville TN 37201. (615)586-0621. **E-mail:** jimhyatt.nashville@gmail.com. **Website:** www.blackcrowmusicgroup.com. **Contact:** Jim Hyatt. Offers options for recording an album or recording singles. Black Crow Music Group is a full-service music production and talent management company.

MUSIC Any genre, but mostly **country, pop,** and **R&B.** Has worked with Colin Lockey, Brittni Renee, Colt Prather, Arianna Reiter, and more.

◯ BLUES ALLEY RECORDS

Rt. 1, Box 288, Clarksburg WV 26301. (304)598-2583. **E-mail:** hswiger@bluesalleymusic.com. **Website:** www.bluesalleymusic.com. Record producer, record company and music publisher (Blues Alley Publishing/BMI). Prices for production services start at $30/hour for studio time, plus additional fees for mastering.

MUSIC Mostly **country, pop, Christian,** and **rock.** Produced *Monongalia*, recorded by The New Relics (country), 2009; *Chasing Venus*, recorded by The New Relics (acoustic rock), 2006; *Sons of Sirens*, recorded by Amity (rock), 2004; and *It's No Secret*, recorded by Samantha Caley (pop country), 2004.

CLIFF BRODSKY

Beverly Hills CA **E-mail:** cliff@brodskyentertainment.com. **Website:** www.brodskyentertainment.com.

MUSIC Has worked with Rose Rossi, Daize Shayne, Jason Kirk, Burning Retna, Future Kings of Spain, Jordy Towers, Brentley Gore, Cat Switzer, Justin Lanning, Warner Brothers, Universal, Sony, MCA, Virgin, Interscope. **Music: indie, pop, rock.**

BOB BULLOCK

E-mail: bob@bobbullock.net. **Website:** www.bobbullock.net. Bob Bullock was born in Oakland, California, and began his lifelong career in the music business while still a senior in high school. Living in the Los Angeles area, he made his way up the ranks as a studio engineer, training under such greats as Humberto Gatica, Reggie Dozier, Barney Perkins, Roy Haley and Roger Nichols. He quickly became a top engineer himself and worked with a variety of acts, including The Tubes, Art Garfunkel, Seals and Crofts, Crazy Horse, Chic Corea and REO Speedwagon. In 1981, while working at Lionshare Recording Studio for Kenny Rogers, he was approached by legendary producer Jimmy Bowen to engineer for Warner Bros. Records in Nashville. Bullock commuted from Los Angeles to Nashville until 1984, when he and his family made a permanent move. Bullock's engineering credits while living in Nashville include over 50 gold and platinum albums, including Shania Twain, Reba McEntire, George Strait, Tanya Tucker, Patty Loveless, George Jones, John Anderson, Hank Williams Jr., Jimmy Buffet and Steve Wariner. Having spent the bulk of his 40-year career working with some of music's greatest stars, including Kenny Chesney, Loretta Lynn, and Keith Urban, Bullock has also shifted his focus to include many independent artists, as well. In recent years, Bullock's production work has been almost exclusively with independent artists from all over the world, including Switzerland's Baton Rouge, Norway's Gunslingers, and Canadian acts Tyler Whelan and Friends of Jack.

KIM COPELAND PRODUCTIONS

1216 17th Ave. S., Nashville TN 37212. (615)293-9545 or (615)429-5032. **E-mail:** info@kimcopelandproductions.com. **Website:** www.kimcopelandproductions.com. **Contact:** Kim Copeland, Susan Tucker. "At its core, Kim Copeland Productions is a full-service music production company in the heart of Music Row, perfect for everything from songwriter demos through label pitch packages to mastered albums."

MUSIC Mostly **country**. Has worked with Brenda Lee White, James Kevin O'Connor, Family Tree, Matt Strasner, Lisa Lambert, Maddie Deneault, Tim Sweeney, Sim Balkey, Chris Monaghan, and more.

❶ ERIC CORNE

Los Angeles CA (310)500-8831. **E-mail:** eric@ericcornemusic.com. **Website:** www.ericcornemusic.com. **Contact:** Eric Corne, producer.

MUSIC Has worked with Glen Campbell, Lucinda Willaims, Joanna Wang, Michelle Shocked, DeVotchKa, Instant Karma. **Music: rock, indie, Americana, country, blues, jazz, folk.**

❶ CREATIVE SOUL

Nashville TN 37179. (615) 400-3910. **E-mail:** firstcontact@creativesoulrecords.com. **Website:** www.creativesoulonline.com. Record producer. Produces 10-25 singles and 10-15 albums/year. Fee derived from outright fee from recording artist. Other services include consulting/critique/review and marketing services. *Contact first by e-mail to obtain permission to submit demo.* Prefers 2-3 MP3s via e-mail. Responds only if interested.

MUSIC Mostly **contemporary Christian**, including **pop, rock, jazz, world**, and **ballads** in the **Christian** and **gospel** genre. No southern gospel, rap, or hiphop, please. Produced Afterglow Sky (Christian pop/rock); Kristin King (Christian pop); Konai Adelphe (urban gospel); Gretchen Keskeys (Christian inspirational) all released on Creative Soul Records. Other artists include Becki Bice, Leslie McKee, Stephen Bautista, Stephanie Newton, Frances Drost, and Kelly Gardenhire.

TIPS "Contact us first by e-mail; we are here in Nashville for you. We offer free weekly online information and monthly consults in Nashville for Christian artists and songwriters. We want to meet you and talk with you about your dreams. E-mail us and let's start talking about your music and ministry!"

MARC DESISTO

Sherman Oaks CA. (818)259-4235. **E-mail:** marcdmix@gmail.com. **E-mail:** marcdmix@gmail.com. **Website:** www.marcdesistoaudio.com.

MUSIC Has worked with Dwight Yoakam, Stevie Nicks, Michelle Branch, Melissa Etheridge, Don Henley, Patti Smith, Tom Petty, U2. **Music: rock, alternative, pop, indie**.

JEANNIE DEVA VOICE STUDIOS

Jeannie Deva Enterprises, Inc., P.O. Box 4454, Sunland CA 91041-4554. (818)875-4747. **E-mail:** sing@jeanniedeva.com. **Website:** www.jeanniedeva.com. **Contact:** Joe Scoglio. Vocal coaching and voice lessons.

Ꙩ   Jeannie Deva is deceased but training in her vocal method is still available through her trained teachers and online.

MUSIC Vocal coaching and voice lessons with Deva Method certified instructors.

⊘ JOEL DIAMOND ENTERTAINMENT

3940 Laurel Canyon Blvd., Suite 441, Studio City CA 91604. (818)980-9588. **E-mail:** jdiamond20@aol.com. **Website:** www.joeldiamond.com. **Contact:** Joel Diamond, president and CEO. Record producer, music publisher and manager. Fee derived from sales royalty when song is recorded or outright fee from recording artist or record company.

Ꙩ   Also see the listing for Silver Blue Music/Oceans Blue Music in the Music Publishers section of this book.

MUSIC Mostly **dance, R&B, soul** and **top 40/pop**. The 5 Browns—3 No. 1 CDs for Sony/BMG, David Hasselhoff; produced "One Night In Bangkok" (single by Robey); "I Think I Love You," recorded by Katie Cassidy (daughter of David Cassidy) on Artemis Records; "After the Loving" (single), recorded by E. Humperdinck; "Forever Friends," recorded by Vaneza (featured on Nickelodeon's *The Brothers Garcia*); and "Paradise" (single), recorded by Kaci.

Ꝋ DRE WILLPLAY

Nashville TN **E-mail:** dremonaw@gmail.com. **Website:** www.soundcloud.com/drewillplay. **Contact:** Dre Williams, producer. Dre WillPlay is a Nashville-based multi-instrumentalist and producer who has served as musical director for a nationally touring country artist, worked as an in-house producer at Nashville's revered Sound Kitchen Studios, and worked with multi-platinum-selling R&B and gospel artists. He's also produced numerous independent artists, helping them to craft a sound unique to their musical visions while garnering local and national acclaim. His full-service production company specializes in artist development, demo production, full album production, live show programming, and more.

HOW TO CONTACT E-mail with a brief description of your project and what services you need, and someone will respond with a quote within 48 hours.

LES DUDEK

EFLAT Productions, P.O. Box 726, Auburndale FL 33823-0726. **Website:** www.lesdudek.com.

MUSIC Has worked with Stevie Nicks, Steve Miller Band, Cher, Dave Mason, The Allman Brothers, Mike Finnigan, Bobby Whitlock. **Music: southern rock**.

Ꝋ NICK EIPERS

E-mail: nick@nickeipers.com. **Website:** www.nickeipers.com. "I am a freelance recording engineer and producer, specializing in music. Currently based in the Chicago area, I am on staff at Tranquility One Studios, and am available to work freelance almost anywhere. I have worked at Chicago Recording Co., Studiomedia Recording Co., Hinge Studios, Rax Trax Recording, IV Lab Studios, Gallery of Carpet Recording, Shantyville Recording Studio, Gravity Studios, Studiochicago, Star Trax Recording and Chicago Trax, as well as various remote locations and private studios. We choose the recording space based on the aesthetic and practical needs of your music."

MUSIC Specializing in **jazz, fusion, world, indie, alternative, singer/songwriter, folk, classical**.

FINAL MIX INC.

2219 W. Olive Ave., Suite 102, Burbank CA 91506. **E-mail:** rob@finalmix.com. **Website:** www.finalmix.com. Releases 70 singles and 5-7 LPs and CDs/year. Fee derived from sales royalty when song or artist is recorded.

Ꙩ   *Does not accept unsolicited submissions.*

MUSIC Primarily **pop, rock, dance, R&B,** and **rap**. Produced and/or mixer/remixer for Mary Mary, New Boyz, Kirk Franklin, Charlie Wilson, LeAnn Rimes, Charice, Train, Aaliyah, Hilary Duff, Jesse McCartney, Christina Aguilera, American Idol, Ray Charles, Quincy Jones, Michael Bolton, K-Ci and Jo Jo, Will Smith, and/or mixer/remixer for Janet Jackson, Ice Cube, Queen Latifah, Jennifer Paige, and The Corrs.

Ꝋ ALEX FORBES

E-mail: alexforbesmusic@gmail.com. **Website:** http://www.alexforbesmusic.com/. **Contact:** Alex Forbes. "Alex Forbes has spent many years writing songs (especially singles), producing records (especially vocals), and coaching songwriters (especially committed, talented ones)." Work has also appeared on TV/film projects including *Nurse Jackie*, *Dance Moms*, and *Make It or Break It*.

HOW TO CONTACT In addition to offering production services, Forbes also coaches budding songwriters. Reach out via e-mail for more info.

JUD FRIEDMAN STUDIO

Los Angeles CA **E-mail:** jud@judfriedmanmusic.com. **Website:** www.judfriedmanmusic.com. Jud Friedman is a Los Angeles-based songwriter and producer. He's worked with artists who have had 65 million records sold worldwide, been nominated for 2 Academy Awards, 2 Grammys, 2 Golden Globes, and nominations for 2 more Grammys and a Soul Train Award.

MUSIC Any genre. Has worked with Whitney Houston, Kenny Loggins, Barbra Streisand, Ray Charles, Tina Turner, Rod Stewart, LeAnn Rimes, and more.

◗ CHRIS GAGE

Austin TX (512)751-0235. **E-mail:** chris@moonhousestudio.com. **Website:** http://www.moonhousestudio.com/.

MUSIC Artists produced include 8 1/2 Souvenirs (co-produced with Jack Hazzard for RCA Records) Bill Small, Jody Mills, Steve Brooks, Michael Austin, Cowboy Johnson, Albert and Gage, Christine Albert, Abi Tapia, Rio King, Sharon Bousquet, Lawrence J. Clark, Boyd Bristow, Jimmie Dale Gilmore (2 songs) and Willie Nelson (1 duet with Jimmie Dale Gilmore).

MAURICE GAINEN

4470 Sunset Blvd., Suite 177, Hollywood CA 90027. (323)662-3642. **E-mail:** mauricegainen@gmail.com; info@mauricegainen.com. **Website:** www.mauricegainen.com. "We provide complete start-to-finish CD production, including help in choosing songs and musicians through CD mastering. We also pride ourselves on setting a budget and keeping to it."

MUSIC Has worked with Stacy Golden, Yuka Takara, Donna Loren, James Webber, Andy McKee, Rafael Moreira, Alex Skolnick Trio, Metro, Mel Elias, Shelly Rudolph, Kenny Tex, Rachael Owens. **Music: R&B, jazz, alternative, rock, pop.**

BRIAN GARCIA

Los Angeles CA (626)487-0410. **E-mail:** brian@briangarcia.net; info@briangarcia.net. **Website:** www.briangarcia.net.

MUSIC "Producer-mixer-engineer Brian Garcia specializes in the genres of rock and pop. He has been part of 22 million records sold, debuts at No. 1 in 30 countries, a Grammy-winning album, and a No. 1 single on iTunes as a co-writer/producer/mixer. Brian has taken artists from development to securing record deals and producing albums for EMI and Sony/BMG." Has worked with Our Lady Peace, Earshot, Until June, Galactic Cowboys, Avril Lavigne, Kelly Clarkson, Michelle Branch, Dizmas, Chantal Kreviazuk, King's X, Diana Degarmo, The Library, Pushmonkey, The Daylights, Precious Death, Joy Drop. **Music: rock, pop, indie.**

MCKAY GARNER

1873 Eighth Ave. Suite A, San Francisco CA 94122. **E-mail:** info@mckaygarner.com. **Website:** www.mckaygarner.com.

MUSIC Producer, engineer for hire only that has worked with Red Hot Chili Peppers, Styles of Beyond, Flogging Molly, J Dilla, doppio, Valencia, Mike Shinoda, Michael Bublé, Seth Lael.

CARMEN GRILLO

Big Surprise Music, 16161 Ventura Blvd. Suite C-522, Encino CA 91436. (818)613-3984. **E-mail:** info@carmengrillo.com. **Website:** www.carmengrillo.com.

MUSIC Has worked with Manhattan, Transfer, Chicago, Bill Champlin, Mike Finnigan, Tower of Power. **Music: R&B, pop, rock, jazz, blues.**

H2M SOUND

Nashville TN **E-mail:** howiemoscovitch@yahoo.ca. **Website:** www.howiemoscovitch.com. **Contact:** Howie Moscovitch. "Howie Moscovitch is a Canadian-born writer/producer/multi-instrumentalist working in Nashville. He is comfortable and experienced with all styles but specializes in pop and Top 10 of all charts including hip-hop, dance, and R&B. His productions have very current beats, sounds and arrangements. His influences come from all manner of music."

MUSIC Mostly **rap, hip hop, R&B,** and **pop.**

HEATHER HOLLEY

Los Angeles CA **E-mail:** info@heatherholleymusic.com. **Website:** http://www.heatherholleymusic.com/. Heather Holley is a multi-platinum-selling pop music producer and songwriter based in Los Angeles and New York. She specializes in artist development and is known for her role in launching Christina Aguilera's career. Her songs have been featured in global ad campaigns for Pepsi, Mercedes; feature films and trailers *Pursuit of Happyness*, *Honey*, *Kiss of the Dragon*; TV series *Grey's Anatomy*, *The Office*, *90210*, *Private Practice*, and many more. Her article about the craft of songwriting, "Soaring With Christina Aguilera," was published in *The Wall Street Journal*. Works primarily with artists, not necessarily songwriters only looking to have songs produced and recorded.

MUSIC Has worked with Christina Aguilera, Skylar Grey, Itaal Shur, Katie Costello, Nikki Williams. **Music: pop, dance, indie, R&B.**

JIMMY HUNTER

Hollywood CA (323)655-0615. **E-mail:** jimmy@jimmyhunter.com. **Website:** www.jimmyhunter.com. "When you work with Jimmy Hunter, you find a fellow artist who will help you to achieve and refine your vision. He has the experience and tools to get the ultimate sound for your music and bring out the very best in you."

MUSIC Has worked with Todd Standford, Dr. Alias, Savannah Phillips, Mr. Smoove, Mark R. Kent, Della Reese, Lisa Gold, Jamie Palumbo, The Ramblers. **Music:** rock, pop, R&B.

❶ INTEGRATED ENTERTAINMENT

1815 JFK Blvd., #1612, Philadelphia PA 19103-1713. (267)408-0659. **E-mail:** lawrence@gelboni.com. **Website:** www.gelboni.com. Estab. 1991. Produces up to 6 projects/year. Compensation is derived from outright fee from recording artist or record company and sales royalties.

HOW TO CONTACT Submit demo package by mail. Solicited submissions only. CD only with 3 songs. "Draw a guitar on the outside of envelope so we'll know it's from a songwriter." Will respond if interested.

MUSIC Mostly **rock** and **pop**. Produced *Gold Record* (album), written and recorded by Dash Rip Rock (rock) on Ichiban Records and many others.

CHRIS JULIAN

4872 Topanga Canyon Blvd., Suite 406, Woodland Hills CA 91364. (310)924-7849. **E-mail:** chris@ChrisJulian.com. **Website:** www.chrisjulianproductions.com. "Owned and operated solely by engineer/producer Chris Julian, the studio is oriented toward personal service."

MUSIC Has worked with David Bowie, Vanessa Williams, Jimmy Webb, De La Soul, Queen Latifah, Biz Markie, A Tribe Called Quest, Fat Joe, Peter Moffitt, Art Garfunkel, David Crosby, Danielle Livingston, Ray Davies, Don Was, Bobbi Humphrey, Mint, Just James, Brenda K. Star, Jimmy Webb, Naughty By Nature. **Music: R&B, pop, rock, soul, hip-hop, jazz.**

❶ KAREN KANE PRODUCER/ENGINEER

(910)681-0220. **E-mail:** karenkane@mixmama.com. **Website:** www.mixmama.com. **Contact:** Karen Kane. Record producer and recording engineer. Produces 5-8 CDs/year. Fee derived from outright fee from recording artist or record company. *E-mail first and obtain permission to submit. Unsolicited submissions are not OK.* "Please note: I am not a song publisher. My expertise is in album production." Does not return material. Responds in 1 week.

MUSIC Mostly **acoustic music of any kind**, **rock**, **blues**, **pop**, **alternative**, **R&B/reggae**, **country**, and **bluegrass**. Produced *Good to Me* (album), recorded by Nina Repeta; *Topless* (Juno-nominated album), recorded by Big Daddy G, released on Reggie's Records; *Mixed Wise and Otherwise* (Juno-nominated album), recorded by Harry Manx (blues). Other artists include Tracy Chapman (her first demo), Katarina Bourdeaux, Crys Matthews, Laura Bird, L Shape Lot, The Hip Hop Co-op, Barenaked Ladies (live recording for a TV special), and The Coolidge Band.

TIPS "Get proper funding to be able to make a competitive, marketable product."

TIM DAVID KELLY

Ultradose Music, 10061 Riverside Drive #343, Los Angeles CA 91602. (818)601-7047. **E-mail:** info@ultradosemusic.com. **Website:** http://www.ultradosemusic.com/. Offers: Start-to-finish album production; track mixing and music editing; guitar, synth, bass and drum tracking; songwriting and arrangement; indie artist demos; and custom music cues and themes.

MUSIC Has worked with Kicking Harold, Shiny Toy Guns, Dokken. **Music: alternative, metal, Americana, rock, acoustic pop.**

❶ L.A. ENTERTAINMENT, INC.

7095 Hollywood Blvd., #826, Hollywood CA 90028. **E-mail:** info@warriorrecords.com. **Website:** www.warriorrecords.com. Record producer, record company (Warrior Records [distributed via Universal Music Distribution]) and music publisher (New Entity Music/ASCAP, New Copyright Music/BMI, New Euphonic Music/SESAC). Fee derived from sales royalty when song or artist is recorded. Submit demo package by mail. Unsolicited submissions are OK. Prefers CD and/or DVD with original songs, lyric and lead sheet if available. "We do not review Internet sites. Do not send MP3s, unless requested. All written submitted materials (e.g., lyric sheets, letter, etc.) should be typed." Does not return material unless SASE is included. Responds in 2 months only via e-mail or SASE.

MUSIC All styles. All genres are utilized with music supervision company for film and TV, with the label's original music focus on **rock**, **country**, **jazz**, and **urban genres** (e.g., **R&B**, **rap**, **gospel**).

BEN LINDELL

EMW Music Group, 42 Broadway 22nd Floor, New York NY 10004. **E-mail:** ben@benlindell.com. **Website:** www.benlindell.com. **Contact:** Ben Lindell. Ben Lindell is a New York-based producer/mixer/engineer who has worked with hundreds of artists including MGMT, 50 Cent, Wale, Bebel Giberto and many more. "In addition to being a fantastic musician he is also a tremendous geek. It's his marriage of musical creativity and technical know-how that makes him an in demand producer/mixer/engineer."

HOW TO CONTACT Use online form to contact.

MUSIC Select clients include: 50 Cent, Soulja Boy, Wale, Ryan Leslie, Genasis, Lloyd Banks, Tony Yayo, Roshon, Illmind, Red Cafe, J.Period, Olivia, Kelly Rowland, Locnville, Chromeo, MGMT, Bebel Giberto, Rufus Wainright, Edie Brickell, and more.

BOB LUNA

Los Angeles CA (310)202-8043 or (310)508-1356. **E-mail:** bobluna@earthlink.net. **Website:** http://bobluna-music.net.

MUSIC Music: **live** and **midi orchestration**. Live performance/arranging/recording credits include Paul McCartney, Dionne Warwick, Reba McEntire, Denice Williams, Randy Crawford, Alanis Morissette, Sister Sledge, others.

⊘ COOKIE MARENCO

Blue Coast Music Group, P.O. Box 874, Belmont CA 94002. (650)595-8475. **E-mail:** support@bluecoast-music.com. **Website:** http://bluecoastmusic.com/about-the-founder.

HOW TO CONTACT *"No speculative projects." Does not accept unsolicited material.* Must have budget.

MUSIC Founder Blue Coast Music Group, which includes Blue Coast Records, Downloads NOW!, OTR

Studios, Master Quality Disc and DSD-guide. Five Grammy nominations, 2 gold records. Specializing in acoustic music recording at the highest-quality recording level and releasing as high-resolution files to music lovers.

TIPS Specialists in analog tape and DSD audio from recording to mixing to mastering to distribution and direct delivery.

DENNY MARTIN MUSIC

1004 Regents Park Circle, Antioch TN 37013. (615)361-6073. **E-mail:** dennymartinmusic@comcast.net. **Website:** www.dennymartinmusic.com. **Contact:** Denny Martin. Offers full-service production from "a lifelong music pro," collaborative process with top musicians and singers; takes on all levels of projects from demos to indie projects, guitar/vocal to full band.

MUSIC Any genre. Has worked with Gerald Flemming, Infinitely More, Becca Richter, Don McNatt, Sue Lopez, Paul Hurtado, Todd Kramer, Haley Olivia, Dave Saunders, and more.

○ SCOTT MATHEWS, D/B/A HIT OR MYTH PRODUCTIONS, INC.

246 Almonte Blvd., Mill Valley CA 94941. **E-mail:** scott@scottmathews.com. **Website:** www.scottmathews.com. **Contact:** Scott Mathews, CEO and founder. Record producer, "song doctor," multi-instrumentalist, studio owner, music industry executive, and professional consultant. Produces 3-5 projects/year. Fee derived from recording artist or record company (with royalty points).

Scott Mathews has more than 20 gold and multi-platinum awards for sales of more than 30 million records. He has worked with more than 80 Rock and Roll Hall of Fame inductees and on a combination of nearly 30 Grammy- and Oscar-winning or nominated releases. He is currently working primarily with emerging artists while still making music with his legendary established artists such as Billie Joe Armstrong (Green Day), James Hatfield (Metallica), Pat Monohan (Train), Sammy Hagar, Ann Wilson, Joe Satriani, and Van Dyke Parks. His latest No. 1 Billboard hit came in 2012. His first was in 1976, and he has achieved No. 1 hits in every decade since he began.

HOW TO CONTACT "We are only seeking self-contained artists. We do not place songs with artists because we work with artists that write their own material." Submit artist demo for production consideration by e-mail. "Unsolicited submissions are often the best ones and readily accepted. All early-stage business is conducted via e-mail." Responds in 2 months.

MUSIC Mostly **rock/pop, alternative, country** and **singer/songwriters of all styles**. In 2014, he was awarded 7 more gold and multi-platinum records by Eric Clapton, Van Morrison, David Bowie, B.B. King, The Beach Boys, Bonnie Raitt, and Sammy Hagar. In 2004, Mathews earned a gold album for "Smile" by Brian Wilson. Has produced Elvis Costello, Roy Orbison, Rosanne Cash, Jerry Garcia, Huey Lewis, Sammy Hagar, Bob Weird, and many more iconic artists. Has worked with Barbra Streisand, John Lee Hooker, Keith Richards, George Harrison, Mick Jagger, Van Morrison, Bonnie Raitt, Ringo Starr, Brian Wilson, Zac Brown, Chris Isaak, Eric Clapton, and a long list of music's greatest.

TIPS "If you are not independent, you are dependent. The new artists that are coming up and achieving success in the music industry are the ones that prove they have a vision and can make incredible records without the huge financial commitment of a label. When an emerging artist makes great product for the genre they are in, they are in the driver's seat to be able to make a fair and equitable deal for distribution, be it with a major or independent label. My philosophy is to go where you are loved. The truth is, a smaller label that is completely dedicated to you and shares your vision may help your career far more than a huge label that will not keep you around if you don't sell millions of units. Perhaps no label is needed at all, if you are up for the challenge of wearing a lot of hats. I feel too much pressure is put on emerging artists when they have to pay huge sums back to the label in order to see their first royalty check. We all know those records can be made for a fraction of that cost without compromising quality or commercial appeal and I am proving that every day. I still believe in potential and our company is in business to back up that belief. It is up to us as record makers/visionaries to take that potential into the studio and come out with music that can compete with anything else on the market. Discovering, developing and producing artists that can sustain long careers is our main focus at Hit or Myth Productions. We are proud to be associated with so many legendary and timeless artists and our track record speaks for itself. If you love making music, don't

let anyone dim that light. We look forward to hearing from you if you are an emerging artist looking for production to kick your career into high gear. (Please check out www.scottmathews.com for more info, and also www.wikipedia.org, keyword: Scott Mathews.)"

BILL METOYER

16209 Victory Blvd., #132, Lake Balboa CA 91406. (818)780-5394. **E-mail:** bill@skullseven.com. **Website:** www.skullseven.com.

MUSIC Has worked with Slayer, W.A.S.P., Fates Warning, Six Feet Under, Armored Saint, DRI, COC, Tourniquet, Skrew, Rigor Mortis, Sacred Steel, Cement. **Music: hard rock**, **metal**.

O DEAN MILLER ENTERTAINMENT

Nashville TN **E-mail:** deanmillermusic@gmail.com. **Website:** www.deanmillerentertainment.com. **Contact:** Dean Miller, producer. "We are primarily looking for artists to produce, but we occasionally accept songs for specific artists we are working with. Please start with a query e-mail first."

HOW TO CONTACT "We accept song submissions after an initial e-mail and after we determine if the music fits our artists at that time."

BILLY MITCHELL

P.O. Box 284, S. Pasadena CA 91031. (626)574-5040. **Fax:** (626)446-2584. **E-mail:** billymitchell2k@aol.com. **Website:** www.billy-mitchell.com.

MUSIC Has worked with Chartmaker Records, Vista Records, PRC Records, USA Music Group. **Music: contemporary jazz**, **pop**.

ADAM MOSELEY

Los Angeles CA (323)316-4932. **E-mail:** adammoseley@mac.com. **Website:** www.adammoseley.net.

MUSIC Has worked with Claudio Valenzuela, Lisbeth Scott, Wolfmother, Nikka Costa, Abandoned Pools, John Cale, AJ Croce, Lucybell, The Cure, KISS, Rush, Roxette, Maxi Priest. **Music: rock**, **alternative**, **electronica**, **acoustic**.

O NATION PRODUCTIONS

(610)453-0846. **E-mail:** ericmallon74@gmail.com. **Website:** www.nationproductions.com. **Contact:** Eric Mallon, producer. Services provided include high-quality song demos for songwriters and artists for pitching and plugging to producers, publishers and other artists. Artist development and in-studio co-writing sessions, instrumental tracks for "top line" writers, assistance in melody and song crafting, and TV/film sync.

HOW TO CONTACT E-mail is preferred method of contact.

○ NEU ELECTRO PRODUCTIONS

P.O. Box 1582, Bridgeview IL 60455. (630)254-5833. **E-mail:** neuelectro@e-mail.com. **Website:** www.neuelectro.com. **Contact:** Bob Neumann. Recording Studio and Record Label specializing in EDM, trance, and relaxation music.

HOW TO CONTACT Send a CD to the above address, or a link via e-mail.

MUSIC Mostly **dance**, **house**, **techno**, **rap** and **rock**; also **experimental**, **New Age** and **top 40**. Produced "Juicy" (single), written and recorded by Juicy Black on Dark Planet International Records (house); "Make Me Smile" (single), written and recorded by Roz Baker (house); *Reactovate-6* (album by Bob Neumann), recorded by Beatbox-D on N.E.P. Records (dance); and *Sands of Time* (album), recorded by Bob Neumann (New Age). Other artists include Skid Marx and The Deviants.

CARLA OLSON

11684 Ventura Blvd. Suite 583, Studio City CA 91604. **E-mail:** carlawebsite@aol.com. **Website:** www.carlaolson.com.

MUSIC Has worked with Paul Jones, Jake Andrews, Davis Gaines, Joe Louis Walker, Astrella Celeste, Youngblood Hart, Billy Joe Royal, Kim Wilson.

⊘ PHIL EK

E-mail: info@philek.com. **Website:** www.philek.com. **Contact:** Steve Moir, Moir Entertainment, Inc..

MUSIC Worked with such acts as Fleet Foxes, Band of Horses, Boy & Bear, The Walkmen, The Cave Singers, Run River South, Father John Misty, Shout Out Louds, Modest Mouse, The Dodos, Sea Wolf, Animal Kingdom, Mudhoney, The Shins, Spanish for 100, David Cross, Jana McCall, Dinosaur Jr., Feed, Built to Spill, Sick Bees, Fumes, and others.

PLATINUM STUDIOS

Los Angeles CA (818)994-5368. **E-mail:** paulhilton123@sbcglobal.net. **Website:** www.paulhiltonmusic.com. "Platinum sound at affordable rates."

MUSIC Has worked with Janet Klein, Matt Zane & Society 1, Bon Jovi, Spencer Davis, Big Joe Turner, Billy Vera, Metallica, Ratt, Motley Crue, Morgana King, Jack Mack & the Heart Attack, Rodney O & Joe Cooley, WASP, Carlos Rico, Mera, Sam Glaser. **Music:** **Latin**, **rock**, **blues**.

○ MIKE PUWAL

(248)761-3590. **E-mail:** Univox1@yahoo.com. **Website:** https://www.facebook.com/mikepzugizland?fref=ts. **Contact:** Mike Puwal, producer. Nashville-based songwriter and producer works in multiple genres. Contact via phone or e-mail with more info about your project.

TODD ROSENBERG

Los Angeles CA (310)926-5059. **E-mail:** todd@toddrosenberg.net. **Website:** www.toddrosenberg.net.

MUSIC Has worked with Pressure 45, Devil Driver, Mad Caddies, Motograter, Honda, Mitsubishi, Panasonic, Grooveworks. **Music:** **indie**, **rock**, **Americana**, **country**, **ska**, **punk**.

MARK SAUNDERS

Beat 360 Studios, 630 Ninth Ave., Suite 710, New York NY 10036. **E-mail:** ms@marksaunders.com. **Website:** www.marksaunders.com. **Contact:** Ollie Hammett.

MUSIC Has worked with The Cure, Tricky, Depeche Mode, Marilyn Manson, David Byrne, Cyndi Lauper, Shiny Toy Guns, Yaz, The Mission, John Lydon, The Farm, The Sugarcubes, Gravity Kills, Neneh Cherry. **Music:** **electronic**, **rock**.

○◑ SHELL LANE STUDIOS

RR # 1, Kensington PE C0B 1M0 Canada. **E-mail:** manager@shelllanestudio.com. **Website:** www.shelllanestudio.com. **Contact:** Paul Milner, producer/engineer/mixer: paul@shelllanestudio.com; Matt Wilson, engineer: mattwilson@shelllanestudio.com. Shell Lane Studio is located in a turn-of-the-century farmhouse in Prince Edward Island, Canada, with breathtaking views of Darnley Basin. The area offers some of Canada's best golfing, sea kayaking, biking on the Confederation trail and deep sea fishing. All are within a short drive of the studio and the sandy beach is only a five-minute walk away. This is one of the most relaxing and comfortable environments you could find to work in, free from the distraction and stress of an urban center. Charlottetown, Moncton and Halifax airports makes it easy to get here. This authentic seven-bedroom farmhouse is a fully equipped residential studio offering complete privacy to its clients in a totally unique setting.

MUSIC Mostly **rock**, **A/C**, **alternative** and **pop**; also **Christian** and **R&B**. Produced *COLOUR* (album writ-

ten by J. MacPhee/R. MacPhee/C. Buchanan/D. Mac-
Donald), recorded by The Chucky Danger Band (pop/
rock); winner of ECMA award; *Something In Between*
(album, written by Matt Andersen), recorded by Matt
Andersen and Friends (blues), released on Weather-
box / Andersen; *In A Fever In A Dream* (album, written by Pat Deighan), recorded by Pat Deighan and
The Orb Weavers (rock), released on Sandbar Music;
Saddle River String Band (album, written by Saddle
River Stringband), recorded by Saddle River Stringband (bluegrass) released on Save As Music; winner
of ECMA award.

SKYELAB MUSIC GROUP

247 W. 38th St., Suite 601, New York NY 10018.
(212)789-8942. **E-mail:** info@skyelab.com. **Website:**
www.skyelab.com. **Contact:** Arty Skye. Arty Skye
has worked with major stars such as Will Smith, Madonna, Alicia Keys, Santana, 98 Degrees, Queen Latifah, Missy Elliot, Public Enemy, Wu-Tang Clan and
many more. Arty opened Skyelab Sound Studios in
1994 and has hosted such stars as James Taylor, Tito
Puente, Mya, Pink, Hayle Duff, 98 Degrees, Lil 'Mo
and many more.

SLANG MUSIC GROUP

1915 West Superior St., Chicago IL 60622. (312)482-
9001. **Fax:** (312)482-9007. **Website:** www.slangmusic-
group.com. **Contact:** Vince Lawrence. Chicago-based
music producers that specialize in creating remix and
original music for TV commercials, artists, films, and
gaming. "Noted for achievements in house music,
owner/producer Vince Lawrence has created a destination for electronic music makers of every genre.
The Slang Music Group has multiple producer/artists
and we have received many RIAA gold and platinum
awards. Along with music for commercials, members
of The Slang Music Group have also been working
with burgeoning new talent from all over the world."

HOW TO CONTACT Contact via online form.

TIPS "House music is the heartbeat of every dancer
... no fluff or glitter, just the beat of the drum and the
true passionate voice of a life worth living. House music is a tale of distant lovers trying to get back together,
broken hearts mending, people finding true joy while
they are just getting by. House knows no race, religion
or sexual preference. House music isn't just for the
rich or the poor, dumb or intellectual ... house music
is the backing track to life. It moves in all directions."

SOUND ARTS RECORDING STUDIO

8377 Westview Dr., Houston TX 77055. (713)464-
4653. **E-mail:** brianbaker@soundartsrecording.com.
Website: www.soundartsrecording.com. **Contact:**
Brian Baker.

MUSIC Mostly **pop/rock**, **country** and **blues**. Produced *Texas Johnny Brown* (album), written and re-
corded by Texas Johnny Brown on Quality (blues);
and "Sheryl Crow" (single), recorded by Dr. Jeff and
the Painkillers. Other artists include Tim Nichols,
Perfect Strangers, B.B. Watson, Jinkies, Joe "King"
Carasco (on Surface Records), Mark May (on Ice-
house Records), The Barbara Pennington Band (on
Earth Records), Tempest, Atticus Finch, Tony Vega
Band (on Red Onion Records), Saliva (Island Records),
Earl Gillian, Blue October (Universal Records), and
The Wiggles.

CHRIS STAMEY

Modern Recording, Chapel Hill NC (919)929-5008.
E-mail: mrstamey@gmail.com. **Website:** www.chris-
stamey.com. "The central philosophy behind my production and mixing these days is that the best records
combine the recording of transcendent musical moments with the structuring of the carefully considered
arrangement details that frame those moments. And
the point of recording is to add new entries to that select list of best records." See website for rates.

MUSIC Has worked with Alejandro Excovedo, Ryan
Adams/Whiskeytown, Amy Ray, Yo La Tengo, Squir-
rel Nut Zippers, Patrick Park, Le Tigre, Jeremy Lar-
son, Chatham Country Line. **Music: rock**, **indie**, **alternative**.

STUDIO SEVEN

417 N. Virginia, Oklahoma City OK 73106. (405)236-
0643. **Website:** www.lunacyrecords.com.

MUSIC Mostly **rock**, **jazz-blues**, **country**, and **Native American**.

SURREAL STUDIOS

355 W. Potter Dr., Anchorage AK 99518. (907)562-
3754. **E-mail:** surrealstudiosak@gmail.com. **Website:**
www.surrealstudios.com. **Contact:** Kurt Riemann,
owner/engineer.

MUSIC Produces a variety of music from **native
Alaskan** to **Techno** to **Christmas**.

DAVE TOUGH, PRODUCER SONGWRITER

5801 Tee Pee Dr., Nashville TN 37013. **Website:** www.
davetough.com.

HOW TO CONTACT See website for rates.

MUSIC Dove Award nominee. Has worked with Come & Go, Cindy Alter, Matt Heinecke, Craig Winquist, Jeff Dane, Lost Trailers and 100-plus Film and TV placements. **Music: country, pop, rock, hip-hop**.

TRACK STAR STUDIOS

San Diego CA (619)697-7827. **E-mail:** info@trackstarstudios.com. **Website:** www.trackstarstudios.com. **Contact:** Josquin des Pres. "Josquin des Pres is a lifelong music impresario. As a renowned producer, songwriter, musician, manager, studio owner and prolific author, Josquin has consistently maintained the respect of his peers throughout the music industry."

HOW TO CONTACT Any genre. Has worked with Jack Johnson, Bernie Taupin, Gipsy Kings, Tech N9ne, Peter Frampton, Robert Lamm, and more.

BIL VORNDICK

6090 Fire Tower Rd., Nashville TN 37221. (615)352-1227. **Fax:** (615)353-1235. **E-mail:** bilinstudio@comcast.net. **Website:** www.bilvorndick.com. "Helping artists realize their dreams."

MUSIC Has worked with Alison Krauss, Rhonda Vincent, Jerry Douglas, Bela Fleck, Jim Lauderdale, Ralph Stanley, Claire Lynch, Lynn Anderson, Bob Dylan, John Oates.

○ WARNER WORKS

P.O. Box 167, Old Hickory TN 37138. (615)473-1030. **E-mail:** bill@warnerworks.net. **Website:** http://warnerworks.net. **Contact:** Bill Warner. "A lover of diverse musical styles, Bill Warner keeps a creative edge, working projects ranging from rock, dance/pop, to country and bluegrass. Recent production projects include the country rockers Crossroad Station, Americana artist Jessie Veeder, Ben Robinson of Nick Cannon's boy band, Four Count, country rock band Crossroad Station, and a rock project with The Ryan Michaels Band that had appearances on *The Kardashians* and other reality TV shows. Other credits include mixer on 'The Rust-eze Song' from the Pixar film *Cars* and 'Cotton Eye Joe' from the motion picture *Cowgirls and Angels*, vocal sessions with country hitmakers Lonestar, and Christian artists Avalon. Another interesting project Bill was recently involved in was cutting vocals for Cowboy Troy of Big & Rich fame, performing his hit, 'I Play Chicken With the Train' adeptly performed in Simlish for the classic video game, *The Sims 2*."

○ WEST COAST COUNTRY

(615)669-2212. **E-mail:** bj@brandonjamesmusic.com. **Website:** www.brandonjamesmusic.com. **Contact:** Brandon James, producer. Brandon James is an accomplished vocalist, multi-instrumentalist and songwriter based in Nashville, Tennessee. He produces piano-guitar/vocal tracks, as well as full production demos for other artists and songwriters.

◑ WESTWIRES RECORDING USA

1042 Club Ave., Allentown PA 18109. (610)435-1924. **E-mail:** info@westwires.com. **Website:** www.westwires.com.

MUSIC Mostly **rock, R&B, dance, alternative, folk** and **eclectic**. Produced Ye Ren (Dimala Records), Weston (Universal/Mojo), Zakk Wylde (Spitfire Records). Other artists include Ryan Asher, Paul Rogers, Anne Le Baron, and Gary Hassay.

TIPS "We are interested in singer/songwriters and alternative artists living in the mid-Atlantic area. Must have steady gig schedule and established fan base."

MICHAEL WOODRUM

(818)848-3393. **Website:** www.woodrumproductions.com. "Michael Woodrum is a producer who's also an accomplished engineer. He gets sounds faster than you can think them up. You won't sit around waiting for something to sound right."

MUSIC Has worked with 3LW, Juvenile, 2Pac, Linkin Park, MC Lyte, Mary J. Blige, Eric Clapton, Joss Stone, Snoop Dogg, Bobby Rydell, B2K, Rocio Banquells, Queen Latifah, JoJo, Dr. Dre, John Guess, Tiffany Evans, Samantha Jade. **Music: rock, pop, R&B, rap, hip-hop, alternative, acoustic, indie, Americana, country, soul**.

◑ ZIG PRODUCTIONS

P.O. Box 120931, Arlington TX 76012. **E-mail:** billyherzig@hotmail.com. **Website:** www.zigproductions.com. **Contact:** billy herZIG. "Occasionally I produce a single that is recorded separate from a full CD project." Produces 6-10 albums. Fee derived from sales royalty when song or artist is recorded and/or outright fee from recording artist. "Sometimes there are investors." ◒ Always looking for unique, different, original artists (pop and country), whether they write or don't."

MUSIC Mostly **country, Americana**, and **rock**; also **pop, r&b**, and **alternative**. Produced "Ask Me to Stay" (single by King Cone/Josh McDaniel) from *Gallery*, recorded by King Cone (Texas country/Americana), released on King Cone; "A Cure for Awkward Silence" (single), recorded by Tyler Stock (acoustic rock), released on Payday Records; "Take Me Back" (single) from *Peace, Love & Crabs*, written and recorded by Deanna Dove (folk-rock), released on Island Girl.

Also produced Robbins & Jones (country), Jordan Mycoskie (country), Carla Rhodes (comedy), Four Higher (alternative), Charis Thorsell (country), Shane Mallory (country), Rachel Rodriguez (blues-rock), Jessy Daumen (country), Frankie Moreno (rock/R&B), Shawna Russell (country), and many others.

MANAGERS & BOOKING AGENTS

///

Before submitting to a manager or booking agent, be sure you know exactly what you need. If you're looking for someone to help you with performance opportunities, the booking agency is the one to contact. They can help you book shows either in your local area or throughout the country. If you're looking for someone to help guide your career, you need to contact a management firm. Some management firms also may handle booking; however, it may be in your best interest to look for a separate booking agency. A manager should be your manager—not your agent, publisher, lawyer or accountant.

MANAGERS

Of all the music industry players surrounding successful artists, managers usually are the people closest to the artists themselves. The artist manager can be a valuable contact, both for the songwriter trying to get songs to a particular artist and for the songwriter/performer. A manager and his connections can be invaluable in securing the right publishing deal or recording contract if the writer is also an artist. Getting songs to an artist's manager is yet another way to get your songs recorded, since the manager may play a large part in deciding what material his client uses. For the performer seeking management, a successful manager should be thought of as the foundation for a successful career.

The relationship between a manager and his client relies on mutual trust. A manager works as the liaison between you and the rest of the music industry, and he must know exactly what you want out of your career in order to help you achieve your goals. His handling of publicity, promotion and finances, as well as the contacts he has within the industry, can make or break your career. You should never be afraid to ask questions about any aspect of the relationship between you and a prospective manager.

Always remember that a manager works *for the artist*. A good manager is able to communicate his opinions to you without reservation, and should be willing to explain any confusing terminology or discuss plans with you before taking action. A manager needs to be able to communicate successfully with all segments of the music industry in order to get his client the best deals possible. He needs to be able to work with booking agents, publishers, lawyers and record companies.

Keep in mind that you are both working together toward a common goal: success for you and your songs. Talent, originality, professionalism and a drive to succeed are qualities that will attract a manager to an artist—and a songwriter.

BOOKING AGENTS

The function of the booking agent is to find performance venues for his clients. Booking agents usually represent many more acts than a manager does, and have less contact with their acts. A booking agent charges a commission for his services, as does a manager. Managers usually ask for a 15 to 20 percent commission on an act's earnings; booking agents usually charge around 10 percent. In the area of managers and booking agents, more successful acts can negotiate lower percentage deals than the ones set forth above.

SUBMITTING MATERIAL TO MANAGERS & BOOKING AGENTS

The firms listed in this section have provided information about the types of music they work with and the types of acts they represent. You'll want to refer to the Category Index to find out which companies deal with the type of music you write, and the Geographic Index at the back of the book to help you locate companies near where you live. Then determine whether they are open to your level of experience (see A Sample Listing Decoded in the article "How to Use *Songwriter's Market*"). Each listing also contains submission requirements and information about what items to include in a press kit and also will specify whether the company is a management firm or a booking agency. Remember that your submission represents you as an artist, and should be as organized and professional as possible.

ADDITIONAL MANAGERS & BOOKING AGENTS

There are **more managers & booking agents** located in other sections of the book! Consult the Index to find additional Managers & Booking Agents listings within other sections.

Icons

For more instructional information on the listings in this book, including explanations of symbols, read the article "How To Use *Songwriter's Market*."

○○⊘ ALERT MUSIC INC.

305-41 Britain St., Suite 305, Toronto ON M5A 1R7 Canada. **E-mail:** gabriella@alertmusic.com. **Website:** www.alertmusic.com. **Contact:** Gabriella Lima. *"Please note that Alert Music is not currently hiring or accepting any unsolicited e-mails."* Management firm, record company and recording artist. Represents local and regional individual artists and groups.

MUSIC All types. Works primarily with bands and singer/songwriters. Current acts include Holly Cole (jazz vocalist) and Kim Mitchell (rock singer/songwriter). Also worked with Michael Kaeshammer (pianist/singer) and Rozanne Potvin.

○ AMERICAN BANDS MANAGEMENT

P.O. Box 842103, Houston TX 77284. **Website:** www.americanbandsmanagement.com. **Contact:** John Blomstrom. There is a contact form on the website. Represents groups from anywhere. Receives 15-25% commission. Reviews material for acts.

HOW TO CONTACT Submit demo package by mail prior to making phone contact. Unsolicited submissions are OK. Prefers live videos. If seeking management, press kit should include cover letter, bio, photo, demo CD, press clippings, video, résumé, and professional references with names and numbers. Does not return material. Responds in 1 month.

MUSIC Mostly **rock (all forms)** and **modern country**. Works primarily with bands. Current acts include The Scars Heal In Time, Trey Gadler & Dead Man's Hand, Kenny Cordrey & Love Street, The Standells, Paul Cotton (from Poco), and Pearl (Janis Joplin tribute).

◑ BILL ANGELINI ENTERPRISES/ BOOKYOUREVENT.COM

P.O. Box 132, Seguin TX 78155. (210)363-4978. **Fax:** (484)842-5549. **E-mail:** bill@bookyourevent.com; bookyourevent@att.net. **Website:** www.bookyourevent.com. **Contact:** Bill Angelini, owner. Management firm and booking agency. Represents individual artists and groups from anywhere. Receives 10-15% commission. Reviews material for acts.

HOW TO CONTACT Submit demo package by mail or EPK. Unsolicited submissions are OK. Press kit should include pictures, bio, and discography. Does not return material. Responds in 1 month.

MUSIC Mostly **Latin American**, **Tejano**, and **international**; also **Norteno** and **country**. Current acts include Jay Perez (Tejano), Ram Herrera (Tejano), Mi-

chael Salgado (Tejano), Electric Cowboys (Tex-Mex), Los Caporales (Tejano), Grupo Solido (Tejano), and Texmaniacs (Tex-Mex).

◑ APODACA PROMOTIONS INC.

717 E. Tidwell Rd., Houston TX 77022. (713)691-6677. **Website:** www.apodacapromotions.com. Management firm, booking agency, music publisher (Huina Publishing Co., Inc.). Represents songwriters and groups from anywhere; currently handles 40 acts. Reviews material for acts.

HOW TO CONTACT Submit demo package by mail. Unsolicited submissions are OK. Prefers CD and lyric and lead sheet. Include SASE. Responds in 2 months.

MUSIC Mostly **international** and **Hispanic**; also **rock**. Works primarily with bands and songwriters. Current acts include Alicia Villarreal, Boby Pulldo, Fanny Lu, Elephant, Angel Y Khriz, Golden Horse, and Ninel Conde.

◑ ARTIST REPRESENTATION AND MANAGEMENT

1257 Arcade St., St. Paul MN 55106. (651)483-8754. **Fax:** (651)776-6338. **E-mail:** molly@armentertainment.com. **Website:** www.armentertainment.com. There are different agents to contact depending on where in the country you live. Visit the website's "Contact Us" page for this info. Management firm and booking agency. Estab. 1983. Represents artists from US/Canada. Receives 15% commission. Reviews material for acts.

HOW TO CONTACT Submit CD and DVD by mail. Unsolicited submissions are OK. Please include minimum 3 songs. If seeking management, current schedule, bio, photo, press clippings should also be included. "Priority is placed on original artists with product who are currently touring." Does not return material. Responds only if interested within 30 days.

MUSIC Mostly **melodic rock**. Current acts include Bret Michaels, Warrant, Firehouse, Winger, Skid Row, Head East, Frank Hannon of Tesla, LA Guns featuring Phil Lewis, Dokken, Adler's Appetite, and Vince Neil.

⊘ BILL SILVA

Los Angeles CA **Website:** www.billsilvaentertainment.com. Bill Silva Management (BSM) was formed in 1993 and offers a full house of specialized services helping to guide the careers of an eclectic roster of music artists and producers. "Our roster includes Grammy Award-winning artist Jason Mraz; RCA

Records rapper Brooke Candy; Greyson Chance; Olivia Holt; and Atlantic Records band Night Terrors of 1927. For all of our musical clients we also offer music licensing services by placing their music in television programs, movies, video games and commercials."

HOW TO CONTACT Use online form to contact.

MUSIC Artists include Jason Mraz, Midlake, Annie Stela, Ryan Hewitt, Brooke Candy, Olivia Holt, M. Ward, and many more.

◑ BROTHERS MANAGEMENT ASSOCIATES

141 Dunbar Ave., Fords NJ 08863. (732)738-0880. **Fax:** (732)738-0970. **E-mail:** bmaent@yahoo.com. **Website:** www.bmaent.com. **Contact:** Allen A. Faucera, president. Management firm and booking agency. Represents artists, groups and songwriters; currently handles 25 acts. Receives 15-20% commission. Reviews material for acts.

HOW TO CONTACT *Write first and obtain permission to submit.* Prefers CD or DVD with 3-6 songs and lyric sheets. Include photographs and résumé. If seeking management, include photo, bio, tape, and return envelope in press kit. Include SASE. Responds in 2 months.

MUSIC Mostly **pop**, **rock**, **MOR**, and **R&B**. Works primarily with vocalists and established groups. Current acts include Nils Lofgren of the E Street Band, Cover Girls, Harold Melvin's Blue Notes, and Gloria Gaynor.

TIPS "Submit very commercial material—make demo of high quality."

◑ CLOUSHER PRODUCTIONS

P.O. Box 1191, Mechanicsburg PA 17055. (717)766-7644. **Fax:** (717)766-1490. **E-mail:** cpinfo@msn.com. **Website:** www.clousherentertainment.com. **Contact:** Fred Clousher, owner. Booking agency and production company. Represents groups from anywhere; currently handles more than 100 acts.

HOW TO CONTACT Submit demo package by mail. Please, no electronic press kits. Unsolicited submissions are OK. Prefers CDs or DVD. Press kit should also include bio, credits, pictures, song list, references, and your contact information. Does not return material. "Performer should check back with us!"

MUSIC Mostly **country**, **oldies rock 'n' roll** and **ethnic** (German, Hawaiian, etc.); also **dance bands** (regional), **Dixieland**, and **classical musicians**. "We

work mostly with country, old-time rock 'n' roll, regional variety dance bands, tribute acts, and all types of variety acts." Current acts include Stanky & the Coal Miners (polka), Lee Alverson (tribute artist), and Orville Davis & The Wild Bunch (country/rockabilly).

TIPS "The songwriters we work with are entertainers themselves, which is the aspect we deal with. They usually have bands or do some sort of show, either with tracks or live music. We engage them for stage shows, concerts, etc. We do not review songs you've written. We do not publish music, or submit performers to recording companies for contracts. We strictly set up live performances for them."

◑ DCA PRODUCTIONS

302A 12th St., #330, New York NY 10014. (800)659-2063. **Fax:** (609)259-8260. **E-mail:** info@dcaproductions.com. **Website:** www.dcaproductions.com. Management firm. Represents individual artists, groups, and songwriters from anywhere.

HOW TO CONTACT If seeking management, press kit should include cover letter, bio, photo, demo CD, and video. Prefers CD or DVD with 2 songs. "All materials are reviewed and kept on file for future consideration. Does not return material. We respond only if interested."

MUSIC Mostly **acoustic**, **rock**, and **mainstream**; also **cabaret** and **theme**. Works primarily with acoustic singer/songwriters, top 40 or rock bands. Current acts include And Jam Band (soulful R&B), Lorna Bracewell (singer/songwriter), and Jimmy and The Parrots (Jimmy Buffett cover band). "Visit our website for a current roster of acts."

TIPS "Please do not call for a review of material."

◑◑ DIVINE INDUSTRIES

Unit 191, #101-1001 W. Broadway, Vancouver BC V6H 4E4 Canada. (604)737-0091. **Fax:** (604)737-3602. **E-mail:** allenm@divineindustries.com. **Website:** www.divineindustries.com. **Contact:** Allen Moy. Management firm, production house and music publisher. Represents artists and songwriters; currently handles 5 acts. Reviews material for acts.

HOW TO CONTACT *Write first and obtain permission to submit.* Prefers audio links. "Videos are not entirely necessary for our company. It is certainly a nice touch. If you feel your CD is strong—send the video upon later request." Does not return material. Responds in 2 months.

MUSIC Rock, pop, and **roots**. Works primarily with rock/left-of-center folk show bands. Current acts include 54-40 (rock/pop), Blackie & The Rodeo Kings (folk rock), Ridley Bent, John Mann (of Spirit of the West).

JOHN ECKERT ENTERTAINMENT CONSULTANTS

7723 Cora Dr., Lucerne CA 95458. (323)325-6662. **Contact:** John Eckert, coordinator. Management firm and talent coordination. Represents individual artists and groups; currently handles 12 acts. Receives 15% commission. Reviews material for acts.

HOW TO CONTACT Submit demo package by mail. Unsolicited submissions are OK. "We prefer CD (4 songs). Submit DVD with live performance only." If seeking management, press kit should include an 8x10 photo, a CD of at least 4-6 songs, a bio on group/artist, references, cover letter, press clippings, video, and business card, or a phone number with address. Does not return material. Responds in 5 weeks.

MUSIC Mostly **country**, **country/pop**, and **rock**. Works primarily vocalists, show bands, dance bands, and bar bands. Current acts include The Rose Garden (pop/rock/country band); Sam the Sham (vocalist); The Fifth Estate (pop/rock)

SCOTT EVANS PRODUCTIONS

P.O. Box 814028, Hollywood FL 33081-4028. (954)963-4449. **E-mail:** evansprod@hotmail.com. **Website:** www.facebook.com/pages/Scott-Evans-Productions/. **Contact:** Jeanne K., Internet marketing and sales. Management firm and booking agency. Represents local, regional or international individual artists, groups, songwriters, comedians, novelty acts and dancers; currently handles over 200 acts. Receives 10-50% commission. Reviews material for acts.

HOW TO CONTACT New artists can make submissions through the "Auditions" link located on the website. Unsolicited submissions are OK. "Please be sure that all submissions are copyrighted and not your original copy as we do not return material."

MUSIC Mostly **pop**, **R&B**, and **Broadway**. Deals with "all types of entertainers; no limitations." Current acts include Scott Evans and Company (variety song and dance), Dorit Zinger (female vocalist), Jeff Geist, Actors Repertory Theatre, Entertainment Express, Joy Deco (dance act), Flashback (musical song and dance revue), and Around the World (international song and dance revue).

TIPS "Submit a neat, well-put together, organized press kit."

B.C. FIEDLER MANAGEMENT

53 Seton Park Rd., Toronto ON M3C 3Z8 Canada. (416)421-4421. **Fax:** (416)421-0442. **E-mail:** info@bc-fiedler.com. **Website:** www.bcfiedler.com. **Contact:** B.C. Fiedler. Management firm, music publisher (B.C. Fiedler Publishing) and record company (Sleeping Giant Music, Inc.). Represents individual artists, groups and songwriters from anywhere. Receives 20-25% or consultant fees. Reviews material for acts.

HOW TO CONTACT *Call first and obtain permission to submit.* Prefers CD or DVD with 3 songs and lyric sheet. If seeking management, press kit should include bio, list of concerts performed in past 2 years including name of venue, repertoire, reviews and photos. Does not return material. Responds in 2 months.

MUSIC Mostly **classical/crossover**, **voice** and **pop**. Works primarily with classical/crossover ensembles, instrumental soloists, operatic voice and pop singer/songwriters. Current acts include Gordon Lightfoot, Dan Hill, Quartetto Gelato, and Patricia O'Callaghan.

TIPS "Invest in demo production using best-quality voice and instrumentalists. If you write songs, hire the vocal talent to best represent your work. Submit CD and lyrics. Artists should follow up 6-8 weeks after submission."

FIRST TIME MANAGEMENT

Ebrel House, 2a Penlee Close, Praa Sands, Penzance, Cornwall TR20 9SR England, United Kingdom. 01736-762826. **E-mail:** panamus@aol.com. **Website:** www.panamusic.co.uk / www.digimixrecords.com. **Contact:** R. G. Jones, managing director. Management firm, record company (Digimix Records, Ltd. www.digimixrecords.com, Rainy Day Records, Mohock Records, Pure Gold Records), and music publisher (Panama Music Library, Melody First Music Library, Eventide Music Library, Musik Image Music Library, Promo Sonor International Music Library, Caribbean Music Library, ADN Creation Music Library, Piano Bar Music Library, Corelia Music Library, PSI Music Library, Scamp Music Publishing, First Time Music [Publishing] U.K. [www.panamamusic.co.uk) - registered members of the Mechanical Copyright Protection Society [MCPS] and the Performing Right Society [PRS]). Represents local, regional, and international individual artists, groups, composers,

DJs, and songwriters. Receives 15-25% commission. Reviews material for acts.

○ Also see the listings for First Time Music (Publishing) in the Music Publishers section of this book.

HOW TO CONTACT Submit demo package by mail. Unsolicited submissions are OK. Prefers CD with 3 songs, lyric sheets and also complete album projects where writer/performer has finished masters. If seeking management, press kit should include cover letter, bio, photo, demo tape/CD, press clippings and anything relevant to make an impression. Does not return material. Responds in 1 month only if interested.

MUSIC All styles. Works primarily with songwriters, composers, DJs, rappers, vocalists, bands, groups and choirs. Current acts include Leonie Parker (soul), The Glen Kirton Country Band (country), Bram Stoker (prog rock/gothic rock group), Kevin Kendle (New Age, holistic) Peter Arnold (folk/roots), David Jones (urban/R&B), Shanelle (R&B/dance), AudioJunkie & Stylus (dance/hardcore/funky house/electro house) Ray Guntrip (jazz); DJ Gammer (hardcore/hardhouse/dance); Toots Earl & Clown.

TIPS "Become a member of the Guild of International Songwriters and Composers (www.songwriters-guild. co.uk). Keep everything as professional as possible. Be patient and dedicated to your aims and objectives."

∅ FOUNDATIONS ARTIST MANAGEMENT

307 7th Ave., Suite 403, New York NY 10001. (212)366.4576. **Fax:** (646)607-4305. **E-mail:** info@ foundationsmusic.com. **Website:** www.foundationsmusic.com. Foundations Artist Management was launched in 2000 by Steve Bursky, and has since grown into a full-service artist representation company focusing on building artists' careers from the ground up. The New York-based company prides itself on its work with its acts from the very early stages of their careers, helping them lay the necessary groundwork for a successful future in the music industry. With the addition of Brian Winton in 2004 as partner, and Drew Simmons in 2011 as general manager, Foundations has continued to build on its original vision: providing uncompromising support to great artists, assisting them in growing their careers as it grow its own.

HOW TO CONTACT "*We do not accept unsolicited submissions.* If you would like to submit music for review and consideration, please e-mail us."

MUSIC Represents such acts as Pacific Air, White Rabbits, Foy Vance, Dr. Dog, Dispatch, Owl City, Young The Giant, The Colourist, others.

○ HARDISON INTERNATIONAL ENTERTAINMENT CORP.

P.O. Box 1732, Knoxville TN 37901-1732. (865)293-7062 (prefers e-mail contact). **E-mail:** dennishardison@bellsouth.net. **Website:** www.dynamoreckless. com. **Contact:** Dennis K. Hardison, CEO/founder; Dennis K. Hardison II, president; Travis J. Hardison, president, Denlatrin Record (a division of Hardison International Entertainment Corp.). Management firm, booking agency, music publisher (Denlatrin Music) BMI, record label (Denlatrin Records), and record producer. Represents individual artists from anywhere; currently handles 3 acts. Receives 20% commission. Reviews material for acts. "We are seeking level-minded and patient individuals. Our primary interests are established recording acts with prior major deals."

○ This company has promoted many major acts and unsigned acts for over 40 years.

HOW TO CONTACT Submit demo package by mail. Unsolicited submissions are OK. Prefers CD with 3 songs only. If seeking management, press kit should include bio, promo picture, and CD. Does not return materials. Responds in 6 weeks to the "best material" submitted.

MUSIC Mostly **R&B, hip-hop,** and **rap.** Current acts include Dynamo (hip-hop), Triniti (record producer, Universal Music, Public Enemy, Dynamo, among others; current engineer for Chuck D), and RapStation artists.

TIPS "We respond to the hottest material, so make it hot!"

HUNT TALENT MANAGEMENT

Website: www.hunttalentmanagement.com. **Contact:** Tammy Hunt. Hunt Talent Management brings over 25 years of professional experience in the film and music industry. "As a management firm dedicated to the business side of the entertainment industry, we are determined to assist our clients achieve their career goals. Hunt Talent Management understands how to create a profitable business while strategically marketing your individual talents. We represent talent from all areas of the entertainment industry. In addition, Hunt Talent Management is partners with

Gandolfo-Helin Literary Management to help promote our talented authors."

HOW TO CONTACT Contact via online form.

⊘ INTERNATIONAL ENTERTAINMENT BUREAU

3612 N. Washington Blvd., Indianapolis IN 46205. (317)926-7566. **E-mail:** ieb@prodigy.net. **Website:** leonardscorp.com. **Contact:** David Leonards. Booking agency. Represents individual artists and groups from anywhere; currently handles 145 acts. Receives 20% commission.

HOW TO CONTACT *No unsolicited submissions.*

MUSIC Mostly **rock**, **country**, and **A/C**; also **jazz**, **nostalgia**, and **ethnic**. Works primarily with bands, comedians and speakers. Current acts include Five Easy Pieces (A/C), Scott Greeson (country), and Cool City Swing Band (variety).

◑ KENDALL WEST AGENCY

P.O. Box 1673, Colleyville TX 76034. **E-mail:** Michelle@KendallWestAgency.com. **Contact:** Michelle Vellucci. Booking agency and TV producer. Represents individual artists and groups from anywhere. Receives 20% commission. Reviews material for acts.

HOW TO CONTACT *Write first and obtain permission to submit or write to arrange personal interview.* Prefers CD with 5 songs and lead sheet. If seeking management, press kit should include bio, photo, cover letter, CD and resume. Include SASE. Responds in 1 month.

MUSIC Mostly **country**, **blues/jazz**, and **rock**; also **trios**, **dance** and **individuals**. Works primarily with bands. Current acts include Chris & the Roughnecks (Texas music), Shawna Russell (southern rock), Ty England (country), and Jaz-Vil (jazz/blues).

◯ KUPER PERSONAL MANAGEMENT/ RECOVERY RECORDINGS

515 Bomar St., Houston TX 77006. (713)520-5791. **E-mail:** info@recoveryrecordings.com. **Website:** www.recoveryrecordings.com. **Contact:** Koop Kuper, owner. Management firm, music publisher (Kuper-Lam Music/BMI, Uvula Music/BMI, and Meauxtown Music/ASCAP), and record label (Recovery Recordings). Represents individual artists, groups, and songwriters from Texas. Receives 20% commission. Reviews material for acts.

HOW TO CONTACT Submit demo package by mail. Unsolicited submissions are OK. Prefers CD. If seek-

ing management, press kit should include cover letter, press clippings, photo, bio (1 page) tearsheets (reviews, etc.) and demo CD. Does not return material. Responds in 2 months.

MUSIC Mostly **singer/songwriters**, **AAA**, **roots rock**, and **Americana**. Works primarily with self-contained and self-produced artists.

TIPS "Create a market value for yourself, produce your own master tapes, and create a cost-effective situation."

RICK LEVY MANAGEMENT

4250 A1AS, D-11, St. Augustine FL 32080. (904)806-0817. **E-mail:** rick@ricklevy.com. **Website:** www.ricklevy.com. **Contact:** Rick Levy, president. Management firm, music publisher (Flying Governor Music/BMI), and record company (Luxury Records). Voting member of the Grammys. Represents local, regional, or international individual artists and groups; currently handles 5 acts. Also provides worldwide music promotion services. Receives 15-20% commission. Reviews material for acts.

HOW TO CONTACT *Write or call first and obtain permission to submit.* Prefers CD or DVD with 3 songs and lyric sheet. If seeking management, press kit should include cover letter, bio, demo CD, DVD demo, photo and press clippings. Include SASE. Responds in 2 weeks.

MUSIC Mostly **R&B** (no rap), **pop**, **country**, and **oldies**. Current acts include Jay & the Techniques (1960s hit group), The Limits (pop), Freddy Cannon (1960s), The Fallin Bones (Blues/rock), Tommy Roe (1960s), Wax (rock), The Box Tops (1960s).

TIPS "If you don't have 200% passion and commitment, don't bother. Be sure to contact only companies that deal with your type of music."

◯ LOGGINS PROMOTION

5018 Franklin Pike, Nashville TN 37220. (310)325-2800. **E-mail:** staff@logginspromotion.com. **Website:** www.logginspromotion.com. **Contact:** Paul Loggins, CEO. Loggins Promotion is the leading radio promotion and marketing firm in the US. Working with both major and independent record labels, Loggins Promotion also handles booking and publicity for artists and venues. Management firm and radio promotion. Represents individual artists, groups and songwriters from anywhere; currently handles several acts. Receives 20% commission. Reviews material for artists and bands.

○ Loggins Promotion's clients have included the likes of Pink, Gwen Stefani and Coldplay to Country artists as Brad Paisley, Keith Urban and Sugarland.

HOW TO CONTACT If seeking radio promotion, marketing and/or management, press kit should include finished product, short bio, cover letter, press clippings (if available) and CD (preferred) or MP3 if only a one-song submission. "Mark on CD which cut you, as the artist, feel is the strongest." Does not return material. Responds in 2 weeks.

MUSIC Adult, **top 40** and **AAA**; also **urban**, **rap**, **alternative**, **college**, **smooth jazz** and **Americana**. Works primarily with bands and solo artists.

○❶ THE MANAGEMENT TRUST, LTD.

471 Queen St. E., Unit #1, Toronto ON M5A 1T9 Canada. (416)979-7070. **Fax:** (416)979-0505. **E-mail:** mail@mgmtrust.ca. **Website:** www.mgmtrust.ca. Management firm. Represents individual artists and/or groups.

HOW TO CONTACT "If you wish to submit material, please e-mail us a link to your website, social sites, or online EPK. (Do not send MP3s or other large attachments.) While we try to respond to all submissions, we are not always able to. Please be patient, and we will do our best to get back to you. You can e-mail us the above info to mail@mgmtrust.ca."

MUSIC All types.

MARMOSET

2105 SE 7th Ave., Portland OR 97214. (971)260-0201. **E-mail:** compass@marmosetmusic.com. **Website:** www.marmosetmusic.com. Marmoset is an off-the-beaten path, boutique music agency born among the green, mountainous landscapes of the rain-soaked Pacific Northwest. While we enjoy working on all kinds of inspired and creative endeavors, we spend most of our time crafting original music for story-driven mediums in the public eye. We also curate a hand-picked roster of some of the most fascinating independent artists on the planet whose recordings are made available for licensing. Marmoset is made of real people, living real lives, making a real living crafting music and sound. We're talking about hard-working, blue-collar artists, crafting music with their hands and hearts. While some of these are full-time musicians, many are baristas and bartenders, too. Pro-grammers and farmers. Fathers and mothers. Sisters and brothers.

❶ PARADIGM TALENT AGENCY

360 N. Crescent Dr., North Bldg., Beverly Hills CA 90210. (310)288-8000. **Fax:** (310)288-2000. **Website:** www.paradigmagency.com. **Nashville:** 124 12th Ave. S., Suite 410, Nashville TN 37203. (615)251-4400. **Fax:** (615)251-4401. **New York:** 360 Park Ave. S., 16th Floor, New York NY 10010. (212)897-6400. **Fax:** (212)764-8941. **Monterey:** 404 W. Franklin St., Monterey, CA 93940. (831)375-4889. **Fax:** (831)375-2623. Booking agency. Represents individual artists, groups from anywhere. Receives 10% commission. Reviews material for acts.

HOW TO CONTACT *Does not take unsolicited submissions.*

MUSIC Current acts include Ricky Skaggs, Junior Brown, Toby Keith, Kasey Chambers, Umphrey's Mc-Gee, Black Eyed Peas, Kirk Franklin, Lily Allen, My Chemical Romance, and Lauryn Hill.

∅❀ PRIMARY WAVE

116 E. 16th Street, 9th Floor, New York NY 10003. (212)661-6990. **E-mail:** management@primarywave-music.com. **Website:** www.primarywavemusic.com. "Primary Wave Talent Management passionately and meticulously guides the careers of its clients to enhance, shape, and extend their brand—providing a solid foundation for longevity in an ever-changing industry. From multi-platinum-selling recording artists to hit making songwriters and producers, we represent some of the biggest and brightest brands in entertainment. We leverage the full strength of Primary Wave's internal resources to ensure our clients' creative and commercial success. Our talent management division is powered by all divisions of Primary Wave including our in-house press division, A&R/writer-producer relations team, our branding company Brand Synergy Group, digital marketing arm BrightShop, as well as our in-house film, television, video game, commercial advertising and TV development team." *Does not accept unsolicited submissions.*

MUSIC Primary Wave's unique music repertoire includes an interest in the Beatles songs written by John Lennon, the catalogs of Kurt Cobain/Nirvana, Steven Tyler/Aerosmith, Daryl Hall & John Oates, Chicago, Maurice White (Earth, Wind & Fire), Def Leppard, Steve Earle, Daniel Johnston, Marvin Hamlisch, The Matrix, Lamont Dozier and Steven Curtis Chapman, as well as artists such as Airborne Toxic Event, Albert Hammond Jr., John Forte, The Boxer Rebellion, New Boyz, Taddy Porter, Anberlin, writers such as Gregg Alexander, Ryan & Smitty, LP, RoccStar, among others; as well as marketing and administration agreements with Jimmy Webb, Katrina and The Waves, Graham Parker, Evolution Entertainment/Twisted Pictures, Hammer Films, Matt Serletic and Emblem Music Group, and many others

PRIME TIME ENTERTAINMENT

2430 Research Dr., Livermore CA 94550. (925)449-1724. **Fax:** (925)605-0379. **E-mail:** info@primetimeentertainment.com. **Website:** www.primetimeentertainment.com. Management firm and booking agency. Represents individual artists, groups and songwriters from anywhere. Receives 10-20% commission. Reviews material for acts. This market is based in San Francisco and handles many activities in the Bay area.

HOW TO CONTACT Submit demo package by mail. Unsolicited submissions are OK. Prefers CD with 3-5 songs. If seeking management, press kit should include 8x10 photo, reviews, and CDs/tapes. Include SASE. Responds in 1 month.

MUSIC Mostly **jazz**, **country**, and **alternative**; also **ethnic**.

TIPS "It's all about the song."

RAINBOW TALENT AGENCY LLC

146 Round Pond Lane, Rochester NY 14626. (585)723-3334. **E-mail:** carl@rainbowtalentagency.com; info@rainbowtalentagency.com. **Website:** www.rainbowtalentagency.com. **Contact:** Carl Labate, president. Management firm and booking agency. Represents artists and groups. Receives 15-25% commission.

HOW TO CONTACT Submit demo package by mail. Unsolicited submissions are OK. Prefers CD with minimum 3 songs. May send DVD if available; "a still photo and bio of the act; if you are a performer, it would be advantageous to show yourself or the group performing live. Theme videos are not helpful." If seeking management, include photos, bio, markets established, CD/DVD. Does not return material. Responds in 1 month.

MUSIC Mostly **blues**, **rock**, and **R&B**. Works primarily with touring bands and recording artists. Current acts include Russell Thompkins Jr. & The New Stylistics (R&B), Josie Waverly (country), and Spanky Haschmann Swing Orchestra (high energy swing).

TIPS "My main interest is with groups or performers that are currently touring and have some product. And are at least 50% original. Strictly songwriters should apply elsewhere."

ROBERTSON ENTERTAINMENT

106 Harding Rd. Kendenup 6323, Western Australia Australia. (618)9851-4311. **Fax:** (618)9851-4225. **E-mail:** info@robertsonentertainment.com. **Website:** www.robertsonentertainment.com. **Contact:** Eddie Robertson. Booking agency. Represents individual artists and/or groups; currently handles 50 acts. Receives 20% commission. Reviews material for acts.

HOW TO CONTACT *Write first and obtain permission to submit.* Unsolicited submissions are OK. If seeking management, press kit should include photos, bio, cover letter, press clippings, video, demo, lyric sheets and any other useful information. Does not return material. Responds in 1 month.

MUSIC Mostly **top 40/pop**, **jazz**, and **1960s-1990s**; also **reggae** and **blues**. Works primarily with show bands and solo performers. Current acts include Faces (dance band), Heart & Soul (easy listening), and Ruby Tuesday (contemporary pop/rock/classics).

TIPS "Send as much information as possible. If you do not receive a call after 4-5 weeks, follow up with a letter or phone call."

SANDALPHON MANAGEMENT

P.O. Box 18197, Panama City Beach FL 32417. **E-mail:** sandalphonmusic@yahoo.com. **Contact:** Ruth Otey. Management firm, music publisher (Sandalphon Music Publishing/BMI), and record company (Sandalphon Records). Represents individual artists, groups, songwriters; works with individual artists and groups from anywhere. Receives negotiable commission. Reviews material for acts.

HOW TO CONTACT Submit demo by mail. Unsolicited submissions are fine. Prefers CD with 1-5 songs and lyric sheet, cover letter. Include name, address, and contact information. Include SASE or SAE and IRC for outside the US. Responds in 6-8 weeks.

MUSIC Mostly **rock**, **country**, and **alternative**; also **pop**, **gospel**, and **blues**. "We are looking for singers, bands, and singer/songwriters who are original but would be current in today's music markets. We help singers, bands, and singer-songwriters achieve their personal career goals."

TIPS "Submit material you feel best represents you, your voice, your songs, or your band. Fresh and original songs and style are a plus. We are a South East management company looking for singers, bands, and singer-songwriters who are ready for the next level. We are looking for those with talent who are capable of being national and international contenders."

✪ SERGE ENTERTAINMENT GROUP

P.O. Box 5147, Canton GA 30114. (678)880-8207. **Fax:** (678)494-9289. **E-mail:** sergeent@aol.com. **Website:** www.sergeentertainmentgroup.com. **Contact:** Sandy Serge, president. Management and PR firm and song publishers. Represents individual artists, groups, songwriters from anywhere; currently handles 20 acts. Receives 20% commission for management. Monthly fee required for PR acts.

HOW TO CONTACT *E-mail first for permission to submit.* Submit demo package by mail. Unsolicited submissions are OK. Prefers CD with 4 songs and lyric sheet. If seeking management, press kit should include 8x10 photo, bio, cover letter, lyric sheets, max of 4 press clips, DVD, performance schedule and CD. All information submitted must include name, address and phone number on each item. Does not return material. Responds in 6 weeks if interested.

MUSIC Mostly **rock**, **pop**, and **country**; also **New Age**. Works primarily with singer/songwriters and bands. Current acts include Julius Curcio (alt), Erik Norlander (prog rock), and Lana Lane (prog rock).

☯ SIEGEL ENTERTAINMENT, LTD.

1736 W. 2nd Ave., Vancouver BC V6J 1H6 Canada. (604)736-3896. **Fax:** (604)736-3464. **E-mail:** siegelent@telus.net. **Website:** www.siegelent.com. **Contact:** Robert Siegel, president. There is also a contact form for this market on its website. Management firm and booking agency. Represents individual artists, groups and songwriters from anywhere; currently handles more than 100 acts (for bookings). Receives 15-20% commission. Reviews material for acts.

HOW TO CONTACT *Does not accept unsolicited submissions. E-mail or write for permission to submit.* Does not return material. Responds in 1 month.

MUSIC Mostly **rock**, **pop**, and **country**; also **specialty** and **children's**. Current acts include Johnny Fer-

reira & The Swing Machine, Lee Aaron, Kenny Blues Boss Wayne (boogie) and Tim Brecht (pop/children's).

◯ GARY SMELTZER PRODUCTIONS

P.O. Box 201112, Austin TX 78720-11112. (512)478-6020. **Fax:** (512)478-8979. **E-mail:** info@garysmeltzerproductions.com. **Website:** www.garysmeltzerproductions.com. **Contact:** Gary Smeltzer, president. Management firm and booking agency. Represents individual artists and groups from anywhere. Currently handles 20 acts. "We book about 100 different bands each year—none are exclusive." Receives 20% commission. Reviews material for acts.

HOW TO CONTACT Submit demo package by mail. Unsolicited submissions are OK. Prefers CD or DVD. If seeking management, press kit should include cover letter, résumé, CD/DVD, bio, picture, lyric sheets, press clippings, and video. Does not return material. Responds in 1 month.

MUSIC Mostly **alternative**, **R&B** and **country**. Current acts include Rotel & the Hot Tomatoes (nostalgic 1960s showband).

TIPS "We prefer performing songwriters who can gig their music as a solo or group."

◐ SOUTHEASTERN ATTRACTIONS

1025 23rd St. S., Suite 302, Birmingham AL 35205. (205)307-6790. **Fax:** (205)307-6798. **E-mail:** info@southeasternattractions.com. **Website:** southeasternattractions.com. **Contact:** Agent. Booking agency. Represents groups from anywhere. Receives 20% commission.

HOW TO CONTACT Submit demo package by mail. Unsolicited submissions are OK. Prefers CD or DVD. Does not return material. Responds in 2 months.

MUSIC Mostly **rock**, **alternative**, **oldies**, **country**, and **dance**. Works primarily with bands. Current acts include The Undergrounders (variety to contemporary), The Connection (Motown/dance), and Rollin' in the Hay (bluegrass).

◐ STARKRAVIN' MANAGEMENT

11135 Weddington St., Suite 424, North Hollywood CA 91601. (818)587-6801. **Fax:** (818)587-6802. **E-mail:** bcmclane@aol.com. **Website:** www.benmclane.com. **Contact:** Ben McLane, Esq. Management and law firm. Estab. 1994. Represents individual artists, groups and songwriters. Receives 20% commission (management); $300/hour as attorney.

HOW TO CONTACT Submit demo package by mail. Unsolicited submissions are OK. Prefers CDs. Does not return material. Responds in 1 month if interested. **MUSIC** Mostly **rock**, **pop** and **R&B**. Works primarily with bands.

○ ST. JOHN ARTISTS

P.O. Box 619, Neenah WI 54957-0619. (920)722-2222. **Fax:** (920)725-2405. **E-mail:** jon@stjohn-artists.com; information@stjohn-artists.com. **Website:** www.st-john-artists.com. **Contact:** Jon St. John and Gary Coquoz, agents. Booking agency. Represents local and regional individual artists and groups; currently handles 20 acts. Receives 15-20% commission. Reviews material for acts.

HOW TO CONTACT *Call first and obtain permission to submit.* Prefers CD or DVD. If seeking management, press kit should include cover letter, bio, photo, demo CD, video and résumé. Include SASE.

MUSIC Mostly **rock** and **MOR**. Current acts include Boogie & the Yo-Yo's (1960s to 2000s), Vic Ferrari (Top 40 1980s-2000s), Little Vito & the Torpedoes (variety 1950s-2000s), and Da Yoopers (musical comedy/novelty).

◑ TAS MUSIC CO./DAVID TASSÉ ENTERTAINMENT

N2467 Knollwood Dr., Lake Geneva WI 53147. (888)554-9898; (262)245-1335. **Website:** www.tasseentertainment.com. **Contact:** David Tassé. There is a contact form on the website. Booking agency, record company and music publisher. Represents artists, groups, and songwriters; currently handles 21 acts. Receives 10-20% commission. Reviews material for acts.

HOW TO CONTACT Submit demo by mail. Unsolicited submissions are OK. Prefers CD with 2-4 songs and lyric sheet. Include performance videocassette if available. If seeking management, press kit should include tape, bio and photo. Does not return material. Responds in 3 weeks.

MUSIC Mostly **pop** and **jazz**; also **dance**, **MOR**, **rock**, **soul**, and **top 40**. Works primarily with show and dance bands. Current acts include Maxx Kelly (pop/rock) and Glenn Davis (blues band).

◐◑ THE FELDMAN AGENCY & MACKLAM FELDMAN MANAGEMENT

#200-1505 W. 2nd Ave., Vancouver BC V6H 3Y4 Canada. (604)734-5945. **Fax:** (604)732-0922. **E-mail:** info@mfmgt.com; feldman@slfa.com. **Website:** www.mfmgt.com; www.slfa.com. Booking agency and artist management firm. Agency represents mostly established Canadian recording artists and groups.

HOW TO CONTACT *Write or call first to obtain permission to submit a demo.* Prefers CD, photo and bio. If seeking management, contact Watchdog for consideration and include video in press kit. SAE and IRC. Responds in 2 months.

MUSIC Current Macklam Feldman Management acts include The Chieftains, Diana Krall, Elvis Costello, Better Midler, Sarah McLachlan, Ylvis, James Taylor, Colin James, Ry Cooder, Tommy LiPuma, and Melody Gardot.

WHITESMITH ENTERTAINMENT

E-mail: Info@WhitesmithEnt.com. **Website:** www.whitesmithentertainment.com. **Contact:** Los Angeles: Keri Smith Esguia (keri@whitesmithent.com); New York: Emily White (emily@whitesmithent.com). "Whitesmith Entertainment is a full-service talent management firm based in Los Angeles and New York, spanning the music, comedy, film, television, literary, and sports industries. We take pride in working with artists who have a unique voice, style and meaning to their fans. Whitesmith balances a youthful edge while maintaining a deep knowledge within the fields of touring, merchandising, online marketing, social networking, branding, sponsorship, as well as physical and modern content releases. Whitesmith Entertainment is available for outside consulting services in all areas of artist development, content releases, touring services, online marketing, and beyond."

MUSIC Artists represented include Brandan Benson, The Big Sleep, Hockey, The Autumn Defense, GOLD MOTEL, Urge Overkill, Future Monarchs, and many more.

◑ WORLDSOUND, LLC

17837 1st Ave. S., Suite 3, Seattle WA 98148. (206)444-0300. **Fax:** (206)244-0066. **E-mail:** a-r@worldsound.com. **Website:** www.worldsound.com. **Contact:** Warren Wyatt, A&R manager. Management firm. Represents individual artists, groups and songwriters from anywhere. Receives 20% commission. Reviews material for acts.

HOW TO CONTACT "Online, send us an e-mail containing a link to your website where your songs can be heard and the lyrics are available; **please do not e-mail song files!** By regular mail, unsolicited submissions are OK." Prefers CD with 2-10 songs and lyric sheet. "If seeking management, please send an e-mail with a link to your website—your site should contain song samples, band biography, photos, video (if available), press and demo reviews. By mail, please send the materials listed above and include SASE." Responds in 1 month.

MUSIC Mostly **rock, pop,** and **world**; also **heavy metal, hard rock,** and **top 40.** Works primarily with pop/rock/world artists.

TIPS "Always submit new songs/material, even if you have sent material that was previously rejected; the music biz is always changing."

◑ ZANE MANAGEMENT, INC.

One Liberty Place, 1650 Market St., 56th Floor, Philadelphia PA 19103. (215)790-1155. **Fax:** (215)575-3801. **Website:** www.zanemanagement.com. **Contact:**

Lloyd Z. Remick, Esq., president. Entertainment/sports consultants and managers. Represents artists, songwriters, producers and athletes; currently handles 7 acts. Receives 10-15% commission.

HOW TO CONTACT Submit demo tape by mail. Unsolicited submissions are OK. Prefers CD and lyric sheet. If seeking management, press kit should include cover letter, bio, photo, demo tape and video. Does not return material. Responds in 3 weeks.

MUSIC Mostly **dance, easy listening, folk, jazz (fusion), MOR, rock (hard and country), soul** and **top 40/pop.** Current acts include Bunny Sigler (disco/funk), Peter Nero and Philly Pops (conductor), Pieces of a Dream (jazz/crossover), Don't Look Down (rock/pop), Christian Josi (pop-swing), Bishop David Evans (gospel), Kevin Roth (children's music), and Rosie Carlino (standards/pop).

MUSIC FIRMS

//

It's happened a million times—you hear a jingle on the radio or television and can't get it out of your head. That's the work of a successful jingle writer, writing songs to catch your attention and make you aware of the product being advertised. But the field of commercial music consists of more than just memorable jingles. It also includes background music that many companies use in videos for corporate and educational presentations, as well as films and TV shows.

SUBMITTING MATERIAL

More than any other market listed in this book, the commercial music market expects composers to have made an investment in the recording of their material before submitting. A sparse, piano/vocal demo won't work here; when dealing with commercial music firms, especially audiovisual firms and music libraries, high-quality production is important. Your demo may be kept on file at one of these companies until a need for it arises, and it may be used or sold as you sent it. Therefore, your demo tape or reel must be as fully produced as possible.

The presentation package that goes along with your demo must be just as professional. A list of your credits should be a part of your submission, to give the company an idea of your experience in this field. If you have no experience, look to local television and radio stations to get your start. Don't expect to be paid for many of your first jobs in the commercial music field; it's more important to get the credits and exposure that can lead to higher-paying jobs.

Commercial music and jingle writing can be a lucrative field for the composer/songwriter with a gift for writing catchy melodies and the ability to write in many different music styles. It's a very competitive field, so it pays to have a professional presentation package that makes your work stand out.

Three different segments of the commercial music world are listed here: advertising agencies, audiovisual firms, and commercial music houses/music libraries. Each looks for a different type of music, so read these descriptions carefully to see where the music you write fits in.

ADVERTISING AGENCIES

Ad agencies work on assignment as their clients' needs arise. Through consultation and input from the creative staff, ad agencies seek jingles and music to stimulate the consumer to identify with a product or service.

When contacting ad agencies, keep in mind they are searching for music that can capture and then hold an audience's attention. Most jingles are short, with a strong, memorable hook. When an ad agency listens to a demo, it is not necessarily looking for a finished product so much as for an indication of creativity and diversity. Many composers put together a reel of excerpts of work from previous projects, or short pieces of music that show they can write in a variety of styles.

AUDIOVISUAL FIRMS

Audiovisual firms create a variety of products, from film and video shows for sales meetings, corporate gatherings and educational markets, to motion pictures and TV shows. With the increase of home video use, how-to videos are a big market for audiovisual firms, as are spoken-word educational videos. All of these products need music to accompany them. For your quick reference, companies working to place music in movies and TV shows (excluding commercials) have a ✪ preceding their listing (also see the Film & TV Index for a complete list of these companies).

Like ad agencies, audiovisual firms look for versatile, well-rounded songwriters. When submitting demos to these firms, you need to demonstrate your versatility in writing specialized background music and themes. Listings for companies will tell what facet(s) of the audiovisual field they are involved in and what types of clients they serve. Your demo tape should also be as professional and fully produced as possible; audiovisual firms often seek demo tapes that can be put on file for future use when the need arises.

COMMERCIAL MUSIC HOUSES & MUSIC LIBRARIES

Commercial music houses are companies contracted (either by an ad agency or the advertiser) to compose custom jingles. Since they are neither an ad agency nor an audiovisual firm, their main concern is music. They use a lot of it, too—some composed by in-house songwriters and some contributed by outside, freelance writers.

Music libraries are different in that their music is not custom composed for a specific client. Their job is to provide a collection of instrumental music in many different styles that, for an annual fee or on a per-use basis, the customer can use however he chooses.

In the following listings, commercial music houses and music libraries, which are usually the most open to works by new composers, are identified as such by **bold** type.

The commercial music market is similar to most other businesses in one aspect: experience is important. Until you develop a list of credits, pay for your work may not be high. Don't pass up opportunities if a job is non- or low-paying. These assignments will add to your list of credits, make you contacts in the field, and improve your marketability.

Money & Rights

Many of the companies listed in this section pay by the job, but there may be some situations where the company asks you to sign a contract that will specify royalty payments. If this happens, research the contract thoroughly, and know exactly what is expected of you and how much you'll be paid.

Depending on the particular job and the company, you may be asked to sell one-time rights or all rights. One-time rights involve using your material for one presentation only. All rights means the buyer can use your work any way he chooses, as many times as he likes. Be sure you know exactly what you're giving up, and how the company may use your music in the future.

In the commercial world, many of the big advertising agencies have their own publishing companies where writers assign their compositions. In these situations, writers sign contracts whereby they do receive performance and mechanical royalties when applicable.

ADDITIONAL LISTINGS

For additional names and addresses of ad agencies that may use jingles and/or commercial music, refer to the *Standard Directory of Advertising Agencies* (National Register Publishing). For a list of audiovisual firms, check out the latest edition of *AV Marketplace* (R.R. Bowker). Both these books may be found at your local library. To contact companies in your area, see the Geographic Index at the back of this book.

ADVERTEL, INC.

P.O. Box 18053, Pittsburgh PA 15236-0053. (412)714-4421. **E-mail:** info@advertel.com. **E-mail:** production@advertel.com. **Website:** www.advertel.com. Submit demo of previous work. Prefers CD. "Most compositions are 2 minutes strung together in 6-, 12-, 18-minute-length productions." Does not return material; prefers to keep on file. Responds "right away if submission fills an immediate need." Submit any unsolicited material (instrumental only) via e-mail.

TIPS "Go for volume. We have continuous need for all varieties of music in 2-minute lengths. Advertel produces a religious radio program called 'Prayer-in-the-Air.' Feel free to submit songs with lyrics taken from scripture. We also look for catchy, memorable melodies. For those pro bono submissions, no compensation is offered—only national recognition."

COMMUNICATIONS FOR LEARNING

395 Massachusetts Ave., Arlington MA 02474. (781)641-2350. **E-mail:** comlearn395@gmail.com. **Website:** www.communicationsforlearning.com. **Contact:** Jonathan L. Barkan, executive producer/director. Video, multimedia, exhibit and graphic design firm. Clients include multi-nationals, industry, government, institutions, local, national and international nonprofits. Uses services of music houses and independent songwriters/composers as theme and background music for videos and multimedia. Commissions 1-2 composers/year. Pays $2,000-5,000/job and one-time use fees. Rights purchased vary. Submit demo and work available for library use. Prefers CD to Web links. Does not return material; prefers to keep on file. "For each job we consider our entire collection." Responds in 3 months.

TIPS "Please don't call. Just send your best material available for library use on CD. We'll be in touch if a piece works and negotiate a price. Make certain your name and contact information are on the CD itself, not only on the cover letter."

DBF A MEDIA COMPANY

9683 Charles St., La Plata MD 20646. (301)645-6110. **E-mail:** service@dbfmedia.com. **Website:** www.dbfmedia.com. Video production. Uses the services of music houses for background music for industrial, training, educational, and promo videos, jingles and commercials for radio and TV. Buys all rights. "All genre for MOH, industrial, training, video/photo montages and commercials."

HOW TO CONTACT Submit demo CD of previous work. Prefers CD or DVD with 5-8 songs and lead sheet. Include SASE, but prefers to keep material on file. Responds in 6 months.

K&R ALL MEDIA PRODUCTIONS LLC

28533 Greenfield Rd., Southfield MI 48076. (248)557-8276. **Website:** www.knr.net. Scoring service and **jingle/commercial music production house**. Clients include commercial and industrial firms. Services include sound for pictures (Foley, music, dialogue). Uses the services of independent songwriters/composers and lyricists for scoring of film and video, commercials and industrials and jingles and commercials for radio and TV. Commissions 1 composer/month. Pays by the job. Buys all rights.

HOW TO CONTACT Submit demo tape of previous work. Prefers CD or VHS videocassette with 5-7 short pieces. "We rack your tape for client to judge." Does not return material.

TIPS "Keep samples short. Show me what you can do in 5 minutes. Go to knr.net 'free samples' and listen to the sensitivity expressed in emotional music."

KEN-DEL PRODUCTIONS INC.

1500 First State Blvd., First State Industrial Park, Wilmington DE 19804-3596. (302)999-1111. **E-mail:** info@ken-del.com. **Website:** www.ken-del.com. **Contact:** Paul Janocha. Clients include publishers, industrial firms and advertising agencies, how-to's and radio/TV. Uses services of songwriters for radio/TV commercials, jingles and multimedia. Pays by the job. Buys all rights.

HOW TO CONTACT "Submit all inquiries and demos in any format to general manager." Does not return material. Will keep on file for 3 years. Generally responds in 1 month or less.

✪◐ NOVUS VISUAL COMMUNICATIONS

59 Page Ave., Suite 300, Tower One, Yonkers NY 10704. (212)473-1377. **E-mail:** novuscom@aol.com. **Website:** www.novuscommunications.com. **Contact:** Robert Antonik, managing director. Integrated marketing company. Clients include Fortune 500 companies and nonprofits. Uses the services of music houses, independent songwriters/composers and lyricists for scoring, background music for documentaries, commercials, multimedia applications, website, film shorts, and commercials for radio and TV. Commis-

sions 2 composers and 4 lyricists/year. Pay varies per job. Buys one-time rights.

HOW TO CONTACT *Request a submission of demo.* Query with a brief of sample and songs. Prefers CD with 2-3 songs or link to website. "We prefer to keep submitted material on file, but will return material if SASE is enclosed." Responds in 6 weeks.

MUSIC Uses all styles for a variety of different assignments.

TIPS "Always present your best and don't add quantity to your demo. Novus is a creative marketing and integrated communications company. We also work with special events companies, PR firms, artists' management and media companies."

OMNI COMMUNICATIONS

P.O. Box 302, Carmel IN 46082-0302. (317)846-2345. **Fax:** (317)846-6664. **E-mail:** omni@omniproductions. com. **Website:** www.omniproductions.com. OMNI Productions is an experienced interactive, digital media solutions provider offering the complete infrastructure for production and delivery of digital media services including interactive multipoint Internet training; live event and archived Web casting; video, DVD and CD-ROM production; and encoding, hosting and distribution of streaming video content. OMNI is recognized by Microsoft as a Windows Media Service Provider. This partnership with Microsoft was obtained through vigorous training, testing and experience to ensure that those we serve receive the highest quality service from OMNI's experienced professionals. OMNI's staff includes technology experts certified by Microsoft and other industry vendors.

TIPS "Submit good demo tape with examples of your range to command the attention of our producers."

UTOPIAN EMPIRE CREATIVEWORKS

P.O. Box 9, Traverse City MI 49865. (231)715-1614. **E-mail:** traverse_city@utopianempire.com. **Website:** www.utopianempire.com. Web design, multimedia firm, and motion picture/video production company. Primarily serves commercial, industrial and nonprofit clients. "We provide the following services: advertising, marketing, design/packaging, distribution and booking. Uses services of music houses, independent songwriters/composers for jingles and scoring of and background music for multi-image/multimedia, film and video." Negotiates pay. Buys all or one-time rights.

HOW TO CONTACT Submit CD of previous work, demonstrating composition skills or query with résumé of credits. Prefers CD. Does not return material; prefers to keep on file. Responds only if interested.

MUSIC Uses mostly industrial/commercial themes.

✪ VIDEO I-D, TELEPRODUCTIONS

105 Muller Rd., Washington IL 61571. (309)444-4323. **E-mail:** videoid@videoid.com. **Website:** www.videoid.com. **Contact:** Sam B. Wagner, president. Post production/teleproductions. Clients include law enforcement, industrial and business. Uses the services of music houses and independent songwriters/composers for background music for video productions. Pays per job. Buys one-time rights.

HOW TO CONTACT Submit demo of previous work. Prefers CD with 5 songs and lyric sheet. Does not return material. Responds in 1 month.

PLAY PRODUCERS & PUBLISHERS

//

Finding a theater company willing to invest in a new production can be frustrating for an unknown playwright. But whether you write the plays, compose the music, or pen the lyrics, it is important to remember not only where to start but how to start. Theater in the U.S. is a hierarchy, with Broadway, Off-Broadway, and Off-Off-Broadway being pretty much off-limits to all but the Stephen Sondheims of the world.

Aspiring theater writers would do best to train their sights on nonprofit regional and community theaters to get started. The encouraging news is there are a great number of local theater companies throughout the U.S. with experimental artistic directors who are looking for new works to produce, and many are included in this section. This section covers two segments of the industry: theater companies and dinner theaters are listed under Play Producers, and publishers of musical theater works are listed under the Play Publishers heading. These markets are actively seeking new works of all types for their stages or publications.

BREAKING IN

Starting locally will allow you to research each company carefully and learn about their past performances, the type of musicals they present, and the kinds of material they're looking for. When you find theaters you think may be interested in your work, attend as many performances as possible, so you know exactly what type of material each theater presents. Or volunteer to work at a theater, whether it be moving sets or selling tickets. This will give you valuable insight into the day-to-day workings of a theater and the creation of a new show. On a national level, you will find prestigious organizations offering workshops and apprenticeships covering every subject from arts administration to directing to costuming. But it could be more helpful to look into professional internships at theaters and attend theater workshops in your area. The more knowledgeable you are about the workings of a particular company or theater, the easier it will be to tailor your work to fit its style and the more responsive they will be to you and your work. (See the Workshops & Conferences section for more information.) As a composer for the stage, you need to know as much as possible about a theater and how it works, its history and the different roles played by the people involved in it. Flexibility is the key to successful productions, and knowing how a theater works will only help you in cooperating and collaborating with the director, producer, technical people and actors.

If you're a playwright looking to have his play published in book form or in theater publications, see the listings under the Play Publishers section. To find play producers and publishers in your area, consult the Geographic Index at the back of this book.

ARKANSAS REPERTORY THEATRE

601 Main St., P.O. Box 110, Little Rock AR 72201. (501)378-0445. **Website:** www.therep.org. Produces 6-10 plays and musicals/year. "We perform in a 354-seat house and also have a 99-seat second stage." Pays 5-10% royalty or $75-150 per performance.

HOW TO CONTACT Query with synopsis, character breakdown and set description. Include SASE. Responds in 6 months.

MUSICAL THEATER "Small casts are preferred, comedy or drama, and prefer shows to run 1:45 to 2 hours maximum. Simple is better; small is better, but we do produce complex shows. We aren't interested in children's pieces, puppet shows or mime. We always like to receive a tape of the music with the book."

PRODUCTIONS *Disney's Beauty & the Beast*, by Woolverton/Ashman/Rice/Menken (musical retelling of the myth); *Crowns*, by Taylor/Cunningham/Marberry (on the significance of African-American women's hats); and *A Chorus Line*, by Kirkwood/Hamlisch/Kleban (auditions).

TIPS "Include a good CD of your music, sung well, with the script."

BARTER THEATRE

127 W. Main St., Abingdon VA 24210. (276)628-3991. **E-mail:** dramaturge@bartertheatre.com. **Website:** www.bartertheatre.com. The Barter Players produces professional children's productions with 100% of roles written for adults.

○ *Does not accept unsolicited mss.*

MUSICAL THEATER Prefer small-cast musicals, although have done large-scale projects with marketable titles or subject matter. "We do not accept one-act or juke-box musicals. We use original music in many of our plays."

TIPS "We are looking for material that appeals to diverse, family audiences. We accept no one-act play queries."

CIRCA '21 DINNER PLAYHOUSE

1828 Third Ave., Rock Island IL 61201. (309)786-7733. **Website:** www.circa21.com. Plays produced for a general audience. Three children's works/year, concurrent with major productions. Payment is negotiable.

HOW TO CONTACT Query with synopsis, character breakdown and set description or submit complete manuscript, score and tape of songs. Include SASE. Responds in 3 months.

MUSICAL THEATER "We produce both full-length and one-act children's musicals. Folk or fairy tale themes. Works that do not condescend to a young audience yet are appropriate for entire family. We're also seeking full-length, small-cast musicals suitable for a broad audience." Would also consider original music for use in a play being developed.

PRODUCTIONS *A Closer Walk with Patsy Cline*, *Swingtime Canteen*, *Forever Plaid* and *Lost Highway*.

TIPS "Small, upbeat, tourable musicals (like *Pump Boys*) and bright musically sharp children's productions (like those produced by Prince Street Players) work best. Keep an open mind. Stretch to encompass a musical variety—different keys, rhythms, musical ideas and textures."

DRAMATIC PUBLISHING, INC.

311 Washington St., Woodstock IL 60098. (800)448-7469. **E-mail:** submissionseditor@dpcplays.com. **Website:** www.dramaticpublishing.com. **Contact:** Linda Habjan, submissions editor. Recently published: *Redwall: The Legend of Redwall Abbey*, by Evelyn Swensson, based on the book by Brian Jacques. *Gooney Bird Green and Her True-Life Adventures*, adapted by Kent R. Brown from the book by Lois Lowry; *Anastasia Krupnik*, by Meryl Friedman, based on the book by Lois Lowry; *A Village Fable*, by James Still, adapted from *In the Suicide Mountain*, by John Gardner; *The Little Prince*, adapted by Rick Cummins and John Scoullar.

TIPS "Original plays dealing with hopes, joys and fears of today's children are preferred to adaptations of old classics. No more adapted fairytales."

ELDRIDGE PUBLISHING CO., INC.

P.O. Box 4904, Lancaster PA 17604. (850)385-2463. **E-mail:** info@histage.com. **Website:** www.histage.com; www.95church.com. **Contact:** Meredith Edwards, acquisitions editor. Play publisher. Publishes new plays and musicals for junior and senior high school, community theater, and children's theater (adults performing for children), all genres; also religious plays. Publishes 50 plays and 2-3 musicals. Pays 50% royalty and 10% copy sales. "We're always looking for talented composers, but not through individual songs. We serve the school market (6th through 12th grades); and the church market (Christmas musicals)."

○ Recently published plays: *Just Another High School Play*, by Bryan Starchman for schools; *Wage Warfare*, by Scott Haan for community theatres. Church market is nondenominational, specializing in Christmas plays and musicals. Sample title: *An Unlikely Christmas Shepherd*. Prefers work which has been performed or at least had a staged reading.

HOW TO CONTACT Submit complete ms through appropriate online portal; snail mail a sample of the score and CD of songs or provide a Web link to them. Will consider simultaneous submissions, if noted. Responds in 2 months. "Lead sheets, CDs, and scripts are bests way to submit. Let us see your work!"

MUSICAL THEATER Seeking "large-cast musicals, which appeal to students. We like variety and originality in the music, easy staging and costuming. Also looking for children's theater musicals which have smaller casts and are easy to tour."

PRODUCTIONS *That's Princess...With a Pea!*, written and composed by Elliott Baker.

TIPS "Try to have your work performed, if at all possible, before submitting. We're always on the lookout for comedies, which provide a lot of fun for our customers. But other more serious topics, as well as intriguing mysteries and children's theater programs, are of interest to us, as well. We know there are many new talented playwrights out there, and we look forward to reading their fresh scripts."

ENSEMBLE THEATRE OF CINCINNATI

1127 Vine St., Cincinnati OH 45202. (513)421-3555. **Fax:** (513)562-4104. **E-mail:** script@ensemblecincinnati.org. **Website:** www.ensemblecincinnati.org. **Contact:** D. Lynn Meyers, producing artistic director. Professional year-round theater. Play producer. Produces 6 plays and at least 1 new musical/year. Audience is multi-generational and multi-cultural. 191 seats, proscenium stage. Pays 5-8% royalty (negotiable).

HOW TO CONTACT Please call or write to inquire if ETC is accepting new scripts.

MUSICAL THEATER "All types of musicals are acceptable. Minimum set, please."

PRODUCTIONS *Hedwig & the Angry Inch*, by John Cameron Mitchel (rock star/transgender/love story); *Alice in Wonderland*, by David Kisor and Joe McDonough (update of the classic tale); and *The Frog Princess*, by Joe McDonough and David Kisor (family retelling of classic tale).

TIPS Looking for "creative, inventive, contemporary subjects or classic tales. If we ask you to send your

script, please send materials as complete as possible, including a SASE."

SAMUEL FRENCH, INC.

235 Park Ave. S., 5th Floor, New York NY 10003. (866)598-8449. **Fax:** (212)206-1429. **E-mail:** publications@samuelfrench.com. **Website:** www.samuelfrench.com. Publishes paperback acting editions of plays. *Not currently accepting unsolicited submissions.*

PRODUCTIONS "We publish primarily successful musicals from the New York, London and regional stage."

PUBLICATIONS *Evil Dead: The Musical*, by George Reinblatt—lyrics/book, and Frank Cipolla, Christopher Bond, Melissa Morris, George Reinblatt - music (Horror Movie parody); *Hats! The Musical*, book by Marcia Milgrom Dodge & Anthony Dodge, additional material by Rob Bartlett, Lynne Taylor-Corbett and Sharon Vaughn. Songs by Grammy-, Golden Globe-, and Tony-winning songwriters (musical celebration of turning 50); *Adding Machine: A Musical*, composed by Joshua Schmidt, Libretto by Jason Loewith and Joshua Schmidt (dark comic of *The Adding Machine* by Elmer Rice).

HEUER PUBLISHING LLC

P.O. Box 248, Cedar Rapids IA 52406. (319)368-8008. **Fax:** (319)368-8011. **E-mail:** editor@hitplays.com. **E-mail:** editor@heuerpub.com. **Website:** www.hitplays.com. Publishes plays, musicals, operas/operettas and guides (choreography, costume, production/staging) for amateur and professional markets, including junior and senior high schools, college/university and community theaters. Focus includes comedy, drama, fantasy, mystery and holiday. Pays by percentage royalty or outright purchase. Pays by outright purchase or percentage royalty.

HOW TO CONTACT Query with musical CD or submit complete ms and score. Include SASE. Responds in 2 months.

MUSICAL THEATER "We prefer one-, two-, or three-act comedies or mystery-comedies with a large number of characters."

PUBLICATIONS *Happily Ever After*, by Allen Koepke (musical fairytale); *Brave Buckaroo*, by Renee J. Clark (musical melodrama); and *Pirate Island*, by Martin Follose (musical comedy).

TIPS "We are willing to review single-song submissions as cornerstone pieces for commissioned works.

Special-interest focus in multicultural, historic, classic literature, teen issues, and biographies."

LA JOLLA PLAYHOUSE

P.O. Box 12039, La Jolla CA 92039. (858)550-1070. **Fax:** (858)550-1075. **E-mail:** information@ljp.org. **Website:** www.lajollaplayhouse.org. Produces 6 shows/season including 1-2 new musicals/year. Audience is University of California students to senior citizens. Performance spaces include a large proscenium theater with 492 seats, a 3/4 thrust (384 seats), and a black box with up to 400 seats.

HOW TO CONTACT Query with synopsis, character breakdown, 10-page dialogue sample, demo CD. Include SASE. Responds in 1-2 months.

MUSICAL THEATER "We prefer contemporary music but not necessarily a story set in contemporary times. Retellings of classic stories can enlighten us about the times we live in. For budgetary reasons, we'd prefer a smaller cast size."

PRODUCTIONS *Cry-Baby*, book and lyrics by Thomas Meehan and Mark O'Donnell, music by David Javerbaum and Adam Schlesinger; *Dracula, The Musical*, book and lyrics by Don Black and Christopher Hampton, music by Frank Wildhorn (adaptation of Bram Stoker's novel); *Thoroughly Modern Millie*, book by Richard Morris and Dick Scanlan, new music by Jeanine Tesori, new lyrics by Dick Scanlan (based on the 1967 movie); and *Jane Eyre*, book and additional lyrics by John Cairo, music and lyrics by Paul Gordon (adaptation of Charlotte Bronte's novel).

NORTH SHORE MUSIC THEATRE

62 Dunham Rd., Beverly MA 01915. (978)232-7200. **Fax:** (978)921-9999. **E-mail:** northshoremusictheatre@nsmt.org. **Website:** www.nsmt.org.

HOW TO CONTACT Submit synopsis and CD of songs. Include SASE. Responds within 6 months.

MUSICAL THEATER Prefers full-length adult pieces not necessarily arena-theater oriented. Cast sizes from 1-30; orchestra's from 1-16.

PRODUCTIONS *Tom Jones*, by Paul Leigh, George Stiles; *I Sent A Letter to My Love*, by Melissa Manchester and Jeffrey Sweet; *Just So*, by Anthony Drewe and George Stiles (musical based on Rudyard Kipling's fables); *Letters from 'Nam*, by Paris Barclay (Vietnam War experience as told through letters from GIs); and *Friendship of the Sea*, by Michael Wartofsky & Kathleen Cahill (New England maritime adventure musical).

TIPS "Keep at it!"

PIONEER DRAMA SERVICE, INC.

P.O. Box 4267, Englewood CO 80155-4267. (303)779-4035. **Fax:** (303)779-4315. **E-mail:** editors@pioneerdrama.com. **Website:** www.pioneerdrama.com. **Contact:** Lori Conary, submissions editor. Plays are performed for audiences of all ages. Playwrights paid 50% royalty (10% sales) split when there are multiple authors/composers. Publishes plays that are performed by schools, colleges, community theaters, recreation programs, churches, and professional children's theaters for audiences of all ages. For musicals, query with character breakdown, synopsis and set description or submit full manuscript and CD of music. Include SASE.

HOW TO CONTACT For musicals, query with character breakdown, synopsis and set description or submit full manuscript and CD of music. Include SASE. Responds in 6 months.

MUSICAL THEATER "We seek full-length children's musicals, high school musicals, and one-act children's musicals to be performed by children, secondary school students, and/or adults. We want musicals that are easy to perform, simple sets, many female roles, and very few solos. Must be appropriate for educational market. We are not interested in profanity, themes with exclusively adult interest, sex, drinking, smoking, etc."

TIPS "Check out our website to see what we carry and if your material would be appropriate for our market. Make sure to include proof of productions and a SASE if you want your material returned."

PLAYWRIGHTS HORIZONS

416 W. 42nd St., New York NY 10036. (212)564-1235. **Fax:** (212)594-0296. **E-mail:** lit@phnyc.org. **Website:** www.playwrightshorizons.org. **Contact:** Sarah Lunnie, literary manager. Plays performed Off-Broadway for a literate, urban, subscription audience. Produces about 5 plays and 1 new musical/year. "Adventurous New York theater-going audience." Pays general Off-Broadway contract.

HOW TO CONTACT Submit complete ms and CD of songs. Attn: Sarah Lunnie for plays, Kent Nicholson for musicals. Include SASE. Responds in 8 months.

MUSICAL THEATER American writers. "No revivals, one-acts or children's shows; otherwise, we're flexible. We have a particular interest in scores with a distinctively contemporary and American flavor.

We generally develop work from scratch; we're open to proposals for shows and scripts in early stages of development."

PRODUCTIONS *Me, Myself and I*; *After the Revolution*; *A Small Fire, Kin*.

TIPS "We do not accept one-acts, one-person shows, translations, children's shows, screenplays, or works by non-U.S. writers. We dislike synopses because we accept unsolicited manuscripts. We look for plays with a strong sense of language and a clear dramatic action that truly use the resources of the theater."

PRIMARY STAGES

307 W. 38th St., Suite 1510, New York NY 10018. (212)840-9705. **E-mail:** info@primarystages.org. **Website:** www.primarystages.org. New York theater-going audience representing a broad cross-section, in terms of age, ethnicity, and economic backgrounds. one-hundred-and-ninety-nine-seat, Off-Broadway theater.

HOW TO CONTACT *No unsolicited scripts accepted. Submissions by agents only.* Include SASE. Responds in up to 8 months.

MUSICAL THEATER "We are looking for works of heightened theatricality, that challenge realism—musical plays that go beyond film and television's standard fare. We are looking for small cast-shows under 6 characters total, with limited sets. We are interested in original works, that have not been produced in New York."

PRODUCTIONS *Harbor*, by Chad Beguelin; *Bronx Bombers*, by Fran Kirmser and Eric Simmonson; *The Model Apartment*, by Donald Margulies; *The Tribute Artist*, by Charles Busch.

PRINCE MUSIC THEATER

1412 Chestnut St., Philadelphia PA 19102. **E-mail:** info@princemusictheater.org. **Website:** www.princemusictheater.org. "Professional musical productions. Drawing upon operatic and popular traditions, as well as European, African, Asian, and South American forms, new work and new voices take center stage." Play producer. Produces 4-5 musicals/year. "Our average audience member is in his or her mid-40s. We perform to ethnically diverse houses."

HOW TO CONTACT Submit 2-page synopsis with tape or CD of 4 songs. Include SASE. "May include complete script, but be aware that response is at least 10 months."

TIPS "Innovative topics and use of media, music, technology a plus. Sees trends of arts in technology (interactive theater, virtual reality, sound design); works are shorter in length (1 to 1 and 1/2 hours with no intermissions or 2 hours with intermission)."

THE REPERTORY THEATRE OF ST. LOUIS

130 Edgar Rd., P.O. Box 191730, St. Louis MO 63119. (314)968-7340. **Website:** www.repstl.org. **Contact:** Steven Woolf, artistic director.

HOW TO CONTACT Query with synopsis, character breakdown and set description. Does not return material.

MUSICAL THEATER "We want plays with a small cast and simple setting. No children's shows or foul language. After a letter of inquiry, we would prefer script and demo tape."

PRODUCTIONS *Almost September* and *Esmeralda*, by David Schechter and Steve Lutvak; *Jack*, by Barbara Field and Hiram Titus; and *Young Rube*, by John Pielmeier and Nattie Selman, *Ace* by Robert Taylor and Richard Oberacker.

SECOND STAGE THEATRE

305 W. 43rd St., New York NY 10036. (212)246-4422. **Fax:** (212)399-4115. **E-mail:** cburney@2st.com. **Website:** www.2st.com. **Contact:** Christopher Burney, associate artistic director. "Second Stage Theatre gives new life to contemporary U.S. plays through 'second stagings;' provides emerging authors with their Off-Broadway debuts; and produces world premieres by America's most respected playwrights. Adult and teen audiences." Play producer. Produces 4 plays and 1 musical (1 new musical)/year. Plays are performed in a small, 108-seat Off-Broadway House. Pays per performance.

HOW TO CONTACT Query with synopsis, character breakdown, set description, tape of 5 songs (no more). No unsolicited manuscripts. Include SASE. Responds in 6 months.

MUSICAL THEATER "We are looking for innovative, unconventional musicals that deal with socio-political themes."

PRODUCTIONS *Bachelorette*, by Leslye Headland; *Trust* by Paul Weitz; *By the Way, Meet Vera Stark*, by Lynn Nottage.

TIPS "Submit through agent; have strong references; always submit the best of your material in small quantities: 5 outstanding songs are better than 10 mediocre ones. No biographical or historical dramas, or plays in verse. Writers are realizing that audiences can be entertained while being moved. Patience is a virtue but persistence is appreciated."

THE TEN-MINUTE MUSICALS PROJECT

P.O. Box 461194, West Hollywood CA 90046. **E-mail:** info@tenminutemusicals.org. **Website:** www.tenminutemusicals.org. **Contact:** Michael Koppy, producer. "Plays performed in Equity regional theaters in the U.S. and Canada. Deadline August 31; notification by November 30."

○ All pieces are new musicals. Submit complete ms, score, and CD or DVD of songs. Include SASE. Responds in 3 months.

PRODUCTIONS *Away to Pago Pago*, by Jack Feldman/Barry Manilow/John PiRoman/Bruce Sussman; *The Bottle Imp*, by Kenneth Vega (from the story of the same title by Robert Louis Stevenson); and *The Furnished Room*, by Saragail Katzman (from the story of the same title by O. Henry), and many others.

TIPS "Start with a solid story—either an adaptation or an original idea—but with a solid beginning, middle and end (probably with a plot twist at the climax). We caution that it will surely take much time and effort to create a quality work. (Occasionally a clearly talented and capable writer and composer seems to have almost 'dashed' something off, under the mis-conception that inspiration can carry the day in this format. Works selected in previous rounds all clearly evince that considerable deliberation and craft were invested.) We're seeking short contemporary musical theater material, in the style of what might be found on Broadway, Off-Broadway or the West End. Think of shows like *Candide* or *Little Shop of Horrors*, pop operas like *Sweeney Todd* or *Chess*, or chamber musicals like *Once on this Island* or *Falsettos*. (Even small accessible operas like *The Telephone* or *Trouble in Tahiti* are possible models.) All have solid plots, and all rely on sung material to advance them. Of primary importance is to start with a strong story, even if it means postponing work on music and lyrics until the dramatic foundation is complete."

THUNDER BAY THEATRE

400 N. Second Ave., Alpena MI 49707. (989)354-2267. **E-mail:** tbt@thunderbaytheatre.com; artisticdirector@thunderbaytheatre.com. **Website:** www.thunderbaytheatre.com. **Contact:** Jeffrey Mindock, artistic director.

HOW TO CONTACT Submit complete ms, score and tape of songs. Include SASE.

MUSICAL THEATER Small cast. Not equipped for large sets. Considers original background music for use in a play being developed or for use in a pre-existing play.

CLASSICAL
PERFORMING ARTS

///

Finding an audience is critical to the composer of orchestral music. Fortunately, baby boomers are swelling the ranks of classical music audiences and bringing with them a taste for fresh, innovative music. So the climate is fair for composers seeking their first performance.

Finding a performance venue is particularly important because once a composer has his work performed for an audience and establishes himself as a talented newcomer, it can lead to more performances and commissions for new works. Getting started, however, often can be difficult for those just trying to break in.

BEFORE YOU SUBMIT

Be aware that most classical music organizations are nonprofit groups that don't have a large budget for acquiring new works. It takes a lot of time and money to put together an orchestral performance of a new composition; therefore, these groups are quite selective when choosing new works to perform, so make sure you follow their submission guidelines to the letter. Also, don't be disappointed if the payment offered by these groups is small or even non-existent.

What you gain is the chance to have your music performed for an appreciative audience. Performing in front of that audience could eventually lead to more widespread recognition, reviews, and better opportunities. Sometimes the only way to get started is through word of mouth and local reviews.

Also, realize that many classical groups are understaffed, so it may take longer than expected to hear back on your submission. It pays to be patient, and employ diplomacy, tact and timing in your follow-up. Be courteous, prompt and appreciative in your interactions with staff. They can be some of your biggest champions and most important contacts should you work with them!

In this section you will find listings for classical performing arts organizations throughout the U.S. But if you have no prior performances to your credit, it's a good idea to begin with a small chamber orchestra, for example. Smaller symphony and chamber orchestras are usually more inclined to experiment with new works. A local university or conservatory of music, where you may already have contacts, is a great place to start.

Remember that like any other market in this book (and perhaps more so), you'll need time and patience to break into the classical performing arts.

All of the groups listed in this section are interested in hearing new works from contemporary classical composers. Pay close attention to the music needs of each group, and when you find one you feel might be interested in your music, follow the submission guidelines carefully. To locate classical performing arts groups in your area, consult the Geographic Index at the back of this book.

ACADIANA SYMPHONY ORCHESTRA

P.O. Box 53632, Lafayette LA 70505. (337)232-4277. **Website:** www.acadianasymphony.org. **Contact:** Jenny Krueger, executive director. Estab. 1984. Members are amateurs and professionals. Performs 20 concerts/year, including 1 new work. Commissions 1 new work/year. Performs in 2,230-seat hall with "wonderful acoustics." Pays "according to the type of composition."

HOW TO CONTACT Call first. Does not return material. Responds in 2 months.

MUSIC Full orchestra: 10 minutes at most. Reduced orchestra, educational pieces: short, up to 5 minutes.

PERFORMANCES Quincy Hilliard's *Universal Covenant* (orchestral suite); James Hanna's *In Memoriam* (strings/elegy); and Gregory Danner's *A New Beginning* (full orchestra fanfare).

THE AMERICAN BOYCHOIR

P.O. Box 7468, Princeton NJ 08543. (609)924-5858. E-mail: admissions@americanboychoir.org. **Website:** www.americanboychoir.org. P.O. Box 7468, Princeton NJ 08543. (609)924-5858. **Fax:** (609)924-5812. **E-mail:** admissions@americanboychoir.org. **Website:** www.americanboychoir.org. General Manager: Christie Starrett. Music director: Fernando Malvar-Ruiz. Professional boychoir. Estab. 1937. Members are musically talented boys in grades 4-8. Performs 150 concerts/year. Commissions 1 new work approximately every 3 years. Actively seeks high-quality arrangements. Performs national and international tours, orchestral engagements, church services, workshops, school programs, local concerts, and at corporate and social functions.

HOW TO CONTACT Submit complete score. Include SASE. Responds in 1 year.

MUSIC Choral works in unison, SA, SSA, SSAA or SATB division; unaccompanied and with piano or organ; occasional chamber orchestra or brass ensemble. Works are usually sung by 28-60 boys. Composers must know boychoir sonority.

PERFORMANCES *Four Seasons*, by Michael Torke (orchestral-choral); *Garden of Light*, by Aaron Kernis (orchestral-choral); *Reasons for Loving the Harmonica*, by Libby Larsen (piano); and *Songs Eternity*, by Steven Paulus (piano).

ANDERSON SYMPHONY ORCHESTRA

1124 Meridian Plaza, Anderson IN 46016. **Website:** www.andersonsymphony.org. **Contact:** Dr. Richard Sowers, music director. Symphony orchestra. Estab. 1967. Members are professionals. Performs 7 concerts/year. Performs for typical midwestern audience in a 1,500-seat restored Paramount Theatre. Pay negotiable.

HOW TO CONTACT Query first. Include SASE. Responds in several months.

MUSIC "Shorter lengths better; concerti OK; difficulty level: mod high; limited by typically 3 full-service rehearsals."

THE ATLANTA YOUNG SINGERS OF CALLANWOLDE

1085 Ponce de Leon Ave. NE, Atlanta GA 30306. (404)873-3365. **Fax:** (404)873-0756. **E-mail:** info@aysc.org. **Website:** www.aysc.org. **Contact:** Paige F. Mathis, music director. Children's chorus. Estab. 1975. Performs 3 major concerts/year, as well as invitational performances and co-productions with other Atlanta arts organizations. Audience consists of community members, families, alumni, and supporters. Performs most often at churches. Pay is negotiable.

HOW TO CONTACT Submit complete score and tape of piece(s). Include SASE. Responds in accordance with request.

MUSIC Subjects and styles appealing to 3rd- to 12th-grade boys and girls. Contemporary concerns of the world of interest. Unusual sacred, folk, classic style. Internationally and ethnically bonding. Medium difficulty preferred, with or without keyboard accompaniment.

TIPS "Our mission is to promote service and growth through singing."

AUGSBURG CHOIR

Augsburg College, 2211 Riverside Ave. S., Minneapolis MN 55454. (612)330-1265. **E-mail:** musicdept@augsburg.edu. **Website:** www.augsburg.edu. **Contact:** Peter A. Hendrickson, director of choral activities. Vocal ensemble (SATB choir). Members are amateurs. Performs 25 concerts/year, including 1-6 new works. Commissions 0-2 composers or new works/year. Audience is all ages, "sophisticated and unsophisticated." Concerts are performed in churches, concert halls and schools. Pays for outright purchase.

HOW TO CONTACT Query first. Include SASE. Responds in 1 month.

MUSIC Seeking "sacred choral pieces, no more than 5-7 minutes long, to be sung a cappella or with obbligato instrument. Can contain vocal solos. We have 50-60 members in our choir."

PERFORMANCES Carol Barnett's *Spiritual Journey*; Steven Heitzeg's *Litanies for the Living* (choral/orchestral); and Morton Lanriclsen's *O Magnum Mysteries* (a cappella choral).

BARDAVON

35 Market St., Poughkeepsie NY 12601. (845)473-5288. **Fax:** (845)473-4259. **Website:** www.bardavon.org. Symphony orchestra. Estab. 1969. Members are professionals. Performs 20 concerts/year including 1 new work. "Classical subscription concerts for all ages; pop concerts for all ages; New Wave concerts—crossover projects with a rock 'n' roll artist performing with an orchestra. HVP performs in 3 main theaters, which are concert auditoriums with stages and professional lighting and sound." Pay is negotiable.

HOW TO CONTACT Query first. Include SASE. Responds only if interested.

MUSIC "HVP is open to serious classical music, pop music, and rock 'n' roll crossover projects. Desired length of work: 10-20 minutes. Orchestrations can be varied but should always include strings. There is no limit to difficulty since our musicians are professional. The ideal number of musicians to write for would include up to a Brahms-size orchestra 2222, 4231, T, 2P, piano, harp, strings."

PERFORMANCES Joan Tower's *Island Rhythms* (serious classical work); Bill Vanaver's *P'nai El* (symphony work with dance); and Joseph Bertolozzi's *Serenade* (light classical, pop work).

TIPS "Don't get locked into doing very traditional orchestrations or styles. Our music director is interested in fresh, creative formats. He is an orchestrator, as well and can offer good advice on what works well. Songwriters who are into crossover projects should definitely submit works. Over the past 4 years, HVP has done concerts featuring the works of Natalie Merchant, John Cale, Sterling Morrison, Richie Havens, and R. Carlos Naka (Native American flute player), all reorchestrated by our music director for small orchestra with the artist."

BILLINGS SYMPHONY

2721 Second Ave. N., Suite 350, Billings MT 59101. (406)252-3610. **Fax:** (406)252-3353. **E-mail:** symphony@billingssymphony.org. **Website:** www.billingssymphony.org. **Contact:** Darren Rich, executive director. Symphony orchestra, orchestra and chorale. Estab. 1950. Members are professionals and amateurs. Performs 12-15 concerts/year, including 6-7 new works. Traditional audience. Performs at Alberta Bair Theater (capacity 1,416). Pays by outright purchase (or rental).

HOW TO CONTACT Query first. Include SASE. Responds in 2 weeks.

MUSIC Any style. Traditional notation preferred.

PERFORMANCES 2015-2016 season includes *Around the World and to the Stars*, *Cirque de la Symphonie*, *Resurrection*, and more.

TIPS "Write what you feel (be honest) and sharpen your compositional and craftsmanship skills."

BIRMINGHAM-BLOOMFIELD SYMPHONY ORCHESTRA

P.O. Box 1925, Birmingham MI 48012. (248)352-2276. **E-mail:** info@bbso.org. **Website:** www.bbso.org. **Contact:** John Thomas Dodson, music director and conductor. Symphony orchestra. Estab. 1975. Members are professionals. Performs 5 concerts including 1 new work/year. Commissions 1 composer or new work/year "with grants." Performs for middle- to upper-class audience at Temple Beth El's Sanctuary. Pays per performance "depending upon grant received."

HOW TO CONTACT *Query first.* Does not return material. Responds in 6 months.

MUSIC "We are a symphony orchestra but also play pops. Usually 3 works on program (2 hours). Orchestra size: 65-75. If pianist is involved, he or she must rent piano."

PERFORMANCES Brian Belanger's *Tuskegee Airmen Suite* (symphonic full orchestra); Larry Nazer & Friend's *Music from "Warm" CD* (jazz with full orchestra); and Mark Gottlieb's *Violin Concerto for Orchestra*.

THE BOSTON PHILHARMONIC

295 Huntington Ave., Suite 210, Boston MA 02116. (617)236-0999. **E-mail:** info@bostonphil.org. **Website:** www.bostonphil.org. **Contact:** Benjamin Zander, music director. Symphony orchestra. Estab. 1979. Members are professionals, amateurs and students.

Performs 2 concerts/year. Audience is ages 30-70. Performs at New England Conservatory's Jordan Hall, Boston's Symphony Hall and Sanders Theatre in Cambridge. Both Jordan Hall and Sanders Theatre are small (approximately 1,100 seats) and very intimate.

HOW TO CONTACT *Does not accept new music at this time.*

MUSIC Full orchestra only.

PERFORMANCES Dutilleuxs' *Tout un monde lointain* for cello and orchestra (symphonic); Bernstein's *Fancy Free* (symphonic/jazzy); Copland's *El Salon Mexico* (symphonic); Gershwin's *Rhapsody in Blue*; Shostakovitch's *Symphony No. 10*; Harbison's *Concerto for Oboe*; Holst's *The Planet Suite*; Schwantner's *New Morning for the World*; Berg's *Seven Early Songs*; and Ive's *The Unanswered Question*.

☮ CALGARY BOYS CHOIR

4825 Mt. Royal Gate SW, Calgary AB T3E 6K6 Canada. (403)440-6821. **Fax:** (403)440-6594. **E-mail:** gm.calgaryboyschoir@gmail.com. **Website:** levendis99.wix.com/calgaryboyschoir. **Contact:** Paul Grindlay, artistic director. Boys choir. Estab. 1973. Members are amateurs age 5 and up. Performs 5-10 concerts/year including 1-2 new works. Pay negotiable.

HOW TO CONTACT Query first. Submit complete score and tape of piece(s). Include SASE. Responds in 6 weeks. Does not return material.

MUSIC "Style fitting for boys choir. Lengths depending on project. Orchestration preferable a cappella/for piano/sometimes orchestra."

☮ CANADIAN OPERA COMPANY

227 Front St. E., Toronto ON M5A 1E8 Canada. (800)250-4653. **E-mail:** info@coc.ca; music@coc.ca. **Website:** www.coc.ca. **Contact:** Alexander Neef, general director. Opera company. Estab. 1950. Members are professionals. 68-72 performances, including a minimum of 1 new work/year. Pays by contract.

HOW TO CONTACT Submit complete CDs or DVDs of vocal and/or operatic works. "Vocal works please." Include SASE. Responds in 5 weeks.

MUSIC Vocal works, operatic in nature. "Do not submit works that are not for voice. Ask for requirements for the Composers-In-Residence program."

PERFORMANCES Bellini's *Norma*; *Handel's Ariodante*; Mozart's *The Magic Flute*; Harry Somers' *Louis Riel* ; *Giacomo Puccini's Tosca*.

TIPS "We have a Composers-In-Residence program, which is open to Canadian composers or landed immigrants."

CANTATA ACADEMY

P.O. Box 1958, Royal Oak MI 48084. (313)248-7282. **E-mail:** cantata@cantataacademy.org. **E-mail:** director@cantataacademy.org. **Website:** cantataacademy. org. **Contact:** Susan Catanese, director. Vocal ensemble. Estab. 1961. Members are professionals. Performs 10-12 concerts/year including 1-3 new works. "We perform in churches and small auditoriums throughout the metro Detroit area for audiences of about 500 people." Pays variable rate for outright purchase.

HOW TO CONTACT Submit complete score. Include SASE. Responds in 3 months.

MUSIC Four-part a cappella and keyboard accompanied works, two- and three-part works for men's or women's voices. Some small instrumental ensemble accompaniments acceptable. Work must be suitable for 40-voice choir. No works requiring orchestra or large ensemble accompaniment. No pop.

PERFORMANCES Libby Larsen's *Missa Gaia: Mass for the Earth* (SATB, string quartet, oboe, percussion, 4-hand piano); Dede Duson's *To Those Who See* (SATB, SSA); and Sarah Hopkins' *Past Life Melodies* (SATB with Harmonic Overtone Singing); Eric Whiteacre's *Five Hebrew Love Songs*; Robert Convery's *Songs of the Children*.

TIPS "Be patient. Would prefer to look at several different samples of work at one time."

CARMEL SYMPHONY ORCHESTRA

760 3rd Ave. SW, Suite 102, Carmel IN 46032. (317)844-9717. **Fax:** (317)844-9916. **E-mail:** info@carmelsymphony.org. **Website:** www.carmelsymphony. org. **Contact:** Alan Davis, president/CEO. Symphony orchestra. Estab. 1976. Members are paid and nonpaid professionals. Performs 15 concerts/year, including 1-2 new works. Performs in a 1,600-seat Palladium at the Center for the Performing Arts.

HOW TO CONTACT *Query first.* Include SASE. Responds in 3 months.

MUSIC "Full orchestra works, 5-60 minutes in length. Parents are encouraged to bring a child. 85-piece orchestra, medium difficult to difficult.

PERFORMANCES Brahms' *Concerto in D Major for Violin and Orchestra*, Op. 77; Debussy's "La Mer"; Ravel's Second Suite from "Daphnis and Chloe"; Dvorak's

Carnival Overture, Op. 92; and Sibelius' *Symphony No. 5 in E-flat Major*, Op. 82. Outstanding guest artists include Michael Feinstein, Sylvia McNair, Cameron Carpenter, Dale Clevenger, and Angela Brown.

CHATTANOOGA GIRLS CHOIR

4315 Brainerd Rd., Suite B, Chattanooga TN 37411. (423)296-1006. **E-mail:** chattanoogagirlschoir@gmail.com. **Website:** chattanoogagirlschoir.com. **Contact:** Dale Dye, executive director. Vocal ensemble. Estab. 1986. Members are amateurs. Performs 2 concerts/year including at least 1 new work. Audience consists of cultural and civic organizations and national and international tours. Performance space includes concert halls and churches. Pays for outright purchase or per performance.

HOW TO CONTACT Query first. Include SASE. Responds in 6 weeks.

MUSIC Seeks renaissance, baroque, classical, romantic, twentieth century, folk and musical theater for young voices of up to 8 minutes. Performers include 5 treble choices: 4th grade (2 pts.); 5th grade (2 pts.) (SA); grades 6-9 (3 pts.) (SSA); grades 10-12 (3-4 pts.) (SSAA); and a combined choir: grades 6-12 (3-4 pts.) (SSAA). Medium level of difficulty. "Avoid extremely high Tessitura Sop I and extremely low Tessitura Alto II."

PERFORMANCES Jan Swafford's *Iphigenia Book: Meagher* (choral drama); Penny Tullock's *How Can I Keep from Singing* (Shaker hymn).

CHEYENNE SYMPHONY ORCHESTRA

1904 Thomes Ave., Cheyenne WY 82001. (307)778-8561. **E-mail:** administrative@cheyennesymphony.org. **Website:** www.cheyennesymphony.org. **Contact:** Elizabeth McGuire, executive director. Symphony orchestra. Estab. 1955. Members are professionals. Performs 5-6 concerts/year. "Orchestra performs for a conservative, mid-to-upper-income audience of 1,200 season members."

HOW TO CONTACT Query first to Music Director William Intriligator. Does not return material.

CIMARRON CIRCUIT OPERA COMPANY

P.O. Box 1085, Norman OK 73070. (405)364-8962. **Fax:** (405)321-5842. **E-mail:** info@cimarronopera.org. **Website:** www.cimarronopera.org. **Contact:** Kevin W. Smith, music director. Opera company. Estab. 1975. Members are semiprofessional. Performs 75 concerts/year including 1-2 new works. Commissions 1 or less

new work/year. "CCOC performs for children across the state of Oklahoma and for a dedicated audience in central Oklahoma. As a touring company, we adapt to the performance space provided, ranging from a classroom to a full-raised stage." Pay is negotiable.

HOW TO CONTACT Query first. Does not return material. Responds in 6 months.

MUSIC "We are seeking operas or operettas in English only. We would like to begin including new, American works in our repertoire. Children's operas should be no longer than 45 minutes and require no more than a synthesizer for accompaniment. Adult operas should be appropriate for families, and may require either full orchestration or synthesizer. CCOC is a professional company whose members have varying degrees of experience, so any difficulty level is appropriate. There should be a small to moderate number of principals. Children's work should have no more than four principals. Our slogan is 'Opera is a family thing to do.' If we cannot market a work to families, we do not want to see it."

PERFORMANCES Gilbert & Sullivan's *Patience*; and Barab's *La Pizza Con Funghi*.

TIPS "Forty-five-minute fairy tale-type children's operas with possibly a 'moral' work well for our market. Looking for works appealing to K-8 grade students. No more than 4 principles."

CONNECTICUT CHORAL ARTISTS/CONCORA

233 Pearl St., Hartford CT 06103. **Website:** www.concora.org. **Contact:** Ann Drinan, executive director. Estab. 1974. Professional concert choir. Members are professionals. Performs 5 concerts per year, including 3-5 new works.

HOW TO CONTACT Query first. "No unsolicited submissions accepted." Include SASE. Responds in 1 year.

MUSIC Seeking "works for mixed chorus of 36 singers; unaccompanied or with keyboard and/or small instrumental ensemble; text sacred or secular/any language; prefers suites or cyclical works, total time not exceeding 15 minutes. Performance spaces and budgets prohibit large instrumental ensembles. Works suited for 750-seat halls are preferable. Substantial organ or piano parts acceptable. Scores should be very legible in every way."

PERFORMANCES Don McCullough's *Holocaust Contata* (choral with narration); Robert Cohen's *Sprig* *of Lilac: Peter Quince at the Clavier* (choral); Greg Bartholomew's *The 21st Century: A Girl Born in Afghanistan* (choral).

TIPS "Use conventional notation and be sure MS is legible in every way. Recognize and respect the vocal range of each vocal part. Work should have an identifiable rhythmic structure."

● EUROPEAN UNION CHAMBER ORCHESTRA

Hollick, Yarnscombe, Devon EX31 3LQ United Kingdom. (44)1271-858249. **Fax:** (44)1271-858375. **E-mail:** eucorch1@aol.com. **Website:** www.euco.org. uk. Chamber orchestra. Members are professionals. Performs 70 concerts/year, including 6 new works. Commissions 2 composers or new works/year. Performs regular tours of Europe, Americas and Asia, including major venues. Pays per performance or for outright purchase, depending on work.

HOW TO CONTACT Query first. Does not return material. Responds in 6 weeks.

MUSIC Seeking compositions for strings, 2 oboes and 2 horns with a duration of about 8 minutes.

PERFORMANCES Tim Watts' "Bridge of Sighs;" Jane Wells' "Two wings and a prayer."

TIPS "Keep the work to less than 15 minutes in duration, it should be sufficiently 'modern' to be interesting but not too difficult as this could take up rehearsal time. It should be possible to perform without a conductor."

FONTANA CONCERT SOCIETY

359 S. Kalamazoo Mall, Suite 200, Kalamazoo MI 49007. (269)382-7774. **Fax:** (269)382-0812. **Website:** www.fontanachamberarts.org. Chamber music ensemble presenter. Estab. 1980. Members are professionals. Fontana Chamber Arts presents over 45 events, including the 6-week Summer Festival of Music and Art, which runs from mid-July to the end of August. Regional and guest artists perform classical, contemporary, jazz and nontraditional music. Commissions and performs new works each year. Fontana Chamber Arts presents 7 classical and 2 jazz concerts during the fall/winter season. Audience consists of well-educated individuals who accept challenging new works, but like the traditional, as well. Summer—180-seat hall; fall/winter—various venues, 400-1,500 seats.

HOW TO CONTACT Submit complete score, résumé and tapes of piece(s). Include SASE. Responds in

approximately 1 month. Music chamber music—any combination of strings, winds, piano. No "pop" music, new age type. Special interest in composers attending premiere and speaking to the audience.

TIPS "Provide a résumé and clearly marked tape of a piece played by live performers."

FORT WORTH OPERA

1300 Gendy St., Ft. Worth TX 76107. (817)731-0833. **Fax:** (817)731-0835. **E-mail:** boxoffice@fwopera. org. **Website:** www.fwopera.org. **Contact:** Darren K. Woods, general director. Opera company. Estab. 1946. Members are professionals. Performs over 180 in-school performances/year." Audience consists of elementary school children; performs in major venues for district-wide groups and individual school auditoriums, cafetoriums and gymnasiums. Pays $40/ performance.

HOW TO CONTACT Submit complete score and tape of piece(s). Include SASE. Responds in 6 months.

MUSIC "Familiar fairy tales or stories adapted to music of opera composers, or newly composed music of suitable quality. Ideal length: 40-45 minutes. Piano or keyboard accompaniment. Should include moral, safety, or school issues. Can be ethnic in subject matter and must speak to pre-K and grade 1-6 children. Prefer pieces with good, memorable melodies. Performed by young, trained professionals on 9-month contract. Requires work for 4 performers, doubled roles OK, SATB plus accompanist/narrator. Special interest in biligual (Spanish/English) works."

GREATER GRAND FORKS SYMPHONY ORCHESTRA

P.O. Box 5302, Grand Forks ND 58206. (701)732-0579. **E-mail:** ggfso@ggfso.org. **Website:** www.ggfso.org. **Contact:** Director. Symphony orchestra. Estab. 1908. Members are professionals and/or amateurs. Performs 6 concerts/year. "New works are presented in 2-4 of our programs." Audience is "a mix of ages and musical experience. In 1997-98 we moved into a renovated, 420-seat theater." Pay is negotiable, depending on licensing agreements.

HOW TO CONTACT Submit complete score or complete score and tape of pieces. Include SASE. Responds in 6 months.

MUSIC "Style is open, instrumentation the limiting factor. Music can be scored for an ensemble up to but not exceeding: 3,2,3,2/4,3,3,1/3 perc./strings. Rehearsal time limited to 3 hours for new works."

PERFORMANCES Michael Harwood's *Amusement Park Suite* (orchestra); Randall Davidson's *Mexico Bolivar Tango* (chamber orchestra); and John Corigliano's *Voyage* (flute and orchestra); Linda Tutas Haugen's *Fable of Old Turtle* (saxophone concerto); Michael Wittgraf's *Landmarks*; Joan Tower's *Made in America*.

HEARTLAND MEN'S CHORUS

P.O. Box 32374, Kansas City MO 64171. **Website:** www.hmckc.org. **Contact:** Dustin S. Cates, artistic director. Men's chorus. Estab. 1986. Members are professionals and amateurs. Performs 3 concerts/year; 9-10 are new works. Commissions 1 composer or new works/year. Performs for a diverse audience at the Folly Theater (1,100 seats). Pay is negotiable.

HOW TO CONTACT Query first. Include SASE. Responds in 2 months.

MUSIC "Interested in works for male chorus (ttbb). Must be suitable for performance by a gay male chorus. We will consider any orchestration, or a cappella."

PERFORMANCES Mark Hayes' *Two Flutes Playing* (commissioned song cycle); Andrew Lippa's *I Am Harvey Milk* (co-commissioned oratorio); Jake Heggie's *For a Look or a Touch* (chamber opera).

HELENA SYMPHONY

P.O. Box 1073, Helena MT 59624. (406)442-1860. E-mail: artisticplanning@helenasymphony.org. **Website:** www.helenasymphony.org. **Contact:** Allan R. Scott, music director and conductor. Symphony orchestra. Estab. 1955. Members are professionals and amateurs. Performs 7-10 concerts/year including new works. Performance space is an 1,800-seat concert hall. Payment varies.

HOW TO CONTACT Query first. Include SASE. Responds in 3 months.

MUSIC "Imaginative, collaborative, not too atonal. We want to appeal to an audience of all ages. We don't have a huge string complement. Medium to difficult OK—at frontiers of professional ability we cannot do."

PERFORMANCES Eric Funk's *A Christmas Overture* (orchestra); Donald O. Johnston's *A Christmas Processional* (orchestra/chorale); and Elizabeth Sellers' *Prairie* (orchestra/short ballet piece).

TIPS "Try to balance tension and repose in your works. New instrument combinations are appealing."

HENDERSONVILLE SYMPHONY ORCHESTRA

P.O. Box 1811, Hendersonville NC 28793. (828)697-5884. E-mail: info@hendersonvillesymphony.org. **Website:** www.hendersonvillesymphony.org. Symphony orchestra. Estab. 1971. Members are professionals and amateurs. Performs 6 concerts/year. "We would welcome a new work per year." Audience is a cross-section of retirees, professionals, and some children. Performance space is a 857-seat high school audiorium.

HOW TO CONTACT Query first. Include SASE. Responds in 1 month.

MUSIC "We use a broad spectrum of music (classical concerts and pops)."

PERFORMANCES Nelson's *Jubilee* (personal expression in a traditional method); Britten's "The Courtly Dances" from Glorina (time-tested); and Chip Davis' arrangement for Mannheim Steamroller's *Deck the Halls* (modern adaptation of traditional melody).

TIPS "Submit your work even though we are a community orchestra. We like to be challenged. We have the most heavily patronized fine arts group in the county. Our emphasis is on education."

HERSHEY SYMPHONY ORCHESTRA

P.O. Box 93, Hershey PA 17033. (717)533-8449. **Website:** www.hersheysymphony.org. **Contact:** Dr. Sandra Dackow, music director. Symphony orchestra. Estab. 1969. Members are professionals and amateurs. Performs 8 concerts/year, including 1-3 new works. Commissions "possibly 1-2" composers or new works/year. Audience is family and friends of community theater. Performance space is a 1,900-seat grand old movie theater. Pays commission fee.

HOW TO CONTACT Submit complete score and tape of piece(s). Include SASE. Responds in 3 months.

MUSIC "Symphonic works of various lengths and types that can be performed by a non-professional orchestra. We are flexible but like to involve all our players."

PERFORMANCES Paul W. Whear's *Celtic Christmas Carol* (orchestra/bell choir) and Linda Robbins Coleman's *In Good King Charlie's Golden Days* (overture).

TIPS "Please lay out rehearsal numbers/letter and rests according to phrases and other logical musical divisions rather than in groups of 10 measures, etc., which is very unmusical and wastes time and causes a surprising number of problems. Also, please do not send a score written in concert pitch; use the usual transpositions so that the conductor sees what the players see; rehearsal is much more effective this way. Cross cue all important solos; this helps in rehearsal where instruments may be missing."

INDIANA UNIVERSITY NEW MUSIC ENSEMBLE

Indiana University Bloomington, School of Music, Bloomington IN 47405. **E-mail:** ddzubay@indiana. edu. **Website:** www.indiana.edu/~nme. **Contact:** David Dzubay, director. Performs solo, chamber and large-ensemble works. Estab. 1974. Members are students. Presents 4 concerts/year.

PERFORMANCES Peter Lieberson's *Free and Easy Wanderer*; Sven-David Sandstrom's *Wind Pieces*; Atar Arad's *Sonata*; and David Dzubay's *Dancesing in a Green Bay*.

LEXINGTON PHILHARMONIC SOCIETY

161 N. Mill St., Lexington KY 40507. (859)233-4226. **Website:** www.lexphil.org. **Contact:** Scott Terrell, music director. Symphony orchestra. Estab. 1961. Members are professionals. Series includes "8 serious, classical subscription concerts (hall seats 1,500); 3 concerts called Pops the Series; 3 family concerts; 10 outdoor pops concerts (from 1,500 to 5,000 tickets sold); 5-10 run-out concerts; and 10 children's concerts." Pays via ASCAP and BMI, rental purchase and private arrangements.

HOW TO CONTACT Submit complete score and tape of piece(s). Include SASE.

MUSIC Seeking "good current pops material and good serious classical works. No specific restrictions, but overly large orchestra requirements, unusual instruments and extra rentals help limit our interest."

PERFORMANCES "Visit our website for complete concert season listing."

TIPS "When working on large-format arrangement, use cross cues so orchestra can be cut back if required. Submit good-quality copy, scores and parts. Tape is helpful."

LIMA SYMPHONY ORCHESTRA

133 N. Elizabeth St., Lima OH 45801. (419)222-5701. **Fax:** (419)222-6587. **Website:** www.limasymphony. com. **Contact:** Crafton Beck, music conductor. Symphony orchestra. Estab. 1953. Members are professionals. Performs 17-18 concerts including at least 1 new work/year. Commissions at least 1 composer or new work/year. Middle to older audience; also Young People's Series. Mixture for stage and summer productions. Performs in Veterans' Memorial Civic & Convention Center, a beautiful hall seating 1,670; various temporary shells for summer outdoors events; churches; museums and libraries. Pays $2,500 for outright purchase (anniversary commission) or grants $1,500-5,000.

HOW TO CONTACT Submit complete score if not performed; otherwise submit complete score and tape of piece(s). Include SASE. Responds in 3 months.

MUSIC "Good balance of incisive rhythm, lyricism, dynamic contrast and pacing. Chamber orchestra to full (85-member) symphony orchestra." Does not wish to see "excessive odd meter changes."

PERFORMANCES Frank Proto's *American Overture* (some original music and fantasy); Werner Tharichen's *Concerto for Timpani and Orchestra*; and James Oliverio's *Pilgrimage—Concerto for Brass* (interesting, dynamic writing for brass and the orchestra).

TIPS "Know your instruments, be willing to experiment with unconventional textures, be available for in-depth analysis with conductor, be at more than 1 rehearsal. Be sure that individual parts are correctly matching the score and done in good, neat calligraphy."

LYRIC OPERA OF CHICAGO

20 N. Wacker Dr., Chicago IL 60606. (312)332-2244. **Fax:** (312)419-8345. **Website:** www.lyricopera.org. Opera company. Estab. 1953. Members are professionals. Performs 80 operas/year including 1 new work in some years. Commissions 1 new work every 4 or 5 years. "Performances are held in a 3,563-seat house for a sophisticated opera audience, predominantly 30-plus years old." Payment varies.

HOW TO CONTACT Query first. Does not return material. Responds in 6 months.

MUSIC "Full-length opera suitable for a large house with full orchestra. No musical comedy or Broadway musical style. We rarely perform one-act operas. We are only interested in works by composers and librettists with extensive theatrical experience. We have few openings for new works, so candidates must be of the highest quality. Do not send score or other materials without a prior contact."

PERFORMANCES William Bolcom's *View from the Bridge*; John Corigliano's *Ghosts of Versailles*; and Leonard Bernstein's *Candide*.

TIPS "Have extensive credentials and an international reputation."

MILWAUKEE YOUTH SYMPHONY ORCHESTRA

325 W. Walnut St., Milwaukee WI 53212. (414)267-2950. **Fax:** (414)267-2960. **E-mail:** general@myso.org. **Website:** www.myso.org. **Contact:** Linda Edelstein, executive director. Multiple youth orchestras and other instrumental ensembles. Estab. 1956. Members are students. Performs 12-15 concerts/year including 1-2 new works. "Our groups perform in Uihlein Hall at the Marcus Center for the Performing Arts in Milwaukee plus area sites. The audiences usually consist of parents, music teachers and other interested community members, with periodic reviews in the *Milwaukee Journal Sentinel*." Payment varies.

HOW TO CONTACT Query first. Include SASE. Does not return material. Responds in 1 month.

PERFORMANCES James Woodward's *Tuba Concerto*.

TIPS "Be sure you realize you are working with *students* (albeit many of the best in southeastern Wisconsin) and not professional musicians. The music needs to be on a technical level students can handle. Our students are 8-18 years of age, in 2 full symphony orchestras, a wind ensemble and 2 string orchestras, plus 2 flute choirs, advanced chamber orchestra and 15-20 small chamber ensembles."

MOORES OPERA CENTER

Moores School of Music, University of Houston, 120 School of Music Building, Houston TX 77204. (713)743-3009. **Fax:** (713)743-3166. **E-mail:** bross@uh.edu. **Website:** www.uh.edu/music/Mooresopera. **Director of Opera:** Buck Ross. Opera/music theater program. Members are professionals, amateurs, and students. Performs 12-14 concerts/year including 1 new work. Performs in a proscenium theater that

seats 800. Pit seats approximately up to 75 players. Audience covers wide spectrum, from first-time opera-goers to very sophisticated. Pays per performance.

HOW TO CONTACT Submit complete score and tapes of piece(s). Include SASE. Responds in 6 months.

MUSIC "We seek music that is feasible for high graduate-level student singers. Chamber orchestras are very useful. No more than 2 1/2 hours. No children's operas."

PERFORMANCES *The Grapes of Wrath, Florencia en el Amazonas, Elmer Gantry, A Wedding*.

OPERA MEMPHIS

6745 Wolf River Pkwy., Memphis TN 38120. (901)257-3100. **Fax:** (901)257-3109. **E-mail:** info@operamemphis.org. **Website:** www.operamemphis.org. **Contact:** Ned Canty, general director. Opera company. Estab. 1956. Members are professionals. Performs 5 mainstage shows/year including new works. Occasionally commissions composers. Audience is a mixture of long-time patrons and newcomers to opera drawn in through their "30 Days of Opera" program and Midtown Opera Festival. Pay is negotiable.

HOW TO CONTACT Query first. Include SASE. Responds in 1 year or less.

MUSIC "Accessible practical pieces for educational or second-stage programs. Educational pieces should not exceed 90 minutes or 4-6 performers. We encourage songwriters to contact us with proposals or work samples for theatrical works. We are very interested in works that crossover between musical genres."

PERFORMANCES Mike Reid's *Different Fields* (one-act opera); David Olney's *Light in August* (folk opera); Sid Selvidge's *Riversongs* (one-act blues opera), and *Ghosts of Crosstown* (5 short operas).

TIPS "Spend many hours thinking about the synopsis (plot outline)."

ORCHESTRA SEATTLE/SEATTLE CHAMBER SINGERS

P.O. Box 15825, Seattle WA 98115-0825. (206)682-5208. **E-mail:** info@osscs.org. **Website:** www.osscs.org. **Contact:** Jeremy Johnsen, managing director. Symphony orchestra, chamber music ensemble, and community chorus. Estab. 1969. Members are amateurs and professionals. Performs 8 concerts/year including 2-3 new works. Commissions 1-2 composers or new works/year. "Our audience is made up of both experienced and novice classical music patrons. The median age is 45 with an equal number of males and females in the upper income range. Most concerts now held in Benaroya Hall."

HOW TO CONTACT Query first. Include SASE. Responds in 1 year.

PERFORMANCES Beyer's *The Turns of a Girl*; Bernstein's Choruses from *The Lark*; Edstrom's Concerto for Jazz Piano and Orchestra.

PALMETTO MASTERSINGERS

P.O. Box 7441, Columbia SC 29202. (803)765-0777. **E-mail:** info@palmettomastersingers.org. **Website:** www.palmettomastersingers.org. **Contact:** Walter Cuttino, music director. Eighty voice male chorus. Estab. 1981 by the late Dr. Arpad Darasz. Members are professionals and amateurs. Performs 8-10 concerts/year. Commissions 1 composer of new works every other year (on average). Audience is generally older adults, "but it's a wide mix." Performance space for the season series is the Koger Center (approximately 2,000 seats) in Columbia, South Carolina. More intimate venues also available. Fee is negotiable for outright purchase.

HOW TO CONTACT Query first. Include SASE. Or e-mail to info@palmettomastersingers.org.

MUSIC Seeking music of 10-15 minutes in length, "not too far out tonally. Orchestration is negotiable, but chamber size (10-15 players) is normal. We rehearse once a week and probably will not have more than 8-10 rehearsals. These rehearsals (2 hours each) are spent learning a one-hour program. Only 1-2 rehearsals (max) are with the orchestra. Piano accompaniments need not be simplified, as our accompanist is exceptional."

PERFORMANCES Randal Alan Bass' *Te Deum* (12-minute, brass and percussion); Dick Goodwin's *Mark Twain Remarks* (40-minute, full symphony); and Randol Alan Bass' *A Simple Prayer* (a capella 6 minute).

TIPS "Contact us as early as possible, given that programs are planned by July. Although this is an amateur chorus, we have performed concert tours of Europe, performed at Carnegie Hall, The National Cathedral and the White House in Washington, DC. We are skilled amateurs."

PRINCETON SYMPHONY ORCHESTRA

P.O. Box 250, Princeton NJ 08542. (609)497-0020. **Fax:** (609)497-0904. **E-mail:** info@princetonsymphony.org. **Website:** www.princetonsymphony.org. **Contact:** Rossen Milanov, music director. Symphony orchestra. Estab. 1980. Members are professionals. Performs 6-10 concerts/year including some new works. Commissions 1 composer or new work/year. Performs in a "beautiful, intimate 800-seat hall with amazing sound." Pays by arrangement.

MUSIC "Orchestra usually numbers 40-60 individuals."

PRISM SAXOPHONE QUARTET

257 W. Harvey St., Philadelphia PA 19144. (215)438-5282. **E-mail:** info@prismquartet.com. **Website:** www.prismquartet.com. **Contact:** Matthew Levy. Chamber music ensemble. Estab. 1984. Members are professionals. Performs 80 concerts/year including 10-15 new works. Commissions 4 composers or new works/year. "Ours are primarily traditional chamber music audiences." Pays royalty per performance from BMI or ASCAP or commission range from $100 to $15,000.

HOW TO CONTACT Submit complete score (with parts) and tape of piece(s). Does not return material. Responds in 3 months.

MUSIC "Orchestration—sax quartet, SATB. Lengths—5-25 minutes. Styles—contemporary, classical, jazz, crossover, ethnic, gospel, avant-garde. No limitations on level of difficulty. No more than 4 performers (SATB sax quartet). No transcriptions. The Prism Quartet places special emphasis on crossover works which integrate a variety of musical styles."

PERFORMANCES David Liebman's *The Gray Convoy* (jazz); Bradford Ellis's *Tooka-Ood Zasch* (ethnic-world music); and William Albright's *Fantasy Etudes* (contemporary classical).

SACRAMENTO MASTER SINGERS

P.O. Box 417997, Sacramento CA 95841. (916)788-7464. **E-mail:** smsbusiness@surewest.net. **Website:** www.mastersingers.org. **Contact:** Dr. Ralph Edward Hughes, conductor/artistic director. Vocal ensemble. Estab. 1984. Members are professionals and amateurs. Performs 9 concerts/year including 5-6 new works. Commissions 2 new works/year. Audience is made up of mainly college-aged and older patrons. Performs mostly in churches with 500-900 seating capacity. Pays $200 for outright purchase.

HOW TO CONTACT Submit complete score and tape of piece(s). Include SASE. Responds in 5 weeks.

MUSIC "A cappella works; works with small orchestras or few instruments; works based on classical styles with a 'modern' twist; multi-cultural music; shorter works probably preferable, but this is not a requirement. We usually have 38-45 singers capable of a high level of difficulty, but find that often simple works are very pleasing."

PERFORMANCES Joe Jennings' *An Old Black Woman, Homeless and Indistinct* (SATB, oboe, strings, dramatic).

TIPS "Keep in mind we are a chamber ensemble, not a 100-voice choir."

SAN FRANCISCO GIRLS CHORUS

44 Page St., Suite 200, San Francisco CA 94102. (415)863-1752. **E-mail:** info@sfgirlschorus.org. **Website:** www.sfgirlschorus.org. **Contact:** Lisa Bielawa, artistic director. Choral ensemble. Estab. 1978. Advanced choral ensemble of young women's voices. Performs 8-10 concerts/year including 3-4 new works. Commissions 2 composers or new works/year. Concerts are performed for "choral/classical music lovers, plus family audiences and audiences interested in international repertoire. Season concerts are performed in a 800-seat church with excellent acoustics and in San Francisco's Davies Symphony Hall, a 2,800-seat state-of-the-art auditorium." Pay negotiable for outright purchase.

HOW TO CONTACT Submit complete score and CD recording, if possible. Does not return material. Responds in 6 months.

MUSIC "Music for treble voices (SSAA); a cappella, piano accompaniment, or small orchestration; 3-10 minutes in length. Wide variety of styles; 45 singers; challenging music is encouraged."

PERFORMANCES See website under "Music/Commissions" for a listing of SFGC commissions. Examples: Jake Heggie's *Patterns* (piano, mezzo-soprano soloist, chorus); and Chen Yi's *Chinese Poems* (a cappella).

TIPS "Choose excellent texts and write challenging music. The San Francisco Girls Chorus has pioneered the establishment of girls choral music as an art form in the U.S. The Girls Chorus is praised for its 'stunning musical standard' (*San Francisco Chronicle*) in performances in the San Francisco Bay Area and on tour. SFGC's annual concert season showcases the organization's concert/touring ensemble, Chorissima, in performances of choral masterworks from around the world, commissioned works by contemporary composers, and 18th-century music from the Venetian Ospedali and Mexican Baroque which SFGC has brought out of the archives and onto the concert stage. Chorissima tours through California with partial support provided by the California Arts Council Touring Program and have represented the U.S. and the city of San Francisco nationally and abroad. The chorus provides ensemble and solo singers for performances and recordings with the San Francisco Symphony and San Francisco Opera, Women's Philharmonic, and many other music ensembles. The Chorus has produced many solo CD recordings including: *Voices of Hope and Peace*, a recording that includes 'Anne Frank: A Living Voice' by an American composer Linda Tutas Haugen; *Christmas*, featuring diverse holiday selections; *Crossroads*, a collection of world folk music; and *Music from the Venetian Ospedali*, a disc of Italian Baroque music of which *The New Yorker* described as 'tremendously accomplished.'"

SOLI DEO GLORIA CANTORUM

3402 Woolworth Ave., Omaha NE 68105. (402)341-4111. **Fax:** (402)341-9381. **E-mail:** cantorum@berkey.com. **Website:** www.berkey.com. **Contact:** Linda Gardels, music director. Professional choir. Estab. 1988. Members are professionals. Performs 5-7 concerts/year; several are new works. Commissions 1-2 new works/year. Performance space: "cathedral, symphony hall, smaller intimate recital halls, as well." Payment is "dependent upon composition and composer."

HOW TO CONTACT Submit complete score and tape of piece(s). Include SASE. Responds in 2 months.

MUSIC "Chamber music mixed with topical programming (e.g., all Celtic or all Hispanic programs, etc.). Generally a cappella compositions from very short to extended range (6-18 minutes) or multi-movements. Concerts are of a formal length (approximately 75 minutes) with 5 rehearsals. Difficulty must be balanced within program in order to adequately prepare in a limited rehearsal time. 28 singers. Not seeking orchestral pieces, due to limited budget."

PERFORMANCES Jackson Berkey's *Native Am Ambience* (eclectic/classical); John Rutter's *Hymn to the Creator of Light* (classical); and Arvo Part's *Te Deum* (multi-choir/chant-based classical).

ST. LOUIS CHAMBER CHORUS

P.O. Box 11558, Clayton MO 63105. **Website:** www.chamberchorus.org. **Contact:** Philip Barnes, artistic director. Vocal ensemble, chamber music ensemble. Estab. 1956. Members are professionals and amateurs. Performs 6 concerts/year including 5-10 new works. Commissions 3-4 new works/year. Audience is "diverse and interested in unaccompanied choral work and outstanding architectural/acoustic venues." Performances take place at various auditoria noted for their excellent acoustics—churches, synagogues, schools, and university halls. Pays by arrangement.

HOW TO CONTACT Query first. Does not return material. "Panel of 'readers' submit report to artistic director. Responds in 3 months. 'General Advice' leaflet available on request."

MUSIC "*Only a cappella writing!* No contemporary 'popular' works; historical editions welcomed. No improvisatory works. Our programs are tailored for specific acoustics—composers should indicate their preference."

PERFORMANCES Sir Richard Rodney Bennett's *A Contemplation Upon Flowers* (a cappella madrigal); Ned Rorem's *Ode to Man* (a cappella chorus for mixed voices); and Sasha Johnson Manning's *Requiem* (a cappella oratorio).

TIPS "We only consider a cappella works that can be produced in 5 rehearsals. Therefore, pieces of great complexity or duration are discouraged. Our seasons are planned 2-3 years ahead, so much lead time is required for programming a new work. We will accept handwritten manuscripts, but we prefer typeset music."

SUSQUEHANNA SYMPHONY ORCHESTRA

P.O. Box 963, Abingdon MD 21009. **Fax:** (410)306-6069. **E-mail:** sheldon.bair@ssorchestra.org. **Website:** www.ssorchestra.org. **Contact:** Sheldon Bair, founder/music director. Symphony orchestra. Estab. 1978. Members are amateurs. Performs 6 concerts/year including 1-2 new works. Composers paid depending on the circumstances. "We perform in 1 hall, 600 seats with fine acoustics. Our audience encompasses all ages."

HOW TO CONTACT Query first. Include SASE. Responds in 3 or more months.

MUSIC "We desire works for large orchestra, any length, in a 'conservative 20th- and 21st-century' style. Seek fine music for large orchestra. We are a community orchestra, so the music must be within our grasp. Violin I to 7th position by step only; Violin II—stay within 5th position; English horn and harp are OK. Full orchestra pieces preferred."

PERFORMANCES *Jazz Violin Concerto*, by Scott Routenberg; *Holiday music*, by Toddy Hayden; plus, music by Russell Peck and Neil Anderson-Himmelspach.

◑ TORONTO MENDELSSOHN CHOIR

720 Bathurst St., Suite 404, Toronto ON M5S 2R4 Canada. (416)598-0422. **Fax:** (416)598-2992. **E-mail:** manager@tmchoir.org. **Website:** www.tmchoir.org. **Contact:** Cynthia Hawkins, executive director. Vocal ensemble. Members are professionals and amateurs. Performs 25 concerts/year including 1-3 new works. "Most performances take place in Roy Thomson Hall. The audience is reasonably sophisticated, musically knowledgeable but with moderately conservative tastes." Pays by commission and ASCAP/SOCAN.

HOW TO CONTACT Query first or submit complete score and tapes of pieces. Include SASE. Responds in 6 months.

MUSIC All works must suit a large choir (180 voices) and standard orchestral forces or with some other not-too-exotic accompaniment. Length should be restricted to no longer than 1/2 of a nocturnal concert. The choir sings at a very professional level and can sight-read almost anything. "Works should fit naturally with the repertoire of a large choir that performs the standard choral orchestral repertoire."

PERFORMANCES Holman's *Jezebel*; Orff's *Catulli Carmina*; and Lambert's *Rio Grande*.

◑ VANCOUVER CHAMBER CHOIR

1254 W. 7th Ave., Vancouver BC V6H 1B6 Canada. **E-mail:** info@vancouverchamberchoir.com. **Website:** www.vancouverchamberchoir.com. **Contact:** Jon Washburn, artistic director. Vocal ensemble. Members are professionals. Performs 40 concerts/year including 5-8 new works. Commissions 2-4 composers or new works/year. Pays SOCAN royalty or negotiated fee for commissions.

HOW TO CONTACT Submit complete score and CD of piece(s). Does not return material. Responds in 6 months if possible.

MUSIC Seeks "choral works of all types for small chorus, with or without accompaniment and/or soloists. Concert music only. Choir made up of 20 singers. Large or unusual instrumental accompaniments are less likely to be appropriate. No pop music."

PERFORMANCES The VCC has commissioned and premiered over 200 new works by Canadian and international composers, including Alice Parker's *That Sturdy Vine* (cantata for chorus, soloists and orchestra); R. Murray Schafer's *Magic Songs* (SATB a cappella); and Jon Washburn's *A Stephen Foster Medley* (SSAATTBB/piano).

TIPS "We are looking for choral music that is performable yet innovative, and which has the potential to become 'standard repertoire.' Although we perform much new music, only a small portion of the many scores that are submitted can be utilized."

VIRGINIA OPERA

P.O. Box 2580, Norfolk VA 23501. (757)627-9545. **Website:** www.vaopera.org. **Contact:** Alexandra Stacey, artistic coordinator. Opera company. Estab. 1974. Members are professionals. Performs more than 560 concerts/year. Commissions vary on number of composers or new works/year. Concerts are performed for school children throughout Virginia, grades K-5, 6-8, and 9-12 at the Harrison Opera House in Norfolk and at the Carpenter Theatre in Richmond. Pays on commission.

HOW TO CONTACT Query first. Include SASE. Response time varies.

MUSIC "Audience-accessible style approximately 45 minutes in length. Limit cast list to 3 vocal artists of any combination. Accompanied by piano and/or keyboard. Works are performed before school children of all ages. Pieces must be age appropriate both aurally and dramatically. Musical styles are encouraged to be diverse, contemporary, as well as traditional. Works are produced and presented with sets, costumes, etc." Limitations: "Three vocal performers (any combination). One keyboardist. Medium to difficult acceptable, but prefer easy to medium. Seeking only pieces that are suitable for presentation as part of an opera education program for Virginia Opera's educa-

tion and outreach department. Subject matter must meet strict guidelines relative to Learning Objectives, etc. Musical idiom must be representative of current trends in opera, musical theater. Extreme dissonance, row systems not applicable to this environment."

PERFORMANCES Seymour Barab's *Cinderella*; John David Earnest's *The Legend of Sleepy Hollow*; and Seymour Barab's *The Pied Piper of Hamelin*.

TIPS "Theatricality is very important. New works should stimulate interest in musical theater as a legitimate art form for school children with no prior exposure to live theatrical entertainment. Composer should be willing to create a product that will find success within the educational system."

WHEATON SYMPHONY ORCHESTRA

344 Spring Ave., Glen Ellyn IL 60137. (630)790-1430. **Fax:** (630)790-9703. **E-mail:** info@wheatonsymphony. org. **Website:** www.wheatonsymphony.org. **Contact:** Don Mattison, manager. Symphony orchestra. Estab. 1959. Members are professionals and amateurs. Performs 4 concerts/year in the summer. "No pay for performance but can probably record your piece."

HOW TO CONTACT Send a score and CD. Responds in 1 month.

MUSIC "This is a good amateur orchestra that wants pieces to be performed in the mode of John Williams or Samuel Barber, Corliango, etc. Large-scale works for orchestra only. No avant garde, 12-tone or atonal material. Pieces should be 20 minutes or less and must be prepared in 3 rehearsals. Instrumentation needed for woodwinds in 3s, full brass 4-3-3-1, 4 percussion and strings—full instrumentation only. Selections for full orchestra only. No pay for reading your piece, but we will record it at our expense. We will rehearse and give a world premiere of your piece if it is in the stated orchestration, probably with keyboard added."

PERFORMANCES Richard Williams's *Symphony in G Minor* (4 movement symphony); Dennis Johnson's *Must Jesus Bear the Cross Alone, Azon* (traditional); and Michael Diemer's *Skating* (traditional style).

TIPS "We want pops-type music only."

CONTESTS & AWARDS

///

Participating in contests is a great way to gain exposure for your music. Prizes vary from contest to contest, from cash to musical merchandise to studio time, and even publishing and recording deals. For musical theater and classical composers, the prize may be a performance of your work. Even if you don't win, valuable contacts can be made through contests. Many times, music publishers and other industry professionals judge contests, so your music may find its way into the hands of key industry people who can help further your career. Check the websites for any organizations or publishers hosting competitions—they'll often list the judges for the current competition.

And because your work could find its way into the hands of an industry professional, remember to always put your best work forward in any contest. Think of it as a tryout, because even if you don't win overall, there are plenty of success stories out there where a professional discovered someone through a competition that he or she was judging.

HOW TO SELECT A CONTEST

It's important to remember when entering any contest to do proper research before signing anything or sending any money. We have confidence in the contests listed in *Songwriter's Market*, but it pays to read the fine print. Contests can change from year to year, with different guidelines, judges, and even prizes. You'll want to make sure that you have all the available information before submitting. An incorrect submission, in terms of format or genre, will probably just leave you disqualified, no matter how good your work. It's especially important to double-check the information if you've picked up this copy of *Songwriter's Market* some time after it was first released.

First, be sure you understand the contest rules and stipulations once you receive the entry forms and guidelines. Then you need to weigh what you will gain against what they're asking you to give up. If a publishing or recording contract is the only prize a contest is offering, you may want to think twice before entering. Basically, the company sponsoring the contest is asking you to pay a fee for them to listen to your song under the guise of a contest, something a legitimate publisher or record company would not do. For those contests offering studio time, musical equipment or cash prizes, you need to decide if the entry fee you're paying is worth the chance to win such prizes.

Be wary of exorbitant entry fees, and if you have any doubts whatsoever as to the legitimacy of a contest, it's best to stay away. Songwriters need to approach a contest, award, or grant in the same manner as they would a record or publishing company. Make your submission as professional as possible; follow directions and submit material exactly as stated on the entry form.

Contests in this section encompass all types of music and levels of competition. Read each listing carefully and contact them if the contest interests you. Many contests now have websites that offer additional information and even entry forms you can print. Be sure to read the rules carefully and be sure you understand exactly what a contest is offering before entering.

AGO/ECS PUBLISHING AWARD IN CHORAL COMPOSITION

American Guild of Organists, 475 Riverside Dr., Suite 1260, New York NY 10115. (212)870-2310. **Fax:** (212)870-2163. **E-mail:** competitions@agohq.org. **Website:** www.agohq.org/new-music-competitions-commissions/. **Contact:** Eileen Hunt, DMA. Bian-nual award.

REQUIREMENTS Seeking to draw on particular individual strengths, the committee has developed a procedure wherein composers submit proposals for commission rather than compose for stipulated criteria. See website for details.

AWARDS Prize: $2,000 cash, publication by ECS Publishing, and premiere performance at the AGO National Convention. Further details are published in *The American Organist*.

AGO/MARILYN MASON AWARD IN ORGAN COMPOSITION

American Guild of Organists, 475 Riverside Dr., Suite 1260, New York NY 10115. (212)870-2310. **Fax:** (212)870-2163. **E-mail:** competitions@agohq.org. **Website:** www.agohq.org. **Contact:** Eileen Hunt. For composers and performing artists. Biennial award.

REQUIREMENTS Organ solo.

AMERICAN SONGWRITER LYRIC CONTEST

113 19th Ave. S., Nashville TN 37203. (615)321-6096. **Fax:** (615)321-6097. **E-mail:** info@americansongwriter.com. **Website:** www.americansongwriter.com/lyric-contest/. For songwriters and composers. Award for each bimonthly issue of *American Songwriter* magazine, plus grand prize winner at year-end.

PURPOSE To promote and encourage the craft of lyric writing.

REQUIREMENTS Contest is open to any amateur songwriter. *AS* defines an amateur as one who has not earned more than $5,000 from songwriting related to royalties, advances, or works for hire. Lyrics must be typed and a check per entry must be enclosed. See website for exact dates.

AWARDS Grand Prize: The annual winner, chosen from the 6 contest winners, will receive round-trip airfare to Nashville and a dream co-writing session.

TIPS "You do not have to be a subscriber to enter or win. You may submit as many entries as you like. All genres of music accepted."

ANNUAL NSAI SONG CONTEST

1710 Roy Acuff Place, Nashville TN 37203. (615)256-3354. **Fax:** (615)256-0034. **E-mail:** reception@nash-villesongwriters.com. **Website:** www.nashvillesong-writers.com.

PURPOSE "A chance for aspiring songwriters to be heard by music industry decision makers."

REQUIREMENTS In order to be eligible contestants must not be receiving income from any work submitted—original material only. Mail-in submissions must be in CD form and include entry form, lyrics and melody. Online submissions available. Visit website for complete list of rules and regulations. Deadline is different each year; check website or send for application. Samples are required with application in the format of cassette or CD.

AWARDS Visit website for complete list of rules and prizes.

ARTISTS' FELLOWSHIPS

New York Foundation for the Arts, 20 Jay St., 7th Floor, Brooklyn NY 11201. (212)366-6900. **Fax:** (212)366-1778. **E-mail:** fellowships@nyfa.org. **Website:** www.nyfa.org. For songwriters, composers, and musical playwrights. Annual award, but each category is not funded annually. Check the website to see if songwriting/music is coming up.

PURPOSE Artists' Fellowships are $7,000 grants awarded by the New York Foundation for the Arts to individual originating artists living in the state of New York. The foundation is committed to supporting artists from all over the state of New York at all stages of their professional careers. Fellows may use the grant according to their own needs; it should not be confused with project support.

REQUIREMENTS Must be 18 years of age or older; resident of the state of New York for 2 years prior to application; and cannot be enrolled in any graduate or undergraduate degree program.

AWARDS All Artists' Fellowships awards are for $7,000. Fellowships are awarded on the basis of the quality of work submitted. Applications are reviewed by a panel of 5 composers representing the aesthetic, ethnic, sexual and geographic diversity within the state of New York. The panelists change each year and review all allowable material submitted.

TIPS "Please note that musical playwrights may submit only if they write the music for their plays; librettists must submit in our playwriting category."

ARTIST TRUST FELLOWSHIP AWARD

1835 12th Ave., Seattle WA 98122. (209)467-8734, ext. 11. **Fax:** (866)218-7878. **E-mail:** info@artisttrust.org. **Website:** www.artisttrust.org. **Contact:** Miguel Guillen, program manager. Fellowships award $7,500 to practicing professional artists of exceptional talent and demonstrated ability. The Fellowship is a merit-based, not project-based award. Recipients present at a Meet the Artist event to a community in Washington that has little or no access to the artists and their work. Awards 14 fellowships of $7,500 and 2 residencies with $1,000 stipends at the Millay Colony.

THE ASCAP DEEMS TAYLOR AWARDS

American Society of Composers, Authors & Publishers, One Lincoln Plaza, New York NY 10023. (212)621-6318. **E-mail:** jlapore@ascap.com. **Website:** www.ascap.com/music-career/support/deems-taylor-guidelines.aspx. **Contact:** Julian Lapore. The ASCAP Deems Taylor Awards program recognizes books, articles, broadcasts, and websites on the subject of music selected for their excellence.

PURPOSE Honors the memory of composer/critic/commentator Deems Taylor.

TIPS "The website will answer all questions. Please call (212)621-6318 with any additional questions."

THE BLANK THEATRE COMPANY YOUNG PLAYWRIGHTS FESTIVAL

P.O. Box 38756, Hollywood CA 90038. (323)662-7734. **Fax:** (323)661-3903. **E-mail:** info@theblank.com. **E-mail:** submissions@youngplaywrights.com. **Website:** ypf.theblank.com. For both musical and non-musical playwrights. Annual award.

PURPOSE Purpose is to give young playwrights an opportunity to learn more about playwriting and to give them a chance to have their work mentored, developed, and presented by professional artists.

REQUIREMENTS Playwrights must be 19 years or younger at time of submission. Send legible, original plays of any length and on any subject (co-written plays are acceptable provided all co-writers meet eligibility requirements). Submissions must be postmarked by March 15 and must include a cover sheet with the playwright's name, date of birth, school (if any), home address, home phone number, e-mail address and production history. Pages must be numbered and submitted unbound (unstapled). For musicals, a tape or CD of a selection from the score should be submitted with the script. Manuscripts will not be returned; do not send originals. Semifinalists and winners will be contacted in May.

AWARDS Winning playwrights receive a workshop presentation of their work.

CRS COMPETITION FOR COMPOSERS' RECORDINGS

724 Winchester Rd., Broomall PA 19008. (610)205-9897. **Fax:** (707)549-5920. **E-mail:** crsnews@verizon.net. **Website:** www.crsnews.org. For songwriters, composers, and performing artists. College faculty and gifted artists. Each annual competition is limited to the first 300 applicants—all fees beyond this limit will be returned.

REQUIREMENTS "Each category requires a separate application fee. The work submitted must be non-published (prior to acceptance) and not commercially recorded on any label. The work submitted must not exceed 9 performers. Each composer/performer may submit 1 work for each application submitted. (Taped performances by composers are additionally encouraged.) Composition must not exceed 16 minutes in length. CRS reserves the right not to accept a 1st Place winner. Write with SASE for application or visit website. Add $5 for postage and handling. Must send a detailed résumé with application form available on our Web page under 'Events' category. Samples of work required with application. Send score and parts with optional CD or DAT. Application fee: $50."

AWARDS First place will consist of a commercially distributed new CD recording grant featuring 1 composition along with other distinguished composers and performing artists. Second and third prizes will be awarded honorable mention toward future recordings with CRS and Honorary Life Membership to the society. Applications are judged by panel of judges determined each year.

DELTA OMICRON INTERNATIONAL COMPOSITION COMPETITION

418 W. Main St., Georgetown KY 40324. (865)471-6155. **Fax:** (865)475-9716. **E-mail:** ninabdurr@bellsouth.net. **Website:** www.delta-omicron.org/?q=node/131. **Contact:** Nina Belle Durr, chair, Composition Competition. The 2015 award was for solo piano.

PURPOSE "To encourage composers worldwide to continually add to our wonderful heritage of musical creativity instrumentally and/or vocally."

REQUIREMENTS People from college age on (or someone younger who is enrolled in college). Work must be unpublished and unperformed in public. "View our website for specific submission guidelines such as instrument selection and deadline. Click on ''Composition Competition' on homepage." Manuscripts should be legibly written in ink or processed, signed with *nom de plume*, and free from any marks that would identify the composer to the judges. Entry fee: $25 per composition. Send for application. Composition is required with application.

AWARDS Prize: 1st Place: $1,000 and world premiere at Delta Omicron Triennial Conference. Judged by 2-3 judges (performers, conductors, and/or composers).

EUROPEAN INTERNATIONAL COMPETITION FOR COMPOSERS/IBLA FOUNDATION

568 Grand St., Suite 2001, New York NY 10002. (212)387-0111. **E-mail:** iblanewyork@gmail.com. **Website:** www.ibla.org/comp.composer.eng.php4. **Contact:** Dr. Salvatore Moltisanti, president. For songwriters and composers. Annual award.

PURPOSE "To promote the winners' career through exposure, publicity, recordings with Athena Records, and nationwide distribution with the Empire Group."

REQUIREMENTS Music score and/or recording of 1 work are required with application. Application fee is refunded if not admitted into the program.

AWARDS Winners are presented in concerts in Europe, Japan, US.

GLOBAL SONGWRITING CONTEST

20 Hale Makai Place, Lahaina HI 96761. (808)385-3035. **E-mail:** mail@globalsongwritingcontest.com. **Website:** www.globalsongwritingcontest.com. **Contact:** Gary Robilotta, CEO/founder. Competition awards cash prizes and promotion deals to winners. Awards encourage winners seeking other opportunities in the songwriting business. As a winner, the funds can be used to buy new equipment, assist with touring expenses, or fund a recording project.

TIPS Judges look for originality in melody, its progression, how catchy the song is, and emotion within the composition. Different and original is the key to creating a fresh melody. Looking for material that stands out, written from the heart. Submit something that has a twist to a style. Judges also look for creativity and imagination in words. Think outside the box. Strive to compel the heart and the mind. Make your song genius in overall execution and style. Be different, unique.

GRASSY HILL KERRVILLE NEW FOLK COMPETITION

3876 Medina Hwy., Kerrville TX 78028. (830)257-3600. **Fax:** (830)257-8680. **E-mail:** info@kerrville-music.com. **Website:** http://kerrville-music.com/newfolk.htm. For songwriters. Annual award.

PURPOSE "To provide an opportunity for emerging songwriters to be heard and rewarded for excellence."

AWARDS Thirty-two finalists invited to sing the 2 songs entered during The Kerrville Folk Festival in May. Six writers are chosen as award winners. Initial round of entries judged by the festival producer and a panel of online listeners from the music industry. Thirty-two finalists judged by panel of 3 performer/songwriters.

TIPS "Do not allow instrumental accompaniment to drown out lyric content. Don't enter without complete copy of the rules. Former winners and finalists include Lyle Lovett, Nanci Griffith, Hal Ketchum, John Gorka, David Wilcox, Lucinda Williams and Robert Earl Keen, Tish Hinojosa, Carrie Newcomer, and Jimmy Lafave."

GREAT AMERICAN SONG CONTEST

6312 SW Capitol Hwy., Suite 202, Portland OR 97239. **E-mail:** info@greatamericansong.com. **Website:** www.greatamericansong.com. For songwriters, composers and lyricists. Annual award.

Also see the listing for Songwriters Resource Network in the Organizations section of this book.

PURPOSE To help songwriters get their songs heard by music industry professionals; to generate educational and networking opportunities for participating songwriters; to help songwriters open doors in the music business.

AWARDS Winners receive a mix of cash awards and prizes. The focus of the contest is on networking and educational opportunities. (All participants receive detailed evaluations of their songs by industry professionals.) Songs are judged by knowledgeable music industry professionals, including prominent hit songwriters, producers and publishers.

TIPS "Focus should be on the song. The quality of the demo isn't important. Judges will be looking for good songwriting talent. They will base their evaluations on the song—not the quality of the recording or the voice performance."

IAMA (INTERNATIONAL ACOUSTIC MUSIC AWARDS)

2881 E. Oakland Park Blvd., Suite 414, Fort Lauderdale FL 33306. **E-mail:** info@inacoustic.com. **Website:** www.inacoustic.com. For singer-songwriters, musicians, performing musicians in the acoustic genre.

PURPOSE "The purpose is to promote the excellence in acoustic music performance and songwriting." Genres include: folk, alternative, bluegrass, etc.

REQUIREMENTS Visit website for entry form and details. "All songs submitted must be original. There must be at least an acoustic instrument (voice) in any song. Electric and electronic instruments, along with loops, is allowed, but acoustic instruments (or voice) must be clearly heard in all songs submitted. Contestants may enter as many songs in as many categories as desired but each entry requires a separate CD, entry form, lyric sheet, and entry fee. CDs and lyrics will not be returned. Winners will be chosen by a blue ribbon judging committee composed of music industry professionals, including A&R managers from record labels, publishers and producers. Entries are judged equally on music performance, production, originality, lyrics, melody and composition. Songs may be in any language. Winners will be notified by e-mail and must sign and return an affidavit confirming that winner's song is original and he/she holds rights to the song."

TIPS "Judging is based on music performance, music production, songwriting, and originality/artistry."

KATE NEAL KINLEY MEMORIAL FELLOWSHIP

University of Illinois, College of Fine and Applied Arts, 100 Architecture Bldg., 608 E. Lorado Taft Dr., Champaign IL 61820. (217)333-1661. **E-mail:** faa@illinois.edu. **Website:** http://faa.illinois.edu/kate_neal_kinley_memorial_fellowship. For students of architecture, art or music. Annual award.

PURPOSE Purpose is for the advancement of study in the fine arts.

REQUIREMENTS "The fellowship will be awarded upon the basis of unusual promise in the fine arts. Open to college graduates whose principal or major studies have been in the fields of architecture, art or music." Deadline: December 6. Call or visit website for application. Samples of work are required with application.

AWARDS "One major fellowship, which yields the sum of $20,000, is to be used by the recipients toward defraying the expenses of advanced study of the fine arts in America or abroad." Two or 3 smaller fellowships may also be awarded upon committee recommendations. Good for 1 year. Grant is nonrenewable.

THE JOHN LENNON SONGWRITING CONTEST

180 Brighton Rd., Suite 801, Clifton NJ 07012. (888)884-5572. **E-mail:** info@jlsc.com. **Website:** www.jlsc.com.

PURPOSE "The purpose of the John Lennon Songwriting Contest is to promote the art of songwriting by assisting in the discovery of new talent, as well as providing more established songwriters with an opportunity to advance their careers."

REQUIREMENTS "Each entry must consist of the following: completed and signed application; audio cassette, CD or MP3 containing 1 song only, 5 minutes or less in length; lyric sheet typed or printed legibly (English translation is required when applicable); $30 entry fee per song. Applications can be found in various music-oriented magazines, as well as on our website."

AWARDS Entries are accepted in the following 12 categories: rock, country, jazz, pop, world, gospel/inspirational, R&B, hip-hop, Latin, electronic, folk, and children's music. Winners will receive EMI Publishing contracts, studio equipment from Brian Moore Guitars, Roland, Edirol and Audio Technica, 1,000 CDs in full color with premium six-panel Digipaks courtesy of Discmakers, and gift certificates from Musiciansfriend.com. One entrant will be chosen to tour and perform for 1 week on the Warped Tour. One Lennon Award-winning song will be named "Song of the Year" and take home an additional $20,000 in cash.

MID-ATLANTIC SONG CONTEST

Songwriters Association of Washington, 4200 Wisconsin Ave., NW, PMB 106-137, Washington DC 20016. **E-mail:** contact@saw.org. **Website:** masc.saw.org. For songwriters and composers. Annual award.

PURPOSE "This is one of the longest-running contests in the nation; SAW has organized 27 contests since 1982. The competition is designed to afford rising songwriters (in a wide variety of genres) the opportunity to receive awards and exposure in an environment of peer competition."

REQUIREMENTS Amateur status is important. Applicants should request a brochure/application using the contact information above. Rules and procedures are clearly explained in the brochure and also online. CD and 3 copies of the lyrics are to be submitted with an application form and fee for each entry, or submit MP3 entries by applying online or through Sonicbids. Reduced entry fees are offered to members of Songwriters' Association of Washington; membership can be arranged simultaneously with entering. Multiple song discounts are also offered.

TIPS "Enter the song in the most appropriate category. Make the sound recording the best it can be (even though judges are asked to focus on melody and lyric and not on production). Avoid clichés, extended introductions, and long instrumental solos."

THELONIOUS MONK INTERNATIONAL JAZZ COMPETITION

5225 Wisconsin Ave. NW, Suite 605, Washington DC 20015. (202)364-7272. **Fax:** (202)364-0176. **E-mail:** info@monkinstitute.org. **Website:** www.monkinstitute.org. For songwriters and composers. Check online often for updated details.

PURPOSE "This is the world's most prestigious jazz competition, recognized for discovering the next generation of jazz masters." The competition focuses on a different instrument each year and features an all-star judging panel.

REQUIREMENTS Deadline: See website. Send for application. Submission must include application form, résumé of musical experience, CD or MP3, entry, 4 copies of the full score, and a photo. The composition features a different instrument each year.

NACUSA YOUNG COMPOSERS' COMPETITION

Box 49256 Barrington Station, Los Angeles CA 90049. (541)765-2406. **E-mail:** nacusa@music-usa.org; membership@mail.music-usa.org. **Website:** http://music-usa.org. **Contact:** John Winsor: webmaster@music-usa.org.

PURPOSE Encourages the composition of new American concert hall music.

PULITZER PRIZE IN MUSIC

Columbia University, 709 Pulitzer Hall, 2950 Broadway, New York NY 10027. (212)854-3841. **Fax:** (212)854-3342. **E-mail:** pulitzer@pulitzer.org. **Website:** www.pulitzer.org; www.pulitzer.org/bycat/Music. For composers and musical playwrights. Annual award.

REQUIREMENTS "For distinguished musical composition by an American who has had his or her first performance or recording in the U.S. during the year." Entries should reflect current creative activity. Works that receive their American premiere between January 1 and December 31 of the contest year are eligible. A public performance or the public release of a recording shall constitute a premiere. Samples of work are required with application, biography and photograph of composer, date and place of performance, score or manuscript and recording of the work, entry form, and $50 entry fee.

AWARDS Applications are judged first by a nominating jury, then by the Pulitzer Prize Board.

ROCKY MOUNTAIN FOLKS FESTIVAL SONGWRITER SHOWCASE

Folks Showcase Contest, P.O. Box 769, Lyons CO 80540. (800)624-2422; (303)823-0848. **Fax:** (303)823-0849. **E-mail:** planet@bluegrass.com. **Website:** www.bluegrass.com. For songwriters, composers, and performers. Annual award.

PURPOSE Award based on having the best song and performance.

REQUIREMENTS Rules available on website. Samples of work are required with application. Send CD with $10/song entry fee. Can now submit online at www.sonicbids.com. "Contestants cannot be signed to a major label or publishing deal. No backup musicians allowed."

RICHARD RODGERS AWARDS FOR MUSICAL THEATER

American Academy of Arts and Letters, 633 W. 155 St., New York NY 10032. (212)368-5900. **Fax:** (212)491-4615. **E-mail:** academy@artsandletters.org. **Website:** www.artsandletters.org/awards2_rodgers.php. **Contact:** Jane Bolster, coordinator. "The Richard Rodgers Awards subsidize staged readings, studio productions, and full productions by nonprofit theaters in New York of works by composers and writers who are not already established in the field of musical theater. The awards are only for musicals—songs by themselves are not eligible. The authors must be citizens or permanent residents of the U.S."

ROME PRIZE COMPETITION FELLOWSHIP

American Academy in Rome, 7 E. 60th St., New York NY 10022-1001. (212)751-7200. **Fax:** (212)751-7220. **E-mail:** info@aarome.org. **Website:** www.aarome.org. For composers. Annual award.

PURPOSE "Through its annual Rome Prize Competition, the academy awards up to 30 fellowships in 11 disciplines, including musical composition. Winners of the Rome Prize pursue independent projects while residing at the Academy's 11-acre center in Rome."

REQUIREMENTS "Applicants for 11-month fellowships must be U.S. citizens and hold a bachelor's degree in music, musical composition, or its equivalent." Application guidelines are available through the academy's website.

AWARDS "Up to 2 fellowships are awarded annually in musical composition. Fellowship consists of room, board, and a studio at the academy facilities in Rome, as well as a stipend. In all cases, excellence is the primary criterion for selection, based on the quality of the materials submitted. Winners are announced in mid-April and fellowships generally begin in early September."

TELLURIDE TROUBADOUR CONTEST

Troubadour Competition, P.O. Box 769, Lyons CO 80540. (303)823-0848; (800)624-2422. **Fax:** (303)823-0849. **E-mail:** planet@bluegrass.com. **Website:** www.bluegrass.com/telluride/contests.html. The Telluride Troubadour Competition is a nationally recognized songwriter competition open to anyone who writes and performs original music and who is not currently signed to a major recording or publishing deal. Contestants are judged on the quality of the song's composition, vocal delivery, and the overall performance. Finalists are awarded cash and prizes, as well as critical acclaim, well-deserved recognition, and a chance to perform on the festival main stage.

USA SONGWRITING COMPETITION

2881 E. Oakland Park Blvd., Suite 414, Ft. Lauderdale FL 33306. (954)537-3127. **Fax:** (954)537-9690. **E-mail:** info@songwriting.net. **Website:** www.songwriting.net. **Contact:** Contest Manager. For songwriters, composers, performing artists, and lyricists. Annual award.

PURPOSE "To honor good songwriters/composers all over the world, especially the unknown ones."

REQUIREMENTS Open to professional and beginner songwriters. No limit on entries. Each entry must include an entry fee, a CD, MP3, or audio cassette tape of song(s) and lyric sheet(s). Judged by music industry representatives. Past judges have included record label representatives and publishers from Arista Records, EMI and Warner/Chappell. Deadline: See website. Entry fee: $35 per song. See website or e-mail for entry forms at any time. Samples of work are not required.

AWARDS Prizes include cash and merchandise in 15 different categories: pop, rock, country, Latin, R&B, gospel, folk, jazz, "lyrics only" category, instrumental, and many others.

TIPS "Judging is based on lyrics, originality, melody, and overall composition. CD-quality production is great but not a consideration in judging."

U.S.-JAPAN CREATIVE ARTISTS EXCHANGE FELLOWSHIP PROGRAM

Japan-U.S. Friendship Commission, 1201 15th St. NW, Suite 330, Washington DC 20005. (202)418-9800. **Fax:** (202)418-9802. **E-mail:** jusfc@jusfc.gov; pcottinghamstreater@jusfc.gov. **Website:** www.jusfc.gov/faqs/creative-artists-programs/. For all creative artists. Annual award.

PURPOSE "For artists to go as seekers, as cultural visionaries, and as living liaisons to the traditional and contemporary life of Japan."

REQUIREMENTS "Artists' works must exemplify the best in U.S. arts." Send for application and guidelines. Applications available on website. Samples of work are required with application. Requires 2 pieces on CD or DVD.

AWARDS Five artists are awarded a 3-month residency anywhere in Japan. Awards monthly stipend for living expenses, housing, and professional support services; up to $2,000 for round-trip transportation will be provided for the artist.

TIPS "Applicants should anticipate a highly rigorous review of their artistry and should have compelling reasons for wanting to work in Japan."

WESTERN WRITERS OF AMERICA

271CR 219, Encampment WY 82325. (307)329-8942. **Fax:** (307)327-5465 (call first). **E-mail:** wwa.moulton@gmail.com. **Website:** www.westernwriters.org. **Contact:** Candy Moulton, executive director. Seventeen Spur Award categories in various aspects of the American West.

PURPOSE The nonprofit Western Writers of America has promoted and honored the best in Western literature with the annual Spur Awards, selected by panels of judges. Awards, for material published last year, are given for works whose inspirations, image and literary excellence best represent the reality and spirit of the American West.

Y.E.S. FESTIVAL OF NEW PLAYS

Northern Kentucky University, Department of Theatre and Dance, Nunn Dr., Highland Heights KY 41099-1007. (859)572-6303. **Fax:** (859)572-6057. **E-mail:** forman@nku.edu. **Contact:** Sandra Forman, project director. For musical playwrights. Biennial award (odd numbered years).

PURPOSE "The festival seeks to encourage new playwrights and develop new plays and musicals. Three plays or musicals are given full productions."

REQUIREMENTS "No entry fee. Submit a script with a completed entry form. Musicals should be submitted with a piano/conductor's score and/or a vocal parts score. Scripts may be submitted May 1 through September 30 for the New Play Festival occuring in April of the following year. Send SASE for application."

AWARDS Three awards of $500. "The winners are brought to NKU at our expense to view late rehearsals and opening night." Submissions are judged by a panel of readers.

TIPS "Plays/musicals which have heavy demands for mature actors are not as likely to be selected as an equally good script with roles for 18- to 30-year olds."

ORGANIZATIONS

One of the first places a beginning songwriter should look for guidance and support is a songwriting organization. Offering encouragement, instruction, contacts, and feedback, these groups of professional and amateur songwriters can help an aspiring songwriter hone the skills needed to compete in the ever-changing music industry. Having a community of support, with relevant information and contacts, is one of the most important things a songwriter can have.

The type of organization you choose to join depends on what you want to get out of it. Local groups can offer a friendly, supportive environment where you can work on your songs and have them critiqued in a constructive way by other songwriters, providing valuable feedback for your work. They're also great places to meet collaborators for projects where you might want a co-writer. Larger, national organizations can give you access to music business professionals and other songwriters across the country. The leaders of both local and national organizations may also be able to help you develop contacts, whether it's someone they know and have worked with directly, or a professional they know from one of their own contacts.

JOINING A SONGWRITING ORGANIZATION

Most of the organizations listed in this book are nonprofit groups with membership open to specific groups of people—songwriters, musicians, classical composers, etc. They can be local groups with a membership of fewer than 100 people, or large national organizations with thousands of members from all over the country. In addition to regular meetings, most organizations occasionally sponsor events such as seminars and workshops to which music industry personnel are invited to talk about the business, and perhaps listen to and critique demo tapes.

Check the following listings, bulletin boards at local music stores, and your local newspapers for area organizations. If you are unable to locate an organization within an easy distance of your home, you may want to consider joining one of the national groups. These groups, based in New York, Los Angeles, and Nashville, keep their members involved and informed through newsletters, regional workshops, and large yearly conferences. They can help a writer who feels isolated in his hometown get his music heard by professionals in the major music centers.

In these listings, organizations describe their purpose and activities, as well as how much it costs to join. Before joining any organization, consider what it has to offer and how becoming a member will benefit you. Also, remember to look up each listing online before joining. While we are confident that all of the information in *Songwriter's Market* is accurate, information can change, and often changes quickly. Remember to fact-check membership fees, activities, and the types of songwriters that join these organizations. To locate an organization close to home, see the Geographic Index at the back of this book.

ACADEMY OF COUNTRY MUSIC

5500 Balboa Blvd., Encino CA 91316. (818)788-8000. **Fax:** (818)788-0999. **E-mail:** info@acmcountry.com. **Website:** www.acmcountry.com. There is a contact form for the group on the website. Serves country music industry professionals. Eligibility for professional members is limited to those individuals who derive some portion of their income directly from country music. Each member is classified by one of the following categories: artist/entertainer, club/venue operator, musician, on-air personality, manager, talent agent, composer, music publisher, public relations, publications, radio, TV/motion picture, record company, talent buyer or affiliated (general). The purpose of ACM is to promote and enhance the image of country music. The Academy is involved year-round in activities important to the country music community. Some of these activities include charity fundraisers, participation in country music seminars, talent contests, artist showcases, assistance to producers in placing country music on TV and in motion pictures and backing legislation that benefits the interests of the country music community. The ACM is governed by directors and run by officers elected annually. Applications are accepted throughout the year online. Membership: $75/year.

AMERICAN SOCIETY OF COMPOSERS, AUTHORS AND PUBLISHERS (ASCAP)

1900 Broadway, New York NY 10023. (212)621-6000 (administration). **Fax:** (212)621-8453. **Website:** www. ascap.com. **Regional offices—West Coast:** 7920 W. Sunset Blvd., 3rd Floor, Los Angeles CA 90046, (323)883-1000; **Nashville:** Two Music Square W., Nashville TN 37203, (615)742-5000; **Atlanta:** 950 Joseph E. Lowery Blvd. NW, Suite 23, Atlanta GA 30318, (404)685-8699; **Miami:** 420 Lincoln Rd., Suite 385, Miami Beach FL 33139, (305)673-3446; **London:** 8 Cork St., London W1S 3LJ England, 011-44-207-439-0909; **Puerto Rico:** Ave. Martinez Nadal, c/ Hill Side 623, San Juan, Puerto Rico 00920, (787)707-0782. ASCAP is a membership association of over 240,000 composers, lyricists, songwriters, and music publishers, whose function is to protect the rights of its members by licensing and collecting royalties for the nondramatic public performance of their copyrighted works. ASCAP licensees include radio, TV, cable, live concert promoters, bars, restaurants, symphony orchestras, new media, and other users of music.

ASCAP is the leading performing rights society in the world. All revenues, minus operating expenses, are distributed to members (about 86 cents of each dollar). ASCAP was the first U.S. performing rights organization to distribute royalties from the Internet. Founded in 1914, ASCAP is the only society created and owned by writers and publishers. The ASCAP board of directors consists of 12 writers and 12 publishers, elected by the membership. ASCAP's Member Card provides exclusive benefits geared towards working music professionals. Among the benefits are health, musical instrument and equipment, tour and studio liability, term life and long-term care insurance, discounts on musical instruments, equipment and supplies, access to a credit union, and much more. ASCAP hosts a wide array of showcases and workshops throughout the year, and offers grants, special awards, and networking opportunities in a variety of genres. Visit their website listed above for more information.

ARIZONA SONGWRITERS ASSOCIATION

428 E. Thunderbird Rd. #737, Phoenix AZ 85022. **E-mail:** azsongwriters@cox.net. **Website:** www.azsongwriters.org. **Contact:** John Iger, president. Members are all ages; all styles of music, novice to pro; many make money placing their songs in film and TV. Most members are residents of Arizona. Purpose is to educate about the craft and business of songwriting and to facilitate networking with business professionals and other songwriters, musicians, singers and studios. Offers instruction, e-newsletter, workshops, performance, and song-pitching opportunities. Applications accepted year-round for membership (for a nomimal fee).

☼ ASSOCIATION DES PROFESSIONEL. LE.S DE LA CHANSON ET DE LA MUSIQUE

450 Rideau St., Suite 401, Ottawa ON K1N 5Z4 Canada. (613)745-5642. **Fax:** (613)745-9715. **E-mail:** communications@apcm.ca. **Website:** www.apcm.ca. **Contact:** Mathilde Hountchegnon, head of communications and promotion. Members are French Canadian singers and musicians. Members must be French singing and may have a CD to be distributed. Purpose is to gather French-speaking artists (outside of Quebec; mainly in Ontario) to distribute their material, other workshops, instructions, lectures, etc. Offers instruction, newsletter, lectures, workshops, and distribution.

Applications accepted year-round. Membership fee: $60 (Canadian).

ASSOCIATION OF INDEPENDENT MUSIC PUBLISHERS

P.O. Box 10482, Marina del Rey CA 90295. (818)771-7301. **E-mail:** LAinfo@aimp.org; NYinfo@aimp.org; NAinfo@aimp.org. **Website:** www.aimp.org. The organization's primary focus is to educate and inform music publishers about the most current industry trends and practices by providing a forum for the discussion of the issues and problems confronting the music publishing industry. Offers monthly panels and networking events. Applications accepted year-round. Professional membership fee: $75/year. Online only: $60/year.

AUSTIN SONGWRITERS GROUP

P.O. Box 17786, Austin TX 78760. (512)698-4237. **E-mail:** leeduffy@austinsongwritersgroup.com. **Website:** www.austinsongwritersgroup.com. **Contact:** Lee Duffy, executive director. The Austin Songwriters Group is a nonprofit organization created by songwriters for songwriters. Serves all ages and all levels, from just beginning to advanced. "Prospective members should have an interest in the field of songwriting, whether it be for profit or hobby. The main purpose of this organization is to educate members in the craft and business of songwriting; to provide resources for growth and advancement in the area of songwriting; and to provide opportunities for performance and contact with the music industry." The primary benefit of membership to a songwriter is exposed to music industry professionals, which increases contacts and furthers the songwriter's education in both craft and business aspects. Offers competitions, instruction, lectures, library, newsletter, performance opportunities, evaluation services, workshops and contact with music industry professionals through special guest speakers at meetings, plus our yearly Austin Songwriters Symposium, which includes instruction, song evaluations, and song pitching direct to those pros currently seeking material for their artists, publishing companies, etc." Applications accepted year-round.

TIPS "Our newsletter is top quality, packed with helpful information on all aspects of songwriting-craft, business, recording and producing tips, and industry networking opportunities. Go to our website and sign up for e-mails to keep you informed about ongoing and upcoming events!"

BALTIMORE SONGWRITERS ASSOCIATION

P.O. Box 22496, Baltimore MD 21203. **E-mail:** info@baltimoresongwriters.org. **Website:** www.baltimoresongwriters.org. "The BSA is an inclusive organization with all ages, skill levels and genres of music welcome. We are trying to build a musical community that is more supportive and less competitive. We are dedicated to helping songwriters grow and become better in their craft." Offers instruction, newsletter, lectures, workshops, performance opportunities. Applications accepted year-round; membership not limited to location or musical status. There are meetings every month, as well as (performance) songwriting showcases.

THE BLACK ROCK COALITION

P.O. Box 1054, Cooper Station, New York NY 10276. **E-mail:** brcmembersinfo@gmail.com. **Website:** www.blackrockcoalition.org. **Contact:** Darrell M. McNeil, director of operations. Serves musicians, songwriters—male and female ages 18-40 (average). Also engineers, entertainment attorneys and producers. Looking for members who are "mature and serious about music as an artist or activist willing to help fellow musicians. The BRC independently produces, promotes and distributes black alternative music acts as a collective and supportive voice for such musicians within the music and record business. The main purpose of this organization is to produce, promote, and distribute the full spectrum of black music along with educating the public on what black music is. The BRC is now soliciting recorded music by bands and individuals for Black Rock Coalition Records. Please send copyrighted and original material only." Offers instruction, newsletter, lectures, free seminars and workshops, monthly membership meeting, quarterly magazine, performing opportunities, evaluation services, business advice, full roster of all members. Applications accepted year-round. Bands must submit a tape, bio with picture and a self-addressed, stamped envelope before sending their membership fee. Membership fee: $25. A lifetime fee is $250.

BROADCAST MUSIC, INC. (BMI)

7 World Trade Center, 250 Greenwich St., New York NY 10007. (212)220-3000. **E-mail:** newyork@bmi.com. **Website:** www.bmi.com. **Los Angeles:** 8730 Sunset Blvd., 3rd Floor West, Los Angeles CA 90069. (310)659-9109. **E-mail:** losangeles@bmi.com. **Nashville:** 10 Music Square E., Nashville TN 37203.

(615)401-2000. **E-mail:** nashville@bmi.com. **Miami:** 1691 Michigan Av., Miami FL 33139. (305)673-5148. **E-mail:** miami@bmi.com. **Atlanta:** 3340 Peachtree Rd., NE, Suite 570, Atlanta GA 30326. (404)261-5151. **E-mail:** atlanta@bmi.com. **Puerto Rico:** 1250 Ave. Ponce de Leon, San Jose Building Santurce PR 00907. (787)754-6490. **United Kingdom:** 84 Harley House, Marylebone Rd., London NW1 5HN United Kingdom. 011-44-207-486-2036. **E-mail:** london@bmi.com. President and CEO: Del R. Bryant. Senior vice presidents: Phillip Graham, New York, writer/publisher relations; Alison Smith, rerforming rights. Vice presidents: Charlie Feldman, New York; Barbara Cane and Doreen Ringer Ross, Los Angeles; Paul Corbin, Nashville; Diane J. Almodovar, Miami; Catherine Brewton, Atlanta. Senior executive, London: Brandon Bakshi. BMI is a performing rights organization representing approximately 300,000 songwriters, composers and music publishers in all genres of music, including pop, rock, country, R&B, rap, jazz, Latin, gospel and contemporary classical. "Applicants must have written a musical composition, alone or in collaboration with other writers, which is commercially published, recorded or otherwise likely to be performed." Purpose: BMI acts on behalf of its songwriters, composers and music publishers by ensuring payment for performance of their works through the collection of licensing fees from radio stations, Internet outlets, broadcast and cable TV stations, hotels, nightclubs, aerobics centers and other users of music. This income is distributed to the writers and publishers in the form of royalty payments, based on how the music is used. BMI also undertakes intensive lobbying efforts in Washington D.C. on behalf of its affiliates, seeking to protect their performing rights through the enactment of new legislation and enforcement of current copyright law. In addition, BMI helps aspiring songwriters develop their skills through various workshops, seminars and competitions it sponsors throughout the country. Applications accepted year-round. There is no membership fee for songwriters; a one-time fee of $150 is required to affiliate an individually owned publishing company; $250 for partnerships, corporations and limited-liability companies. "Visit our website for specific contacts, e-mail addresses and additional membership information."

CALIFORNIA LAWYERS FOR THE ARTS

Fort Mason Center, 2 Marina Blvd., Building C, Room 265, San Francisco CA 94123. (415)775-7200. **Fax:** (415)775-1143. **E-mail:** lris@calawyersforthearts.org. **Website:** www.calawyersforthearts.org. CLA's mission is to empower the creative community by providing education, representation and dispute resolution. CLA's vision is that creative artists and arts organizations serve as agents of democratic involvement, innovation, and positive social change, and the growth of an empowered arts sector is essential to healthy communities. CLA's leadership and services strengthen the arts for the benefit of communities throughout California. CLA serves creative artists of all disciplines, skill levels, and ages, supporting individuals, businesses, inventors, and creative arts organizations. CLA also serves groups and individuals who support the arts. CLA works most closely with the California arts and innovation community. Offers online education, newsletters, in-person workshops and seminars, library, mediation and arbitration service, attorney referral service, publications and arts advocacy. Membership fees: $20 for senior citizens and full-time students, $30 for working artists, $45 for general individual, $70 for non-panel attorney, $75 for panel attorney, $100 for patrons; organizations: $50 for small organizations (budget under $100,000), $90 for large organizations (budget of $100,000 or more), $100 for corporate sponsors.

⊙ CANADA COUNCIL FOR THE ARTS/ CONSEIL DES ARTS DU CANADA

150 Elgin St., P.O. Box 1047, Ottawa ON K1P 5V8 Canada. (800)263-5588 or (613)566-4414, ext. 5060. **Fax:** (613)566-4390. **Website:** www.canadacouncil.ca. An independent agency that fosters and promotes the arts in Canada by providing grants and services to professional artists including songwriters and musicians. "Individual artists must be Canadian citizens or permanent residents of Canada, and must have completed basic training and/or have the recognition as professionals within their fields. The Canada Council offers grants to professional musicians to pursue their individual artistic development and creation. There are specific deadline dates for the various programs of assistance. Visit our website for more details."

✪ CANADIAN ACADEMY OF RECORDING ARTS AND SCIENCES (CARAS)

345 Adelaide St. W., 2nd Floor, Toronto ON M5V 1R5 Canada. (416)485-3135. **Fax:** (416)485-4978. **E-mail:** info@carasonline.ca; jaclyn@junoawards.ca. **Website:** www.carasonline.ca. Membership is open to all employees (including support staff) in broadcasting and record companies, as well as producers, personal managers, recording artists, recording engineers, arrangers, composers, music publishers, album designers, promoters, talent and booking agents, record retailers, rack jobbers, distributors, recording studios, and other music industry-related professions (on approval). Applicants must be affiliated with the Canadian recording industry. Offers newsletter, nomination and voting privileges for Juno Awards and discount tickets to Juno Awards show. "CARAS strives to foster the development of the Canadian music and recording industries and to contribute toward higher artistic standards." Applications accepted year-round. Membership fee: $75/year (Canadian) + HST. Applications accepted from individuals only, not from companies or organizations.

✪ CANADIAN COUNTRY MUSIC ASSOCIATION

120 Adelaide St. E., Suite 200, Toronto ON M5C 1K9 Canada. (416)947-1331. **Fax:** (416)947-5924. **E-mail:** country@ccma.org. **Website:** www.ccma.org. Members are artists, songwriters, musicians, producers, radio station personnel, managers, booking agents, and others. Offers newsletter, workshops, performance opportunities, and the CCMA Awards every September. "Through our newsletters and conventions, we offer a means of meeting and associating with artists and others in the industry. The CCMA is a federally chartered, nonprofit organization, dedicated to the promotion and development of Canadian country music throughout Canada and the world and to providing a unity of purpose for the Canadian country music industry." See website for membership information and benefits. Membership dues start at $75 for 1 year.

CENTRAL CAROLINA SONGWRITERS ASSOCIATION (CCSA)

131 Henry Baker Rd., Zebulon NC 27597. (919)727-6647. **Website:** www.ccsa-raleigh.com. There is a contact form on the site. "CCSA welcomes songwriters of all experience levels, from beginner to professional, within the local RDU/Triad/eastern area of North Carolina to join our group. Our members' musical backgrounds vary, covering a wide array of musical genres. CCSA meets monthly in Raleigh. We are unable to accept applications from incarcerated persons or those who do not reside in the local area, as our group's primary focus is on songwriters who are able to attend the monthly meetings—to ensure members get the best value for their yearly dues." CCSA strives to provide each songwriter and musician a resourceful organization where members grow musically by networking and sharing with one another. Offers annual songwriters forum, periodic workshops, critiques at the monthly meetings, opportunities to perform and network with fellow members. Applications are accepted year-round. Dues are $24/year (pro-rated for new members at $2/month by date of application) with annual renewal each January.

THE COLLEGE MUSIC SOCIETY

312 E. Pine St., Missoula MT 59802. (406)721-9616. **Fax:** (406)721-9419. **E-mail:** cms@music.org. **Website:** www.music.org. **Contact:** Shannon Devlin, member services. The College Music Society promotes music teaching and learning, musical creativity and expression, research and dialogue, and diversity and interdisciplinary interaction. A consortium of college, conservatory, university, and independent musicians and scholars interested in all disciplines of music, the Society provides leadership and serves as an agent of change by addressing concerns facing music in higher education." Offers an online journal, newsletter, lectures, workshops, performance opportunities, job listing service, databases of organizations and institutions, music faculty, and mailing lists. Applications accepted year-round. Membership fees: $70 (regular dues), $35 (student dues), $35 (retiree dues).

CONNECTICUT SONGWRITERS ASSOCIATION

P.O. Box 511, Mystic CT 06355. **E-mail:** info@ctsongs.com. **Website:** www.ctsongs.com. **Contact:** Bill Pere, president and executive director. "We are an educational, nonprofit organization dedicated to improving the art and craft of original music. Founded in 1979, CSA has had almost 2,000 active members and has become one of the best-known and most-respected songwriters' associations in the country. Membership in the CSA admits you to 12-18 seminars/workshops/song critique sessions per year throughout Connecticut and surrounding region. Out-of-state members may mail in songs for free critiques at our meetings. Noted professionals deal with all aspects of the craft and business of music, including lyric writing, music theory, music technology, arrangement and production, legal and business aspects, performance techniques, song analysis and recording techniques." CSA offers song screening sessions for members and songs that pass become eligible for inclusion on the CSA sampler anthology through various retail and online outlets and are brought to national music conferences. CSA is well connected in both the independent music scene and the traditional music industry. CSA also offers showcases and concerts that are open to the public and designed to give artists a venue for performing their original material for an attentive, listening audience. CSA benefits local soup kitchens, group homes, hospice, world hunger, libraries, nature centers, community centers and more. CSA encompasses ballads to bluegrass and Bach to rock. Membership fee: $45/year (there are student and senior discounts).

DALLAS SONGWRITERS ASSOCIATION

Sammons Center for the Arts, 3630 Harry Hines Blvd. #20, Dallas TX 75219. (214)750-0916. **E-mail:** info@dallassongwriters.org. **Website:** dallassongwriters.org. DSA is a nonprofit organization dedicated to providing learning opportunities on the craft and business of songwriting. All styles of music are welcome in the DSA, and membership includes writers of all ages. DSA monthly activities include meetings with guest speakers, song critiques and performance showcases that are open to the public. In addition, the DSA supports and promotes workshops and contests and publishes a monthly newsletter. Check the website for open mic information, as well as workshops and more. New membership is $50.

THE DRAMATISTS GUILD OF AMERICA, INC.

1501 Broadway, Suite 701, New York NY 10036. (212)398-9366. **Fax:** (212)944-0420. **E-mail:** rtec@dramatistsguild.com. **Website:** www.dramatistsguild.com. **Contact:** Roland Tec, director of membership. For over 3/4 of a century, The Dramatists Guild has been the professional association of playwrights, composers and lyricists, with more than 6,000 members across the country. All theater writers, whether produced or not, are eligible for associate membership ($90/year); students enrolled in writing-degree pro-

grams at colleges or universities are eligible for student membership ($45/year); writers who have been produced on Broadway, Off-Broadway or on the main stage of a LORT theater are eligible for active membership ($130/year). The Guild offers its members the following activities and services: use of the Guild's contracts (including the approved production contract for Broadway, the Off-Broadway contract, the LORT contract, the collaboration agreements for both musicals and drama, the 99-seat theatre plan contract, the small theatre contract, commissioning agreements, and the underlying rights agreements contract; advice on all theatrical contracts including Broadway, Off-Broadway, regional, showcase, equity-waiver, dinner theater and collaboration contracts); a nationwide toll-free number for all members with business or contract questions or problems; advice and information on a wide spectrum of issues affecting writers; free and/or discounted ticket service; symposia led by experienced professionals in major cities nationwide; access to health insurance programs; and a spacious meeting room that can accommodate up to 50 people for readings and auditions on a rental basis. The Guild's publications are: *The Dramatist*, a bimonthly journal containing articles on all aspects of the theater (which includes *The Dramatists Guild Newsletter*, with announcements of all Guild activities and current information of interest to dramatists); and an annual resource directory with up-to-date information on agents, publishers, grants, producers, playwriting contests, conferences and workshops, and an interactive website that brings our community of writers together to exchange ideas and share information.

THE FIELD

75 Maiden Lane, Suite 906, New York NY 10038. (212)691-6969. **E-mail:** claire@thefield.org. **Website:** www.thefield.org. **Contact:** Claire Baum, artist services associate. "Founded by artists for artists, The Field has been dedicated to providing impactful services to thousands of performing artists in New York and beyond since 1986. From fostering creative exploration to stewarding innovative fundraising strategies, we are delighted to help artists reach their fullest potential. More than 1,900 performing artists come to The Field annually to build their businesses, 2,000-plus new artworks are developed under our stewardship each year, and our services are replicated in 11 cities across the U.S. and in Europe. At the same time,

we remain true to our grassroots origin and artist-centered mission: to strategically and comprehensively serve the myriad artistic and administrative needs of independent performing artists and companies who work in the fields of dance, theater, music, text, and performance art. Our core values of affordability, accessibility and rigorous delivery infuse all of our interactions. Field services include career-building workshops (grant writing, touring, Internet strategies, etc.), fiscal sponsorship, creative residences in New York and out of town, an 'Artists' Kinkos' resource center, and membership benefits." Offers fiscal sponsorship, arts management and creative workshops, residencies, and performance opportunities. Applications accepted year-round. Membership fee: $100/year.

TIPS "The Field offers the most affordable and accessible fiscal sponsorship program in New York. The Sponsored Artist Program offered by The Field enables performing artists and groups to accumulate the funds they need to make their artistic and career goals a reality. Fiscal sponsorship provides independent performing artists and groups with: eligibility to apply for most government, foundation, and corporate grants that require a 501(c)(3), nonprofit status; eligibility to receive tax-deductible donations of both money and goods from individuals; and other services where 501(c)(3) status is necessary."

✪ FILM MUSIC NETWORK

13101 Washington Blvd., Suite 466, Los Angeles CA 90066. **Website:** www.filmmusic.net. "The Film Music Network, established in 1997, is a leading worldwide professional association of composers, songwriters, bands, recording artists, and more who are seeking to place their music or compose custom music for film or television projects. One of the Film Music Network's most popular member benefits is providing leads for projects seeking music or composers, including film projects, television projects, corporate videos, music libraries, and more. Additional member benefits include a free introductory legal consultation, discounted move theater and event tickets, resources including a directory of film music agents and managers, our film music salary and rate survey, and more." Full membership fee: $11.95/month. Audio-only fee: $4.95/month.

◗ There is a contact form online. Responds to inquiries with 24 hours.

FLORIDA SONGWRITERS ASSOCIATION

200 S. Harbor City Blvd., Suite 403, Melbourne FL 32901. **E-mail:** info@flsw.org. **Website:** www.flsw.org. Florida Songwriters Association is a collaboration of several companies in the industry. We all share the common goal of helping to further educate, motivate, and elevate songwriters. More information online. Annual memberships start at $100 per year.

TIPS "Learn what it takes to be a songwriter. Not just how to write songs, but how to protect your works, as well. Register with a Performing Rights Organization (PRO) and do your research on how the business works. This will go a long way when dealing with industry professionals."

FORT WORTH SONGWRITERS' ASSOCIATION

P.O. Box 330233, Fort Worth TX 76163. (817)654-5400. **E-mail:** fwsanewsletter@gmail.com. **Website:** www.fwsa.com. Members are beginners up to and including published writers. Interests cover gospel, country, western swing, rock, pop, bluegrass, and blues. Purpose is to allow songwriters to become more proficient at songwriting; to provide an opportunity for their efforts to be performed before a live audience; to provide songwriters an opportunity to meet co-writers. "We provide our members free critiques of their efforts. We provide a monthly newsletter outlining current happenings in the business of songwriting. We offer competitions and mini-workshops with guest speakers from the music industry. We promote a weekly open mic for singers of original material, and hold invitational songwriter showcase events a various times throughout the year. Each year, we hold a Christmas song contest, judged by independent music industry professionals. We also offer free Web pages for members or links to member websites." Applications accepted year-round. Membership fee: $40 as of 2015.

◗ There is a contact form on the website.

GLOBAL SONGWRITERS CONNECTION

P.O. Box 140623, Nashville TN 37214. (615)732-8832. **E-mail:** info@globalsongwriters.com. **Website:** www.globalsongwriters.com. Global Songwriters Connection is an association for singer/songwriters founded by music industry professional, career coach, mentor, motivational speaker, and teacher Sheree Spoltore. Sheree is passionate about encouraging, equipping, and empowering songwriters around the world to be their personal best. "GSC's personalized career mentoring services provide singers, songwriters, and artists in all genres and at every level, with industry connections and an individualized plan to help the artist reach the next step. Whether it is song crafting, career, or artist development, GSC's mentoring services focus on personal songwriter development first." Mermbership fee: $50.

GOSPEL MUSIC ASSOCIATION

4012 Granny White Pike, Nashville TN 37204-3924. (615)242-0303. **Fax:** (615)254-9755. **E-mail:** jackie@ gospelmusic.org. **E-mail:** info@gospelmusic.org. **Website:** www.gospelmusic.org. Serves songwriters, musicians and anyone directly involved in or who supports gospel music. Professional members include advertising agencies, musicians, songwriters, agents/managers, composers, retailers, music publishers, print and broadcast media, and other members of the recording industry. Associate members include supporters of gospel music and those whose involvement in the industry does not provide them with income. The primary purpose of the GMA is to expose, promote, and celebrate the gospel through music. A GMA membership offers newsletters, performance experiences and workshops, as well as networking opportunities. Applications accepted year-round. Membership fees: $95/year for professionals; $25/year for iMembers (supporters of gospel music and those whose involvement in the industry does not provide them a source of income).

❺ THE GUILD OF INTERNATIONAL SONGWRITERS & COMPOSERS

Northland House, 32 Hillgarth, Castleside, Consett Durham DH8 9QD United Kingdom. (01) (207)500825. **E-mail:** songmag@aol.com; gisc@bt-connect.com. **Website:** www.songwriters-guild.co.uk. The Guild of International Songwriters & Composers is an international music industry organization based in England. Guild members are songwriters, composers, lyricists, poets, performing songwriters, musicians, music publishers, studio owners, managers, independent record companies, music industry personnel, etc., from many countries throughout the world. The Guild of International Songwriters & Composers has been publishing *Songwriting and Composing Magazine* since 1986, which is issued free to all Guild members throughout their membership. The Guild offers advice, guidance, assistance, copyright protection service, information, encouragement, contact information, intellectual property/copyright protection of members' works through the Guild's Copyright Registration Centre along with other free services and more to Guild members with regard to helping members achieve their aims, ambitions, progression, and advancement in respect to the many different aspects of the music industry. Information, advice and services available to Guild members throughout their membership includes assistance, advice and help on many matters and issues relating to the music industry in general.

INTERNATIONAL BLUEGRASS MUSIC ASSOCIATION (IBMA)

608 W. Iris Dr., Nashville TN 37204. (615)256-3222 or (888)438-4262. **Fax:** (615)256-0450. **E-mail:** info@ ibma.org. **Website:** www.ibma.org. Serves songwriters, musicians and professionals in bluegrass music. "IBMA is a trade association composed of people and organizations involved professionally and semiprofessionally in the bluegrass music industry, including performers, agents, songwriters, music publishers, promoters, print and broadcast media, local associations, recording manufacturers, and distributors. Voting members must be currently or formerly involved in the bluegrass industry as full- or part-time professionals. A songwriter attempting to become professionally involved in our field would be eligible. Our mission statement reads: *IBMA: Working together for high standards of professionalism, a greater appreciation for our music, and the success of the worldwide bluegrass music community.* IBMA holds an annual trade show/convention with a songwriter's showcase in the fall, represents our field outside the bluegrass music community, and compiles and disseminates databases of bluegrass-related resources and organizations. Market research on the bluegrass consumer is available and we offer "Bluegrass in the Schools" information and matching grants. The primary value in this organization for a songwriter is having current information about the bluegrass music field and contacts with other songwriters, publishers, musicians and record companies." Offers workshops, liability insurance, rental car discounts, consultation and databases of record companies, radio stations, press, organizations and gigs. Applications accepted year-round. Membership fee: for a non-voting patron, $40/year; for an individual voting professional, $75/year; for an organizational voting professional, $205/year.

INTERNATIONAL SONGWRITERS ASSOCIATION, LTD.

P.O. Box 46, Limerick City, Ireland 00-353-61-228837 United Kingdom. (01)(71)486-5353. **E-mail:** jliddane@songwriter.iol.ie. **Website:** www.songwriter.co.uk. **Contact:** Bill Miller, Ray Coleman, membership department. Serves songwriters and music publishers. "The ISA headquarters is in Limerick City, Ireland, and from there it provides its members with assessment services, copyright services, legal and other advisory services, and an investigations service, plus a magazine for 1 yearly fee. Our members are songwriters in more than 60 countries worldwide, of all ages." There are conditions for membership — see the website. "We provide information and assistance to professional or semiprofessional songwriters. Our publication, *Songwriter*, which was founded in 1967, features detailed exclusive interviews with songwriters and music publishers, as well as directory information of value to writers." Applications accepted year-round. Membership fee for European writers is £19.95; for non-European writers, $30.

JUST PLAIN FOLKS MUSIC ORGANIZATION

5327 Kit Dr., Indianapolis IN 46237. **E-mail:** JPFolksPro@aol.com. **Website:** www.justplainfolks.org. "Just Plain Folks is among the world's largest music organizations. Our members cover nearly every musical style and professional field, from songwriters, artists, publishers, producers, record labels, entertainment attorneys, publicists and PR experts, performing rights organization staffers, live and recording engineers, educators, music students, musical instrument manufacturers, television, radio and print media, and almost every major Internet music entity. Representing all 50 U.S. states and more than 160 countries worldwide, we have members of all ages, musical styles and levels of success, including winners and nominees of every major music industry award, as well as those just starting out. A complete demographics listing of our group is available on our website. Whether you are a No. 1 hit songwriter or artist, or the newest kid on the block, you are welcome to join. Membership *does* require an active e-mail account." The purpose of this organization is "to share wisdom, ideas and experiences with others who have been there, and to help educate those who have yet to make the journey. Just Plain Folks provides its members with a friendly networking and support community that uses the power of the Internet and combines it with good old-fashioned human interaction. We help promote our members' success and educate those still learning." Membership is free.

LOS ANGELES MUSIC NETWORK

P.O. Box 2446, Toluca Lake CA 91610. (818)769-6095. **E-mail:** info@lamn.com. **Website:** www.lamn.com. "Our emphasis is on sharing knowledge and information, giving you access to top professionals and promoting career development. LAMN is an association of music industry professionals, i.e., artists, singers, songwriters, and people who work in various aspects of the music industry with an emphasis on the creative. Members are ambitious and interested in advancing their careers. LAMN promotes career advancement, communication and education among artists and creatives. LAMN sponsors industry events and educational panels held at venues in the Los Angeles area and now in other major music hubs around the country (New York, Las Vegas, Phoenix, and San Francisco). LAMN Jams are popular among our members. Experience LAMN Jams in Los Angeles or New York by performing your original music in front of industry experts who can advance your career by getting your music in the hands of hard-to-reach music supervisors. The singer-songwriter contest gives artists an opportunity to perform in front of industry experts and receive instant feedback on their music, lyrics, and performance. Offers performance opportunities, instruction, newsletters, lectures, seminars, music industry job listings, career counseling, résumé publishing, mentor network, and many professional networking opportunities. See our website for current job listings and a calendar of upcoming events." Applications accepted year-round. Annual membership fee as of 2015: $25.

LOUISIANA SONGWRITERS ASSOCIATION

P.O. Box 82009, Baton Rouge LA 70884. **E-mail:** info@louisianamusichalloffame.org. **Website:** http://louisianamusichalloffame.org/content/view/154/168/. Membership fee: $25/year. "The purposes of the registration and membership process are simply to create a database of Louisiana's songwriters and other industry people, to organize songwriters as part of our efforts to help build the music industry of Louisiana, provide a verifiable actual number of interested, dues-paying songwriters to seek programs and business partners to aid the musicians of Louisiana, and to create a verifiable 'force' in the music business by doing the following: showing the number of songwriters with legitimate interest in the business, providing a path for communications to, from and between songwriters, musicians and other industry workers, helping to network for bookings, gigs, etc., and giving songwriters an advocate and voice to help build our music industry."

ⓒ MANITOBA MUSIC

1-376 Donald St., Winnipeg MB R3B 2J2 Canada. (204)942-8650. **Fax:** (204)942-6083. **E-mail:** info@manitobamusic.com. **Website:** www.manitobamusic.com. Organization consists of "songwriters, producers, agents, musicians, managers, retailers, publicists, radio, talent buyers, media, record labels, etc. (no age limit, no skill level minimum). Must have interest in the future of Manitoba's music industry." The main purpose of Manitoba Music is to foster growth in all areas of the Manitoba music industry, primarily through education, promotion and lobbying. Offers newsletter, extensive website, directory of Manitoba's music industry, workshops, and performance opportunities. Manitoba Music is also involved with the Western Canadian Music Awards festival, conference and awards show. Applications accepted year-round. Membership fee: $50 (Canadian). Other membership levels, such as band ($75) and youth ($35), available, as well.

MINNESOTA ASSOCIATION OF SONGWRITERS

P.O. Box 285, Hopkins MN 55343. **E-mail:** info@mn-songwriters.org. **Website:** www.mnsongwriters.org. "Includes a wide variety of members, ranging in age from 18 to 80; type of music is very diverse, ranging from alternative rock to folk, blues, theatrical and contemporary Christian; skill levels range from beginning songwriters to writers with recorded and published material. Main requirement is an interest in songwriting. Although most members come from the Minneapolis-St. Paul area, others come from nearby Wisconsin and other parts of the country. Some members are full-time musicians, but most represent a wide variety of occupations. MAS is a nonprofit community of songwriters that informs, educates, inspires, and assists its members in the art and business of songwriting." Offers instruction, workshops with pro songwriters, public performance opportunities, online and in-meeting evaluation services, In-

ternet radio, and a public-access TV show being aired around the nation. Applications accepted year-round. Membership fee: $35. Student membership: $20. Other membership options listed online.

TIPS "Members are kept current on resources and opportunities. Original works are played at meetings or submitted via e-mail, then reviewed by involved members. Through this process, writers hone their skills and gain experience and confidence in refining their works and putting them into the music market."

ⓒ MUSIC BC INDUSTRY ASSOCIATION

#100-938 Howe St., Vancouver BC V6Z 1N9 Canada. (604)873-1914. **Fax:** (604)873-9686. **E-mail:** info@musicbc.org. **Website:** www.musicbc.org. Music BC (formerly PMIA) is a nonprofit society that supports and promotes the spirit, development, and growth of the British Columbia music community provincially, nationally, and internationally. Music BC provides education, resources, advocacy, opportunities for funding, and a forum for communication. Visit website for membership benefits. There are several levels of membership (all with different pricing). A basic individual membership is $56.

MUSICIANS CONTACT

29684 Masters Dr., Murrieta CA 92563. (818)888-7879. **E-mail:** information@musicianscontact.com. **Website:** www.musicianscontact.com. "The primary source of paying jobs for musicians and vocalists nationwide. Job opportunities are posted daily on the Internet. Also offers exposure to the music industry for solo artists and complete acts seeking representation." Offers a newsletter.

NASHVILLE SONGWRITERS ASSOCIATION INTERNATIONAL (NSAI)

1710 Roy Acuff Place, Nashville TN 37203. (615)256-3354. **E-mail:** nsai@nashvillesongwriters.com. **Website:** www.nashvillesongwriters.com. Purpose: a nonprofit service organization for both aspiring and professional songwriters in all fields of music. Membership: spans the US and several foreign countries. Songwriters may apply in 1 of 3 annual categories: *active* ($200 US currency for songwriters are actively working to improve in the craft of writing and/or actively pursing a career within the songwriting industry); *professional* ($100 US currency for songwriters who are staff writers for a publishing company or earn 51% of their annual income from songwriting, whether from advances, royalties, or performances, or are generally regarded as a professional songwriter within the music industry); *lifetime* (please contact NSAI for details). Membership benefits: music industry information and advice, song evaluations, eNews, access to industry professionals through weekly Nashville workshops and several annual events, regional workshops, use of office facilities, and discounts on books and NSAI's 3 annual events. There are also "branch" workshops of NSAI. Workshops must meet certain standards and are accountable to NSAI.

○   There is a contact form on the website.

THE NATIONAL ASSOCIATION OF COMPOSERS/USA (NACUSA)

P.O. Box 49256, Barrington Station, Los Angeles CA 90049. **E-mail:** nacusa@music-usa.org; gregsteinke@ mail.music-usa.org. **Website:** www.music-usa.org/ nacusa. **Contact:** Greg A. Steinke, Ph.D., membership coordinator. "We are of most value to the concert hall composer. Members are serious music composers of all ages and from all parts of the country, who have a real interest in composing, performing, and listening to modern concert hall music. The main purpose of our organization is to perform, publish, broadcast and write news about composers of serious concert hall music—mostly chamber and solo pieces. Composers may achieve national notice of their work through our newsletter and concerts, and the fairly rare feeling of supporting a noncommercial music enterprise dedicated to raising the musical and social position of the serious composer. Ninety-nine percent of the money earned in music is earned, or so it seems, by popular songwriters who might feel they owe the art of music something, and this is one way they might help support that art. It's a chance to foster fraternal solidarity with their less prosperous, but wonderfully interesting, classical colleagues at a time when the very existence of serious art seems to be questioned by the general populace." Offers competitions, lectures, performance opportunities, library and newsletter. Applications accepted year-round. Membership fee: National (regular): $30; National (students/ seniors): $15.

TIPS Also see the listing for NACUSA Young Composers' Competition in the Contests section of this book.

NEW MUSIC USA

90 Broad St., Suite 1902, New York NY 10004. (212)645-6949. **Fax:** (646)490-0998. **E-mail:** info@ newmusicusa.org. **Website:** www.newmusicusa.org. "New Music USA was formed by the merger of the American Music Center and Meet the Composer. We provide over $1 million each year in grant support for the creation and performance of new work and community building throughout the country. We amplify the voice of the new music community through New-MusicBox, profiling the people and ideas that energize and challenge music makers today. We stream a wide-ranging catalog of new music around the clock on Counterstream Radio and provide an online home for composers to feature their own music. This is not a membership organization; all musicians are eligible for support." Offers grant programs and information services. Deadlines vary for each grant program.

OPERA AMERICA

330 Seventh Ave., New York NY 10001. (212)796-8620. **Fax:** (212)796-8631. **E-mail:** info@operaamerica.org; SSnook@operaamerica.org. **Website:** www. operaamerica.org. Members are composers, librettists, musicians, singers, and opera/music theater producers. Offers conferences, workshops, and seminars for artists. Publishes online database of opera/music theater companies in the US and Canada, database of opportunities for performing and creative artists, online directory of opera and musical performances worldwide and US, and an online directory of new works created and being developed by current-day composers and librettists, to encourage the performance of new works. Applications accepted year-round. Publishes quarterly magazine and a variety of electronic newsletters. Membership fees are on a sliding scale by membership level. 2016 Opera Conference is May 18-21.

○   There is a contact form on the website.

OUTMUSIC

1206 Pacific St., Suite 3D, New York NY 11216. **E-mail:** info@outmusicfoundation.org. **Website:** www. outmusicfoundation.org. "OUTMUSIC—The LGBT Academy of Recording Artists (LARA) is a 501(c)(3) nonprofit, charitable foundation that serves as an advocacy and awareness platform, and offers programming to support its mission to promote the advancement and appreciation of LGBT music culture and heritage, create opportunities to support the development of young aspiring artists, increase the viability and visibility of the LGBT music and entertainment platform and honor, document and archive the contributions and achievements of out and proud LGBT music artists." Offers newsletter, lectures, workshops, performance opportunities, networking, industry leads. Sponsors OUTMUSIC Awards. Applications accepted year-round. Membership: $100 for individual artist; $150 for duo or group; $100 for individual patrons; $150 for business patrons.

PORTLAND SONGWRITERS ASSOCIATION

P.O. Box 28355, Portland OR 97228. **E-mail:** info@portlandsongwriters.org. **Website:** portlandsongwriters.org. "The PSA is a nonprofit organization providing education and opportunities that will assist writers in creating and marketing their songs. The PSA offers an annual national songwriting contest, monthly workshops, songwriter showcases, special performance venues, quarterly newsletters, mail-in critique service, discounted seminars by music industry pros." Membership fee: $25 (no eligibility requirements).

TIPS "Although most of our members are from the Pacific Northwest, we offer services that can assist songwriters anywhere. Our goal is to provide information and contacts to help songwriters grow artistically and gain access to publishing, recording and related music markets. For more information, please check the website or e-mail."

RHODE ISLAND SONGWRITERS' ASSOCIATION

P.O. Box 9246, Warwick RI 02889. **E-mail:** generalinformation@risongwriters.com; memberships@risongwriters.com. **Website:** www.risongwriters.com. "Membership consists of novice and professional songwriters. RISA provides opportunities to the aspiring writer or performer, as well as the established regional artists who have recordings, are published and perform regularly. The only eligibility requirement is an interest in the group and the group's goals. Non-writers are welcome, as well." The main purpose is to "encourage, foster and conduct the art and craft of original musical and/or lyrical composition through education, information, collaboration and performance." Offers instruction, a newsletter, lectures, workshops, performance opportunities, and evaluation services. Applications accepted year-round. Membership fees: $25/year (individual); $35/year (family/band). "The group holds twice-monthly critique sessions; twice-monthly performer showcases (one performer featured) at a local coffeehouse; songwriter showcases

(usually 6-8 performers); weekly open mics; and a yearly songwriter festival called 'Hear In Rhode Island,' featuring approximately 50 Rhode Island acts, over 2 days."

SAN DIEGO SONGWRITERS GUILD

3952 Clairemont Mesa Blvd, D413, San Diego CA 92117. (858)376-7374. **Website:** http://sdsongwriters.org. There is a contact form on the website. Use it to e-mail them. "Members range with a variety of skill levels. Several members perform and work full time in music. Many are published and have songs recorded. Some are getting major artist record cuts. Most members are from San Diego County. New writers are encouraged to participate and meet others. All musical styles are represented." The purpose of this organization is to "serve the needs of songwriters and artists, especially helping them in the business and craft of songwriting through industry guest appearances." Offers competitions, newsletters, workshops, performance opportunities, discounts on services offered by fellow members, in-person song pitches and evaluations by publishers, producers and A&R executives. Applications accepted year-round. Individual membership dues: $50/year.

SESAC INC.

55 Music Square E., Nashville TN 37203. (615)320-0055. **Fax:** (615)963-3527. **Website:** www.sesac.com. There is a contact form on the website. "SESAC is a selective organization taking pride in having a repertory based on quality rather than quantity. Serves writers and publishers in all types of music who have their works performed by radio, television, nightclubs, cable television, etc. Purpose of organization is to collect and distribute performance royalties to all active affiliates. As a SESAC affiliate, the individual may obtain equipment insurance at competitive rates. Music is reviewed upon invitation by the Writer/Publisher Relations department."

○ SOCAN

41 Valleybrook Dr., Toronto ON M3B 2S6 Canada. (866)307-6226. **E-mail:** info@socan.ca; members@socan.ca. **Website:** www.socan.ca. "SOCAN is the Canadian copyright collective for the communication and performance of musical works. We administer these rights on behalf of our members (composers, lyricists, songwriters, and their publishers) and those of affiliated international organizations by licensing this use of their music in Canada. The fees collected

are distributed as royalties to our members and to affiliated organizations throughout the world. We also distribute royalties received from those organizations to our members for the use of their music worldwide. SOCAN has offices in Toronto, Montreal, Vancouver, and Dartmouth."

SOCIETY OF COMPOSERS & LYRICISTS

8447 Wilshire Blvd., Suite 401, Beverly Hills CA 90211. (310)281-2812. **Fax:** (310)284-4861. **E-mail:** execdir@thescl.com; office@thescl.com. **Website:** www.thescl.com. The professional nonprofit trade organization for members actively engaged in writing music/lyrics for films, TV, and/or video games, or are students of film composition or songwriting for film. Primary mission is to advance the interests of the film and TV music community. Offers an award-winning quarterly publication, educational seminars, screenings, special member-only events, and other member benefits. Applications accepted year-round. Membership fees: $135 full membership (composers, lyricists, songwriters—film/TV music credits must be submitted); $85 associate/student membership for composers, lyricists, songwriters without credits only; $135 sponsor/special friend membership (music editors, music supervisors, music attorneys, agents, etc.).

✪Ⓞ SODRAC INC.

Tower B, Suite 1010, 1470 Peel, Montreal QC H3A 1T1 Canada. (514)845-3268. **Fax:** (514)845-3401. **E-mail:** sodrac@sodrac.ca; members@sodrac.ca. **Website:** www.sodrac.ca. "SODRAC is a reproduction rights collective society facilitating the clearing of rights on musical and artistic works based on the Copyright Board of Canada tariffs or through collective agreements concluded with any users. It is responsible for the distribution of royalties to its national and international members. The society counts more than 6,000 Canadian members and represents musical repertoire originating from nearly 100 foreign countries and manages the rights of 25,000 Canadian and foreign visual artists. SODRAC is the only reproduction rights society in Canada where both songwriters and music publishers are represented, equally and directly." Serves those with an interest in songwriting and music publishing no matter their age or skill level. "Members must have written or published at least 1 musical work that has been reproduced on an audio or audiovisual support, or published 5 musical works that have been recorded and used for com-

mercial purposes. The new member will benefit from a society working to secure his reproduction rights (mechanicals) and broadcast mechanicals." Applications accepted year-round.

SONGWRITERS' ASSOCIATION OF WASHINGTON

4200 Wisconsin Ave. NW, PMB 106-137, Washington DC 20016. **E-mail:** contact@SAW.org. **Website:** www.saw.org. The Songwriters' Association of Washington (SAW) is a nonprofit organization established in 1979 to benefit aspiring and professional songwriters. "Our mission: Strengthen the craft of songwriting; foster the talents of our members; provide an active forum for songwriters and their work; celebrate the power of music." Membership: $35/year, $20/year for students.

THE SONGWRITERS GUILD OF AMERICA

5120 Virginia Way, Suite C22, Brentwood TN 37027. (615)742-9945. **Fax:** (615)630-7501. **E-mail:** membership@songwritersguild.com. **Website:** www.songwritersguild.com. "The Songwriters Guild of America Foundation offers a series of workshops with discounts for some to SGA members, including online classes and song critique opportunities. There is a charge for some songwriting classes and seminars; however, online classes and some monthly events may be included with an SGA membership. Charges vary depending on the class or event. Current class offerings and workshops vary. Visit website to sign up for the newsletter and e-events, and for more information on current events and workshops. Some current events in Nashville are the Ask-a-Pro and ProCritique sessions that give SGA members the opportunity to present their songs and receive constructive feedback from industry professionals. Various performance opportunities are also available to members, including an SGA showcase at the Bluebird. The New York office hosts a weekly Pro-Shop, which is coordinated by producer/musician/award-winning singer Ann Johns Ruckert. For each of 6 sessions an active publisher, producer or A&R person is invited to personally screen material from SGA writers. Participation is limited to 10 writers and an audit of 1 session. Audition of material is required. Various performance opportunities and critique sessions are also available from time to time. SGAF Week is held periodically and is a week of scheduled events and seminars of interest to songwriters that includes workshops, seminars and showcases."

SONGWRITERS HALL OF FAME (SONGHALL)

330 W. 58th St., Suite 411, New York NY 10019. (212)957-9230. **Fax:** (212)957-9227. **E-mail:** info@songhall.org. **Website:** www.songhall.org. **Contact:** Jimmy Webb, chairman. "SongHall membership consists of songwriters of all levels, music publishers, producers, record company executives, music attorneys, and lovers of popular music of all ages. There are different levels of membership, all able to vote in the election of inductees, except associates, who pay only $25 in dues (respectively), but are unable to vote. SongHall's mission is to honor the popular songwriters who write the soundtrack for the world, as well as provide educational and networking opportunities to our members through our workshop and showcase programs." Offers: newsletters, workshops, performance opportunities, networking meetings with industry pros and scholarships for excellence in songwriting. Applications accepted year-round. Membership fees: $25 and up.

SONGWRITERS OF WISCONSIN INTERNATIONAL

P.O. Box 1027, Neenah WI 54957. **E-mail:** sowi2012@gmail.com. **Website:** www.SongwritersOfWisconsin.org. Serves songwriters. "Membership is open to songwriters writing all styles of music. Residency in Wisconsin is recommended but not required. Members are encouraged to bring tapes and lyric sheets of their songs to the meetings, but it is not required. We are striving to improve the craft of songwriting in Wisconsin. Living in Wisconsin, a songwriter would be close to any of the workshops and showcases offered each month at different towns. The primary value of membership for a songwriter is in sharing ideas with other songwriters, being critiqued and helping other songwriters." Offers competitions, field trips, instruction, lectures, newsletters, performance opportunities, social outings, workshops, and critique sessions. Applications accepted year-round. Membership dues: $30/year.

SONGWRITERS RESOURCE NETWORK

Portland OR **E-mail:** info@songwritersresourcenetwork.com. **Website:** www.songwritersresourcenetwork.com. "For songwriters and lyricists of every kind, from beginners to advanced." No eligibility requirements. "Purpose is to provide free information to help songwriters develop their craft, market

their songs, and learn about songwriting opportunities. We provide leads to publishers, producers and other music industry professionals." Visit website for more information.

SOUTHWEST VIRGINIA SONGWRITERS ASSOCIATION

P.O. Box 698, Salem VA 24153. **E-mail:** info@svsasongs.com. **Website:** www.svsasongs.com. Accepts members of all ages and skill levels in all genres of music. SVSA helps regional members improve their songwriting knowledge and skills through song critiques, workshops and discussions of related topics in an encouraging and supportive environment. SVSA offers performance opportunities, instruction, monthly meetings and a monthly newsletter. Applications accepted year-round. Membership fee: $20/year.

TEXAS ACCOUNTANTS & LAWYERS FOR THE ARTS

PO Box 144722, Austin TX 78714. (512)459-8252. **E-mail:** info@talarts.org; centraltexas@talarts.org. **Website:** www.talarts.org. TALA's members include accountants, attorneys, museums, theater groups, dance groups, actors, artists, musicians, and filmmakers. Our members are of all age groups and represent all facets of their respective fields. TALA is a nonprofit organization that provides *pro bono* legal and accounting services to income-eligible artists from all disciplines and to nonprofit arts organizations. TALA also provides mediation services for resolving disputes as a low-cost, non-adversarial alternative to litigation. Offers newsletters, lectures, library, and workshops. Applications accepted year-round. Annual membership fees: students, $30; artists, $75; nonprofit organizations, $250.

TIPS TALA's speakers program presents low-cost seminars on topics such as the music business, copyright and trademark, and the business of writing. These seminars are held annually at a location in Houston. TALA's speakers program also provides speakers for seminars by other organizations.

TEXAS MUSIC OFFICE

P.O. Box 13246, Austin TX 78711. (512)463-6666. **Fax:** (512)463-4114. **E-mail:** music@governor.state.tx.us. **Website:** http://governor.state.tx.us/music. **Contact:** Casey J. Monahan, director. "The Texas Music Office (TMO) is a state-funded business promotion office and information clearinghouse for the Texas music industry. The TMO assists more than 14,000 individual clients each year, ranging from a new band trying to make statewide business contacts to BBC journalists seeking information on "down south hip-hop." The TMO is the sister office to the Texas Film Commission, both of which are within the Office of the Governor. The TMO serves the Texas music industry by using its business referral network: Texas music industry (7,880 Texas music businesses in 96 music business categories); Texas music events (625 Texas music events); Texas talent register (8,036 Texas recording artists); Texas radio stations (942 Texas stations); U.S. music contacts; classical Texas (detailed information for all classical music organizations in Texas); and international (1,425 foreign businesses interested in Texas music). Provides referrals to Texas music businesses, talent, and events in order to attract new business to Texas and/or to encourage Texas businesses and individuals to keep music business in-state. Serves as a liaison between music businesses and other government offices and agencies. Publicizes significant developments within the Texas music industry."

○ There is a contact form on the website.

◑ TORONTO MUSICIANS' ASSOCIATION

15 Gervais Dr., Suite 500, Toronto ON M3C 1Y8 Canada. (416)421-1020. **Fax:** (416)421-7011. **E-mail:** info@tma149.ca; rsinnaeve@tma149.ca. **Website:** www.torontomusicians.org. "Local 149 of the American Federation of Musicians of the United States and Canada is the professional association for musicians in the greater Toronto Area. A member-driven association of 3,500 members, the TMA represents professional musicians in all facets of music in the greater Toronto area. Dedicated to the development of musical talent and skills, the Toronto Musicians' Association has for the past 100 years fostered the opportunity through the collective efforts of our members for professional musicians to live and work in dignity while receiving fair compensation." Joining fee: $225; thereafter, members pay $63.75 per quarter.

VOLUNTEER LAWYERS FOR THE ARTS

1 E. 53rd St., 6th Floor, New York NY 10022. (212)319-2787, ext. 1. **Fax:** (212)752-6575. **E-mail:** vlany@vlany.org. **Website:** www.vlany.org. Purpose of organization: Volunteer Lawyers for the Arts is dedicated to providing free arts-related legal assistance to low-income artists and nonprofit arts organizations in all creative fields. Over 1,000 attorneys in the New York area donate their time through VLA to artists

and arts organizations unable to afford legal counsel. Everyone is welcome to use VLA's Art Law Line, a legal hotline for any artist or arts organization needing quick answers to arts-related questions. VLA also provides clinics, seminars, and publications designed to educate artists on legal issues that affect their careers. Members receive discounts on publications and seminars, as well as other benefits.

WASHINGTON AREA MUSIC ASSOCIATION

6263 Occoquan Forest Dr., Manassas VA 20112. (703)368-3300. **Fax:** (703)393-1028. **E-mail:** dcmusic@wamadc.com. **Website:** www.wamadc.com. Serves songwriters, musicians and performers, managers, club owners and entertainment lawyers; "all those with an interest in the Washington music scene." The organization is designed to promote the Washington DC scene and increase its visibility. Its primary value to members are seminars and networking opportunities. Offers lectures, newsletter, performance opportunities, and workshops. WAMA sponsors the annual Washington Music Awards (The Wammies; the 2015 awards were held in February) and The Crosstown Jam or annual showcase of artists in the DC area. Applications accepted year-round. Membership fee: $35/year.

WEST COAST SONGWRITERS

1724 Laurel St., Suite 120, San Carlos CA 94070. (650)654-3966. **E-mail:** info@westcoastsongwriters.org; ian@westcoastsongwriters.org. **Website:** www.westcoastsongwriters.org. "Our 1,200 members are lyricists and composers from ages 16-80, from beginners to professional songwriters. No eligibility requirements. Our purpose is to provide the education and opportunities that will support our writers in creating and marketing outstanding songs. WCS provides support and direction through local networking and input from Los Angeles and Nashville music industry leaders, as well as valuable marketing opportunities. Most songwriters need some form of collaboration, and by being a member they are exposed to other writers, ideas, critiques, etc." Offers annual West Coast Songwriters Conference, "the largest event of its kind in northern California. This 2-day event held the second weekend in September features 16 seminars, 50 screening sessions (over 1,200 songs listened to by industry professionals) and a sunset concert with hit songwriters performing their songs." Also offers monthly visits from major publishers, songwriting classes, competitions, seminars conducted by hit songwriters (online), song screening service for members who cannot attend due to time or location, a monthly e-newsletter, monthly performance opportunities and workshops Applications accepted year-round. Membership fees: $40/year for students; $90/year, regular individual; $119, bands; $150-plus, contributing members. The 2016 dates of the conference are September 24-25.

TIPS "WCS's functions draw local talent and nationally recognized names together. This is of a tremendous value to writers outside a major music center. We are developing a strong songwriting community in Portland, and in northern and southern California. We serve the San Jose, Monterey Bay, East Bay, San Francisco, Los Angeles, Sacramento and Portland areas."

RETREATS & COLONIES

This section provides information on retreats and artists' colonies. These are places for creatives, including songwriters, to find solitude and spend concentrated time focusing on their work. While a residency at a colony may offer participation in seminars, critiques, or performances, the atmosphere of a colony or retreat is much more relaxed than that of a conference or workshop. Also, a songwriter's stay at a colony is typically anywhere from one to twelve weeks (sometimes longer), while time spent at a conference may only run from one to fourteen days.

Like conferences and workshops, however, artists' colonies and retreats span a wide range. Yaddo, perhaps the most well-known colony, limits its residencies to artists "working at a professional level in their field, as determined by a judging panel of professionals in the field." The Brevard Music Center offers residencies only to those involved in classical music. Despite different focuses, all artists' colonies and retreats have one thing in common: They are places where you may work undisturbed, usually in nature-oriented, secluded settings.

SELECTING A COLONY OR RETREAT

When selecting a colony or retreat, the primary consideration for many songwriters is cost, and you'll discover that arrangements vary greatly. Some colonies provide residencies, as well as stipends for personal expenses. Some suggest donations of a certain amount. Still others offer residencies for substantial sums but have financial assistance available.

When investigating the various options, consider meal and housing arrangements and your family obligations. Some colonies provide meals for residents, while others require residents to pay for meals. Some colonies house artists in one main building; others provide separate cottages. A few have provisions for spouses and families. Others prohibit families altogether.

Overall, residencies at colonies and retreats are competitive. Since only a handful of spots are available at each place, you often must apply months in advance for the time period you desire. A number of locations are open year-round, and you may find planning to go during the "off-season" lessens your competition. Other colonies, however, are only available during certain months. In any case, be prepared to include a sample of your best work with your application. Also, know what project you'll work on while in residence and have alternative projects in mind in case the first one doesn't work out once you're there.

Each listing in this section details fee requirements, meal and housing arrangements, and space and time availability, as well as the retreat's surroundings, facilities and special activities. Of course, before making a final decision, send a SASE to the colonies or retreats that interest you to receive their most up-to-date details. Costs, application requirements, and deadlines are particularly subject to change.

MUSICIAN'S RESOURCE

For other listings of songwriter-friendly colonies, see *Musician's Resource* (available from Watson-Guptill—www.watsonguptill.com), which not only provides information about conferences, workshops, and academic programs but also residencies and retreats. Also check the Publications of Interest section in this book for newsletters and other periodicals providing this information.

☻ THE TYRONE GUTHRIE CENTRE

Annaghmakerrig, Newbliss, County Monaghan Ireland. **E-mail:** info@tyroneguthrie.ie. **Website:** www.tyroneguthrie.ie. Offers year-round residencies. Artists may stay for up to 1 month in the Big House, or for up to 2 months at a time in one of the 5 self-catering houses in the old farmyard. Open to artists of all disciplines (music, dance, performing arts). For Irish and European artists. To qualify for a residency, it is necessary to show evidence of a significant level of achievement in the relevant field.

THE HAMBIDGE CENTER

105 Hambidge Court, Rabun Gap GA 30568. (706)746-5718. **Fax:** (706)746-9933. **E-mail:** center@ hambidge.org; director@hambidge.org. **Website:** www.hambidge.org. **Contact:** Debra Sanders, office manager; Jamie Badoud, executive director. Hambidge provides a residency program that empowers talented artists to explore, develop, and express their creative voices. Situated on 600 acres in the mountains of north Georgia, Hambidge is a sanctuary of time and space that inspires artists working in a broad range of disciplines to create works of the highest caliber. Hambidge's Residency Program opens the first week of February and closes mid-to late-December through the month of January. Application deadlines are: January 15 for May-August; April 15 for September-December; September 15 for March-April of the following year.

COSTS Several scholarships are available.

ISLE ROYALE NATIONAL PARK ARTIST-IN-RESIDENCE PROGRAM

800 E. Lakeshore Dr., Houghton MI 49931. (906)482-0984. **Fax:** (906)482-8753. **E-mail:** Greg_Blust@nps.gov. **Website:** www.nps.gov/getinvolved/artist-in-residence.htm. Offers 2-3 week residencies from mid-June to mid-September. Open to all art forms. Accommodates 1 artist with 1 companion at 1 time. Personal living quarters include cabin with shared outhouse. A canoe is provided for transportation. Offers a guest house at the site that can be used as a studio. The artist is asked to contribute a piece of work representative of their stay at Isle Royale, to be used by the park in an appropriate manner. During their residency, artists will be asked to share their experience (1 presentation per week of residency, about 1 hour/week) with the public by demonstration, talk, or other means.

REQUIREMENTS Deadline: applications should be postmarked or delievered by February 16. Send for application forms and guidelines. Accepts inquiries via fax or e-mail. A panel of professionals from various disciplines and park representatives will choose the finalists. The selection is based on artistic integrity, ability to reside in a wilderness environment, a willingness to donate a finished piece of work inspired by the island, and the artist's ability to relate and interpret the park through their work.

KALANI OCEANSIDE RETREAT

RR2, P.O. Box 4500, Pahoa HI 96778. (808)965-7828. **Fax:** (808)965-0527. **Website:** www.kalani.com.

☻   "Kalani Honua means harmony of heaven and earth, and this is what we aspire to. We welcome all in the spirit of aloha and are guided by the Hawaiian tradition of `ohana (extended family), respecting our diversity yet sharing in unity. We invite you to open your heart to the Big Island of Hawaii at Kalani Oceanside Retreat."

SITKA CENTER FOR ART & ECOLOGY

56605 Sitka Dr., Otis OR 97368. (541)994-5485. **Fax:** (541)994-8024. **E-mail:** info@sitkacenter.org. **Website:** www.sitkacenter.org.

COSTS Residency and housing provided. The resident is asked to provide some form of community service on behalf of Sitka.

VIRGINIA CENTER FOR THE CREATIVE ARTS

154 San Angelo Dr., Amherst VA 24521. (434)946-7236. **Fax:** (434)946-7239. **E-mail:** vcca@vcca.com. **Website:** www.vcca.com. Offers residencies year-round, typical residency lasts 2 weeks to 2 months. Open to originating artists: composers, writers, and visual artists. Accommodates 25 at one time.

COSTS Application fee: $40. Deadline as of 2016: May 15 for October-January residency; September 15 for February-May residency; January 15 for June-September residency. For application form, download from website. Applications are reviewed by panelists. "Artists are accepted at VCCA without consideration for their financial situation. We ask fellows to contribute according to their ability. The actual cost to us of a residency is $180 per day."

WORKSHOPS & CONFERENCES

For a songwriter just starting out, conferences and workshops can provide valuable learning opportunities. At conferences, songwriters can have their songs evaluated, hear suggestions for further improvement, and receive feedback from music business experts. They also are excellent places to make valuable industry contacts. Workshops can help a songwriter improve his craft and learn more about the business of songwriting. They may involve classes on songwriting and the business, as well as lectures and seminars by industry professionals.

Each year, hundreds of workshops and conferences take place all over the country. Songwriters can choose from small regional workshops held in someone's living room to large national conferences such as South by Southwest in Austin, Texas, which hosts more than 6,000 industry people, songwriters and performers. Many songwriting organizations—national and local—host workshops that offer instruction on just about every songwriting topic imaginable, from lyric writing and marketing strategy to contract negotiation. Conferences provide songwriters the chance to meet one-on-one with publishing and record company professionals and give performers the chance to showcase their work for a live audience (usually consisting of industry people) during the conference. There are conferences and workshops that address almost every type of music, offering programs for songwriters, performers, musical playwrights and much more.

This section includes national and local workshops and conferences with a brief description of what they offer, when they are held, and how much they cost to attend. Write or call any that interest you for further information. To find out what workshops or conferences take place in specific parts of the country, see the Geographic Index at the end of this book.

ASCAP HAROLD ADAMSON SONGWRITERS WORKSHOP

7920 Sunset Blvd., 3rd Floor, Los Angeles CA 90046. **Website:** www.ascap.com/music-career/workshops. aspx. Annual workshop for advanced songwriters sponsored by the ASCAP Foundation. Renamed to honor great lyricist and Music Hall of Fame member Harold Adamson, the workshop is designed to enrich participants' knowledge of the industry, help them establish contacts and confidence, and expand their collaborative partnerships. Workshop dates and deadlines vary from year to year. Applicants must submit 2 digital song files with lyrics, brief bio or résumé, and short explanation as to why they would like to participate, e-mail address, and telephone number. Limited number of participants are selected each year. This is one of many ASCAP workshops.

ASCAP I CREATE MUSIC EXPO

1 Lincoln Plaza, New York NY 10023. **E-mail:** expo@ ascap.com. **Website:** www.ascap.com. "The ASCAP I Create Music EXPO puts you face-to-face with some of the world's most successful songwriters, composers, producers and music business leaders, all who willingly share their knowledge and expertise and give you the know-how to take your music to the next level." For more info and to register, visit the website.

ASCAP MUSICAL THEATRE WORKSHOP

1 Lincoln Plaza, New York NY 10023. (212)621-6264. **Website:** www.ascap.com/music-career/workshops. aspx. Workshop is for musical theater composers and lyricists only. Its purpose is to nurture and develop new musicals for the theatre. Offers programs for songwriters. Offers programs annually, usually April through May. Events take place in New York. Four musical works are selected. Others are invited to audit the workshop. Participants are amateur and professional songwriters, composers and musical playwrights. Participants are selected by demo CD submission. Deadline: see website. Also available: the annual ASCAP/Disney Musical Theatre Workshop in Los Angeles. It takes place in January and February. Deadline is late November. Details similar to New York workshop, as above.

THE BMI LEHMAN ENGEL MUSICAL THEATRE WORKSHOP

7 World Trade Center, 250 Greenwich St., New York NY 10007. (212)230-3000. **Fax:** (212)262-2824. **E-mail:** theatreworkshop@bmi.com. **Website:** www. bmi.com/theatre_workshop. **Contact:** Patricia Cook, director. "BMI is a music licensing company that collects royalties for affiliated writers and publishers. We offer programs to musical theater composers, lyricists and librettists. The BMI-Lehman Engel Musical Theatre Workshops were formed in an effort to refresh and stimulate professional writers, as well as to encourage and develop new creative talent for the musical theater. Each workshop meets 1 afternoon a week for 2 hours at BMI, New York. Participants are professional songwriters, composers and playwrights. The BMI Lehman Musical Theatre Workshop Showcase presents the best of the workshop to producers, agents, record and publishing company executives, press and directors for possible option and production. Visit the website for application. Tape and lyrics of 3 compositions required with applications."

TIPS BMI also sponsors a jazz composers workshop. For more information, contact Raette Johnson at rjohnson@bmi.com.

BYRDCLIFFE ARTS COLONY

34 Tinker St., Woodstock NY 12498. (845)679-2079. **Fax:** (845)679-4529. **E-mail:** info@woodstockguild. org. **Website:** www.woodstockguild.org. Offers 1-month residencies June-September. Open to composers, writers, and visual artists. Accommodates 15 at 1 time. Personal living quarters include single rooms, shared baths, and kitchen facilities. Offers separate private studio space. Composers must provide their own keyboard with headphone. Activities include open studio and readings for the Woodstock community at the end of each session. The Woodstock Guild, parent organization, offers music and dance performances and gallery exhibits.

COSTS $650/month; fellowships available. Residents are responsible for own meals and transportation. $40 application fee.

CMJ MUSIC MARATHON & FILM FESTIVAL

1201 Broadway, Suite 706, New York NY 10001. (212)277-7120. **Fax:** (212)719-9396. **E-mail:** marketing@cmj.com; editorial@cmj.com. **Website:** www. cmj.com/marathon. "Premier annual alternative music gathering of more than 9,000 music business and film professionals. Features 5 days and nights of more than 75 panels and workshops focusing on every facet of the industry; exclusive film screenings; keynote speeches by the world's most intriguing and controversial voices; exhibition area featuring live performance stage; over 1,000 of music's brightest and most visionary talents (from the unsigned to the legendary) performing over 5 evenings at more than 80 of New York's most important music venues." Participants are selected by submitting demonstration tape.

CUTTING EDGE C.E.

Cutting Edge HQ, 1524 N. Claiborne Ave., New Orleans LA 70116. (504)322-3540. **E-mail:** eric@cuttingedgenola.com. **Website:** www.cuttingedgenola.com. Cutting Edge C.E. (formerly the Cutting Edge Music Business Conference) will again discuss "Hot Topics" and "Current Trends" in today's entertainment business. Attend conference sessions on Entertainment law, music business, film financing and tax credits, roots music, and the new works showcases. Check out the NOLA Downtown Festival and Cruisin' New Orleans Pro Gear Show at the Historic Carver Theater. Held at the InterContinental Hotel and the Historic Carver Theater in New Orleans. 2016 dates: August 25-27. Schedule and speaker lineup are available online.

FOLK ALLIANCE ANNUAL CONFERENCE

509 Delaware St. #101, Kansas City MO 64105. (816)221-3655. **Fax:** (816)221-3658. **E-mail:** fai@folk.org. **Website:** ww.folkalliance.org/conference. Conference/workshop topics change each year. Conference takes place late-February and lasts 4 days at a different location each year. Two-thousand-plus attendees include artists, agents, arts administrators, print/broadcast media, folklorists, folk societies, merchandisers, presenters, festivals, recording companies, etc. Artists wishing to showcase should contact the office for a showcase application form.

INDEPENDENT MUSIC CONFERENCE

304 Main Ave., PMB 287, Norwalk CT 06851. (203)606-4649. **E-mail:** IMC@intermixx.com. **Website:** www.independentmusicconference.com. "The purpose of the IMC is to bring together rock, hip hop and acoustic music for panels and showcases. Offers programs for songwriters, composers and performers. Two-hundred-and-fifty showcases at 20 clubs around the city. Also offer a DJ cutting contest." Held annually in the fall. Three thousand amateur and professional songwriters, composers, individual vocalists, bands, individual instrumentalists, attorneys, managers, agents, publishers, A&R, promotions, club owners, etc., participate each year. Check the website for an application.

◯ Formerly the Philadelphia Music Conference.

KERRVILLE FOLK FESTIVAL

Kerrville Festivals, Inc., 3876 Medina Hwy, Kerrville TX 78028. **E-mail:** info@kerrville-music.com. **Website:** www.kerrvillefolkfestival.com. Hosts three-day songwriters' school, a four-day music business school and New Folk concert competition. Festival produced in late spring and early summer. Spring festival lasts 18 days and is held outdoors at Quiet Valley Ranch. One-hundred-and-ten or more songwriters participate. Performers are professional songwriters and bands. Participants selected by submitting demo, by invitation only. Send cassette, or CD, promotional material and list of upcoming appearances. "Songwriter and music schools include lunch, experienced professional instructors, camping on ranch and concerts. Rustic facilities. Food available at reasonable cost. Audition materials accepted at above address. These three-day and four-day seminars include noon meals, handouts and camping on the ranch. Usually held during Kerrville Folk Festival, first and second week in June. Write or check the website for contest rules, schools and seminars information, and festival schedules. Also establishing a Phoenix Fund to provide assistance to ill or injured singer/songwriters who find themselves in distress."

◯ This organization also organizes the Kerrville Fall Music Festival.

LAMB'S RETREAT FOR SONGWRITERS

presented by Springfed Arts, a nonprofit organization, P.O. Box 304, Royal Oak MI 48068-0304. (248)589-3913. **E-mail:** johndlamb@ameritech.net; info@springfed.org. **Website:** www.springfed.org. **Contact:** John D. Lamb, director. Offers programs for songwriters on annual basis; 2016 dates are November 3-6, November 10-13, and November 5-15 at The Birchwood Inn, Harbor Springs, Michigan. Sixty songwriters/musicians participate in each event. Participants are amateur and professional songwriters. Anyone can participate. Send for registration or e-mail. Deadline: 2 weeks before event begins. Faculty are noted songwriters.

◑ THE MACDOWELL COLONY

100 High St., Peterborough NH 03458. (603)924-3886. **Fax:** (603)924-9142. **E-mail:** admissions@macdowellcolony.org. **Website:** www.macdowellcolony.org. Open to writers, playwrights, composers, visual art-

WORKSHOPS & CONFERENCES

ists, film/video artists, interdisciplinary artists and architects. Applicants submit information and work samples for review by a panel of experts in each discipline. Application form submitted online at macdowellcolony.org/apply.html.

COSTS Travel reimbursement and stipends are available for participants of the residency, based on need. There are no residency fees.

MANCHESTER MUSIC FESTIVAL

P.O. Box 33, 42 Dillingham Ave., Manchester VT 05254. (802)362-1956. **Fax:** (802)362-0711. **E-mail:** info@mmfvt.org. **Website:** www.mmfvt.org. **Contact:** Joana Genova, education director. Offers classical music education and performances. Summer program for young professional musicians offered in tandem with a professional concert series in the mountains of Manchester, Vermont. Up to 23 young professionals, ages 19 and up, are selected by audition for the Young Artists Program, which provides instruction, performance and teaching opportunities, with full scholarship for all participants. Commissioning opportunities for new music, and performance opportunities for professional chamber ensembles and soloists for both summer and fall/winter concert series.

THE NEW HARMONY PROJECT

P.O. Box 58, New Harmony IN 47631. (317)464-1103. **E-mail:** info@newharmonyproject.org. **Website:** www.newharmonyproject.org. **Contact:** Mead Hunter, artistic director; Joel Grynheim, project director.

"The purpose of The New Harmony Project shall be to create, nurture, and promote new works for stage, television and film that sensitively and truthfully explore the positive aspects of life. Our goal is to bring the writers who seek to produce uplifting, high-quality entertainment alternatives to our conference, surround them with professional resources, provide them with the opportunity to develop these works in a supportive and life-affirming environment that further enables their writing creativity, and help each writer to tell their story well." 2015 dates: May 22-31.

NEWPORT FOLK FESTIVAL

New Festival Productions, LLC, P.O. Box 3865, Newport RI 02840. **E-mail:** newportfolkfest@gmail.com. **Website:** www.newportfolk.org. An annual folk festival. 2016 dates: July 22-24.

NEWPORT JAZZ FESTIVAL

New Festival Productions, LLC, Newport RI **E-mail:** jazz@newportjazzfest.org. **Website:** www.newportjazzfest.org. An annual jazz festival. 2016 dates: July 29-31. "Hailed by *The New York Times* as the festival that put jazz festivals on the map, the Newport Jazz Festival was founded by jazz pianist George Wein in 1954 as the first outdoor music festival of its kind devoted entirely to jazz, and is now universally acknowledged as the grandfather of all jazz festivals. During the last half-century, the name Newport has become synonymous with the best in jazz music. In its long, illustrious history, the Newport Jazz Festival has presented a virtual pantheon of jazz immortals alongside an array of rising young artists: Duke Ellington's 1956 rebirth framing Paul Gonzalves' epic solo; subject of the classic 1958 documentary *Jazz on a Summer's Day*; origin of famous recordings by Thelonious Monk, John Coltrane and Miles Davis; showcase for emerging young masters including Wynton Marsalis, Diana Krall, Joshua Redman and Esperanza Spalding. Referred to as a Mecca of Jazz, the event draws thousands of people from all over the world to its uniquely picturesque outdoor stages at the International Tennis Hall of Fame and Fort Adams State Park."

NORFOLK CHAMBER MUSIC FESTIVAL

P.O. Box 208246, New Haven CT 06520. **E-mail:** norfolk@yale.edu. **Website:** www.yale.edu/norfolk. Festival season of chamber music. Offers programs for composers and performers. Offers programs summer only. Approximately 45 fellows participate. Participants are up-and-coming composers and instrumentalists. Participants are selected following a screening round. Auditions are held in New Haven, Connecticut. "Held at the Ellen Battell Stoeckel Estate, the festival offers a magnificent music shed with seating for 1,000, practice facilities, music library, dining hall, laundry and art gallery. Nearby are hiking, bicycling and swimming."

NORTH BY NORTHEAST MUSIC FESTIVAL AND CONFERENCE

189 Church St., Lower Level, Toronto ON M5B 1Y7 Canada. (416)863-6963. **Fax:** (416)863-0828. **E-mail:** info@nxne.com. **Website:** www.nxne.com. 2016 dates: June 13-19. "Our festival takes place mid-June at over 30 venues across downtown Toronto, drawing over 2,000 conference delegates, 500 bands and 50,000 music fans. Musical genres include everything

from folk to funk, roots to rock, polka to punk and all points in between, bringing exceptional new talent, media frontrunners, music business heavies and music fans from all over the world to Toronto." Participants include emerging and established songwriters, vocalists, composers, bands and instrumentalists. Festival performers are selected by submitting a CD and accompanying press kit or applying through sonicbids.com. Application forms are available by website or by calling the office. Submission period each year is from November 1 to the third weekend in January.

NSAI SONG CAMPS

1710 Roy Acuff Place, Nashville TN 37023. (800)321-6008; (615)256-335. **Fax:** (615)256-0034. **E-mail:** events@nashvillesongwriters.com; reception@nashvillesongwriters.com. **Website:** www.nashvillesongwriters.com. 2016 dates: July 15-17. Offers programs strictly for songwriters. Events held in late July in Nashville. "We provide most meals and lodging is available. We also present an amazing evening of music presented by the faculty." Camps are 3-4 days long, with 36-112 participants, depending on the camp. "There are different levels of camps, some having preferred prerequisites. Each camp varies. Please call, e-mail or refer to website. It really isn't about the genre of music, but the quality of the song itself. Song Camp strives to strengthen the writer's vision and skills, therefore producing the better song. Song Camp is known as 'boot camp' for songwriters. It is guaranteed to catapult you forward in your writing! Participants are all aspiring songwriters led by a pro faculty. We do accept lyricists only and composers only with the hopes of expanding their scope." Participants are selected through submission of 2 songs with lyric sheet. Song Camp is open to NSAI members, although anyone can apply and upon acceptance join the organization.

COSTS $425 for members; $525 for non-members.

✪ ORFORD FESTIVAL

Orford Arts Centre, 3165 chemin du Parc, Orford QC J1X 7A2 Canada. (819)843-9871; (800)567-6155. **Fax:** (819)843-7274. **E-mail:** info@arts-orford.org. **Website:** www.orford.mu. 2016 dates: May 9-16. The Orford Arts Centre plays host to a world-class Academy of Music, which offers advanced training to particularly gifted young musicians who are at the beginning of a professional career in classical music. Together with internationally renowned professors and artists

who are devoted to training the next generation, we are committed to providing our students with pedagogical activities that are as unique as they are enriching. In pursuit of its mission, the Centre abides by the following values: excellence, discipline, dedication, open-mindedness, respect and the will to surpass individual expectations.

◐ REGGAE SUMFEST

Shops 9 & 10 Parkway Plaza, Rose Hall, Montego Bay Jamaica. (876)953-8360. **Website:** reggaesumfest.com. 2016 dates: July 17-23. "Reggae Sumfest is a musical event to which we welcome 30,000-plus patrons each year. The festival showcases the best of dancehall and reggae music, as well as top R&B/hip-hop performers. The festival also offers delicious Jamaican cuisine, as well as arts and crafts from all over the island. The main events of the festival are held at Catherine Hall, Montego Bay, Jamaica over a three-day period, which usually falls in the third week of July, from Sunday to Saturday." Reggae Sumfest is presented by Summerfest Productions and accepts press kit submissions from persons wishing to perform at the festival between November and January each year.

SOUTH BY SOUTHWEST MUSIC CONFERENCE

SXSW Headquarters, P.O. Box 685289, Austin TX 78768. **E-mail:** sxsw@sxsw.com. **Website:** sxsw.com/music/about. 2016 dates: March 15-20. South by Southwest (SXSW) is a private company based in Austin, Texas, with a year-round staff of professionals dedicated to building and delivering conference and festival events for entertainment and related media industry professionals. Since 1987, SXSW has produced the internationally recognized music and media conference and festival SXSW. As the entertainment business adjusted to issues of future growth and development, in 1994, SXSW added conferences and festivals for the film industry (SXSW Film), as well as for the blossoming interactive media (SXSW Interactive Festival). Now 3 industry events converge in Austin during a Texas-sized week, mirroring the ever-increasing convergence of entertainment/media outlets. The next SXSW Music Conference and Festival will be held in March. Offers panel discussions, "Crash Course" educational seminars and nighttime showcases. SXSW Music seeks out speakers who have developed unique ways to create and sell music. The conference includes over 50 sessions including a panel of label heads discussing strategy, interviews with notable artists, topical discussions, demo listening sessions and the mentor program. And when the sun goes down, a multitude of performances by musicians and songwriters from across the country and around the world populate the SXSW Music Festival, held in venues in central Austin. Write, e-mail or visit website for dates and registration instructions.

TIPS "Visit the website in August to apply for showcase consideraton. SXSW is also involved in North by Northeast (NXNE), held in Toronto, Canada, in late spring."

THE SWANNANOA GATHERING— CONTEMPORARY FOLK WEEK

Warren Wilson College, P.O. Box 9000, Asheville NC 28815-9000. (828)298-3434. **Fax:** (828)298-3434. **E-mail:** gathering@warren-wilson.edu. **Website:** www.swangathering.com. "For anyone who ever wanted to make music for an audience, we offer a comprehensive week in artist development, including classes in songwriting, performance, and vocal coaching." For a brochure or other info, contact The Swannanoa Gathering. There are several programs that happen in the summer (July and August), such as Celtic Week, Fiddle Week, and Guitar Week. Annual program of The Swannanoa Gathering Folk Arts Workshops.

WEST COAST SONGWRITERS CONFERENCE

1724 Laurel St., Suite 120, San Carlos CA 94070. (650)654-3966. **E-mail:** info@westcoastsongwriters.org; ian@westcoastsongwriters.org. **Website:** www.westcoastsongwriters.org. 2016 dates: September 24-25. "Conference offers opportunity and education; 16 seminars, 50 song screening sessions (1,500 songs reviewed), performance showcases, one-on-one sessions and concerts." Offers programs for lyricists, songwriters, composers and performers. "During the year we have competitive, live songwriter competitions. Winners go into the playoffs. Winners of the playoffs perform at the sunset concert at the conference." Event takes place second weekend in September

at Foothill College, Los Altos Hills, California. More than 500 songwriters/musicians participate in this event. Participants are songwriters, composers, musical playwrights, vocalists, bands, instrumentalists and those interested in a career in the music business.

WESTERN WIND WORKSHOP IN ENSEMBLE SINGING

263 W. 86th St., New York NY 10024. (212)873-2848. **E-mail:** workshops@westernwind.org; info@westernwind.org. **Website:** www.westernwind.org/workshops.html. Participants learn the art of ensemble singing—no conductor. Workshops focus on blend, diction, phrasing, and production. Offers programs for performers. Limited talent-based scholarship available. Offers programs annually. Takes place June and August in the music department at Smith College, Northampton, Massachussetts. Seventy-80 songwriters and/or musicians participate in each event. Participants are amateur and professional vocalists. Anyone can participate. Send for application or register on their website. (2016 dates: Session 1 is June 24-26 and June 27 - July 2. Session 2 is July 29-31 and August 1-6.)

WINTER MUSIC CONFERENCE, INC.

3450 NE 12 Terrace, Ft. Lauderdale FL 33334. (954)563-4444. **Fax:** (954)563-1599. **E-mail:** info@wintermusicconference.com. **Website:** www.wintermusicconference.com. Features educational seminars and showcases for dance, hip hop, alternative, and rap. Offers programs for songwriters and performers. Offers programs annually. Event takes place March of each year in Miami, Florida. Three-thousand songwriters/musicians participate in each event. Participants are amateur and professional songwriters, composers, musical playwrights, vocalists, bands and instrumentalists. Participants are selected by submitting demo tape. Send SASE, visit website or call for application. Deadline: February. Event held at either nightclubs or hotel with complete staging, lights and sound. 2016 dates were March 21-24.

VENUES

//

924 GILMAN

924 Gilman St., Berkeley CA 94710. (510)525-9926. **E-mail:** booking@924gilman.org. **Website:** www.924gilman.org. Punk rock music venue. 924 Gilman books shows on Friday, Saturday and Sunday. Booking is often confirmed months in advance. Send a recorded form of your music to the booking address: Alternative Music Foundation, P.O. Box 1058, Berkeley, CA 94710.

ABG'S BAR

190 W. Center St., Provo UT 84601. (801)373-1200. **E-mail:** bigdanet@gmail.com. **Website:** abgsbar.com. Music: rock, alt-country, alternative, folk, blues, jazz.

ANDERSON FAIR RETAIL RESTAURANT

2007 Grant St., Houston TX 77006. (832)767-2785. **Website:** andersonfair.net. Features original, eclectic music performed largely by Texas singer/songwriters.

ANTONE'S

305 E. Fifth St., Austin TX 78701. (512)814-0361. **E-mail:** booking@antonesnightclub.com. **Website:** www.antonesnightclub.com. "Antone's Nightclub was founded by legendary promoter Clifford Antone and has hosted such blues 'greats' as Muddy Waters, B.B. King, Buddy Guy, John Lee Hooker, Pinetop Perkins, James Cotton, and countless others."

THE ARK

316 S. Main St., Ann Arbor MI 48104. (734)761-1800. **Website:** www.theark.org. **Contact:** Anya Siglin. The Ark is Michigan's nonprofit home for folk and roots music. Considered one of the top music clubs in the world, The Ark is renowned for the quality and breadth of its programming. The Ark is an intimate 400-seat club presenting performers ranging from young up-and-comers to classic figures of the folk genre. With live music over 300 nights each year in one of the best listening rooms anywhere, The Ark is a sure bet for a memorable evening of enriching entertainment, musical artistry, and personal warmth. "Over the course of a year, The Ark staff reviews on average 1,200 unsolicited demos. We listen to all the demos we receive and give the group or performer a rating. Time constraints make it impossible for us to contact performers after we review their demos or to return their CDs or tapes. Demos are reviewed 3 times a year: April, August, and December. Performers can contact us after submitting their materials to find out their ratings. Keep in mind that of the performers whose demos we review, only a very small number are selected to appear at The Ark—perhaps 10 each year. Hint: Put your best stuff up-front. While we respect all forms of music, we focus primarily on acoustic genres. We request that you forgo submitting materials to The Ark if your music could best be described by the following terms: cover band, hard rock, heavy metal, hip hop, rap, and reggae. To submit, send your stuff to: Attn: Anya Siglin, The Ark, 117 N. First St., Suite 40, Ann Arbor, MI 48104."

ARLENE'S GROCERY

95 Stanton St., New York NY 10001. **E-mail:** booking@arlenesgrocery.net. **Website:** www.arlenesgrocery.net. Music: rock, alternate, indie, old school, new school, etc. When submitting band for consideration, include band name and instrumentation, links to streaming music (Soundcloud, Bandcamp, etc.), links to social media, links to any press, history in New York, and requested dates for a show.

TIPS "Booking is done by e-mail only. We do not review CD demos, press packages, or anything dropped off or mailed to the club."

ART BAR

1211 Park St., Columbia SC 29201. (803)929-0198. **Website:** artbarsc.com. Booking guidelines and contact form available on website. Music: alternative, indie.

ASHLAND COFFEE AND TEA

100 N. Railroad Ave., Ashland VA 23005. (804)798-1702. **Fax:** (804)798-2573. **Website:** ashlandcoffeeandtea.com. "Join us most Thursdays, Fridays, and Saturdays in our intimate 'Listening Room' for an evening of Americana, bluegrass, folk, blues, jazz, pop—you never know what we'll have on tap with our wide range of performers. Don't miss 'Homegrown Wednesday,' featuring local Virginia talent, or the 'Songwriter's Showdown,' a songwriting and vocal performance competition every Tuesday."

TIPS For booking, contact the venue via online form.

AUSTIN CITY LIMITS LIVE AT THE MOODY THEATER

310 W. Willie Nelson Blvd., Austin TX 78701. (512)225-7999. **E-mail:** info@acl-live.com. **Website:** www.acl-live.com. Austin City Limits Live at the Moody Theater (ACL Live) is a state-of-the-art, 2,750-person capacity live-music venue that hosts approximately 100 concerts a year.

BACKBOOTH

37 W. Pine St., Orlando FL 32801. (407)999-2570. **E-mail:** booking@backbooth.com. **Website:** www.backbooth.com. "BackBooth's reputation as a music venue has grown to being named one of the best live-music venues in the city, according to *Orlando Weekly*, and still boasts the most impressive draft selection in downtown. With a capacity of 350, a large stage, a powerful sound/lighting system, balcony, and back bar area, the club still maintains a very comfortable and inviting, almost pub-like, atmosphere with Old English décor, including woodwork and dark curtains throughout. As a venue, BackBooth continues to play host to many popular national and regional acts, while remaining a favorite among locals. The club is also known for its dance parties, which are among the most popular and recognized in town. Whether for an intimate live performance, a rousing rock show, or a night of dancing and drinks, BackBooth is established in the heart of the central Florida community as a favorite destination." Music: reggae, acoustic, alternative, indie, pop, hip-hop, jam, roots, soul, gospel, funk, dubstep, country, rock, metal.

BACK EAST BAR & GRILL

9475 Briar Village Point, Colorado Springs CO 80920. (719)264-6161. **Website:** www.backeastbarandgrill.com/briargate/index.cfm. "We have created the perfect place for you to watch your favorite game and enjoy the incredible food and flavors that we have brought from home. We know you will enjoy every minute that you share with us. So sit back and have a drink, eat some great food, and enjoy your favorite team on one of our many TVs." Music: rock, alternative, R&B, blues, country, pop.

THE BARLEY STREET TAVERN

2735 N. 62nd St., Omaha NE 68104. (402)408-0028. **E-mail:** bookings@barleystreet.com. **Website:** www.barleystreet.com. "We have live music performances on scheduled nights, featuring some great local and regional performers, as well as national touring acts. This is the music venue to find the best in all music styles." Music: rock, alternative, folk, indie, country, pop, Americana.

THE BELL HOUSE

149 Seventh St., Brooklyn NY 11215. (718)643-6510. **E-mail:** info@thebellhouseny.com. **E-mail:** booking@thebellhouseny.com. **Website:** www.thebellhouseny.com. "In fall 2008, a 1920s warehouse was converted into The Bell House. Called 'a welcome oasis' by *TimeOut*, The Bell House is a magnificent two-room music and events venue located in the Gowanus section of Brooklyn. The Main Room boasts 25-foot wooden arched ceilings, a 450-square foot stage, and unobstructed views from any part of the room."

BELLY UP

143 S. Cedros Ave., Solana Beach CA 92075. (858)481-8140. **E-mail:** booking@bellyup.com. **Website:** bel-

lyup.com. "Belly Up is a live-music venue located in Solana Beach, California. We have all types of music almost every night and serve bar food and alcohol (and some tasty soft drinks), as well."

TIPS "Please do not send promo kits or show up randomly to the club with gifts; please save your money and the environment. Simply e-mail booking@bellyup.com with your band's Web page, with audio or a social media page, along with a band bio and listing of clubs in San Diego and other acts you have played over the last year."

BERKELEY CAFE

217 W. Martin St., Raleigh NC 27601. (919)828-9190. **E-mail:** lakeboonee@bellsouth.net. **Website:** www.berkeleyraleigh.blogspot.com. **Contact:** Jim Shires. Music: rock, bluegrass, alternative, blues, punk, folk.

THE BIG EASY SOCIAL AND PLEASURE CLUB

5731 Kirby Dr., Houston TX 77005. (713)523-9999. **E-mail:** bigeasyblues@pando.org. **Website:** www.thebigeasyblues.com. Music: rhythm, blues.

BILLY'S LOUNGE

1437 Wealthy St. SE, Grand Rapids MI 49506. (616)459-5757. **E-mail:** booking@billyslounge.com. **Website:** www.billyslounge.com. **Contact:** Lyndi Charles, booking manager. "Billy's Lounge is a local hot spot in the Eastown Community. With our live music, fully stocked bar, and dirt-cheap drink specials on a nightly basis, you can see why! Billy's has a strong history in keeping with the tradition of service and entertainment. We pride ourselves on our support of local music, our abilities to drink, and the atmospheres we produce." Music: blues, rock, R&B, Americana, hip-hop, jazz.

BIMBO'S 365 CLUB

1025 Columbus Ave., San Francisco CA 94133. (415)474-0365. **E-mail:** info@bimbos365club.com. **E-mail:** booking@bimbos365club.com. **Website:** www.bimbos365club.com. Has featured Adele, 10,000 Maniacs, A Tribe Called Quest, Air, Ben Harper, Black Eyed Peas, Brian McKnight, Brian Setzer Orchestra, Coldplay, Iron and Wine, Jack Johnson, Jewel, Nelly Furtado, Pink Martini, She & Him, The Raconteurs, The Strokes, The Wallflowers, Van Morrison, and many more.

BLIND PIG

208 N. First St., Ann Arbor MI 48104. (734)996-8555. **E-mail:** jason@goodshowlive.com; jessica@goodshowlive.com. **Website:** www.blindpigmusic.com. **Contact:** Jason Berry, senior talent buyer; Jessica Levy, junior talent buyer. The Blind Pig, a popular local nightclub and concert venue, has played an instrumental role in the ushering in and showcasing of musical activity in Ann Arbor.

BLUE

650 Congress St., Portland ME 04101. (207)774-4111. **E-mail:** booking@portcityblue.com. **Website:** portcityblue.com. "Located in the heart of Portland's Arts District, Blue is Portland's most intimate live-music venue. We present an array of music such as Celtic, Middle Eastern, blues, old time, jazz, folk, and more."

○ For booking requests, e-mail electronic press kit to booking@portcityblue.com.

THE BLUE DOOR

2805 N. McKinley Ave., Oklahoma City OK 73106. (405)524-0738. **E-mail:** bluedoorokc@gmail.com. **Website:** www.bluedoorokc.com. **Contact:** Greg Johnson. "We have grown to become Oklahoma's premier venue for performing songwriters, hosting such legends as Jimmy Webb, Joe Ely, Ramblin' Jack Elliott, David Lindley, and Tom Rush. We love working with new songwriters who are developing their audience, and we always welcome the best in bluegrass, folk, rock, country, and blues."

BLUE MOOSE TAP HOUSE

211 Iowa Ave., Iowa City IA 52240. (319)358-9206. **E-mail:** bluemoosebooking@gmail.com. **Website:** www.bluemusicic.com. The Blue Moose doubles as an exciting dual-stage music venue. The upstairs stage can hold shows with crowds of over 200 people, and the downstairs stage can host shows of up to 600 people. Contact via e-mail to request a media sheet, which will aid in local promotions, or a sound sheet with a complete inventory of sound equipment and stage dimensions.

BLUE WHALE BAR

123 Astronaut E. S. Onizuka St., Ste. 301, Los Angeles CA 90012. (213)620-0908. **E-mail:** info@bluewhalemusic.com. **Website:** bluewhalemusic.com. Blue Whale is a live jazz bar located in the heart of Little Tokyo, Los Angeles.

BOGART'S

2621 Vine St., Cincinnati OH 45219. (513)872-8801. **Fax:** (513)872-8805. **E-mail:** robthomas@livenation. com. **Website:** www.bogarts.com. **Contact:** Rob Thomas. The venue holds approximately 1,500 people, has 6 bars, 3 levels for concert viewing, 2 entrances, and an elevated stage. Bogart's has been recognized on the international stage for bringing the newest and best music and entertainment to the public for over 2 decades. Today, it is operated by Live Nation Inc., and continues the tradition of quality live entertainment that has been its forte since the building was built in 1890.

BOHEMIAN BIERGARTEN

2017 13th St., Boulder CO 80302. (720)328-8328. **E-mail:** events@bohemianbiergarten.com. **Website:** www.bohemianbiergarten.com. Estab. 2013. Interested in polka and acoustic artists. Contact via e-mail for booking information.

BOOTLEG THEATER

2220 Beverly Blvd., Los Angeles CA 90057. **E-mail:** info@bootlegtheater.com. **E-mail:** booking@bootlegtheater.org. **Website:** www.bootlegtheater.org. "Bootleg Theater is a year-round inclusive art space for original, boundary-defying live theater, music, and dance performances born from the diverse cultural and artistic landscape of Los Angeles. Bootleg supports and collaborates with the best of established and emerging music, theater, and dance artists to create daring multidisciplinary live experiences that are striking, contemporary, and nontraditional."

TIPS "For booking inquiries, please provide your name, the band's name, a phone number, and e-mail address in all correspondences. Please list your targeted show dates, or even some details on how you got referred. Please don't e-mail MP3s and such as attachments; just e-mail the appropriate URL or soundclip address."

THE BOTTLENECK

737 New Hampshire, Lawrence KS 66044. (785)841-5483. **E-mail:** booking@pipelineproductions.com. **Website:** www.thebottlenecklive.com. "The Bottleneck is considered by many to be a rock 'n' roll historical landmark. The Bottleneck cemented its status as a scheduled stop on many major-city, national tours, giving nearby University of Kansas students access to some of the best names in modern music." Music: indie, rock, alternative, folk, country, jazz, blues, funk, dance, ska, psychedelic.

THE BOTTLETREE

3719 Third Ave. S., Birmingham AL 35222. (205)533-6288. **Fax:** (205)533-7565. **E-mail:** booking@thebottletree.com. **Website:** www.thebottletree.com. **Contact:** Merrilee Challiss. Music: punk, indie, folk, rock, country, soul, alternative.

TIPS All booking is done via e-mail.

BOTTOM OF THE HILL

1233 17th St., San Francisco CA 94107. (415)626-4455. **Fax:** (415)861-1615. **E-mail:** booking@bottomofthehill.com. **Website:** bottomofthehill.com. **Contact:** Ramona Downey, Lynn Schwarz, Ben Flanagan, bookers. "Chosen by *Rolling Stone* magazine as 'the best place to hear live music in San Francisco,' the Bottom of the Hill presents some of the finest original artists, 7 nights a week. Featuring up-and-coming acts from around the globe, as well as in our own backyard, the music spans the spectrum from alternative, rockabilly, punk, and hard rock to folk, funk, and pop." Music: alternative, rock, rockabilly, punk, hard rock.

BOWERY BALLROOM

6 Delancey St., New York NY 10002. **E-mail:** info@boweryballroom.com. **Website:** www.boweryballroom.com. **Contact:** Eddie Bruiser.

TIPS "Please list a New York show history and allow 4-6 weeks before following up with an e-mail."

THE BRASS RAIL

1121 Broadway, Fort Wayne IN 46802. (260)267-5303. **E-mail:** corey@brassrailfw.com. **Website:** www.brassrailfw.com. Music: rock, garage punk, metal, country, rockabilly, surf, '60s soul, indie rock, ska, reggae.

TIPS "All booking is conducted through the website; do not call the bar."

THE BRICKYARD

129 N. Rock Island Rd., Wichita KS 67202. (316)263-4044. **E-mail:** booking@brickyardoldtown.com. **Website:** www.brickyardoldtown.com. Music: rock, indie, alternative, punk, classic rock, country.

BROOKLYN BOWL

61 Wythe Ave., Brooklyn NY 11249. (718)963-3369. **E-mail:** rock.androll@brooklynbowl.com. **E-mail:** booking@brooklynbowl.com. **Website:** www.brooklynbowl.com. "Brooklyn Bowl redefines the enter-

tainment experience for the 21st century. Centered around a 16-lane bowling alley, 600-capacity performance venue with live music 7 nights a week and food by Blue Ribbon, Brooklyn Bowl stakes out expansive new territory, literally and conceptually, in the 23,000-square-foot former Hecla Iron Works (1882), 1 block from the burgeoning waterfront." Music: rock, indie, hip-hop, R&B, alternative, punk, funk, folk, reggae, soul.

THE BROTHERHOOD LOUNGE
119 Capitol Way N., Olympia WA 98501. (360)352-4153. **Website:** thebrotherhoodlounge.com. Music: soul, funk, rock, pop, hip-hop, R&B.

THE CACTUS CLUB
2496 S. Wentworth Ave., Milwaukee WI 53207. (414)897-0663. **E-mail:** cactusclubshows@gmail.com. **Website:** www.cactusclubmilwaukee.com. "Milwaukee's Cactus Club has been among the finest live-music venues in the Midwest, featuring such acts as The White Stripes, Queens of the Stone Age, Interpol, Death Cab for Cutie, The Sword, High On Fire, The Faint, Bright Eyes, Eyedea & Abilities, Red Fang, Sylvan Esso, Redd Kross, Sharon Van Etten, Polica, Russian Circles, King Tuff, and countless other national, international, and local bands." Music: punk, rock, alternative, indie, funk, psychedelic.

CAFE NINE
250 State St., New Haven CT 06510. (203)789-8281. **E-mail:** bookcafenine@gmail.com. **Website:** www. cafenine.com. **Contact:** Paul Mayer, booker. "Cafe Nine features live music from national, regional, and local acts 7 nights a week. Catch some of your favorites getting back to their roots in our intimate setting, or see tomorrow's stars on their way to the stadiums." Music: indie, rock, alternative, jazz, punk, garage, alt-country.

CALEDONIA LOUNGE
256 W. Clayton St., Athens GA 30601. **E-mail:** caledonialounge@gmail.com. **Website:** caledonialounge. com. Music: indie, rock, alternative, folk.

THE CANOPY CLUB
708 S. Goodwin Ave., Urbana IL 61801. (217)344-2263. **E-mail:** mikea@jaytv.com. **Website:** www.canopy-club.com. **Contact:** Mike Armintrout. "In striving to achieve the highest level of entertainment, the Canopy Club prides itself on being able to offer entertainment for all walks of life. Whether you like rock, coun-

try, hip-hop, jazz, funk, indie, or anything in between, the Canopy Club has something to offer you. If you're a fan of live music and entertainment, the Canopy Club is your home in central Illinois!"

THE CAVE
452 1/2 W. Franklin St., Chapel Hill NC 27516. (919)968-9308. **E-mail:** cavencbooking@gmail.com. **Website:** caverntavern.com. Music: pop, rock, country, twang, folk, acoustic, funk, indie, punk, blues, bluegrass.

CHELSEA'S CAFE
2857 Perkins Rd., Baton Rouge LA 70808. (225)387-3679. **E-mail:** dave@chelseascafe.com. **Website:** www. chelseascafe.com. "Chelsea's Cafe is Baton Rouge's favorite place to relax, offering good food, drinks, and live music in an intimate, casual atmosphere." Music: rock, indie, alternative, soul.

CHILKOOT CHARLIE'S
2435 Spenard Rd., Anchorage AK 99503. (907)272-1010. **E-mail:** kootsparties@gmail.com. **Website:** www.koots.com. "Chilkoot Charlie's features a rustic Alaska atmosphere with sawdust-covered floors, 3 stages, 3 dance floors, and 10 bars (11 in the summertime!) with padded tree stumps and beer kegs for seating. Literally filled to the rafters with such things as famous band photos and autographs, huge beer can collections, hilarious gags, and tons of Alaska memorabilia, a person could wander around Chilkoot Charlie's for days and still not see everything." Music: rock, punk, metal, ska.

CHURCHILL'S
5501 NE 2nd Ave., Miami FL 33137. (305)757-1807. **Website:** www.churchillspub.com. Music: rock, alternative, indie, pop, jazz, hip-hop, electronica, acoustic. **TIPS** Book through online booking form: www. churchillspub.com/page/contact.

CITY TAVERN
1402 Main St., Dallas TX 75201. **E-mail:** info@citytaverndowntown.com. **E-mail:** booking@citytaverndowntown.com. **Website:** www.citytaverndowntown. com. Music: country, rock, jam, pop, alternative.

CLUB CONGRESS
311 E. Congress St., Tucson AZ 85701. (520)622-8848. **Fax:** (520)792-6366. **E-mail:** bookingashow@hotel-congress.com. **Website:** www.hotelcongress.com. **Contact:** David Slutes, entertainment and booking director. "From its 1985 inception as a once-weekly

showcase for downtown Tucson's creative community, to its current status as 'One of the 10 best rock clubs in the United States,' Club Congress has continuously striven to be a catalyst for art. In addition to showcasing music's cutting edge, the Club Congress has earned repeated accolades as the city's best dance club." Music: rock, alternative, indie, folk, Americana.

THE CLUBHOUSE

1320 E. Broadway Rd., Tempe AZ 85282. (460)968-3238. **E-mail:** clubhousegigs@hotmail.com. **Website:** www.clubhousemusicvenue.com. "A club that features the best in local, touring, and regional acts. Voted Best Local Music Venue by *The New Times Magazine*, we host shows for all age groups on a nightly basis." Music: rock, punk, metal, alternative.

THE COMET

4579 Hamilton Ave., Cincinnati OH 45223. (513)541-8900. **E-mail:** cometbarbooking@gmail.com. **Website:** cometbar.com. Estab. 1996. "Rooted in drink, rock 'n' roll, and shared ideas between persons of original thought."

CRYSTAL CORNER

1302 Williamson St., Madison WI 53715. (608)256-2953. **E-mail:** crystalcornerbooking@gmail.com. **Website:** www.thecrystalcornerbar.com. With a long history of being a favorite neighborhood hangout, the Crystal Corner Bar offers some of the best music in town.

D.B.A.

618 Frenchmen St., New Orleans LA 70116. (504)942-3731. **E-mail:** booking@dbaneworleans.com. **Website:** www.dbaneworleans.com. "We are proud to present some of New Orleans' and the region's greatest musicians and are privileged to have had appearances on our stage by greats such as Clarence 'Gatemouth' Brown, David 'Honeyboy' Edwards, Jimmy Buffet, and Stevie Wonder. When in New Orleans, get away from the tourist traps of Bourbon Street and head down to the 'Marigny,' just downriver from the French Quarter, voted with Williamsburg, Brooklyn, and the Inner Mission in San Francisco as one of the hippest neighborhoods in the country." Music: blues, jazz, R&B, Cajun.

TIPS "We currently have a heavy rotation of local and regional bands that play d.b.a. On occasion we will add new bands to that rotation or if need a late fill-in."

THE DOCK

415 Taughannock Blvd., Ithaca NY 14850. (607)319-4214. **E-mail:** bookingthedock@gmail.com. **Website:** www.thedockithaca.com. The Dock is Ithaca's premier live music venue. Located at the foot of Cayuga Lake in the home of the former Castaways. Contact for booking via form on website or e-mail address.

THE DOGFISH BAR & GRILLE

128 Free St., Portland ME 04101. (207)772-5483. **E-mail:** michele@thedogfishcompany.com. **Website:** www.thedogfishcompany.com. **Contact:** Michele Arcand. "Great food, drink, and service in a casual and unpretentious atmosphere and a great place to hear live local artists. The Dogfish Bar and Grille is an intimate, informal restaurant with a great dinner menu and daily specials. We have 2 very comfortable decks for those who enjoy eating outside, a dining room upstairs, and a friendly tavern on the ground floor. The Dogfish Bar and Grille books local, regional, and national talent most evenings of the week. The music is mostly acoustic, blues, and jazz. There is never a cover charge." Music: jazz, bebop, blues, soul, jam, acoustic.

THE DOUBLE DOOR INN

1218 Charlottetowne Ave., Charlotte NC 28204. (704)376-1446. **E-mail:** maxxmusic2@gmail.com. **Website:** www.doubledoorinn.com. **Contact:** Gregg McCraw, talent buyer/promoter. "Established in 1973 and recognized as the 'Oldest Live Music Venue East of the Mississippi,' the Double Door Inn oozes musical tradition. Looking at our walls, packed with 35 years of autographed photos, has been described as 'viewing a timeline for live music in the Queen City.' Also holding the title 'Oldest Blues Club in the U.S. Under Original Ownership,' the Double Door Inn strives to bring the best in local, regional, and national touring and recording artists to the discriminating music lover. Legendary performers like Eric Clapton, Stevie Ray Vaughn, Dave Alvin, Leon Russell, Buddy Guy, Junior Brown, Bob Margolin, and others have graced the stage of our historic and intimate venue." Music: blues, rock, soul, pop, funk, jazz, bluegrass, acoustic, folk, alt-country, R&B, Americana, reggae.

DOUG FIR LOUNGE

830 E. Burnside St., Portland OR 97214. (503)231-9663. **E-mail:** inquiries@dougfirlounge.com. **E-mail:** booking@dougfirlounge.com. **Website:** www.doug-

firlounge.com. Music: rock, alternative, indie, funk, garage, pop, dance, folk, bluegrass, soul, Americana.

THE DRINKERY

1150 Main St., Cincinnati OH 45202. (513)827-9357. **E-mail:** drinkerybooking@icloud.com. **Website:** www.drinkeryotr.com. **Contact:** Matt Ogden, booking. The Drinkery OTR is a music venue featuring local draft beer, quality craft bottles, and soothing, warm bourbons.

DUFFY'S TAVERN

1412 O St., Lincoln NE 68508. (402)474-3543. **E-mail:** management@duffyslincoln.com. **Website:** www.duffyslincoln.com. "We're known for a lot of things, but if you ask any of us, we will tell you that we're a music venue. Many national acts have graced our stage, including Nirvana, 311, Bright Eyes, the Boss Martians, Slobberbone, Wesley Willis, and many others. A lot of us think some of the local acts are even better, and on any Sunday or Wednesday night, you can be assured Duffy's stage will be jumping with some of the best original music around." Music: rock, folk, Americana, indie, psychedelic, pop, hard rock.

THE ECHO

1822 Sunset Blvd., Los Angeles CA 90026. (213)413-8200. **Website:** www.theecho.com. Music: funk, punk, rock, indie, folk, hip-hop, electronica, Mexicana, pop.

EL REY THEATRE

5515 Wilshire Blvd., Los Angeles CA 90036. (323)936-6400. **E-mail:** booking@theelrey.com. **Website:** www.theelrey.com. "The El Rey Theatre is an original art deco theater in the heart of the Miracle Mile, one of Los Angeles' preserved art deco districts. After over 50 years as a first-run movie house, the El Rey was converted into a live-music venue in 1994."

THE EMPTY BOTTLE

1035 N. Western Ave., Chicago IL 60622. (773)276-3600. **E-mail:** brent@emptybottle.com. **Website:** www.emptybottle.com. **Contact:** Brent Heyl, talent buyer. Music: rock, indie, psychedelic, anti-pop, garage, metal, country, dance, electronica, soul, blues, folk.

TIPS "We strongly prefer electronic booking requests to physical packages."

THE EMPTY GLASS

410 Elizabeth St., Charleston WV 25311. (304)345-3914. **E-mail:** booking@emptyglass.com. **Website:**

www.emptyglass.com. "Located under a three-story house in Charleston's historically diverse East End. Here you will find delicious food, great conversation, friendly spirits, and live original music from all over the planet!" Music: blues, jazz, rock, folk, bluegrass, indie.

EXIT/IN

2208 Elliston Place, Nashville TN 37203. (615)891-1781. **Website:** www.exitin.com. "The Exit/In began its role as a Nashville music venue back in 1971. Since then, countless shows and great memories have happened within these walls." Music: rock, country, alt-country, folk, punk, pop, psychedelic.

TIPS Booking via online submissions form: www.exitin.com/contact.

THE FILLMORE

1805 Geary Blvd., San Francisco CA 94115. (415)346-3000. **E-mail:** thefillmore@livenation.com. **Website:** thefillmore.com. Has featured The Smashing Pumpkins, Gin Blossoms, Brian Setzer Orchestra, Huey Lewis and the News, Blues Traveler and Soul Hat, Tom Petty and the Heartbreakers, and more.

THE FINELINE MUSIC CAFE

318 1st Ave. N., Minneapolis MN 55401. (612)338-8100. **Fax:** (612)337-8416. **E-mail:** fineline@minneapoliseventcenters.com. **Website:** www.finelinemusic.com. Music: rock, acoustic, indie, folk, alternative.

FIREHOUSE SALOON

5930 Southwest Freeway, Houston TX 77057. (281)513-1995. **E-mail:** info@firehousesaloon.com. **E-mail:** rebecca@firehousesaloon.com. **Website:** firehousesaloon.com. **Contact:** Rebecca Harrington, talent buyer. "Our musical guests range from up-and-coming artists in the country scene to renowned favorites. You can discover new stars here before anyone else! Miranda Lambert played the Firehouse stage more than 17 times before being catapulted to superstardom. We not only showcase country music, but ALL types of music, because we are first and foremost a music venue."

TIPS "An opening band must be able to draw at least 50 people. In order to get a headlining spot, the band must be able to draw 150 people."

40 WATT CLUB

285 W. Washington St., Athens GA 30601. (706)549-7871. **E-mail:** velenavego@gmail.com. **Website:**

www.40watt.com. **Contact:** Velena Vego, talent buyer. Music: indie, rock, alternative.

THE 4TH AVENUE TAVERN

210 E. 4th Ave., Olympia WA 98501. (360)951-7887. **E-mail:** the4thave@gmail.com. **Website:** www.the4thave.com. Music: indie, alternative, funk, rock, punk. "The 4th Ave is home to one of the largest stages in Olympia. Booking is very selective. Only contact if you have a large draw in the South Sound area."

FREIGHT & SALVAGE COFFEEHOUSE

2020 Addison St., Berkeley CA 94704. (510)644-2020, ext. 118. **E-mail:** folk@freightandsalvage.org. **E-mail:** booking@freightandsalvage.org. **Website:** www.thefreight.org. Music: folk, bluegrass, acoustic, jazz, Celtic, experimental.

FREIGHT & SALVAGE COFFEEHOUSE

2020 Addison St., Berkeley CA 94704. (510)644-2020. **E-mail:** booking@freightandsalvage.org. **Website:** www.thefreight.org. The Freight & Salvage Coffeehouse is an all-ages venue located in Berkeley, California. It is a nonprofit arts organization dedicated to promoting the understanding and appreciation of traditional and roots music. Contact via e-mail for more info on booking.

THE FREQUENCY

121 W. Main St., Madison WI 53703. (608)819-8777. **Fax:** (608)819-8778. **E-mail:** madisonfrequency@gmail.com. **Website:** www.madisonfrequency.com. "A live-music venue and a nightclub located in downtown Madison near the capital square. We host a wide variety of live music 7 nights a week, featuring local, regional, national, and international acts playing rock, punk, metal, bluegrass, jazz, and indie."

THE FREQUENCY

121 W. Main St., Madison WI 53703. (608)819-8777. **E-mail:** madisonfrequency@gmail.com. **Website:** www.madisonfrequency.com. Hosting shows 7 nights/week, The Frequency hosts local, regional, national, and international acts. All booking is done exclusively via e-mail. Requested dates should be listed as the subject line of the e-mail. If you are not looking for a specific date, expect a 3–4-week response time.

GABE'S

330 E. Washington St., Iowa City IA 52240. (319)351-9175. **E-mail:** booking@icgabes.com. **Website:** www.icgabes.com. "Welcome to the legendary bar known as Gabe's. What first started as The Pub in the early 1970s, then became Fox and Sam's then Gabe and Walker's then Gabe's Oasis, then the Picador, and now back to Gabe's. And while it has gone through many transformations, it is strangely the same—except that it is probably now in the best shape that it has ever been. We are bringing high-quality local, regional and national shows to Iowa City and have made the downstairs and the beer garden a great place to hang out again. One of our favorite things about this place is that you can do ANY type of music upstairs. It is not uncommon to see a punk show followed by a metal show with a jam band show the next night and a hip hop show the night after. We have giant EDM and indy and rock shows, too—anything goes." Contact via e-mail with links to your music online. Cannot guarantee that they can book your band. Not interested in cover bands.

GEORGE'S MAJESTIC LOUNGE

519 W. Dickson St., Fayetteville AR 72701. (479)527-6618. **Fax:** (479)527-6611. **E-mail:** saxsafe@aol.com. **Website:** www.georgesmajesticlounge.com. **Contact:** Brian Crowne, owner/operator/booking. "George's is perhaps best known for the incredible musicians that have graced stages, bringing the best in local, regional, and national acts through its doors. Some artists of note that have performed at George's through the years include Robert Cray, Leon Russell, Little River Band, Delbert McClinton, Eddie Money, Pat Green, Derek Trucks, Sam Bush, Tower of Power, Leftover Salmon, Bob Margolin, Chubby Carrier, Tommy Castro, Coco Montoya, Anthony Gomes, Bernard Allison, Michael Burks, Charlie Robison, Cross Canadian Ragweed, Jason Boland, Dark Star Orchestra, Steve Kimock, Martin Fierro, North Mississippi Allstars, Robert Randolph, David Lindley, Big Smith, Cate Brothers, Oteil Burbridge, and so many more." Music: rock, folk, alternative, country, bluegrass, punk.

THE GOLDEN FLEECE TAVERN

132 W. Loockerman St., Dover DE 19904. (302)674-1776. **E-mail:** info@goldenfleecetavern.com. **Website:** www.thegoldenfleecetavern.com. Music: rock, indie, classic rock, pop, alternative.

THE GRAMOPHONE

4243 Manchester Ave., St. Louis MO 63110. (314)531-5700. **E-mail:** gramophonestl@gmail.com. **Website:** thegramophonelive.com. "The Gramophone features an eclectic schedule of live music and DJs in an intimate concert setting." Music: hip-hop, funk, soul, indie, rock, Americana.

GREAT AMERICAN MUSIC HALL
859 O'Farrell St., San Francisco CA 94109. (415)885-0750. **Website:** www.slimspresents.com. **Contact:** Dana Smith, booking. "The past 3 decades at the Great American Music Hall have been full of music, with artists ranging from Duke Ellington, Sarah Vaughan, and Count Basie to Van Morrison, the Grateful Dead, and Bobby McFerrin." Music: contemporary pop, indie, jazz, folk, rock, alternative, Americana.

THE GREAT NORTHERN BAR & GRILL
27 Central Ave., Whitefish MT 59937. (406)862-2816. **E-mail:** info@greatnorthernbar.com. **Website:** www. greatnorthernbar.com. "The Great Northern Bar & Grill is the premier destination in the Flathead Valley for good food, good music, and good times." Music: rock, alternative.

GREAT SCOTT
1222 Commonwealth Ave., Allston MA 02134. (617)566-9014. **E-mail:** submissions@greatscottboston.com. **Website:** www.greatscottboston.com. **Contact:** Carl Lavin, booking agent. Music: rock, metal, alternative, indie.

GREEK THEATRE
2700 N. Vermont Ave., Los Angeles CA 90027. (323)665-5857. **Fax:** (323)666-8202. **E-mail:** yourcontact@greektheatrela.com. **Website:** www.greektheatrela.com. Music: theatrical, pop, family, rock, ethnic, comedy. Has booked Bruce Springsteen, Dave Matthews Band, Crosby, Stills, Nash & Young, James Taylor, Journey, and more.

THE GREEN LANTERN
497 W. 3rd St., Lexington KY 40508. (859)252-9539. **E-mail:** greenlanternbooking@gmail.com. **Website:** greenlanternlexington.tumblr.com. "Making the best neighborhood bar in Lex a reality." Music: rock, alternative, indie, folk, punk, metal.

GUNPOWDER LODGE
10092 Bel Air Rd., Kingsville MD 21087. (410)256-2626. **E-mail:** info@thegunpowderlodge.com. **Website:** www.thegunpowderlodge.com. Music: rock, indie, acoustic, classic rock.

HAL & MAL'S
200 S. Commerce St., Jackson MS 39204. (601)948-0888. **E-mail:** booking@halandmals.com. **Website:** www.halandmals.com. "The most talked-about, upscale honky tonk in all of Mississippi. Here, art is made, music is played, and locals gather to share community and celebrate the very best of Mississippi's creative spirit." Music: honky-tonk, country, rock, blues, classic rock, alternative.

HALFWAY INN
730 Church St., East Quad, Ann Arbor MI 48109. (734)764-1626. **E-mail:** eqmc@umich.edu. The Halfway Inn serves as a student café during the day and as an all-ages club on weekends. Friday and Saturday shows are the norm, but Sunday shows are not out of the question. All shows end by midnight (university rules). Shows are booked by the East Quad Music Coop. Contact via e-mail for more information.

HANK'S CAFE
1038 Nuuanu Ave., Honolulu HI 96817. (808)526-1411. **Website:** hankscafehawaii.com. Music: rock, doo-wop, dance, country, pop.

THE HAUNT
702 Willow Ave., Ithaca NY 14850. (607)275-3447. **E-mail:** info@dansmallpresents.com. **Website:** www.thehaunt.com. The Haunt is Ithaca's home for live music. E-mail for information on booking.

THE HAVEN
6700 Aloma Ave., Winter Park FL 32792. (407)673-2712. **E-mail:** maniacal_mojo_records@yahoo.com. **Website:** www.thehavenrocks.com. **Contact:** John "Clint" Pinder. The Haven is a 350-plus capacity venue with a full-liquor bar located in the Aloma Square Shopping Center in Winter Park, Florida. Music: alternative, classic rock, cover band, funk, jam band, metal, punk, reggae, rock, and singer/songwriter—all types of live music with local, regional, and national bands, and most shows are ages 18 and up.

TIPS See house P.A., stage and lighting specs, mains, monitors, microphones, stage dimensions, and lighting specs at: www.thehavenrocks.com/specs.

HEADLINERS MUSIC HALL
1386 Lexington Rd., Louisville KY 40206. (502)584-8088. **Website:** headlinerslouisville.com. "Locally owned and operated, Headliners Music Hall is the premier live entertainment venue of Louisville, Kentucky. We bring the best local and national acts to our stage, with fantastic sound and a fun atmosphere. We've had the privilege of hosting some amazing rock, metal, acoustic, hip-hop, and alternative bands such

as My Morning Jacket, Jimmy Eat World, Neko Case, Clutch, Sharon Jones & The Dap Kings, Umphrey's McGee, Old Crow Medicine Show, Kings of Leon, Talib Kweli, Girl Talk, and more." Music: rock, indie, punk, folk, reggae, soul, R&B, psychedelic.

⬭   For booking information, contact using the online submission form.

THE HIDEOUT

1354 W. Wabansia, Chicago IL 60642. (773)227-4433. **Website:** www.hideoutchicago.com.

HIGH NOON SALOON

701A E. Washington Ave., Madison WI 53703. (608)268-1122. **Fax:** (608)268-1121. **E-mail:** info@high-noon.com. **E-mail:** booking@high-noon.com. **Website:** www.high-noon.com. **Contact:** Cathy Dethmers, owner and manager. "Founded in 2004 in downtown Madison, Wisconsin, High Noon Saloon is a live-music venue that features many different styles of music, including rock, alternative, metal, indie, alt-country, pop, punk, bluegrass, folk, jam, world music, and more. We host large national acts, smaller touring bands from around the world, and lots of local music."

HIGH NOON SALOON

701A E. Washington Ave., Madison WI 53703. (608)268-1122. **E-mail:** booking@high-noon.com. **Website:** www.high-noon.com. **Contact:** Cathy Dethmers, booking manager. High Noon Saloon books bands from all over the world in a variety of genres, including rock, indie, metal, alt-country, pop, punk, bluegrass, folk, jam, and world music. "If you want your band to be considered for a show at High Noon Saloon, please send an EPK or a link to a website or media page where we can check out your music, along with a band bio, contact information, and desired show date. Feel free to send along any press you have received. It is helpful to let us know when and where you have previously played in Madison, and what days of the week you are available to play. Press kits via e-mail are preferred. Please refrain from sending multiple MP3s via e-mail—a link to a site where we can listen to your music is greatly preferred. Please allow at least 2-3 weeks for us to review your band before following up with us. We do listen to every submission, but since we often receive over 100 submissions a month, it takes some time to get through them. If you are looking for a last-minute show, we'll do what we can, but you should indicate what date you need in the subject line of your e-mail. We generally book

about 6-14 weeks in advance, so please plan accordingly when looking for a specific tour date."

HI-TONE CAFE

412-414 N. Cleveland St., Memphis TN 38104. (901)490-0335. **E-mail:** thehitonecafe@gmail.com. **Website:** hitonememphis.com. Music: rock, alternative, indie, pop, alt-country, Americana, psych, metal, hip-hop, rap.

TIPS "All booking is handled via e-mail; do not call. Keep in mind that we book 6-8 weeks in advance."

HOTEL CAFE

1623 1/2 N. Cahuenga Blvd., Los Angeles CA 90028. **E-mail:** marko@hotelcafe.com. **Website:** www.hotelcafe.com.

TIPS "For booking, e-mail a link to your website or online press kit. Include where you are from, other places you've played in Los Angeles, and your current draw in the Los Angeles area. Allow up to several weeks for a response and at least 1-2 months for a booking."

HOWLER'S PITTSBURGH

4509 Liberty Ave., Pittsburgh PA 15224. (412)682-0320. **Website:** www.howlerspittsburgh.com. "Howler's Pittsburgh is an independent mid-level music venue and bar in Pittsburgh's east end, hosting local and national acts of all genres 5 days a week." Music: rock, alternative, pop, dance, blues, alt-country, punk, jam, psychedelic, folk, indie.

HUMPY'S

610 W. 6th Ave., Anchorage AK 99517. (907)276-2337. **E-mail:** play@humpysalaska.com. **Website:** www.humpys.com. Music: folk, rock, metal, blues, Americana.

HURRICANE HARRY'S

313 College Ave., College Station TX 77840. (979)846-3343. **E-mail:** info@bcsclubs.com. **Website:** harrys.bcsclubs.com. Estab. 1992. Hurricane Harry's is famous for country western dancing and live concerts.

JEREMIAH BULLFROGS LIVE

2940 SW Wanamaker Rd., Topeka KS 66614. (785)272-3764. **E-mail:** bullfrogslive@gmail.com. **Website:** www.bullfrogslive.com. Music: blues, soul, rock, alternative, dance.

KILBY COURT

741 S. Kilby Court, Salt Lake City UT 84101. **Fax:** (801)364-3538. **E-mail:** will@sartainandsaunders.

com. **Website:** www.kilbycourt.com. **Contact:** Will Sartain, owner/talent buyer. Music: rock, alternative, Americana, indie, pop, ska, punk.

LARIMER LOUNGE

2721 Larimer St., Denver CO 80205. (303)296-1003. **E-mail:** tony@larimerlounge.com. **Website:** www.larimerlounge.com; www.booklarimer.com. **Contact:** Tony Mason, booking manager. Music: rock, pop, electronica, indie, garage, alternative.

LAST CONCERT CAFÉ

1403 Nance St., Houston TX 77003. (713)226-8563; (832)422-5561. **E-mail:** lastconcertcafe@sbcglobal. net. **E-mail:** dawnfudge@lastconcert.com. **Website:** www.lastconcert.com. "Last Concert Café is Houston's favorite place to see live music 7 days a week. From world-class bands to local residents participating in our Sunday Jam Circle, you're sure to find your favorite entertainment at Last Concert Café!"

LAUNCHPAD

618 Central Ave. SW, Albuquerque NM 87102. (505)764-8887. **Website:** www.launchpadrocks.com. Music: rock, punk, reggae, alternative.

LEADBETTERS TAVERN

1639 Thames St., Baltimore MD 21231. (410)675-4794. **E-mail:** leadbetterstavern2@gmail.com. **Website:** www.leadbetterstavern.com. Music: blues, rock, soul, jazz, punk, alternative, funk, pop, indie.

LIQUID LOUNGE

405 S. 8th St., Boise ID 83702. (208)941-2459. **E-mail:** liquidbooking@gmail.com. **Website:** www.liquidboise.com. Music: rock, reggae, funk, ska, bluegrass, dance, soul, folk, punk.

LOCAL 506

506 W. Franklin St., Chapel Hill NC 27516. (919)942-5506. **E-mail:** booking@local506.com. **Website:** www.local506.com. Only does booking via e-mail. Include your band name, hometown, and a link to access your music. Subject of e-mail should include band name, as well as dates you're inquiring about. Generally books 2-3 months in advance.

THE LOFT

2506 W. Colorado Ave. #C, Colorado Springs CO 80904. (719)445-9278. **Website:** www.loftmusicvenue.com. "We are here to bring you the best musical experience in Colorado Springs with an intimate atmosphere, amazing sound, and great music. We hope

you come often and tell your friends about our place." Music: rock, pop, country, acoustic, indie, blues, jazz, bluegrass, folk.

THE LOST LEAF BAR & GALLERY

914 N. 5th St., Phoenix AZ 85004. (602)481-4004. **E-mail:** solnotes@hotmail.com. **Website:** www.thelostleaf.org. **Contact:** Tato Caraveo. Music: Latin, blues, salsa, hip-hop, R&B, funk, outlaw country, Americana.

LOT 10

106 S. Cayuga St., Ithaca NY 14850. (607)272-7224. **E-mail:** book@lot-10.com. **Website:** www.lot-10.com. "Any band/musician looking to play a show at Lot 10 is responsible for setting up a minimum of 1 local support act for the show. If we have given you a hold or confirmed with you that you have the night, we allow a three-week window, that if we are contacted by a booking agent, or major touring act, and they request the night that you have been given, we will contact you within the three-week window and your show will be moved to another date. No calls please—we will only respond to e-mails. If we are interested in booking your band, we will e-mail you back. Please do not e-mail MP3s or other music files for booking consideration, instead please include links to your music."

THE LOUNGE AT HOTEL DONALDSON

101 N. Broadway, Fargo ND 58102. (701)478-1000; (888)478-8768. **E-mail:** info@hoteldonaldson.com. **Website:** www.hoteldonaldson.com. Music: Americana, folk, indie, country, bluegrass.

LOW SPIRITS

2823 2nd St. NW, Albuquerque NM 87107. **Website:** www.lowspiritslive.com. Music: rock, indie, blues, alternative, folk.

LUCKEY'S CLUB CIGAR STORE

933 Olive St., Eugene OR 97401. (541)687-4643. **Website:** www.luckeysclub.com. "Today, Luckey's combines art nouveau decor, saloon sensibilities, serious pool players, cutting-edge music, and a chair for everyone in the community. It still has echoes of the sounds, smells, pool games, and conversations from the past 100 years. It's like a time capsule with a hip twist." Music: folk, acoustic, blues, indie, Americana, rock.

MAD ANTHONY BREWING COMPANY

2002 Broadway, Ft. Wayne IN 46802. (260)426-2537. **Website:** www.madbrew.com. "A cool, laid-back atmosphere, full food menu, and weekly live music." Music: rock, jam, jazz, blues, funk, soul, pop.

THE MAJESTIC/MAGIC STICK

4140 Woodward Ave., Detroit MI 48201. (313)833-9700. **Website:** www.majesticdetroit.com. "The Majestic Theatre is steeped in history. Designed by C. Howard Crane, it opened in 1915 as the largest theater in the world of its kind. Since the mid 1980s, The Majestic Theatre has been the site of memorable concerts featuring live music and entertainment from touring indie rock, blues, jazz, folk, hip-hop and worldbeat artists. The Majestic has produced shows for The Black Keys, George Clinton, Black Eyed Peas, Flaming Lips, Wilco, Sheryl Crow, Dr. John, Yo La Tengo, Patti Smith, Sublime, Matt & Kim, Drake, Fleet Foxes, The Decemberists, Yeah Yeah Yeahs, Foster The People, Jimmy Cliff, 311, Sonic Youth, Fela Kuti, and many more."

MAJESTIC THEATRE

115 King St., Madison WI 53703. (608)255-0901. **E-mail:** info@majesticmadison.com. **Website:** www.majesticmadison.com. Estab. 1906. The Majestic Theatre is a world-class venue located in Madison, Wisconsin, that hosts major national touring acts. Seeks established local and regional acts to open for high-profile headlining acts. Music: acoustic, alternative, Americana, classic rock, country, electronic/dance/DJ, folk, funk, hip-hop/rap, jam band, metal, pop, punk, reggae, rock, singer/songwriter, spoken word, urban/R&B.

TIPS Contact/submit online at website.

THE MANGY MOOSE RESTAURANT & SALOON

PO Box 590, Teton Village WY 83025. (307)733-4913. **E-mail:** management@mangymoose.com. **E-mail:** booking@mangymoose.com. **Website:** mangymoose.com. Music: funk, punk, electronica, indie, folk, rock, bluegrass.

MAXWELL'S

1039 Washington St., Hoboken NJ 07030. (201)653-7777. **E-mail:** bookings@maxwellsnj.com. **Website:** www.maxwellsnj.com. "We're about music, arts, a friendly atmosphere, great food and drink, and an exceptional Hoboken neighborhood experience. Come join us!" Music: rock, alternative, blues, punk, indie.

TIPS "Send a brief bio and some links to recorded music or recent performances."

MELODY INN

3826 N. Illinois St., Indianapolis IN 46208. (317)923-4707. **E-mail:** melodyinn2001@gmail.com. **Website:** www.melodyindy.com. Music: punk, rock, metal, indie, pop, rockabilly, bluegrass.

MEMPHIS ON MAIN

55 E. Main St., Champaign IL 61820. (217)398-1097. **E-mail:** info@memphisonmain.com. **Website:** memphisonmain.com. Music: rock, classic rock, R&B, blues, soul, funk, folk, country, metal, rockabilly, punk, reggae.

MERCURY LOUNGE

1747 S. Boston Ave., Tulsa OK 74119. **E-mail:** mercuryloungetulsa@gmail.com. **Website:** www.mercurylounge918.com. Estab. 2005. Music: country, alt-country, Americana, blues, jazz, rock, reggae, rockabilly, pop.

MERCY LOUNGE/THE CANNERY BALLROOM

1 Cannery Row, Nashville TN 37203. (615)251-3020. **Fax:** (651)252-2527. **E-mail:** info@mercylounge.com. **E-mail:** booking@mercylounge.com. **Website:** mercylounge.com. **Contact:** Todd Ohlhauser, owner. "Since the doors to the Mercy Lounge first opened back in January of 2003, the cozy little club on Cannery Row has been both locally favored and nationally renowned. Building a reputation for showcasing the best in burgeoning buzz bands and renowned national talents, the club has maintained its relevance by consistently offering reliable atmosphere and entertainment." Music: pop, country, rock, folk, Americana, indie, funk, soul, psychedelic.

THE MET

1005 Main St., Pawtucket RI 02860. (401)729-1005. **E-mail:** info@themetri.com. **Website:** themetri.com. Music: rock, funk, folk, blues, soul, punk, alternative.

THE MIDDLE EAST NIGHTCLUB

472 Massachusetts Ave., Cambridge MA 02139. (617)864-3278, ext. 225. **E-mail:** booking@mideastclub.com; lionel@mideastclub.com; jason@mideastclub.com; mideastcorner@gmail.com; abby@mideastclub.com. **Website:** www.mideastclub.com. **Contact:** Lionel Train (downstairs booking); Jason Trefts (upstairs booking); Abby Bower (ZUZU! Live booking). Downstair's room capacity is 575. Upstairs is 194. Parking garage is attached to the Meridian Hotel.

Music: funk, rock, alternative, dance, pop, hip-hop, punk, Americana.

MILLER THEATRE

Columbia University School of the Arts, 2960 Broadway, MC 1801, New York NY 10027. (212)854-6205. **E-mail:** miller-arts@columbia.edu. **Website:** www.millertheatre.com. **Contact:** Melissa Smey, executive director. "Miller Theatre's mission is to develop the next generation of cultural consumers, to reinvigorate public enthusiasm in the arts nationwide by pioneering new approaches to programming, to educate the public by presenting specialized, informative programs inviting to a broad audience, to discover new and diverse repertoire and commission new works, and to share Columbia University's intellectual riches with the public." Music: dance, contemporary and early music, jazz, opera, performance.

THE MINT

6010 W. Pico Blvd., Los Angeles CA 90035. (323)954-9400. **Fax:** (323)938-2994. **E-mail:** booking@themint-la.com. **Website:** themintla.com. "In a city where history is measured in months instead of decades, the Mint is a real cultural treasure. The bar has been presenting live music ever since it opened in 1937, and Stevie Wonder, Macy Gray, Ray Charles, Zigaboo Modeliste, Leo Nocentelli, Royal Crown Revue, and the Wallflowers are among the many notable musicians who've performed on its small stage."

MISSISSIPPI STUDIOS

3939 N. Mississippi, Portland OR 97227. (503)288-3895. **E-mail:** info@mississippistudios.com. **E-mail:** booking@mississippistudios.com. **Website:** www.mississippistudios.com. **Contact:** Matt King, senior talent buyer. "Portland's premier concert venue, offering guests the best sound and an intimate concert experience." Music: indie, folk, rock, Americana, alternative, pop, blues.

MOHAWK

912 Red River St., Austin TX 78701. **E-mail:** cody@mohawkaustin.com; patrick@mohawkaustin.com. **Website:** mohawkaustin.com. **Contact:** Cody R. Cowan, general manager; Patrick Waites, booking and events. Venue known for rock shows. Values creative expression, originality, and work ethic. Contact Patrick Waites with MP3 links only to be considered for booking.

THE MOHAWK PLACE

47 E. Mohawk St., Buffalo NY 14203. (716)312-9279. **E-mail:** buffalosmohawkplace@gmail.com. **Website:** www.buffalosmohawkplace.com. Music: indie, rock, alternative, punk.

"We book shows predominantly through e-mail. Please understand we get a high volume of e-mails daily. In most cases, local bands get priority. If we are interested we will get back to you."

MOJO 13

1706 Philadelphia Pike, Wilmington DE 19809. (302)746-7033. **E-mail:** mojo13booking@gmail.com. "We play host to local and touring music acts as well as a whole host of other forms of entertainment that cater to the rock 'n' roll lifestyle. We're looking to become the home-away-from-home for the alternative-minded music community here in Delaware and beyond. So if you've got a band, are a musician, entertainer, or just a fan, please join us." Music: punk, rock, alternative, indie.

THE MONKEY HOUSE

30 Main St., Winooski VT 05404. (802)655-4563. **E-mail:** monkeybarmusic@gmail.com. **Website:** monkeyhousevt.com. Music: folk, indie, hard rock, punk, rock, alternative, Americana, funk, blues.

MOTR PUB

1345 Main St., Cincinnati OH 45202. (513)381-6687. **Website:** motrpub.com. Music: rock, alternative, folk, indie, Americana.

MUSE MUSIC CAFE

247 W. Center St., Provo UT 84601. **Website:** musemusiccafe.com. "The hub of Music, Art and Culture in Utah Valley." Music: rock, hard rock, hip-hop, electronica, indie, alternative, pop, Americana.

Use contact form at musemusicprovo.com/contact-us-booking/.

THE MUSIC HALL AT CAPITAL ALE HOUSE

623 E. Main St., Richmond VA 23219. (804)780-2537. **E-mail:** audrey@capitalalehouse.com. **Website:** capitalalehouse.com. **Contact:** Audrey Finney. Music: indie, rock, jazz, blues, pop.

MUSIC HALL OF WILLIAMSBURG

The Bowery Presents, 66 N. Sixth St., Brooklyn NY 11211. **E-mail:** info@bowerypresents.com. **Website:**

www.musichallofwilliamsburg.com. **Contact:** Eddie Bruiser. "The best way to get a show at a Bowery Presents club is to send your press pack to: The Bowery Presents, c/o Eddie Bruiser, 156 Ludlow St., New York, NY 10002. Please list a New York show history and allow 4-6 weeks before following up with an e-mail."

NATASHA'S

112 Esplanade Alley, Lexington KY 40507. **Website:** bistro.beetnik.com. "Natasha's has hosted a wide variety of acts, including jazz, rock, world, comedy, pop, country, Americana, folk, singer/songwriter, indie, and blues. Over the Rhine, Punch Brothers, Vienna Teng, Sara Watkins, Michelle Shocked, Richard Shindell, Patty Larkin, and Nellie McKay have all played recently on our stage."

○ Use online submission form for booking inquiries.

NECTAR'S

188 Main St., Burlington VT 05401. (802)658-4771. **E-mail:** booking@liveatnectars.com. **Website:** live-atnectars.com. "A long-standing landmark on Main Street in Burlington, Nectar's restaurant and bar has been the headquarters for thousands of local (and not-so-local) music acts. From Phish to Led Loco, from reggae to rock, Nectar's Bar and Lounge is the place to see live music in downtown Burlington." Music: blues, Americana, folk, rock, alternative, punk, indie, jazz, pop, dance, funk, psychedelic.

NEUMOS

925 E. Pike St., Seattle WA 98122. (206)709-9442. **Fax:** (206)219-5644. **E-mail:** evan@neumos.com; eli@neumos.com. **Website:** neumos.com. "The showroom side of the business has always been our priority and the lifeline to all other things that surround it. We pride ourselves on our always-relevant and carefully curated music calendar, lighting production, and state-of-the-art sound system. The Neumos showroom has 3 full-service bars and a second floor with a nicely seated mezzanine and balcony overlooking the stage. The showroom is fitted with an ample-sized stage, merch area, and superior unobstructed sight lines. We play host to several musical genres, by national and local artists alike, including indie rock, hip-hop, punk rock, DJ's, metal, singer/songwriters, country, and much more. Downstairs, below Neumos, is Barboza, a second, more intimate showroom."

NEUROLUX

111 N. 11th St., Boise ID 83702. (208)343-0886. **Fax:** (208)336-5034. **E-mail:** info@neurolux.com. **Website:** www.neurolux.com. Music: funk, indie, rock, reggae, folk, country, bluegrass.

THE NICK ROCKS

2514 10th Ave. S., Birmingham AL 35205. (205)252-3831. **Website:** www.thenickrocks.com. **Contact:** Dan Nolen, talent buyer. "The music heard almost every night of the week includes local, regional, and national acts. The diverse range of acts add to the appeal of an evening at the Nick. One can hear blues, rock, punk, emo, pop, country, metal, bluegrass, rock-a-billy, roots rock, or whatever your genre of choice. The Nick has had it all. It is an up-close-and-personal room voted 3 times in a row as Birmingham's best live music venue by *Birmingham Weekly*."

○ To contact, use online form at www.thenickrocks.com/info/contact/book-your-band.

NIETZSCHE'S

248 Allen St., Buffalo NY 14201. (716)886-8539. **Website:** www.nietzsches.com. Call for information regarding booking. Music: blues, jazz, rock, alternative, funk, soul.

NORTHSIDE TAVERN

4163 Hamilton Ave., Cincinnati OH 45223. (513)542-3603. **E-mail:** northsidetavern@gmail.com. **Website:** www.northsidetav.com/cincy. Neighborhood tavern and free, original, live music venue in Cincinnati.

NORTH STAR BAR & RESTAURANT

2639 Poplar St., Philadelphia PA 19130. **Website:** www.northstarbar.com. Music: rock, indie, psychedelic, pop, funk, jam, ska, punk, alternative.

TIPS Contact via online submissions form: www.northstarbar.com/contact.

THE OLD ROCK HOUSE

1200 S. 7th St., St. Louis MO 63104. (314)588-0505. **E-mail:** info@oldrockhouse.com. **Website:** oldrockhouse.com. **Contact:** Tim Weber, co-owner. Music: rock, indie, alternative, punk, folk, pop.

ONE TRICK PONY GRILL & TAPROOM

136 E. Fulton, Grand Rapids MI 49503. (616)235-7669. **Website:** www.onetrick.biz. **Contact:** Dan Verhil, owner. Music: acoustic, rock, country, blues.

ON STAGE DRINKS & GRINDS

802 Kapahulu Ave., Honolulu HI 96816. (808)738-0004. "On Stage is our ultimate living room. A cool, 'off the beaten path,' fun, and comfortable spot to hang and chill. Equipped with a stage area complete with sound system, guitars, congas, and drums. We feature live music, and, at times, surprise jams by well-known local artists that pop in. A kind of neat, underground music scene." Music: blues, rock, Hawaiian, acoustic.

PARADISE ROCK CLUB

967 Commonwealth Ave., Boston MA 02115. (617)547-0620. **E-mail:** informationdise@crossroadspresents.com. **E-mail:** bookinginquiriesparadise@crossroadspresents.com. **Website:** crossroadspresents.com/paradise-rock-club. **Contact:** Lee Zazofsky, general manager. Music: pop, reggae, alternative, rock, indie, punk, hip-hop, Americana.

TIPS "Booking is handled by Crossroads Presents."

PARAMOUNT CENTER FOR THE ARTS

518 State St., Bristol TN, 37620. (423)274-8920. **E-mail:** paramountcenter@btes.tv. **Website:** www.theparamountcenter.com. "Built in 1931 and restored to its original splendor in 1991, the Paramount continues to grow as the Mountain Empire's premier performing arts center. Listed on the National Register of Historic Places, the Paramount is an excellent example of the art deco motion picture palaces built in the late 1920s and early 1930s. The restoration retained the Paramount's opulent, richly embellished interior. The original Venetian-styled murals and the art deco ambience were faithfully recreated. The auditorium holds 756."

PARISH

214 E. 6th Street, Austin TX 78701. **E-mail:** austen@theparishaustin.com. **Website:** www.theparishaustin.com. **Contact:** Austen Bailey, director of entertainment/booking. "Located in the heart of downtown Austin, in the historic district of 6th Street, The Parish is arguably the best indoor live-music venue in Austin that offers the highest-quality production for artists and events alike. With a 450 capacity, The Parish has hosted musical legends such as Pete Townshend, Slash, and Perry Farrell, as well as independent artists such as Grizzly Bear and Yeasayer. It is an all-genres venue that provides an intimate, live-music experience for all music fans."

PETE'S CANDY STORE

709 Lorimer St., Brooklyn NY 11211. **E-mail:** booking@petescandystore.com. **Website:** www.petescandystore.com. **Contact:** Jake Silver.

TIPS "We listen to all submissions and contact those acts that we are planning on booking. This follow-up may take anywhere from a week to a month. We do not confirm submissions, nor follow up with acts that we are not planning on booking. Please do not contact us to see if we received your submission, as the volume is quite high. We prefer to receive links to websites with songs/videos. Please do not include links to Myspace sites. Please do not send audio files."

PJ'S LAGER HOUSE

1254 Michigan Ave., Detroit MI 48226. (313)961-4668. **E-mail:** lagerhousebookings@gmail.com. **Website:** www.pjslagerhouse.com. "PJ's features the best of Detroit's original rock 'n' roll. Up-and-coming and established acts along with a variety of touring bands occupy PJ's stage most nights." Music: rock, alternative, hard rock, pop, folk, indie, punk.

PLOUGH AND STARS

912 Massachusetts Ave., Cambridge MA 02139. (617)576-0032. **Website:** www.ploughandstars.com. "The Plough and Stars Irish pub and restaurant in Cambridge has become a favorite of locals and visitors alike. With its warm, cozy atmosphere and great music scene, The Plough has become a staple of the Cambridge community. There is live music nearly every night." Music: alternative, pop, rock, indie, psychedelic, acoustic, folk.

POSITIVE PIE

22 State St., Montpelier VT 05602. (802)229-0453. **E-mail:** music@positivepie.com. **Website:** www.positivepie.com. Music: hip-hop, pop, R&B.

THE POUR HOUSE

1977 Maybank Hwy., Charleston SC 29412. (843)571-4343. **E-mail:** alexharrispoho@gmail.com. **Website:** www.charlestonpourhouse.com. **Contact:** Alex Harris, owner/booking. Music: bluegrass, classic rock, indie, rock, funk, folk, country.

THE RAVE/EAGLES CLUB

2401 W. Wisconsin Ave., Milwaukee WI 53233. (414)342-7283. **E-mail:** perform@therave.com. **Website:** www.therave.com/main.asp. "The Rave/Eagles

Club is a multi-room entertainment complex. Bands like Pearl Jam, Dave Matthews Band, and Creed all played their first gig at The Rave on The Rave Bar stage. Music: rock, alternative, pop, indie, hip-hop, funk, metal.

RECORD BAR

1520 Grand Blvd., Kansas City MO 64108. (816)753-5207. **Website:** www.therecordbar.com. "We strive to provide our guests with diverse live entertainment, special events, and gourmet food in a comfortable atmosphere. You'll see the best of the Kansas City music scene, as well as nationally known touring artists." Music: rock, punk, indie, jazz, swing, folk, pop, alternative.

TIPS Book your band through the online submission form: www.therecordbar.com/booking.

THE REDMOOR

3817 Linwood Ave., Cincinnati OH 45208. (513)871-6789. **Website:** www.theredmoor.com. "Some venues demand performance. In an intimate, acoustically engineered atmosphere, musicians connect with their audiences with distinctive energy. From blue notes to chords that swing, live music lives here."

THE RED ROOM AT CAFE 939

939 Boylston St., Boston MA 02115. **E-mail:** 939booking@berklee.edu. **Website:** www.berklee.edu/redroom-cafe-939. "Cafe 939 showcases Berklee's emerging student performers and local Boston artists, as well as national acts seeking a more intimate, personal space in which to connect with their fans. The venue is open to the general public and aims to attract musicians and music fans from all walks of life." Music: rock, jazz, folk, Americana, bluegrass, hip-hop, electronica, pop, indie.

RED SQUARE

136 Church St., Burlington VT 05401. (802)859-8909. **E-mail:** info@redsquarevt.com. **E-mail:** booking@redsquarevt.com. **Website:** www.redsquarevt.com. Music: jazz, blues, rock, reggae.

REVOLUTION CAFE & BAR

211 B S. Main St., Bryan TX 77806. (979)823-4044. **Website:** www.facebook.com/revolutionbcs. Revolution is the alternative to most bars in Bryan/College Station, welcoming everything involving culture and most things counterculture. Revolution takes pride in consistently booking the highest-quality music that you will hear in the area. Revolution Cafe and Bar specializes in jazz, funk, and reggae. It features a full bar, premium coffees, gourmet paninis, and a large outdoor patio.

RHYTHM & BREWS

2308 4th St., Tuscaloosa AL 35401. (205)750-2992. **Website:** www.rhythmnbrews.com. "Rhythm & Brews first opened in Tuscaloosa, Alabama. The club has the reputation of being the premier location for the best live bands in the region. From dance music to performances by Nashville recording artists, the music you find at Rhythm & Brews will please all. We are committed to bringing you a fun and friendly atmosphere by offering a wide variety of drinks, great service, and great entertainment." Music: pop, rock, country, blues.

RICK'S BAR

2721 Main Ave., Fargo ND 58103. (701)232-8356. **Fax:** (701)232-1095. **E-mail:** meghanc@ricks-bar.com. **Website:** www.ricks-bar.com. **Contact:** Meghan Carik. Music: rock, metal, alternative.

ROCK ISLAND LIVE

101 N. Rock Island, Wichita KS 67202. **E-mail:** rockislandlivemusic@gmail.com. **E-mail:** JaredParson@yahoo.com. **Website:** rockislandlive.tumblr.com. "Rock Island Live is a nationally recognized music venue in historic old town." Music: rock, alternative, pop, indie, dance.

ROCKWOOD MUSIC HALL

196 Allen St., New York NY 10002. (212)477-4155. **E-mail:** info@rockwoodmusichall.com. **Website:** www.rockwoodmusichall.com. "Those interested in booking should send an e-mail with links to their Web pages, official and social, audio and video. Do not include attachments, only links. Each submission is reviewed, and responses are sent if/when there is an opening."

SAINT VITUS BAR

1120 Manhattan Ave., Brooklyn NY 11222. **E-mail:** saintvitusbar@gmail.com. **E-mail:** bookingsaintvitusbar@gmail.com. **Website:** www.saintvitusbar.com. "Saint Vitus, a gothic-themed bar in Greenpoint, Brooklyn, named after a Black Sabbath song, is actually a welcoming spot for downing cheap beers and listening to Pantera."

SAM BONDS GARAGE

407 Blair, Eugene OR 97402. (541)431-6603. **E-mail:** booking@sambonds.com. **Website:** www.sambonds.com. "Since in 1995, we've strived to represent the

uniqueness of the neighborhood with a warm, laid-back atmosphere, always changing local and regional microbrew selection, a full bar, quality vittles, and, of course, one of the West Coast's best places to see diverse local, regional, and worldly entertainment." Music: bluegrass, rock, Irish jam, funk, alternative, folk, Americana.

SANTA FE SOL

37 Fire Place, Santa Fe NM 87508. **Website:** www.sol-santafelive.com. Music: rock, Mexicana, Latin, alternative.

SCHUBAS TAVERN

3159 N. Southport Ave., Chicago IL 60657. (773)525-2508. **Fax:** (773)525-4573. **E-mail:** demos@schubas.com. **Website:** www.schubas.com. **Contact:** Matt Rucins, talent buyer; Sam Andolsen, production manager. Schubas presents a diverse lineup of live music 7 nights a week, from honky tonk to indie rock, from Americana to jazz, from pop to country.

○   The building is a brick and masonry neo-Gothic neighborhood landmark built in 1903.

TIPS "Have a confirmed show? Use the Media Listl link on the website to help better promote your show. Advance your show with our Production Manager, Sam Andolsen. Send any promotional materials (posters, CDs, bios, photos) to Jud Eakin."

SHANK HALL

1434 N. Farwell Ave., Milwaukee WI 53202. (414)276-7288. **E-mail:** shank@wi.rr.com. **Website:** www.shankhall.com. **Contact:** Peter Jest. Music: indie, rock, alternative, Americana, pop, folk, bluegrass.

THE SHED

7501 Hwy 57, Ocean Springs MS 39565. (228)875-8577. **E-mail:** contact@theshedbbq.com; booking@theshedbbq.com. **Website:** theshedbbq.com. Music: blues, folk, country, bluegrass, rock, alternative.

SILVER DOLLAR

478 King St., Charleston SC 29403. (843)722-7223. **Website:** www.charlestoncocktail.com/silverdollar.html. Music: rock, pop, dance, hip-hop, R&B, funk.

THE SLOWDOWN

729 N. 14th St., Omaha NE 68102. (402)345-7569. **Website:** www.theslowdown.com. Music: rock, indie, alternative, psychedelic, punk, folk, pop.

TIPS "Send us a demo of your music (CD, vinyl, or tape is fine; we have all sorts of players). Your pack-age should contain pertinent information about your band: contact name/number, where you have played, and whatever else you think we should know." Accepts mail or drop-off submissions.

THE SMILING MOOSE

1306 E. Carson St., Pittsburgh PA 15203. (412)431-4668. **Website:** www.smiling-moose.com. Music: rock, alt-country, indie, country, acoustic, pop, garbage, funk, hip-hop, metal.

TIPS Booking via online submissions form: www.smiling-moose.com/contact/index.php#.

SMITH'S OLDE BAR

1578 Piedmont Ave. NE, Atlanta GA 30307. (404)875-1522. **E-mail:** seanmcphrsn@yahoo.com; office@nolenreevesmusic.com. **Website:** www.smithsoldebar.com. **Contact:** Sean McPherson, talent buyer; Brittany Burdett, assistant talent buyer. "Smith's Olde Bar is an Atlanta institution, offering some of the best music to be found anywhere in the city. Our atmosphere is very relaxed, and you can find something good to eat and something fun to do almost every night." Music: rock, indie, punk, hip-hop, alternative, garage, bluegrass, reggae, jazz, funk.

THE SOUTHGATE HOUSE REVIVAL

111 E. 6th St., Newport KY 41071. (859)431-2201. **E-mail:** sghbooking@gmail.com. **Website:** www.southgatehouse.com. **Contact:** Morrella. "The Southgate House Revival is a three-in-one music venue, with the Sanctuary, the Revival Room, and the Lounge serving audiences from 85-500. Located in a renovated historic church, the venue presents an eclectic lineup of independent music (and other events) up to 7 nights a week."

THE SPACE

295 Treadwell St., New Haven CT 06514. (203)288-6400. **E-mail:** spacebooking@gmail.com. **Website:** www.thespacect.com. **Contact:** Nicholas Firine, promoter and talent buyer. "The Space (since 2003) exists to build a safe, positive community for people of all ages through music and the arts. Physically, we are a listening room venue located in an unlikely industrial park in a sleepy suburb of New Haven." Music: alternative, rock, blues, Latin, folk, pop, indie, dance, hip-hop, Americana.

THE SPANISH MOON

1109 Highland Rd., Baton Rouge LA 70802. (225)383-6666. **E-mail:** moonbooking@hotmail.com. **Website:**

www.thespanishmoon.com. **Contact:** Aaron Scruggs, talent buyer/booking manager. Music: rock, pop, dubstep, indie, alternative, Americana.

THE SPOT UNDERGROUND

180 Pine St., 1st Floor, Providence RI 02903. (401)383-7133. **E-mail:** 725@thespotprovidence.com. **E-mail:** thespotunderground@gmail.com. **Website:** www.thespotunderground.com. Music: rock, indie, world, hip-hop, R&B, funk, dance, jam, pop.

THE STARRY PLOUGH

3101 Shattuck Ave., Berkeley CA 94705. (510)841-0188. **E-mail:** starryploughbooking@yahoo.com. **Website:** www.thestarryplough.com. "The Starry Plough is a full-service restaurant, pub and nightclub that has been a staple of the East Bay scene since 1973. With deep roots as an Irish revolutionary watering hole, the history of protest runs as deep today as it did when we opened 4 decades ago. Shows are booked 2-3 months in advance. Please review the calendar before requesting a date that falls on a Friday-Saturday night or Sunday matinee. Sunday-Thursday nights are regular weekly events and are never available. Genres include: Celtic, Americana, rock 'n' roll, Balkan, garage, indie rock, bluegrass, soul, old-time, post punk, avant-rock, ska, psychedelic, shoegaze, folk, country, Latin, blues, power-pop, gypsy jazz and a myriad of variations on these."

STRANGE BREW TAVERN

88 Market St., Manchester NH 03101. (603)666-4292. **E-mail:** strangebrewtavern@gmail.com. **Website:** strangebrewtavern.net. Music: blues, acoustic, rock, alternative.

SULLY'S PUB

2071 Park St., Hartford CT 06106. (860)231-8881. **E-mail:** sully@sullyspub.com; rob@sullyspub.com. **Website:** www.sullyspub.com. **Contact:** Darrel "Sully" Sullivan, owner; Rob Salter, manager. "This mantra is an important one in any community: Original music must be supported on every level of society. Sully's is proud to stand on the front lines of musical evolution, blazing a trail with the very musicians composing and performing." Music: pop, rock, alternative, indie.

SWEETWATER MUSIC HALL

19 Corte Madera Ave., Mill Valley CA 94941. (415)388-3850. **E-mail:** info@swmh.com. **E-mail:** booking@swmh.com. **Website:** www.sweetwatermusichall.com. "The much-anticipated Sweetwater Music Hall—a community gathering place and live-music venue dedicated to bringing back the Sweetwater's musical legacy to Mill Valley—opened in late January 2012. The opening of Sweetwater Music Hall marked a rebirth of the landmark roots music venue and Bay Area treasure originally opened on November 17, 1972. The Sweetwater Music Hall is a state-of-the-art nightclub and café that not only presents nationally recognized, top-quality entertainment but also provides a comfortable home venue for local and emerging talent to perform and experiment."

TIN ROOF

160 Freedom Way, Suite 150, Cincinnati OH 45202. (513)381-2176. **E-mail:** infocincinnati@tinroofbars.com. **Website:** www.tinroofbars.com/home/cincinnati. Tin Roof is a live-music restaurant and bar with a laid-back atmosphere.

TOAD

1912 Massachusetts Ave., Cambridge MA 02140. (617)497-4950. **E-mail:** info@toadcambridge.com. **E-mail:** bookagig@toadcambridge.com. **Website:** www.toadcambridge.com. **Contact:** Billy Beard. "Toad is a small neighborhood bar and music club featuring live music 7 nights a week." Music: folk, alternative, rock, acoustic, Americana, indie.

TRACTOR TAVERN

5213 Ballard Ave. NW, Seattle WA 98107. (206)789-3599. **E-mail:** booking@tractortavern.com. **Website:** www.tractortavern.com. "The Tractor hosts live shows 5-7 nights a week featuring a wide range of local and national acts. Check out all of your favorite rock, alternative country, rockabilly, groove and psychedelia, Celtic, cajun and zydeco, folk, blues, jazz, and bluegrass acts, to name a few."

THE TREE BAR

887 Chambers Rd., Columbus OH 43212. (614)725-0955. **E-mail:** booking@treebarcolumbus.com. **Website:** treebarcolumbus.com. Music: rock, classic rock, alternative, indie, Americana, folk, pop.

TIPS "You must include in your e-mail: the date you're interested in, the lineup you propose for the night, and links to your music."

TRIPLE ROCK SOCIAL CLUB

629 Cedar Ave., Minneapolis MN 55454. (612)333-7399. **Fax:** (612)333-7703. **E-mail:** booking.triplerock@gmail.com. **Website:** www.triplerocksocialclub.com. Estab. 2003. The Triple Rock has become

one of the big destination punk, indie rock, and underground hip-hop clubs in the Twin Cities—a good-sized music venue with a capacity of 400. The Triple Rock is owned and operated by the members of punk rock band Dillinger Four. Music: acoustic, alternative, blues, classic rock, country, cover band, electronic/dance/DJ, folk, funk, Goth, hip-hop/rap, jam band, metal, pop, punk, reggae, rock, singer/songwriter, soul, and urban/R&B.

TROCADERO

1003 Arch St., Philadelphia PA 19107. (215)922-6888. **E-mail:** trocadero@thetroc.com. **Website:** www.thetroc.com. Music: pop, indie, Americana, alternative, rock, hip-hop, rap, folk, bluegrass.

TROUBADOUR

9081 Santa Monica Blvd., West Hollywood CA 90069. **Website:** www.troubadour.com. Estab. 1958. "The Troubadour is rich with musical history. Elton John, Billy Joel, James Taylor, and Joni Mitchell have all made debuts at the Troubadour. The legendary musical lineups at the Troubadour continue until today. The Troubadour schedule features a wide arrangement of musical performances. Nada Surf, Bob Schneider, The Morning Benders, and Manchester Orchestra were some of the performances featured on the Troubadour schedule for 2010." Music: pop, indie, alternative, rock, hip-hop, Americana, jazz, blues.

To contact, use form online at www.troubadour.com/contact-booking. See also lighting plot, stage layout, technical rider links at same site.

TURF CLUB

1601 University Ave., St. Paul MN 55104. (651)647-0486. **E-mail:** booking@turfclub.net. **Website:** www.turfclub.net. "Turf Club is a perfect setting for rock. The long, prominent bar scales one side of the narrow interior, the stage is at the back, and the entire space is enveloped in dark woods. The music is loud, the crowd is devoted." Music: rock, indie, alternative, punk, classic rock.

UNDERGROUND 119

119 S. President St., Jackson MS 39201. (601)352-2322. **E-mail:** underground119music@gmail.com. **Website:** www.underground119.com. Music: blues, jazz, bluegrass, country, funk, rock, alternative.

UNION POOL

484 Union Ave., Brooklyn NY 11211. **E-mail:** booking@union-pool.com. **Website:** www.union-pool.com. Music: rock, indie, alternative, Americana.
TIPS Venue guidelines and tech specs on website.

UPSTATE CONCERT HALL

1208 NY-146, Clifton Park NY 12065. (518)371-0012. **E-mail:** dave@upstateconcerthall.com. **Website:** www.upstateconcerthall.com.
TIPS To book your own show, please e-mail dave@upstateconcerthall.com. To get booked on an existing bill, please e-mail: tetoll@nycap.rr.com.

URBAN LOUNGE

241 S. 500 E., Salt Lake City UT 84102. (801)746-0557. **E-mail:** will@sartainandsaunders.com. **Website:** www.theurbanloungeslc.com. **Contact:** Will Sartain. "The Urban Lounge has been a staple in the Salt Lake City, Utah, music community for more than a decade. What started off as a local live-music bar has flourished into a regular stop for headlining national acts, hosting a variety of music from independent artists of all genres, including rock, hip-hop, folk, electronic, reggae, and experimental. Nearly every night of the week you can find a fresh take on a familiar scene."

VAUDEVILLE MEWS

212 4th St., Des Moines IA 50309. **E-mail:** booking@vaudevillemews.com. **Website:** www.vaudevillemews.com. Music: folk, pop, blues, rock, alternative, Americana, hip-hop, soul, rap, country, hard rock, electronica.

THE VISULITE THEATRE

1615 Elizabeth Ave., Charlotte NC 28204. (704)358-9200. **Fax:** (704)358-9299. **E-mail:** boxoffice@visulite.com. **Website:** www.visulite.com. Music: rock, pop, funk, Americana, indie, blues, folk.

THE WAY STATION

683 Washington Ave., Brooklyn NY 11238. (347)627-4949. **E-mail:** bookingtws@gmail.com. **Website:** waystationbk.blogspot.com. **Contact:** Andy Heidel, proprietor. "For booking, send an e-mail with a short introduction and a link to hear your music or watch videos. Looking for 1 set of 40-45 minutes. Books 3 months in advance. If your band has already played at The Way Station, contact gailaheidel@yahoo.com with 2-3 dates to rebook."

THE WEBSTER UNDERGROUND

31 Webster St., Hartford CT 06114. (860)246-8001. E-mail: booking@webstertheater.com. Website: www.webstertheater.com. "The Main Theater is a great room for sizeable events or concerts. Book now and share the same stage that launched careers such as Staind, Marilyn Manson, Sevendust, Incubus, 311, Jay Z, Method Man, Godsmack, Fall Out Boy, and many more. The Underground is our intimate room equipped for shows and more—perfect for national, regional, and locals that are looking to create their own show in a historic room." Music: rock, reggae, punk, alternative, pop, soul, indie, funk, hard rock.

WHISKY A GO-GO

8901 W. Sunset Blvd., West Hollywood CA 90069. (310)652-4202, ext. 11; (310)652-4202, ext. 17. E-mail: mproductionsrocks@gmail.com; erika@whiskyagogo.com. Website: www.whiskyagogo.com. Contact: Luke Iblings and Jake Perry, national talent buyers; Erika Gimenes, booking agent. "As long as there has been a Los Angeles rock scene, there has been the Whisky A Go-Go. An anchor on the Sunset Strip since its opening in 1964, the Whisky A Go-Go has played host to rock 'n' roll's most important bands, from the Doors, Janis Joplin, and Led Zeppelin to today's up-and-coming new artists." Music: hip-hop, rock, punk, metal, alternative, reggae, pop, classic rock, indie, Americana.

WHITE WATER TAVERN

2500 W. 7th St., Little Rock AR 72205. E-mail: whitewaterbooking@gmail.com. Website: www.whitewatertavern.com. Music: rock, country, alternative, Americana, punk.

THE WILTERN

3790 Wilshire Blvd., Los Angeles CA 90010. (213)388-1400. Website: www.thewiltern.net. Music: rock, pop.

WOLF PEN CREEK AMPHITHEATER

1015 Colgate Dr., College Station TX 77840. (979)764-3486. E-mail: parks@cstx.gov. Website: cstx.gov/index.aspx?page=1414. Estab. 1993. The Wolf Pen Creek Amphitheater is located in the heart of Texas in College Station, home of Texas A&M University. Serving the southeast Texas market area, with a local population of approximately 184,000 people, the amphitheater's potential is unlimited with the University enrollment being stable at 47,800-plus students.

WOODLANDS TAVERN

1200 W. 3rd Ave., Columbus OH 43212. (614)299-4987. Website: woodlandstavern.com. Music: bluegrass, acoustic, psychedelic, reggae, jam, funk, rock, classic rock, jazz, blues.

TIPS Submit booking inquiries through online submission form: woodlandstavern.com/find-contact-us.

WORMY DOG SALOON

311 E. Sheridan Ave., Oklahoma City OK 73104. (405)601-6276. E-mail: booking@wormydog.com. Website: www.wormydog.com. Music: country, bluegrass, rock, Americana, rockabilly, folk.

YOUNG AVENUE DELI

2119 Young Ave., Memphis TN 38104. (901)278-0034; (901)274-7080. E-mail: youngave@youngavenuedeli.com. Website: www.youngavenuedeli.com. Music: rock, country, pop, folk.

TIPS Booking via online submissions form: www.youngavenuedeli.com/contact.

STATE & PROVINCIAL GRANTS

//

Arts councils in the U.S. and Canada provide assistance to artists (including songwriters) in the form of fellowships or grants. These grants can be substantial and confer prestige upon recipients; however, **only state or province residents are eligible**. Because deadlines and available support vary annually, query first or check websites for updated guidelines.

UNITED STATES ARTS AGENCIES

ALABAMA STATE COUNCIL ON THE ARTS, 201 Monroe St., Suite 110, Montgomery AL 36104. (334)242-4076. Website: www.arts.state.al.us.

ALASKA STATE COUNCIL ON THE ARTS, 161 Klevin St., Suite 102, Anchorage AK 99508-1506. (907)269-6610 or (888)278-7424. E-mail: aksca.info@alaska.gov. Website: www.eed.state.ak.us/aksca.

ARIZONA COMMISSION ON THE ARTS, 417 W. Roosevelt St., Phoenix AZ 85003-1326. (602)771-6501. E-mail: info@azarts.gov. Website: www.azarts.gov.

ARKANSAS ARTS COUNCIL, 323 Center St., Suite 1500, Little Rock AR 72201-2606. (501)324-9766. Website: www.arkansasarts.org.

CALIFORNIA ARTS COUNCIL, 1300 I St., Suite 930, Sacramento CA 95814. (916)322-6555 or (800)201-6201. E-mail: info@arts.ca.gov. Website: www.cac.ca.gov.

CONNECTICUT OFFICE OF CULTURE & TOURISM, Office of the Arts, One Constitution Plaza, 2nd Floor, Hartford CT 06103. (860)256-2800. Website: www.cultureandtourism.org.

COLORADO CREATIVE INDUSTRIES, 1625 Broadway, Suite 2700, Denver CO 80202. (303)892-3840. E-mail: online form. Website: www.coloradocreativeindustries.org.

DELAWARE DIVISION OF THE ARTS, Carvel State Office Bldg., 4th Floor, 820 N. French St., Wilmington DE 19801. (302)577-8278. E-mail: delarts@state.de.us. Website: www.artsdel. org.

DC COMMISSION ON THE ARTS AND HUMANITIES, 200 I St., SE, Washington, DC 20003. (202)724-5613. E-mail: cah@dc.gov. Website: www.dcarts.dc.gov.

FLORIDA DIVISION OF CULTURAL AFFAIRS, R.A. Gray Building, 500 S. Bronough St., Tallahassee FL 32399. (850)245-6470. E-mail: webmaster@dos.myflorida.com. Website: www.florida-arts.org.

GEORGIA COUNCIL FOR THE ARTS, Technology Square, 75 Fifth St., NW, Suite 1200, Atlanta GA 30308. E-mail: gaarts@gaarts.org. Website: www.gaarts.org.

GUAM COUNCIL ON THE ARTS & HUMANITIES AGENCY, P.O. Box 2950, Hagatna GU 96932. (671)300-1204. Website: www.guamcaha.org.

HAWAII STATE FOUNDATION ON CULTURE AND THE ARTS, 250 S. Hotel St., 2nd Floor, Honolulu HI 96813. (808)586-0300. Website: sfca.hawaii.gov.

IDAHO COMMISSION ON THE ARTS, P.O. Box 83720, Boise ID 83720-0008. (208)334-2119 or (800)278-3863. E-mail: online form. Website: www.arts.idaho.gov.

ILLINOIS ARTS COUNCIL AGENCY, James R. Thompson Center, 100 W. Randolph, Suite 10-500, Chicago IL 60601. (312)814-6750 or (800)237-6994. E-mail: iac.info@illinois.gov. Website: www.arts.illinois.gov.

INDIANA ARTS COMMISSION, 100 N. Senate Ave., Room N505, Indianapolis IN 46204. (317)232-1268. E-mail: indianaartscommission@iac.in.gov. Website: www.in.gov/arts.

IOWA ARTS COUNCIL, 600 E. Locust St., Des Moines IA 50319-0290. (515)281-5111. Website: www.iowaartscouncil.org.

KANSAS CITY - ARTSKC - REGIONAL ARTS COUNCIL, 106 Southwest Blvd., Kansas City MO 64108. (816)221-1777. E-mail: theartscouncil@artskc.orgWebsite: www.artskc.org.

KENTUCKY ARTS COUNCIL, 21st Floor, Capital Plaza Tower, 500 Mero St., Frankfort KY 40601-1987. (502)564-3757 or (888)833-2787. Website: www.artscouncil.ky.gov.

LOUISIANA DIVISION OF THE ARTS, P.O. Box 44247, Baton Rouge LA 70804-4247. (225)342-8180. E-mail: arts@crt.la.gov. Website: www.crt.state.la.us/cultural-development/arts/.

MAINE ARTS COMMISSION, 193 State St., 25 State House Station, Augusta ME 04333-0025. (207)287-2724 or (877)887-3878. E-mail: mainearts.info@maine.gov. Website: www.mainearts.maine.gov.

MARYLAND STATE ARTS COUNCIL, 175 W. Ostend St., Suite E, Baltimore MD 21230. (410)767-6555 or (800)735-2258. Website: www.msac.org.

MASSACHUSETTS CULTURAL COUNCIL, 10 St. James Ave., 3rd Floor, Boston MA 02116. (617)858-2700 or (800)232-0960. Website: www.massculturalcouncil.org.

MICHIGAN COUNCIL FOR ARTS AND CULTURAL AFFAIRS, Michigan Economic Development Corp., 300 N. Washington Square, Lansing MI 48913. (517)241-4011 Website: www.michiganbusiness.org/community/council-arts-cultural-affairs.

MINNESOTA STATE ARTS BOARD, Park Square Court, Suite 200, 400 Sibley St., St. Paul MN 55101-1928. (651)215-1600 or (800)866-2787. E-mail: msab@arts.state.mn.us. Website: www.arts.state.mn.us.

MISSISSIPPI ARTS COMMISSION, 501 N. West St., Suite 1101A, Woolfolk Bldg., Jackson MS 39201. (601)359-6030. Website: www.arts.state.ms.us.

MISSOURI ARTS COUNCIL, 815 Olive St., Suite 16, St. Louis MO 63101-1503. (314)340-6845 or (866)407-4752. E-mail: moarts@ded.mo.gov. Website: www.missouriartscouncil.org.

MONTANA ARTS COUNCIL, P.O. Box 202201, Helena MT 59620-2201. (406)444-6430. E-mail: mac@mt.gov. Website: www.art.mt.gov.

NATIONAL ASSEMBLY OF STATE ARTS AGENCIES, 1200 18th St. NW, Suite 1100, Washington, DC 20036. (202)347-6352. E-mail: nasaa@nasaa-arts.org. Website: www.nasaa-arts.org.

THE NATIONAL MUSEUM OF PUERTO RICAN ARTS & CULTURE, 3015 W. Division St., Chicago IL 60622. (773)486-8345. E-mail: info@NMPRAC.org. Website: www.iprac.org.

NEBRASKA ARTS COUNCIL, 1004 Farnam St., Omaha NE 68102. (402)595-2122 or (800)341-4067. E-mail: nac.info@nebraska.gov. Website: www.nebraskaartscouncil.org.

NEVADA ARTS COUNCIL, 716 N. Carson St., Suite A, Carson City NV 89701. (775)687-6680. Website: www.nac.nevadaculture.org.

NEW HAMPSHIRE STATE COUNCIL ON THE ARTS, 19 Pillsbury St., 1st Floor, Concord NH 03301. (603)271-2789 or (800)735-2964. Website: www.nh.gov/nharts.

NEW JERSEY STATE COUNCIL ON THE ARTS, P.O. Box 306, Trenton NJ 08625-0306. (609)292-6130. Website: www.artscouncil.nj.gov.

NEW MEXICO ARTS, Bataan Memorial Bldg., 407 Galisteo St., Suite 270, Santa Fe NM 87501. (505)827-6490 or (800)879-4278. Website: www.nmarts.org.

NEW YORK STATE COUNCIL ON THE ARTS, 300 Park Ave. S., 10th Floor, New York NY 10010. (212)459-8800 or (800)510-0021. Website: www.nysca.org.

NORTH CAROLINA ARTS COUNCIL, MSC #4632, Depart. of Cultural Resources, Raleigh NC 27699-4632. (919)807-6500. E-mail: ncarts@ncdcr.gov. Website: www.ncarts.org.

NORTH DAKOTA COUNCIL ON THE ARTS, 1600 E. Century Ave., Suite 6, Bismarck ND 58503-0649. (701)328-7590. E-mail: comserv@nd.gov. Website: www.nd.gov/arts.

OHIO ARTS COUNCIL, 30 E. Broad St., 33rd Floor, Columbus OH 43215-3414. (614)466-2613. Website: www.oac.state.oh.us.

OKLAHOMA ARTS COUNCIL, P.O. Box 52001-2001, Oklahoma City, OK 73152-2001. (405)521-2931. E-mail: okarts@arts.ok.gov. Website: www.arts.ok.gov.

OREGON ARTS COMMISSION, 775 Summer St. NE, Suite 200, Salem OR 97301-1280. (503)986-0082. E-mail: oregon.artscomm@state.or.us. Website: www.oregonartscommission.org.

PENNSYLVANIA COUNCIL ON THE ARTS, 216 Finance Bldg., Commonwealth & North Streets, Harrisburg PA 17120. (717)787-6883. E-mail: RA-arts@pa.gov Website: www.arts.pa.gov.

RHODE ISLAND STATE COUNCIL ON THE ARTS, One Capitol Hill, 3rd Floor, Providence RI 02908. (401)222-3880. Website: www.arts.ri.gov.

SOUTH CAROLINA ARTS COMMISSION, 1026 Sumter St., Suite 200, Columbia SC 29201-3746. (803)734-8696. Website: www.southcarolinaarts.com.

SOUTH DAKOTA ARTS COUNCIL, 711 E. Wells Ave., Pierre SD 57501. (800)952-3625. E-mail: sdac@state.sd.us. Website: www.artscouncil.sd.gov.

TENNESSEE ARTS COMMISSION, 401 Charlotte Ave., Nashville TN 37243. (615)741-6395. Website: www.tn.gov/arts.

TEXAS COMMISSION ON THE ARTS, P.O. Box 13406, Austin, TX 78711-3406. (512)463-5535 or (512)475-3327. E-mail: front.desk@arts.texas.gov. Website: www.arts.texas.gov.

UTAH DIVISION OF ARTS & MUSEUMS, 617 E. South Temple, Salt Lake City UT 84102. (801)236-7555. Website: www.heritage.utah.gov/utah-division-of-arts-museums.

VERMONT ARTS COUNCIL, 136 State St., Montpelier VT 05633-6001. (802)828-3291. E-mail: info@vermontartscouncil.org. Website: www.vermontartscouncil.org.

VIRGIN ISLANDS COUNCIL ON THE ARTS, 5070 Norre Gade, Suite 1, St. Thomas VI 00802-6762. (340)774-5984. Website: www.vicouncilonarts.org.

VIRGINIA COMMISSION FOR THE ARTS, 1001 E. Broad St., Suite 330, Richmond VA 23219. (804)225-3132. E-mail: arts@vca.virginia.gov. Website: www.arts.virginia.gov.

WASHINGTON STATE ARTS COMMISSION-ARTSWA, P.O. Box 42675, Olympia WA 98504-2675. (360)753-3860. E-mail: online form. Website: www.arts.wa.gov.

WEST VIRGINIA COMMISSION ON THE ARTS, The Culture Center, Capitol Complex, 1900 Kanawha Blvd. E., Charleston WV 25305-0300. (304)558-0220 or (304)558-3562. Website: www.wvculture.org/arts.

WISCONSIN ARTS BOARD, P.O. Box 8690, Madison WI 53708-8690. (608)266-0190. E-mail: artsboard@wisconsin.gov. Website: www.artsboard.wisconsin.gov.

WYOMING ARTS COUNCIL, 2301 Central Ave., Barrett Bldg., 2nd Floor, Cheyenne WV 82002. (307)777-7742. Website: http://wyoarts.state.wy.us.

CANADIAN PROVINCIAL ARTS AGENCIES

ALBERTA FOUNDATION FOR THE ARTS, 10708-105 Ave., Edmonton, AB T5H 0A1. (780)427-9968. E-mail: online form. Website: www.affta.ab.ca.

ARTSNB, 634 Queen St., 2nd Floor, Fredericton, NB E3B 1C3. (506)444-4444 or (866)460-2787. Website: www.artsnb.ca.

BRITISH COLUMBIA ARTS COUNCIL, P.O. Box 9819, Stn. Prov. Govt., Victoria, BC V8W 9W3. (250)356-1718. E-mail: bcartscouncil@gov.bc.ca. Website: www.bcartscouncil.ca.

CANADA COUNCIL FOR THE ARTS, 150 Elgin St., P.O. Box 1047, Ottawa, ON K1P 5V8. (613)566-4414 or (800)263-5588. E-mail: info@canadacouncil.ca. Website: www.canadacouncil.ca.

MANITOBA ARTS COUNCIL, 525-93 Lombard Ave., Winnipeg, MB R3B 3B1. (204)945-2237 or (866)994-2787. E-mail: info@artscouncil.mb.ca. Website: www.artscouncil.mb.ca.

NEWFOUNDLAND AND LABRADOR ARTS COUNCIL, P.O. Box 98, St. John's, NL A1C 5H5. (709)726-2212 or (866)726-2212. Website: www.nlac.ca.

NOVA SCOTIA DEPARTMENT OF COMMUNITIES, CULTURE AND HERITAGE, 1741 Brunswick St., 3rd Floor, P.O. Box 456, STN Central, Halifax, NS B3J 2R5. (902)424-2170. E-mail: cch@novascotia.ca. Website: https://cch.novascotia.ca.

ONTARIO ARTS COUNCIL, 121 Bloor St. E., 7th Floor, Toronto, ON M4W 3M5. (416)969-7429 or (800)387-0058, ext. 7429. E-mail: jlambrakos@arts.on.ca. Website: www.arts.on.ca.

THE PRINCE EDWARD ISLAND COUNCIL OF THE ARTS, 115 Richmond St., Charlottetown, PE C1A 1H7. (888)734-2784. Website: www.peiartscouncil.com.

QUÉBEC COUNCIL FOR ARTS & LITERATURE, 79 boul. René-Lévesque Est, 3e étage, Québec, QC G1R 5N5. (418)643-1707 or (800)608-3350 (in Québec). E-mail: info@calq.gouv.qc.ca. Website: www.calq. gouv.qc.ca.

SASKATCHEWAN ARTS BOARD, 1355 Broad St., Regina, SK S4R 7V1. (306)787-4056 or (800)667-7526 (in Saskatchewan). E-mail: info@saskartsboard.ca. Website: www.artsboard.sk.ca.

YUKON ARTS FUND, Cultural Services Branch, Dept. of Tourism and Culture, Government of Yukon, P.O. Box 2703 (L-3), Whitehorse, YT Y1A 2C6. (867)667-3535 or (800)661-0408, ext. 3535. E-mail: artsfund@gov.yk.ca. Website: www.tc.gov.yk.ca/af.

PUBLICATIONS OF INTEREST

Knowledge about the music industry is essential for both creative and business success, and staying informed requires keeping up with constantly changing information. Updates on the evolving trends in the music business are available to you in the form of music magazines, music trade papers, and books. There is a publication aimed at almost every type of musician, songwriter, and music fan, from the most technical knowledge of amplification systems to gossip about your favorite singer. These publications can enlighten and inspire you, and provide information vital in helping you become a more well-rounded, educated, and, ultimately, successful musical artist.

What follows is a cross-section of all types of magazines and books you may find interesting. From songwriters' newsletters and glossy music magazines to tip sheets and how-to books, there should be something listed here that you'll enjoy and benefit from.

PERIODICALS

ALTERNATIVE PRESS, 1305 W. 80th St., Suite 214, Cleveland OH 44102-3045. (216)631-1510. E-mail: editorial@altpress.com. Website: http://altpress.com. *Reviews, news, and features for alternative and indie music fans.*

AMERICAN SONGWRITER, P.O. Box 90187, Long Beach CA 90809. (888)881-5861. E-mail: info@americansongwriter.com. Website: www.americansong writer.com. *Bimonthly publication for and about songwriters.*

ARTROCKER, 43 Chute House, Stockwell Park Road, Brixton, SW9 0DW. E-mail: info@artrockermagazine.com. Website: http://artrockermagazine.com. *Monthly magazine involved in music promotion and publishing.*

BACKSTAGE (NYC), 45 Main St., Brooklyn NY 11201. (212)725-6367. E-mail: editorial@ backstage.com. Website: www.backstage.com. *Weekly East and West Coast performing-artist trade papers.*

BACKSTAGE (LA), 5700 Wilshire Blvd., Los Angeles CA 90036. (323)525-2358. Website: www.backstage.com.

BASS PLAYER, 28 E. 28th St., 12th Floor, New York NY 10016. (212)378-0400. Website: www.bassplayer.com. *Monthly magazine for bass players with lessons, interviews, articles, and transcriptions.*

BILLBOARD, P.O. Box 15, Congers NY 10920. (800)684-1873. E-mail: subscriptions@billboard.com. Website: www.billboard.com. *Weekly industry trade magazine.*

CANADIAN MUSICIAN, 4056 Dorchester Rd., Suite 202, Niagara Falls, ON L2E 6M9 Canada. (905)374-8878. E-mail: mail@nor.com. Website: www.canadianmusician.com. *Bimonthly publication for amateur and professional Canadian musicians.*

CCM MAGAZINE, 402 BNA Dr., Suite 400, Nashville TN 37217. (800)527-5226. E-mail: online form. Website: www.ccmmagazine.com. *Online magazine focusing on Christian singers and performers.*

CHART ATTACK, 200-41 Britain St., Toronto, ON M5A 1R7 Canada. E-mail: Online form. Website: www.chartattack.com. *Monthly magazine covering the Canadian and international music scenes.*

CMJ NEW MUSIC REPORT, 115 E. 23rd St., 3rd Floor, New York NY 10113. Website: www. cmj.com. *Weekly college radio and alternative music tip sheet.*

COUNTRY LINE MAGAZINE, 9508 Chisholm Trail, Austin TX 78748. (512)292-1113. E-mail: sandra@countrylinemagazine.com. Website: www.countrylinemagazine.com. *Monthly Texas-only country music cowboy and lifestyle magazine.*

ENTERTAINMENT LAW & FINANCE, Website: www.lawjournalnewsletters.com/ljn_entertainment/. *Monthly newsletter covering music industry contracts, lawsuit filings, court rulings, and legislation.*

EXCLAIM!, 849A Bloor St. W., Toronto, ON M6G 1M3 Canada. (416)535-9735. E-mail: exclaim@exclaim.ca. Website: https://exclaim.ca. *Canadian music monthly covering all genres of non mainstream music.*

GAMUT: ONLINE JOURNAL OF THE MUSIC THEORY SOCIETY OF THE MID-ATLANTIC, Website: http://trace.tennessee.edu/gamut. *Peer-reviewed online journal of the Music Theory Society of the Mid-Atlantic. A journal of criticism, commentary, research, and scholarship.*

GUITAR PLAYER, 28 E. 28th St., 12th Floor, New York NY 10016. (212)378-0400. Website: www.guitarplayer.com. *Monthly guitar magazine with transcriptions, columns, and interviews, including occasional articles on songwriting.*

JAZZTIMES, 10801 Margate Rd., Silver Spring MD 20901. (617)315-9155. E-mail: Online form. Website: www.jazztimes.com. *Ten issues/year; magazine covering the American jazz scene.*

MOJO, Bauer Media, Endeavour House, 189 Shaftesbury Ave., London, United Kingdom WC2H 8JG. E-mail: mojo@bauermedia.co.uk. Website: www.mojo4music.com. *Monthly UK maagzine focusing on classic rock acts, as well as emerging rock and indie bands.*

MUSIC CONNECTION MAGAZINE, 3441 Ocean View Blvd., Glendale CA 91208. (818)995-0101. E-mail: Online form. Website: www.musicconnection.com. *Monthy music industry trade publication.*

MUSIC ROW MAGAZINE, 1231 17th Ave. S., Nashville TN 37212. (615)349-2171. E-mail: info@musicrow.com. Website: www.musicrow.com. *Biweekly Nashville industry publication.*

MUSIC WEEK, New Bay Media UK Ltd., c/o Abacus eMedia, 3rd Floor, 10 Furnival St., London EC4A1YH. +44(0) 20 8955 7020. E-mail: musicweek@abacusemedia.com Website: www.musicweek.com. *UK industry publication with music news, data, analysis, and opinions.*

NEW MUSICAL EXPRESS (NME), NME, 8th Floor, Blue Fin Bldg., London, United Kingdom SE1 0SU. Website: www.nme.com. *UK weekly publication of music journalism.*

OFFBEAT MAGAZINE, 421 Frenchman St., Suite 200, New Orleans LA 70116. (504)944-4300. E-mail: offbeat@offbeat.com. Website: www.offbeat.com. *Monthly magazine covering Louisiana music and artists.*

PERFORMER MAGAZINE, P.O. Box 348, Somerville MA 02143. E-mail: editorial@performermag.com. Website: www.performermag.com. *Focuses on independent musicians, those unsigned and on small labels, and their success in a DIY environment.*

THE PERFORMING SONGWRITER, Performing Songwriter Enterprises, LLC, P.O. Box 158989, Nashville TN 37215. E-mail: lydia@performingsongwriter.com. Website: www.performingsongwriter.com. *Bimonthly songwriters' magazine.*

SING OUT!, P.O. Box 5460, Bethlehem PA 18015-0460. (610)865-5366 or (888)sing-out. Fax: (215)895-3052. E-mail: info@singout.org. Website: www.singout.org. *Quarterly folk music magazine.*

SOCAN, 41 Valleybrook Dr., Toronto, ON M3B 2S6 Canada. (416)445-8700. Website: www. socan.ca. *Monthly songwriters' magazine.*

SONG CAST, SongCast, Inc., 2926 State Rd., Suite 111, Cuyahoga Falls OH 44223. E-mail: info@songcastmusic.com. Website: www.songcastmusic.com *Offers assistance selling music through online retail sites like iTunes or Amazon.*

SONGLINK INTERNATIONAL, 23 Belsize Crescent, London NW3 5QY United Kingdom. +44(0)207-794-2540. E-mail: Online form. Website: www.songlink.com. *Ten issues/year; newsletter including details of recording artists looking for songs; contact details for industry sources; also news and features on the music business.*

SOUND ON SOUND, Media House, Trafalgar Way, Bar Hill, Cambridge, CB23 8SQ, United Kingdom. +44(0)1954 789888. Website: www.soundonsound.com. *Monthly music technology magazine with online forum.*

VARIETY, 11175 Santa Monica Blvd., Los Angeles CA 90025. (323)617-9100. E-mail: variety@ pubservice.com. Website: www.variety.com. *Weekly entertainment trade newspaper.*

BOOKS & DIRECTORIES

1000 SONGWRITING IDEAS: MUSIC PRO GUIDES, by Lisa Aschmann, Hal Leonard Corp., P.O. Box 13819, Milwaukee WI 53213. E-mail: Online form. Website: www.halleonard-books.com.

101 SONGWRITING WRONGS & HOW TO RIGHT THEM, by Pat & Pete Luboff, Writer's Digest Books, 10151 Carver Rd., Suite 200, Blue Ash OH 45242. (855)840-5124. Website: www.writersdigestshop.com.

THE A&R REGISTRY, by Ritch Esra, SRS Publishing, 7510 Sunset Blvd., Suite 1041, Los Angeles CA 90046-3400. (800)377-7411 or (800)552-7411. E-mail: musicregistry@com-puserve.com.

THE BILLBOARD GUIDE TO MUSIC PUBLICITY, rev. ed., by Jim Pettigrew, Jr.

BREAKIN' INTO NASHVILLE, by Jennifer Ember Pierce, Madison Books, University Press of America, 4501 Forbes Road, Suite 200, Lanham MD 20706.

CMJ DIRECTORY, 1201 Broadway, Suite 706, New York, NY 10001. Website: www.cmj.com.

THE CRAFT AND BUSINESS OF SONGWRITING, by John Braheny, Writer's Digest Books, 10151 Carver Rd., Suite 200, Blue Ash OH 45242. (855)840-5124. Website: www.writersdi-gestshop.com.

THE CRAFT OF LYRIC WRITING, by Sheila Davis, Writer's Digest Books, 10151 Carver Rd., Suite 200, Blue Ash OH 45242. (855)840-5124. Website: www.writersdigestshop.com.

HOLLYWOOD CREATIVE DIRECTORY. *Lists producers in film and TV.*

THE HOLLYWOOD REPORTER, The Writers Store, 3510 W. Magnolia Blvd., Burbank CA, 91505. (800)272-8927. Website: www.writersstore.com.

HOW TO GET SOMEWHERE IN THE MUSIC BUSINESS FROM NOWHERE WITH NOTHING, by Mary Dawson, CQK Books, CQK Music Group, 2221 Justin Rd., Suite 119-142, Flower Mound TX 75028. (972)317-2760. Website: www.fromnowherewithnothing.com.

HOW TO PROMOTE YOUR MUSIC SUCCESSFULLY ON THE INTERNET, by David Nevue, Midnight Rain Productions. Website: www.rainmusic.com.

HOW TO MAKE IT IN THE NEW MUSIC BUSINESS: LESSONS, TIPS, & INSPIRATIONS FROM MUSIC'S BIGGEST AND BEST, by Robert Wolff, Billboard Books, 1745 Broadway, New York NY 10019. Website: www.billboard.com.

HOW YOU CAN BREAK INTO THE MUSIC BUSINESS: WITHOUT BREAKING YOUR HEART, YOUR DREAM, OR YOUR BANK ACCOUNT, by Marty Garrett, Lonesome Wind Corp.

LOUISIANA MUSIC DIRECTORY, OffBeat, Inc., 421 Frenchmen St., Suite 200, New Orleans LA 70116. (504)944-4300. Website: www.louisianamusicdirectory.com.

LYDIAN CHROMATIC CONCEPT OF TONAL ORGANIZATION, VOLUME ONE: THE ART AND SCIENCE OF TONAL GRAVITY, by George Russell, Concept Publishing Co. E-mail: postmaster@lydiancromaticconcept.com. Website: www.lydianchromaticconcept.com.

MELODY IN SONGWRITING, by Jack Perricone, Berklee Press, 1140 Boylston St., Boston MA 02215. (617)747-2146. E-mail: support@online.berklee.com. Website: www.berklee-press.com.

MUSIC ATTORNEY LEGAL & BUSINESS AFFAIRS REGISTRY, by Ritch Esra and Steve Trumbull, SRS Publishing, 7510 Sunset Blvd., Suite #1041, Los Angeles CA 90046-3400. (800)552-7411. E-mail: musicregistry@compuserve.com or srspubl@aol.com.

THE MUSIC BUSINESS REGISTRY, by Ritch Esra, SRS Publishing, 7510 Sunset Blvd., Suite #1041, Los Angeles CA 90046-3400. (800)552-7411. E-mail: info@musicregistry.com. Website: www.musicregistry.com.

MUSIC DIRECTORY CANADA, Norris-Whitney Communications, Inc., 4056 Dorchester Rd., Suite 202, Niagara Falls, ON L2E 6M9 Canada. (905)374-8878 or (877)RING-NWC. E-mail: mail@nor.com. Website: http://nor.com or www.musicdirectorycanada.com.

MUSIC LAW: HOW TO RUN YOUR BAND'S BUSINESS, by Richard Stim, Nolo Press, 950 Parker St., Berkeley CA 94710. (510)549-1976. Website: www.nolo.com.

MUSIC, MONEY AND SUCCESS: THE INSIDER'S GUIDE TO THE MUSIC INDUSTRY, by Jeffrey Brabec and Todd Brabec, Schirmer Trade Books, 257 Park Ave. S., Suite 20, New York NY 10010. (212) 254-2100.

THE MUSIC PUBLISHER REGISTRY, by Ritch Esra, SRS Publishing, 7510 Sunset Blvd. #1041, Los Angeles CA 90046-3400. (800)552-7411. E-mail: info@musicregistry.com.

MUSIC PUBLISHING: A SONGWRITER'S GUIDE, rev. ed., by Randy Poe, Writer's Digest Books, 10151 Carver Rd., Suite 200, Blue Ash OH 45242. (855)840-5124. Website: www. writersdigestshop.com.

THE MUSICIAN'S GUIDE TO MAKING & SELLING YOUR OWN CDS & CASSETTES, by Jana Stanfield, Writer's Digest Books, 10151 Carver Rd., Suite, 200, Blue Ash OH 45242. (855)840-5124. Website: www.writersdigestshop.com.

MUSICIANS PHONE BOOK, THE LOS ANGELES MUSIC INDUSTRY DIRECTORY, Get Yourself Some Publishing, 28336 Simsalido Ave., Canyon Country CA 91351.

NASHVILLE MUSIC BUSINESS DIRECTORY, by Mark Dreyer, NMBD Publishing, 9 Music Square S., Suite 210, Nashville TN 37203. (615)826-4141. E-mail: Online form. Website: www.nashvilleconnection.com.

NASHVILLE'S UNWRITTEN RULES: INSIDE THE BUSINESS OF COUNTRY MUSIC, by Dan Daley, Overlook Press, 141 Wooster St., New York NY 10012. (212) 673-2210. E-mail: sales@overlookny.com. Website: www.overlookpress.com

THE REAL DEAL—HOW TO GET SIGNED TO A RECORD LABEL FROM A TO Z, by Daylle Deanna Schwartz, Billboard Books.

RECORDING INDUSTRY SOURCEBOOK, Music Books Plus, 4600 Witmer Industrial Estates, Suite 6, Niagara Falls NY 14305. (800)265-8481. Website: www.musicbooksplus.com.

REHARMONIZATION TECHNIQUES, by Randy Felts, Berklee Press, 855 Boylston St., 7th Floor, Boston MA 02216. (617)747-2146. E-mail: support@online.berklee.edu. Website: www.berkleepress.com.

THE SONGWRITERS IDEA BOOK, by Sheila Davis, Writer's Digest Books, 10151 Carver Rd., Suite 200, Blue Ash OH 45242. (855)840-5124. Website: www.writersdigestshop.com.

SONGWRITER'S MARKET GUIDE TO SONG & DEMO SUBMISSION FORMATS, Writer's Digest Books, 10151 Carver Rd., Suite 200, Blue Ash OH 45242. (855)840-5124. Website: www.writersdigestshop.com.

SONGWRITER'S PLAYGROUND—INNOVATIVE EXERCISES IN CREATIVE SONGWRITING, by Barbara L. Jordan, BookSurge Publishing. Website: www.songwritersplayground.com

THE SONGWRITER'S WORKSHOP: HARMONY, by Jimmy Kachulis, Berklee Press, 855 Boylston St., 7th Floor, Boston MA 02216. (617)747-2146. E-mail: support@online.berklee.edu. Website: www.berkleepress.com.

THE SONGWRITER'S WORKSHOP: MELODY, by Jimmy Kachulis, Berklee Press, 855 Boylston St., 7th Floor, Boston MA 02216. (617)747-2146. E-mail: support@online.berklee.edu. Website: www.berkleepress.com.

SONGWRITING AND THE CREATIVE PROCESS, by Steve Gillette, Sing Out! Publications, P.O. Box 5460, Bethlehem PA 18015-0460. (610)865-5366 or (888)sing-out. E-mail: sing-out@libertynet.org.

SONGWRITING: ESSENTIAL GUIDE TO LYRIC FORM AND STRUCTURE, by Pat Pattison, Berklee Press, 855 Boylston St., 7th Floor, Boston MA 02216. (617)747-2146. E-mail: support@online.berklee.edu. Website: www.berkleepress.com.

SONGWRITING: ESSENTIAL GUIDE TO RHYMING, by Pat Pattison, Berklee Press, 855 Boylston St., 7th Floor, Boston MA 02216. (617)747-2146. E-mail: support@online.berklee.edu. Website: www.berkleepress.com.

THE SONGWRITING SOURCEBOOK: HOW TO TURN CHORDS INTO GREAT SONGS, by Rikky Rooksby, Hal Leonard Corp., P.O. Box 13819, Milwaukee WI 53213. E-mail: Online form. Website: www.halleonardbooks.com.

SONGWRITING STRATEGIES: A 360-DEGREE APPROACH, by Mark Simos, 855 Boylston St., 7th Floor, Boston MA 02216. (617)747-2146. E-mail: support@online.berklee.edu. Website: www.berkleepress.com.

SONGWRITING WITHOUT BOUNDARIES, by Pat Pattison, 10151 Carver Rd., Suite 200, Blue Ash OH 45242. (855)840-5124. Website: www.writersdigestshop.com.

THE SOUL OF A WRITER, by Susan Tucker with Linda Lee Strother, Journey Publishing Co.

SUCCESSFUL LYRIC WRITING, by Sheila Davis, Writer's Digest Books, 10151 Carver Rd., Suite 200, Blue Ash OH 45242. (855)840-5124. Website: www.writersdigestshop.com.

THIS BUSINESS OF MUSIC MARKETING AND PROMOTION, by Tad Lathrop, Billboard Books, The Crown Publishing Group, 1745 Broadway, New York NY 10019. (212)782-9000. E-mail: crownosm@penguinrandomhouse.com.

TIM SWEENEY'S GUIDE TO RELEASING INDEPENDENT RECORDS, by Tim Sweeney, TSA Books, 31805 Temecula Pkwy., Suite 551, Temecula CA 92592. (951)303-9506. E-mail: sweeney@timsweeney.com. Website: www.timsweeney.com.

TEXAS MUSIC INDUSTRY DIRECTORY, Texas Music Office, Office of the Governor, P.O. Box 13246, Austin TX 78711. (512)463-6666. E-mail: Online form. Website: gov.texas.gov/musicdirectory/.

TUNESMITH: INSIDE THE ART OF SONGWRITING, by Jimmy Webb, Hachette Book Group, 1290 Avenue of the Americas, New York NY 10104. (800)759-0190.

VOLUNTEER LAWYERS FOR THE ARTS GUIDE TO COPYRIGHT FOR MUSICIANS AND COMPOSERS, by Timothy Jensen, One E. 53rd St., 6th Floor, New York NY 10022. (212)319-2787.

WRITING BETTER LYRICS, by Pat Pattison, Writer's Digest Books, 10151 Carver Rd., Suite 200, Blue Ash OH 45242. (855)840-5124. Website: www.writersdigestshop.com.

WRITING MUSIC FOR HIT SONGS, by Jai Josefs, Schirmer Trade Books, 257 Park Ave. S., Suite 20, New York NY 10010. (212)254-2100.

THE YELLOW PAGES OF ROCK, The Album Network, 120 N. Victory Blvd., Burbank CA 91502. Fax: (818)955-9048. E-mail: ypinfo@yprock.com.

WEBSITES OF INTEREST

The Internet provides a wealth of information for songwriters and performers, and the number of sites devoted to music grows each day. Below is a list of websites that can offer you information, links to other music sites, contact with other songwriters, and places to showcase your songs. Due to the dynamic nature of the online world, this is certainly not a comprehensive list, but it gives you a place to start on your Internet journey as you search for opportunities to get your music heard.

ABOUT.COM MUSICIANS' EXCHANGE

www.musicians.about.com

Site features headlines and articles of interest to independent musicians and songwriters, as well as links and label profiles.

AMERICAN SOCIETY OF COMPOSERS, AUTHORS AND PUBLISHERS (ASCAP)

www.ascap.com

Database of works in ASCAP's repertoire. Includes performer, songwriter, and publisher information, as well as membership information and industry news.

AMERICAN SONGWRITER MAGAZINE HOMEPAGE

www.americansongwriter.com

This is the official homepage for *American Songwriter* magazine. Features an online article archive, e-mail newsletter, and links.

BANDCAMP

www.bandcamp.com

An online music store and platform for artist promotion that caters mainly to independent artists.

BEAIRD MUSIC GROUP DEMOS

www.beairdmusicgroup.com

Nashville demo service that offers a variety of demo packages.

BILLBOARD

www.billboard.com

Industry news and searchable online database of music companies by subscription.

THE BLUES FOUNDATION

www.blues.org

Nonprofit organization located in Memphis, Tennessee; website contains information on the foundation, membership, and events.

BROADCAST MUSIC, INC. (BMI)

www.bmi.com

Offers lists of song titles, writers, and publishers of the BMI repertoire. Includes membership information and general information on songwriting and licensing.

THE BUZZ FACTOR

www.thebuzzfactor.com

Website offers free tips on music marketing and self-promotion.

BUZZNET

www.buzznet.com

Searchable networking and news site featuring music, pop culture, photos, videos, concert reviews, and more.

CDBABY

www.cdbaby.com

An online CD store dedicated to the sales of independent music.

CADENZA

www.cadenza.org

Online resource for contemporary and classical music and musicians, including methods of contacting other musicians.

CHORUS AMERICA

www.chorusamerica.org

The website for Chorus America, a national organization for professional and volunteer choruses. Includes job listings and professional development information.

CHORUS.FM

www.absolutepunk.net

Searchable online community focusing on punk and rock music, including news, reviews, articles, interviews, and forums to discuss music and pop culture.

FILM MUSIC NETWORK

www.filmmusicworld.com or www.filmmusic.net

Network of links, news, and job listings within the film music world.

GET SIGNED

www.getsigned.com

Interviews with musicians, songwriters, and industry veterans, how-to business information, and more.

GOVERNMENT LIAISON SERVICES, INC.

www.trademarkinfo.com

An intellectual property research firm. Offers a variety of trademark searches.

GUITAR NINE

www.guitar9.com

Offers articles on songwriting, music theory, guitar techniques, etc.

GOOGLE

www.google.com

Online search engine can be used to look up music, information, lyrics.

HARMONY CENTRAL

www.harmony-central.com

Online community for musicians with in-depth reviews and discussions.

HARRY FOX AGENCY (HFA)

www.harryfox.com

Offers a comprehensive FAQ about licensing songs for use in recording, performance, and film.

INDEPENDENT DISTRIBUTION NETWORK (IDN)

www.idnmusic.com

Website of independent bands distributing their music with advice on everything from starting a band to finding labels.

INDEPENDENT SONGWRITER WEB MAGAZINE

www.independentsongwriter.com

Independent music reviews, classifieds, message board, and chat sessions.

INDIE-MUSIC.COM

www.indie-music.com

Website of how-to articles, record label directory, links to musicians and venue listings.

JAZZ CORNER

www.jazzcorner.com

Portal for the websites of jazz musicians and organizations. Includes the jazz video share, jukebox, and the "Speakeasy" bulletin board.

JUST PLAIN FOLKS

www.jpfolks.com or www.justplainfolks.org

Website for songwriting organization featuring message boards, lyric feedback forums, member profiles, music, contact listings, chapter homepages, and more.

LAST.FM

www.last.fm

Music tracking and social networking site.

HAL'S GUIDE FOR SONGWRITERS IN L.A.

www.halsguide.com

Website for songwriters with information on clubs, publishers, books, etc. Links to other songwriting sites.

LIVEJOURNAL

www.livejournal.com

Social networking community using open-source technology, music communities providing news, interviews, and reviews.

LOS ANGELES GOES UNDERGROUND

www.lagu.somaweb.org

Website dedicated to underground rock bands from Los Angeles and Hollywood.

LYRIC IDEAS FOR SONGWRITERS

www.lyricideas.com

Offers songwriting prompts, themes, and creative techniques for songwriting.

MI2N (MUSIC INDUSTRY NEWS NETWORK)

www.mi2n.com

Offers news on happenings in the music industry and career postings.

THE MUSE'S MUSE

www.musesmuse.com

Classifieds, catalog of music samples, songwriting articles, newsletter, and chat room.

MUSIC BOOKS PLUS

www.musicbooksplus.com

Online bookstore dedicated to music books on every music-related topic, plus a free newsletter.

MUSIC PUBLISHERS ASSOCIATION OF THE UNITED STATES

www.mpa.org

Offers directories for music publishers and imprints, copyright resource center, and information on the organization.

MUSIC YELLOW PAGES

www.musicindustrybuyersguide.com

Listings of music-related businesses.

MYSPACE

www.myspace.com

Social networking site featuring music web pages for musicians and songwriters.

NASHVILLE SONGWRITERS ASSOCIATION INTERNATIONAL (NSAI)

www.nashvillesongwriters.com

Official NSAI homepage. Offers news, links, online registration, and message board for members.

NATIONAL ASSOCIATION OF COMPOSERS/USA (NACUSA)

www.music-usa.org/nacusa

A nonprofit organization devoted to the promotion and performance of American concert hall music.

NATIONAL MUSIC PUBLISHERS ASSOCIATION (NMPA)

www.nmpa.org

Organization's online site filled with information about copyright, legislation, and other concerns of the music publishing world.

NEW MUSIC USA ONLINE LIBRARY

library.newmusicusa.org

Classical and jazz archives. Includes a list of organizations and contacts for composers.

ONLINE ROCK

www.onlinerock.com

Range of membership options including a free option, offers web page services, articles, chat rooms, links, and more.

OPERA AMERICA

www.operaamerica.org

Website of OPERA America features information on advocacy and awareness programs, publications, conference schedules, and more.

PANDORA

www.pandora.com

A site created by the founders of the Music Genome Project; a searchable music radio/streaming audio site.

PERFORMER MAGAZINE

www.performermag.com

Offers articles, music, industry news, classifieds, and reviews.

PERFORMING SONGWRITER MAGAZINE HOMEPAGE

www.performingsongwriter.com

Official home page for the magazine features articles and links.

PITCHFORK

www.pitchforkmedia.com

Offers indie news, reviews, media, and features.

PUBLIC DOMAIN INFORMATION PROJECT

www.pdinfo.com

Articles on public domain works and copyright, including public domain song lists, research sources, tips, and FAQs.

PUMP AUDIO

www.pumpaudio.com

License music for film and television on a nonexclusive basis. No submission fees, rights retained by songwriter.

PUREVOLUME

www.purevolume.com

Music hosting site with searchable database of songs by signed and unsigned artists. Musicians and songwriters can upload songs and events.

THE RECORDING PROJECT

www.recordingproject.com

Online community for musicians and recording artists; every level welcome.

ROCK AND ROLL HALL OF FAME + MUSEUM

www.rockhall.com

Website for the Rock and Roll Hall of Fame and Museum, including events listings, visitor info, and more.

SESAC INC.

www.sesac.com

Website for performing rights organization with songwriter profiles, industry news updates, licensing information, and links to other sites.

SLACKER RADIO

www.slacker.com

Internet radio/streaming audio. User can create personalized channels and playlists online.

SOMA FM

www.somafm.com

Internet underground/alternative radio with commercial-free broadcasting from San Francisco.

SONGLINK INTERNATIONAL

www.songlink.com

Offers opportunities to pitch songs to music publishers for specific recording projects and industry news.

SONGSALIVE!

www.songsalive.org

Online songwriters organization and community.

SONGWRITER 101

www.songwriter101.com

Offers articles, industry news, and message boards.

SONGWRITER'S GUILD OF AMERICA (SGA)

www.songwritersguild.com

Industry news, member services information, newsletters, contract reviews, and more.

SONGWRITER'S RESOURCE NETWORK

www.songwritersresourcenetwork.com

News and education resource for songwriters, lyricists, and composers.

SONGWRITERUNIVERSE

www.songwriteruniverse.com

In-depth articles, business information, education, and recommended reading.

SONIC BIDS

www.sonicbids.com

Features an online press kit with photos, bio, music samples, date calendar. Free trial period first month for artists/bands to sign up, newsletter.

SOUNDCLOUD

www.soundcloud.com

An online audio distribution platform that allows collaboration, promotion, and distribution of audio recordings.

STARPOLISH

www.starpolish.com

Features articles and interviews about the music industry.

SUMMERSONGS SONGWRITING CAMPS

www.summersongs.com

Information about songwriting camps, staff, and online registration.

TAXI

www.taxi.com

Independent A&R vehicle that shops demos to A&R professionals.

TUNECORE

www.tunecore.com

Service that allows musicians to sell their music digitally via online retailers such as iTunes, Amazon, Spotify, and more.

UNITED STATES COPYRIGHT OFFICE

www.copyright.gov

Homepage for the U.S. Copyright Office. Offers information on registering songs.

WEIRDO MUSIC

www.weirdomusic.com

Online music magazine with articles, reviews, downloads, and links to Internet radio shows.

YAHOO!

www.news.yahoo.com

Search engine with radio station guide, music industry news, and listings.

YOUTUBE

www.youtube.com

Social networking site that hosts audiovisual content. Searchable database provides links to music videos, interviews, and more.

GLOSSARY

A CAPPELLA. Choral singing without accompaniment.

AAA FORM. A song form in which every verse has the same melody, often used for songs that tell a story.

AABA, ABAB. A commonly used song pattern consisting of two verses, a bridge, and a verse, or a repeated pattern of verse and bridge, where the verses are musically the same.

A&R DIRECTOR. Record company executive in charge of the Artists and Repertoire Department who is responsible for finding and developing new artists and matching songs with artists.

A/C. Adult contemporary music.

ADVANCE. Money paid to the songwriter or recording artist, which is then recouped before regular royalty payment begins. Sometimes called "up-front" money, advances are deducted from royalties.

AFIM. Association for Independent Music (formerly NAIRD). Organization for independent record companies, distributors, retailers, manufacturers, etc.

AFM. American Federation of Musicians. A union for musicians and arrangers.

AFTRA. American Federation of Television and Radio Artists. A union for performers.

AIMP. Association of Independent Music Publishers.

AIRPLAY. The radio broadcast of a recording.

AOR. Album-Oriented Rock. A radio format that primarily plays selections from rock albums as opposed to hit singles.

ARRANGEMENT. An adaptation of a composition for a recording or performance, with consideration for the melody, harmony, instrumentation, tempo, style, etc.

ASCAP. American Society of Composers, Authors, and Publishers. A performing rights society. (See the "Organizations" section.)

ASSIGNMENT. Transfer of song rights from writer to publisher.

AUDIO VISUAL INDEX (AVI). A database containing title and production information for cue sheets which are available from a performing rights organization. Currently, BMI, ASCAP, SOCAN, PRS, APRA, and SACEM contribute their cue-sheet listings to the AVI.

AUDIOVISUAL. Refers to presentations that use audio backup for visual material.

BACKGROUND MUSIC. Music used that creates mood and supports the spoken dialogue of a radio program or visual action of an audiovisual work. Not feature or theme music.

B&W. Black and white.

BED. Prerecorded music used as background material in commercials. In rap music, often refers to the sampled and looped drums and music over which the rapper performs.

BLACK BOX. Theater without fixed stage or seating arrangements, capable of a variety of formations. Usually a small space, often attached to a major theater complex, used for workshops or experimental works calling for small casts and limited sets.

BMI. Broadcast Music, Inc. A performing rights society. (See the "Organizations" section.)

BOOKING AGENT. Person who schedules performances for entertainers.

BOOTLEGGING. Unauthorized recording and selling of a song.

BUSINESS MANAGER. Person who handles the financial aspects of artistic careers.

BUZZ. Attention an act generates through the media and word of mouth.

B/W. Backed with. Usually refers to the B-side of a single.

C&W. Country and western.

CATALOG. The collected songs of one writer or all songs handled by one publisher.

CD. Compact Disc.

CD-R. A recordable CD.

CD-ROM. Compact Disc-Read Only Memory. A computer information storage medium capable of holding enormous amounts of data. Information on a CD-ROM cannot be deleted. A computer user must have a CD-ROM drive to access a CD-ROM.

CHAMBER MUSIC. Any music suitable for performance in a small audience area or chamber.

CHAMBER ORCHESTRA. A miniature orchestra usually containing one instrument per part.

CHART. The written arrangement of a song.

CHARTS. The trade magazines' lists of the best-selling records.

CHR. Contemporary Hit Radio. Top-40 pop music.

COLLABORATION. Two or more artists, writers, etc., working together on a single project; for instance, a playwright and a songwriter creating a musical together.

COMPACT DISC. A small disc (about 4.7 inches in diameter) holding digitally encoded music that is read by a laser beam in a CD player.

COMPOSERS. The men and women who create musical compositions for motion pictures and other audiovisual works or the creators of classical music compositions.

COPUBLISH. Two or more parties own publishing rights to the same song.

COPYRIGHT. The exclusive legal right giving the creator of a work the power to control the publishing, reproduction, and sales of the work. Although a song is technically copyrighted at the time it is written, the best legal protection of that copyright comes through registering the copyright with the Library of Congress.

COPYRIGHT INFRINGEMENT. Unauthorized use of a copyrighted song or portions thereof.

COVER RECORDING. A new version of a previously recorded song.

CROSSOVER. A song that becomes popular in two or more musical categories (e.g., country and pop).

CUT. Any finished recording; a selection from an LP. Also, to record.

DAT. Digital Audio Tape. A professional and consumer audiocassette format for recording and playing back digitally encoded material. DAT cassettes are approximately one-third smaller than conventional audiocassettes.

DCC. Digital Compact Cassette. A consumer audio cassette format for recording and playing back digitally encoded tape. DCC tapes are the same size as analog cassettes.

DEMO. A recording of a song submitted as a demonstration of a writer's or artist's skills.

DERIVATIVE WORK. A work derived from another work, such as a translation, musical arrangement, sound recording, or motion-picture version.

DISTRIBUTOR. Wholesale marketing agent responsible for getting records from manufacturers to retailers.

DONUT. A jingle with singing at the beginning and end and an instrumental background in the middle. Ad copy is recorded over the middle section.

E-MAIL. Electronic mail. Computer address where a company or individual can be reached via modem.

ENGINEER. A specially trained individual who operates recording studio equipment.

ENHANCED CD. General term for an audio CD that also contains multimedia computer information. It is playable in both standard CD players and CD-ROM drives.

EP. Extended-Play record, CD, or cassette containing more selections than a standard single, but fewer than a standard album.

EPK. Electronic press kit. Usually contains photos, sound files, bio information, reviews, tour dates, etc., posted online. Sonicbids.com is a popular EPK hosting website.

FINAL MIX. The art of combining all the various sounds that take place during the recording session into a two-track stereo or mono tape. Reflects the total product and all of the energies and talents the artist, producer, and engineer have put into the project.

FLY SPACE. The area above a stage from which set pieces are lowered and raised during a performance.

FOLIO. A softcover collection of printed music prepared for sale.

FOLLOWING. A fanbase committed to going to gigs and buying albums.

FOREIGN RIGHTS SOCIETIES. Performing rights societies other than domestic that have reciprocal agreements with ASCAP and BMI for the collection of royalties accrued by foreign radio, television airplay, and other public performance of the above groups' writer members.

HARRY FOX AGENCY. Organization that collects mechanical royalties.

GRAMMY. Music industry awards presented by the National Academy of Recording Arts and Sciences.

HIP-HOP. A dance-oriented musical style derived from a combination of disco, rap, and R&B.

HIT. A song or record that achieves Top-40 status.

HOOK. A memorable "catch" phrase or melody line that is repeated in a song.

HOUSE. Dance music created by remixing samples from other songs.

HYPERTEXT. Words or groups of words in an electronic document that are linked to other text, such as a definition or a related document. Hypertext also can be linked to illustrations.

INDIE. An independent record label, music publisher, or producer.

INFRINGEMENT. A violation of the exclusive rights granted by the copyright law to a copyright owner.

INTERNET. A worldwide network of computers that offers access to a wide variety of electronic resources.

IPS. Inches per second, a speed designation for tape recording.

IRC. International reply coupon, necessary for the return of materials sent out of the country. Available at most post offices.

JINGLE. Usually a short verse set to music, designed as a commercial message.

LEAD SHEET. Written version (melody, chord symbols, and lyric) of a song.

LEADER. Plastic (nonrecordable) tape at the beginning and between songs for ease in selection.

LIBRETTO. The text of an opera or any long choral work. The booklet containing such text.

LISTING. Block of information in this book about a specific company.

LP. Designation for long-playing record played at 33⅓ rpm.

LYRIC SHEET. A typed or written copy of a song's lyrics.

MARKET. A potential song or music buyer. Also a demographic division of the record-buying public.

MASTER. Edited and mixed tape used in the production of records; the best or original copy of a recording from which copies are made.

MD. MiniDisc. A 2.5-inch disk for recording and playing back digitally encoded music.

MECHANICAL RIGHT. The right to profit from the physical reproduction of a song.

MECHANICAL ROYALTY. Money earned from record, tape, and CD sales.

MIDI. Musical instrument digital interface. Universal standard interface that allows musical instruments to communicate with each other and computers.

MINI DISC. (see **MD**, above.)

MIX. To blend a multi-track recording into the desired balance of sound, usually to a two-track stereo master.

MODEM. MOdulator/DEModulator. A computer device used to send data from one computer to another via telephone line.

MOR. Middle of the road. Easy-listening popular music.

MP3. File format of a relatively small size that stores audio files on a computer. Music saved in MP3 format can be played only with an MP3 player (which can be downloaded onto a computer).

MS. Manuscript.

MULTIMEDIA. Computers and software capable of integrating text, sound, photographic-quality images, animation, and video.

MUSIC BED. (see **BED**, above.)

MUSIC JOBBER. A wholesale distributor of printed music.

MUSIC LIBRARY. A business that purchases canned music, which can then be bought by producers of radio and TV commercials, films, videos, and audiovisual productions to use however they wish.

MUSIC PUBLISHER. A company that evaluates songs for commercial potential, finds artists to record them, finds other uses (such as television or film) for the songs, collects income generated by the songs, and protects copyrights from infringement.

MUSIC ROW. An area of Nashville, Tennessee, encompassing Sixteenth, Seventeenth and Eighteenth avenues where most of the major publishing houses, recording studios, mastering labs, songwriters, singers, promoters, etc., practice their trade.

NARAS. National Academy of Recording Arts and Sciences.

THE NATIONAL ACADEMY OF SONGWRITERS (NAS). The largest U.S. songwriters' association. (See the "Organizations" section.)

NEEDLE-DROP. Refers to a type of music library. A needle-drop music library is a licensed library that allows producers to borrow music on a rate schedule. The price depends on how the music will be used.

NETWORK. A group of computers electronically linked to share information and resources.

NMPA. National Music Publishers Association.

ONE-OFF. A deal between songwriter and publisher that includes only one song or project at a time. No future involvement is implicated. Many times a single-song contract accompanies a one-off deal.

ONE-STOP. A wholesale distributor who sells small quantities of records to "mom-and-pop" record stores, retailers, and jukebox operators.

OPERETTA. Light, humorous, satiric plot, or poem set to cheerful, light music with occasional spoken dialogue.

OVERDUB. To record an additional part (vocal or instrumental) onto a basic multi-track recording.

PARODY. A satirical imitation of a literary or musical work. Permission from the owner of the copyright is sometimes required before commercial exploitation of a parody.

PAYOLA. Dishonest payment to broadcasters in exchange for airplay.

PERFORMING RIGHTS. A specific right granted by U.S. copyright law protecting a composition from being publicly performed without the owner's permission.

PERFORMING RIGHTS ORGANIZATION. An organization that collects income from the public performance of songs written by its members and then proportionally distributes this income to the individual copyright holder based on the number of performances of each song.

PERSONAL MANAGER. A person who represents artists to develop and enhance their careers. Personal managers may negotiate contracts, hire and dismiss other agencies and personnel relating to the artist's career, review material, help with artist promotions, and perform many other services.

PIRACY. The unauthorized reproduction and selling of printed or recorded music.

PITCH. To attempt to solicit interest for a song by audition.

PLAYLIST. List of songs a radio station will play.

POINTS. A negotiable percentage paid to producers and artists for records sold.

PRODUCER. Person who supervises every aspect of a recording project.

PRODUCTION COMPANY. Company specializing in producing jingle packages for advertising agencies. May also refer to companies specializing in audiovisual programs.

PROFESSIONAL MANAGER. Member of a music publisher's staff who screens submitted material and tries to get the company's catalog of songs recorded.

PROSCENIUM. Permanent architectural arch in a theater that separates the stage from the audience.

PUBLIC DOMAIN. Any composition with an expired, lapsed, or invalid copyright, therefore belonging to everyone.

PURCHASE LICENSE. Fee paid for music used from a stock music library.

QUERY. A letter of inquiry to an industry professional soliciting his interest.

R&B. Rhythm and blues.

RACK JOBBER. Distributors who lease floor space from department stores and put in racks of albums.

RATE. The percentage of royalty as specified by contract.

RELEASE. Any record issued by a record company.

RESIDUALS. In advertising or television, payments to singers and musicians for use of a performance.

RIAA. Recording Industry Association of America.

ROYALTY. Percentage of money earned from the sale of records or use of a song.

RPM. Revolutions per minute. Refers to phonograph turntable speed.

SAE. Self-addressed envelope (with no postage attached).

SASE. Self-addressed stamped envelope.

SATB. The abbreviation for parts in choral music, meaning Soprano, Alto, Tenor, and Bass.

SCORE. A complete arrangement of all the notes and parts of a composition (vocal or instrumental) written out on staves. A full score, or orchestral score, depicts every orchestral part on a separate staff and is used by a conductor.

SELF-CONTAINED. A band or recording act that writes all its own material.

SESAC. A performing rights organization, originally the Society of European Stage Authors and Composers. (see the "Organizations" section.)

SFX. Sound effects.

SHOP. To pitch songs to a number of companies or publishers.

SINGLE. 45rpm record with only one song per side. A 12£ single refers to a long version of one song on a 12£ disc, usually used for dance music.

SKA. Up-tempo dance music influenced primarily by reggae and punk, usually featuring horns, saxophone, and bass.

SOCAN. Society of Composers, Authors and Music Publishers of Canada. A Canadian performing rights organization. (see the "Organizations" section.)

SOLICITED. Songs or materials that have been requested.

SONG PLUGGER. A songwriter representative whose main responsibility is promoting uncut songs to music publishers, record companies, artists, and producers.

SONG SHARK. Person who deals with songwriters deceptively for his own profit.

SOUNDSCAN. A company that collates the register tapes of reporting stores to track the actual number of albums sold at the retail level.

SOUNDTRACK. The audio, including music and narration, of a film, videotape, or audiovisual program.

SPACE STAGE. Open stage that features lighting and, perhaps, projected scenery.

SPLIT PUBLISHING. To divide publishing rights between two or more publishers.

STAFF SONGWRITER. A songwriter who has an exclusive agreement with a publisher.

STATUTORY ROYALTY RATE. The maximum payment for mechanical rights guaranteed by law that a record company may pay the songwriter and his publisher for each record, CD, or tape sold.

SUBPUBLISHING. Certain rights granted by a U.S. publisher to a foreign publisher in exchange for promoting the U.S. catalog in his territory.

SYNCHRONIZATION. Technique of timing a musical soundtrack to action on film or video.

TAKE. Either an attempt to record a vocal or instrumental part or an acceptable recording of a performance.

TEJANO. A musical form begun in the late 1970s by regional bands in south Texas, its style reflects a blended Mexican-American culture. Incorporates elements of rock, country, R&B, and jazz, and often features accordion and 12-string guitar.

THRUST STAGE. Stage with audience on three sides and a stagehouse or wall on the fourth side.

TOP 40. The first forty songs on the pop music charts at any given time. Also refers to a style of music which emulates that heard on the current Top 40.

TRACK. Divisions of a recording tape (e.g., 24-track tape) that can be individually recorded in the studio, and then mixed into a finished master.

TRADES. Publications covering the music industry.

12-SINGLE. A 12-inch record containing one or more remixes of a song, originally intended for dance club play.

UNSOLICITED. Songs or materials that were not requested and are not expected.

VOCAL SCORE. An arrangement of vocal music detailing all vocal parts and condensing all accompanying instrumental music into one piano part.

WEBSITE. An address on the World Wide Web that can be accessed by computer modem. It may contain text, graphics, and sound.

WING SPACE. The offstage area surrounding the playing stage in a theater, unseen by the audience, where sets and props are hidden, actors wait for cues, and stagehands prepare to change sets.

WORLD MUSIC. A general music category that includes most musical forms originating outside the U.S. and Europe, including reggae and calypso. World music finds its roots primarily in the Caribbean, Latin America, Africa, and the South Pacific.

WORLD WIDE WEB (WWW). An Internet resource that utilizes hypertext to access information. It also supports formatted text, illustrations, and sounds, depending on the user's computer capabilities.

GENERAL INDEX

GEOGRAPHIC INDEX

CATEGORY INDEX